# Is the Bible True?

JEFFERY L. SHELER

# IS THE

# BIBLE

# TRUE?

## HOW MODERN DEBATES
## AND DISCOVERIES
## AFFIRM THE ESSENCE OF
## THE SCRIPTURES

HarperSanFrancisco
Zondervan

*Is the Bible True?* is available from HarperSanFrancisco and Zondervan Publishing House.

HarperCollins books may be purchased for educational, business, or sales promotional use. For information please write: Special Markets Department, HarperCollins Publishers, 10 East 53rd Street, New York, NY 10022.

HarperCollins Web Site: http://www.harpercollins.com

HarperCollins®, ■ ®, and HarperSanFrancisco™ are trademarks of HarperCollins Publishers Inc.

FIRST EDITION

Library of Congress Cataloging-in-Publication Data
Sheler, Jeffery L.
    Is the Bible true?: how modern debates and discoveries affirm the essence of the Scriptures / Jeffery L. Sheler. — 1st ed.
        p.  cm.
    Includes bibliographical references and index.
    ISBN 0–06–067541–1 (cloth)
    ISBN 0–06–067542–X (pbk.)
    1. Bible—History of contemporary events. 2. Bible—Antiquities. 3. Jesus Christ—Historicity. I. Title.
Historicity.   I. Title.
    BS635.2 .S  1999

                                                                    99-16882
                                                                      CIP

99  00  01  02  03  ❖ RRD(H)  10  9  8  7  6  5  4  3  2  1

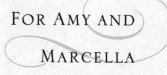

FOR AMY AND
MARCELLA

# CONTENTS

# ACKNOWLEDGMENTS

I OWE A GREAT DEBT OF GRATITUDE TO A HOST OF PEOPLE WHO, WHETHER they know it or not, were a tremendous help to me in the research and writing of this book.

First and foremost, I must thank my editors at *U.S. News & World Report* for permitting me these past ten years to cover the fascinating world of religion and for actually putting what I have written in their magazine. Several of the chapters here are based on cover stories that have appeared in *U.S. News & World Report* since 1989. I thank the editors especially for their encouragement and for allowing me the time and the resources to complete this book. I must also thank two of my *U.S. News* colleagues: Mike Tharp, for his help in producing the profile of Marcus Borg in Chapter 19, and Joannie Schrof, for her research assistance in the section on religion and science in Chapter 4. And finally, I must thank the talented staff of the *U.S. News* library, who continue to amaze me with their research magic.

As a journalist rather than a scholar, I have relied heavily in the preparation of this book on the work and wisdom of distinguished experts in fields such as biblical studies, archaeology, and ancient history. And while I take full responsibility for the manner in which the material is presented here, I must credit the invaluable contributions of those whose names you will see in the text and notes to follow.

I especially want to acknowledge Eugene Ulrich and James VanderKam of the University of Notre Dame, both leading experts on the Dead Sea Scrolls, for their authoritative written works and for subjecting themselves repeatedly to my interviews. On matters involving the scrolls and biblical archaeology in general, I am indebted to Hershel Shanks and to the many fine books and publications of his Biblical Archaeology Society; also to William G. Dever of the University of Arizona, James K. Hoffmeier of Wheaton College, and Barry Beitzel of Trinity Evangelical Divinity School.

My research into the quest for the historical Jesus could not have proceeded without the help and cooperation of John Meier of the University of Notre Dame, Don A. Carson of Trinity Evangelical Divinity School, Donald Hagner of Fuller Theological Seminary, Gregory Boyd of Bethel College, and Robert

Funk and the scholars of the Jesus Seminar. Indispensable as well were the written works of ancient historian Paul Maier and New Testament scholars N. T. Wright, Raymond E. Brown, Marcus Borg, John Dominic Crossan, and Craig Blomberg.

For the section on the Bible code, I must gratefully acknowledge the contributions of authors Michael Drosnin and Jeffrey Satinover, whose popular books put the phenomenon on the nation's radar screen, and those authors' chief antagonists: Brendan McKay of Australian National University and Jeffrey Tigay of the University of Pennsylvania. I offer a special thanks to McKay, Robert E. Kass of Carnegie Mellon University, and Leon J. Gleser of the University of Pittsburgh, editor of the mathematics journal *Statistical Science,* for graciously allowing me prepublication access to a forthcoming journal article critiquing the Bible-code phenomenon. The article, quoted in Chapter 24, should be out by the time this book appears in print.

This book has been a labor of love, and the labor has been made less burdensome thanks to the efforts of my editor at HarperSanFrancisco, John Loudon, whose wise counsel, deft editing, and endless patience are most appreciated. Thanks also to his assistant, Lisa Porfirio, and her predecessor, Karen Levine. Special thanks to my agent, Gail Ross, for helping me to conceive of the book and for making it happen, and to Mark Chimsky, formerly of HarperSanFrancisco, and Lyn Cryderman of Zondervan, for their willingness to hear my initial proposal and to take a chance that it just might work.

And finally, while I owe my wife Doreen much more than thanks, in this medium words will have to do. Her unrelenting support and encouragement and her remarkable patience throughout the course of the project have reminded me anew how fortunate I am to have her as my friend and partner.

# INTRODUCTION

WHAT ARE WE TO MAKE OF THE BIBLE IN THESE MODERN TIMES? IS IT, AS so many millions throughout the centuries have believed, the divinely inspired Word of God, accurate and trustworthy in every detail? Or is it, as others contend, merely a collection of ancient fables, fantasies, and folklore that has little credibility or relevance in a scientific age? Or could it be, as some have suggested recently, a divinely encrypted oracle whose significance lies not in its timeless teachings and spiritual insights but in a hidden grid of dramatic predictions that are decipherable only by computer?

Never before has the Bible been subjected to as much scholarly and scientific scrutiny or to as many sensational and conflicting claims as it is today. Archaeologists are making dramatic discoveries that cast surprising new light on the Bible's accounts of history. Anthropologists and sociologists examining the cultural contexts of biblical times are challenging some long-held notions about societal influences on the life of Jesus and the early church. Bible scholars and historians poring over the Dead Sea Scrolls and other ancient manuscripts are drawing some startling conclusions about the integrity and authenticity of some biblical texts and the origins of Christianity and modern Judaism. Some New Testament scholars have judged the gospels so devoid of reliable information that they have begun looking to other sources in their quest for the historical Jesus.

For many people, this explosion of modern research and speculation has forever changed how the Bible is regarded and how it is to be read and understood. For some it has made a purely literal approach to the Scriptures untenable, while for others it has made the Bible more credible and concrete in its connectedness to verifiable history. Those who had hoped that modern science and archaeology would discover some incontestable proof of the Bible's veracity have been disappointed. Yet so have those who once arrogantly anticipated the Bible's collapse under the weight of post-Enlightenment rationalism. All too often, the result of all this scrutiny has seemed conflicting and ambiguous, the scholarly conclusions complex and disappointing in their lack of consensus. What sense can average readers, whether believers or nonbelievers, hope to make of it all?

This book attempts to fill the gap. As a journalist who has covered the world's religious scene for more than a decade, I have endeavored here to put into meaningful perspective a wide array of recent developments in the fields of archaeology, biblical studies, and other disciplines and to evaluate the evidence they present both for and against the historical accuracy and integrity of the Bible.

This is not a book about theology or the Bible's theological claims. Its interest is not so much in ascertaining, for example, whether Jesus is "the way, the truth, and the life" as it is in learning whether he might have *said* he is. It is a book mainly about history and about the evidence and arguments that scholars have raised in recent years that pertain to the Bible as history. As we sort through all of the discoveries and debates in the pages that follow, the guiding questions that will be asked are these: In the light of the evidence, what can be known about the Bible? What can be proved? What is reasonable for modern readers to believe about the Bible's authority, its authenticity, and its origins? In that respect, is the Bible true?

Nearly a decade of research has gone into this book. Much of what you will read is the direct result of my reporting in the United States and abroad for the weekly newsmagazine *U.S. News & World Report,* for whom over the years I have written on many of the subjects covered here. The information presented in these pages is based on extensive interviews with leading Bible experts, archaeologists, and other authorities, as well as surveys of some of the latest and most authoritative written works.

As will quickly become apparent, this is not a technical, scholarly work— although I hope it will demonstrate sufficient precision as to fairly represent the views of the scholars it cites. I am neither a Bible scholar nor a theologian, but a journalist. The questions that this study brings to the Bible and its historical claims are fundamentally journalistic ones: What really happened and why? What was really said? How reliable are the sources? These, roughly summarized, are the very questions that have been at the heart of most of the critical biblical scholarship of the past two centuries.

If this book were merely a survey of recent scholarship it might prove useful, particularly to those who do not have the time or inclination to wade through the proliferating stacks of biblical and archaeological research literature, or to those who have found the occasional newspaper or magazine stories on biblical topics tantalizing but ultimately unsatisfying. Certainly survey and summary are important features of this book. But if those features were all it had to offer, it should be judged a failure. The questions being raised, the evidence marshaled, and the issues argued in modern biblical research today are far too important to be given the customary "on-the-one-hand/on-the-other-hand" journalistic treatment.

Consequently, wherever possible I have attempted to follow the arguments and the evidence to their most reasonable conclusions. In most cases, those conclusions reflect the studied judgments of renowned and respected scholars, and occasionally they represent what at least approaches a scholarly consensus. But on many of the most pressing issues there is nothing close to a consensus of expert opinion. The evidence in hand often is simply too equivocal: reasonable scholars, examining the same available data, arrive at different conclusions.

In other instances where consensus is reputed to exist, the assumptions and premises that underlie the conventional wisdom are subject to reasonable challenge. In biblical scholarship, as in many fields of academic inquiry, the majority is not always right. Sometimes it is the contrarian—the "voice calling in the wilderness"—who ultimately is found to have a firmer grasp on reality. For our purposes here, then, it will not do to simply invoke "the majority of scholars" as the decisive factor on matters of dispute (as if there were scientific polling data that would enable one to say such a thing in the first place!).

What follows in these pages is not a fundamentalist manifesto. Anyone hoping to find a ringing defense of biblical literalism should look elsewhere. Nor should this be viewed as the author's personal statement of faith—or lack thereof. I am, like many people, a lifelong reader of the Bible. And many of my own personal impressions of the Bible I have gained from participating in faith communities of the Protestant tradition. There is much in the Bible that I, as a Christian, find worthy of belief even though I cannot make a convincing case for it based on hard historical data. You would not care to read, nor would I care to offer, what I merely believe to be true about the Bible. In any event, that is not what this book is about.

As will become apparent in the discussions that follow, some of the Bible's claims are mainly theological in nature and as such are simply beyond the reach of historical inquiry. Those necessarily will be left alone. Other claims—and there are many—that *do* lend themselves to historical inquiry but for which scholars currently find no corroboration, or for which there is conflicting evidence, will be fairly and honestly treated even when doing so challenges traditional views. And when the Bible's claims and the weight of historical evidence are found to neatly coincide, as happens more often than one might expect judging from the skeptical viewpoint prevalent in so much of modern scholarship, that too will be duly noted.

Lest some jump to the conclusion that exposing the Bible to historical inquiry is at best futile or at worst inimical to faith, we should be mindful at the outset that there need be no shrinking from the difficult questions thrust at the Bible. History is, after all, as the British biblical scholar N. T. Wright has observed, "the sphere where we find, at work to judge and to save, the God who made the world." Historical inquiry into the Bible's claims may well "challenge us radically, in the church as well as outside it," says Wright. "But only if we start out with the presupposition that we already know all there is to be known about God should it puzzle or alarm us."[1]

It is with that in mind that we begin, in Part One, by considering why the question of the title needs to be asked in the first place. We will explore how and why the conflict arose over the reliability of the Bible as a source of history. Then we will look at what modern scholarship has revealed about the Bible's own history—who wrote the widely diverse documents of the Old and New Testaments and how those documents came to be viewed as Holy Scripture.

In Part Two we will examine what modern archaeology has brought to the debate over the historical accuracy of the Bible. We will explore some of the more recent and significant discoveries that have shed light on major eras of biblical history, from the age of the patriarchs and the exodus from Egypt to the days of Jesus. We will note how some modern discoveries, such as the "House of David" inscription found in upper Galilee or the tomb of Caiaphas unearthed in Jerusalem, tend to affirm the historical accuracy of Scripture. But we also will weigh findings that seem to challenge traditional understandings of some biblical narratives—archaeological evidence uncovered at Jericho, for example, that appears to conflict with Old Testament accounts of a military conquest of Canaan by the Israelites.

Without a doubt, the greatest Bible-related archaeological find of the twentieth century was the discovery in 1947 of the Dead Sea Scrolls. That is the subject of Part Three. We will see how the mysterious manuscripts from the Judean desert not only have provided important corroboration of the Bible but continue to offer valuable new insight into the religious and social milieu that gave rise to Christianity and modern Judaism. We will explore a bit of the background of the Dead Sea Scrolls—who wrote them, how they were found, and why they have stirred so much controversy. Then we will inquire into what they have revealed about the formation and content of the Hebrew Bible and what connection they have to the New Testament and the rise of Christianity.

In Part Four we will turn our attention to the quest for the historical Jesus. As the explosion of books and articles on the subject during the past decade attests, this quest has become a major focus of both scholarly and popular attention. We will trace its origins and evolution, noting how it has spawned what has sometimes seemed an ideology-driven debate over the reliability of the gospels. We will consider some of the main characters involved in the quest and examine some of their methods and agendas. We will look at, among others, the leaders of the Jesus Seminar, a group that has attracted much attention in recent years with its media savvy and zealous efforts to redefine not only the person of

Jesus but the biblical canon and the Christian faith. Then we will survey in some detail the reliability of the biblical evidence concerning the life, death, and resurrection of Jesus of Nazareth.

In Part Five we will consider the phenomenon of the so-called Bible code. Since the release of Michael Drosnin's *The Bible Code* in 1997, tens of thousands of readers have been tantalized and terrified by what appear to be predictions of assassinations, wars, and natural disasters buried in encrypted form in the first five books of the Bible and extractable now only by computer. Are these, as some contend, secret messages from God designed to convince modern skeptics of the Bible's divine origins? Or is the whole theory, as others argue, a nefarious hoax that encourages thinking of the Bible as something akin to a Ouija board rather than a book of inspired teachings. We will look at how the code works, and how it doesn't. We will see, for example, how one scholar obtained amazing results by applying the same technique to Herman Melville's classic *Moby Dick*.

In the final section, Part Six, we will attempt to draw what I believe are reasonable conclusions about the nature and the stature of the Bible—its reliability as a historical witness and as a testimony of timeless faith. After all of the scholarly scrutiny, the Bible emerges affirmed but not unscathed, a credible but complex chronicle of humanity's encounter with God.

# PART ONE

# THE BIBLE
# AND
# HISTORY

## CHAPTER 1

# CENTURIES
# OF CONFLICT

## THE BATTLE

## FOR THE BIBLE

In the beginning
was the Word.

*John 1:1*

LATE IN THE SECOND CENTURY CE, DURING A RELATIVE LULL IN ROME'S violent persecution of the early church, a Platonist philosopher named Celsus fanned the smoldering embers of anti-Christian sentiment by writing a long and derisive critique of the Scriptures of Christianity and Judaism. He entitled his work *True Doctrine*. From the story of creation to the accounts of the resurrection, Celsus wrote, the teachings of the Scriptures were "altogether absurd."[1] The gospel accounts of the life of Jesus were a deception. Those who believed the writings of Moses to be authentic were "deluded by vulgar deceits, and so supposed that there was one God."[2] Christianity, Celsus concluded, was a pernicious cult that appealed mainly to the simpleminded and the superstitious—and to top it off, it encouraged disloyalty to Rome.

Celsus's searing attack on the Bible did not go unanswered. The Alexandrian church father Origen, a renowned biblical scholar and prolific theologian of the third century, responded with an eight-volume treatise that he aptly entitled *Against Celsus*. Origen's point-by-point rebuttal of the pagan philosopher and his carefully crafted defense of the Scriptures would be remembered as one of the most cogent Christian apologies ever written.[3]

But the battle for the Bible would hardly end there. Within a few decades, in 303 CE, the Roman emperor Diocletian would launch a more direct offensive. Hoping to eradicate Christianity from the imperial capital once and for all, he ordered the burning of all the Bibles in the city, along with any churches or houses in which they were found. Christians who refused to offer sacrifices to the pagan gods were to be jailed. Rome's prisons filled quickly, but the faith did not die, nor did the Bible disappear. Within three years Diocletian would be gone and the new emperor, Constantine, would welcome both Christianity and its Scriptures to the very apex of the Roman Empire.

These had not been the first assaults on the Bible, nor certainly would they be the last. Through the ensuing centuries, the Bible and its claims would continue to stir debate and controversy, not only between the church and its antagonists but within and among communities of faith, as believers wrestled to understand and apply the essence of the Scriptures in their own times.

Yet from the days of Constantine to the cusp of the modern era, the Bible would enjoy a unique and reverential status that previously had existed only within the confines of the nascent church and the synagogue. Its colorful stories and symbols would be woven into the rich tapestry of the emerging Western culture, influencing its art, music, and literature and informing its politics, philosophy, and economics. In the popular mind the Bible would become synonymous with "Holy Scripture," and broad assent would be granted its claim to divine inspiration. As they do today, countless millions over the centuries would encounter in its pages the Creator of the universe disclosed in the history of the people of Israel.

But in the broader culture of the modern world, two centuries of post-Enlightenment skepticism have exacted a toll. While the Bible maintains its ubiquitous presence and continues to be the best-selling book of all time, the cultural consensus for the Bible has weakened. Many long-held assumptions regarding its content and authority seem no longer to pertain. In the pews and on Main Street, an overwhelming majority of Americans still say they believe the Bible to be God's inspired word.[4] But many harbor varying degrees of doubt about the veracity of a book whose accounts of miracles, theophanies, and divine interventions they find somehow out of sync with a modern scientific worldview.

Fueling that skepticism has been a steady stream of scholarly writings and pronouncements over the years that have assailed the Bible's historical reliability and integrity. But in contrast to the days of Celsus, these modern assaults in most instances have come not from professed enemies of the church but from learned professors of the Bible whose approach to the Scriptures reflects the largely secular mindset that has come to characterize much of the biblical academy in the twentieth century.

In earlier times, when biblical scholarship was largely the domain of the clergy, the primary concern was to relate the Scriptures to questions of faith and practice. Exegetical study was geared mainly at elucidating the literary and historical context of the sacred texts. Today it is a field dominated by professional academicians who tend to regard biblical studies more as an empirical and academic pursuit than as a devotional discipline. They approach the Bible much as they would any other ancient text, or so they claim. The questions they pose often are those of the historian or the literary critic: Did this really happen? Did it happen in just this way? What is the evidence? What is the author's purpose in telling this story? What are the sources? Little weight is given to a text's internal or traditional claims to authority. Instead, scholars apply what now are widely accepted historical-critical techniques of textual analysis as they attempt to snoop out whatever "real history" may be buried within the layers of religious myth and theological propaganda that many in the academy assume permeate the Scriptures. We will examine some of those techniques and their philosophical premises in later chapters.

That is not to say that modern "secular" scholars were the first (or only) ones to ask tough questions of the Bible. As early as the second century, church leaders struggled to sort out what they recognized were difficult passages of Scripture, not the least of which were apparent discrepancies in the four gospel accounts of Jesus' life. Late in that century, a Syrian Christian named Tatian offered a solution by blending the gospels into a single harmonized narrative that he called the *Diatessaron* (a label derived from the Greek and meaning "through four"). The results were not altogether satisfactory, however, and church leaders continued to debate whether and how the gospels could be made to agree.[5] It is a debate that persists to the present, as we shall see in Chapter 3.

But underlying those early critical inquiries within the church was an unshakable confidence in the ultimate authority of the Scriptures and a belief that future study would somehow offer more satisfying solutions. No such deference is given the Scriptures in many quarters of modern biblical scholarship.

The skeptical mindset that generally dominates the field today can be understood as a natural and, in many ways, benign outgrowth of Enlightenment rationalism. The enormous scientific and intellectual advances of the seventeenth and eighteenth centuries forever changed the way many in the West would understand the natural world and the forces at work in history. For many, faith in science and reason had superseded religious frames of reference and made belief in revelation and the supernatural no longer tenable. The only certain reality, in the Enlightenment view, was that which could be observed, measured, or duplicated. In an age of reason and empiricism, it would no longer suffice to invoke divine inspiration or ecclesiastical tradition as special pleadings for biblical authority. The historical claims of the Bible would have to stand or fall on their own merits.

Out of that post-Enlightenment empiricism arose the historical-critical approach to the study of the Bible in the eighteenth and nineteenth centuries. At the great universities of Europe (and later in North America and elsewhere), scholars began applying the methodologies of "objective science"—although just how objective and scientific would be hotly disputed—to questions of biblical origins and historicity, questions that continue to be asked today. Who were the real writers of the Bible, and what were their sources? How accurate is the history of ancient Israel as recorded in the Old Testament? How reliable are the gospels in reporting the words and deeds of Jesus? Is there any verifiable history at all in the Bible, or should the Scriptures be regarded as religious myth and legend from start to finish?

From the opening words of Genesis to the final phrases of Revelation, not a verse of Scripture was left unchallenged. And as one might expect from such an inquiry, many of the answers that emerged tended to present a picture of the Bible radically different from that of the Jewish and Christian traditions—a Bible that was as flawed and as fallible as those anonymous ancient writers and editors who it was assumed had composed it.

Defenders of tradition in those early scholarly debates increasingly seemed outnumbered, if not outgunned. Their voices tended to get lost in the rising din of skepticism. The field of biblical scholarship had become thoroughly polarized between the dominant "minimalists," who saw little or no history in the Bible, and the "maximalists," for whom the Bible contained a wealth of reliable historical data. And the field was about to become even more lopsided.

It was largely in reaction to the ascendant skepticism in biblical academia in the late nineteenth and early twentieth centuries that a large segment of conservative Protestantism opted out of the discourse altogether and withdrew into the isolated bulwark of biblical literalism and religious fundamentalism. In a series of pamphlets entitled *The Fundamentals,* published in the second decade of the twentieth century, the movement's leaders confidently asserted, among other things, that the Bible had been verbally inspired by God, word for word, and was therefore free of error and contradiction, not only in matters of faith but in matters of history, geography, and science. Their position was based largely on "common sense" and syllogism: "The Bible is God's word; God, being perfect, cannot err; therefore, the Bible cannot err" (at least not in its original form).[6] Attaching that last qualification made it possible for fundamentalists to explain away what few anomalies they would acknowledge in the biblical text as errors of translation or transmission rather than of the Scriptures themselves. Having so asserted, there was no further need to consider the "evidence" or arguments of the skeptics. It was a position that later would be summed up in a bumper-sticker slogan: "God said it. I believe it. That settles it!"

With the fundamentalists disengaged and off talking amongst themselves at their own Bible institutes and seminaries, the mainstream of biblical academia in the first half of the century was left with even fewer conservative voices to challenge the growing hegemony of the liberals and the skeptics. By midcentury, under the significant influence of the German scholar Rudolf Bultmann, it had become a standard assumption in New Testament studies that the gospels were suffused with mythology and contained little if any verifiable history. In Old Testament studies, there were few scholars left who would dare argue that Moses had actually written the five books that tradition ascribed to him. Some questioned that he had ever even lived. What would later be called a "hermeneutic of suspicion" had settled like a dense fog over the field of biblical scholarship. The Bible's claims had to be corroborated before they could be considered historical. In other words, the Scriptures were considered "guilty until proven innocent."[7]

But in the second half of the twentieth century, refreshing winds of change began to blow across the biblical-studies landscape—change that would profoundly affect the debates over the Bible. The fledgling field of biblical archaeology had come into its own as a mature discipline and produced breathtaking discoveries that would shed dramatic new light on the historicity of the Scriptures. In some instances, the material evidence provided important new corroboration of biblical episodes that minimalist scholars had long since written off as nonhistorical. We will examine some of that evidence in Part Two. But even when it did not prove decisive, biblical archaeology brought new data and vigor to debates that previously had hinged on innovative refinements of arguments that had grown old and stale after centuries of repeated use.

At the same time, a new generation of biblical scholars, historians, and theologians emerged from the ranks of conservative evangelicalism who rejected the isolationism of their fundamentalist forebears and who increasingly became engaged in the scholarly discourse. Their renewed involvement in organizations such as the American Academy of Religion and the Society of Biblical Literature gave an important new voice to a high view of Scripture that had been sorely lacking in the academic mainstream during much of the century.

There were other encouraging signs that the hyper-skepticism that had come to characterize much of the biblical academy was beginning to lose its cachet. Scholars from Harvard and Yale were joining those from such bastions of conservatism as Wheaton College in Illinois and Fuller Theological Seminary in California in challenging the ideological filters that too often have seemed to apply in biblical research.[8] If the Bible, like other ancient texts, is to be subjected to critical examination, scholars insisted, then it should be treated fairly and "without condescension."[9] As William Hallo of Yale has argued, the Bible must be "scrutinized like other historiographical traditions of the ancient Near East, neither exempted from the standards demanded of those other traditions, nor subjected to severer ones than they are."[10] While there are limits to the evidentiary value of any ancient text, he says, "surely there are also limits to skepticism."[11]

If these developments are indicative of a pendulum swing, of a new direction in biblical research, then it bodes well for the future of the enterprise. This is so not because it presumes where those studies will lead or what they ultimately will conclude, but because it would seem to assure a reasoned and more balanced examination of the arguments and evidence for the Bible.

As the twentieth century draws to a close, the spirit of post-Enlightenment skepticism unquestionably continues to dominate the biblical academy. But it is a skepticism seemingly less rigid and dogmatic than it has been at times in the past. As we shall see in Part Four, there are many scholars today of a decidedly "secular" nature who nonetheless appreciate the possibility of realities, some of which are represented in the Bible, that are beyond the scope of nature and of natural explanation. And while there still are some, as we shall discover, who like Celsus pose polemical arguments in order to debunk the Bible and dispel traditional belief, they are the exception in what is for most a reasonable and legitimate scholarly inquiry into important questions of history, fact, and faith.

The evidence uncovered and the conclusions drawn in this modern quest for biblical truth often are complex and should not be oversimplified. Seldom do they line up neatly as "for" or "against" the Bible. Yet as will become apparent as we proceed, there is much in the debates and discoveries that affirms the biblical record as a credible historical witness.

To begin to understand the Bible's historical claims and to properly weigh the arguments and evidence, we must first consider the Bible's own history—who wrote it, how it came to be understood as Holy Scripture, and what types of literature it contains. As one might imagine, these are hotly contested questions in and of themselves—questions to which we now shall turn.

## CHAPTER 2

# CANON AND CONTENT

## THE BIBLE AS

## SACRED SCRIPTURE

> All Scripture is inspired by God and is useful for
> teaching, for reproof, for correction, and for training
> in righteousness, so that everyone who belongs to God
> may be proficient, equipped for every good work.
>
> *2 Timothy 3:16–17*

WHEN THE WORDS OF THE ABOVE EPIGRAPH WERE WRITTEN SOMETIME in the second half of the first century CE, the only Scripture known to the apostle Paul and the early church was the Hebrew Bible, the core of what Christians now call the Old Testament. It would be nearly a century after the death of Jesus before the concept of a distinctly Christian Scripture would begin to emerge. And it would take longer still before any formal consensus would arise as to which writings should be included in the biblical canon—the list of officially recognized books. Who made these decisions? How did some writings come to be regarded as Scripture while others did not? What confidence can we have today in the judgments of the ancient men who defined the borders of what many would come to believe to be the very Word of God?

Regardless of what one thinks today of the notion of divine inspiration and the role it played in the composition of the Bible, it is clear that the process of canon formation was very much a human and historical process. Already in Paul's time it was widely believed that the status "inspired by God" is what set the sacred Scriptures apart from other meritorious texts. But there were myriad religious writings circulating at the time that also claimed that status and yet would never make it into the biblical canon of either Judaism or Christianity. To understand the processes at work, it is helpful to consider what the Bible looked like in the days of Jesus and Paul and how it was regarded at this crucial stage in the Bible's own history.

## THE HEBREW CANON

As it is today, the Hebrew Bible at the turn of the era was a diverse assortment of sacred Jewish literature—law and history, liturgy and poetry, proverb and prophecy—composed by different hands and in different places over hundreds of years. It existed then as it had for centuries as a collection of loose parchment or papyrus scrolls, each normally containing no more than one "book" of the Bible. By then there were no surviving manuscripts from the hand of an original author. Each scroll had been painstakingly copied from an earlier copy, over and over again, generation after generation.

The scrolls probably were kept together as a collection in boxes or other containers at the Jewish synagogue or library or at the "house church" where Christians worshiped. While they may have been arranged "in order," any significance that was attached to the sequence of the books was not fully reflected physically until centuries later, when the codex, with its bound pages set in place one after another, would require a deliberate ordering of the biblical material.[1] It is somewhat misleading, then, to think of the early Bible as a neatly defined "book" in the sense of a single unified literary work, or even as an anthology. In reality, it was an ancient library whose components together had come to be recognized as the inspired and authoritative Scriptures of the people of Israel.

The extent to which the boundaries of that collection already were fixed in the first century is a matter of some conjecture. Some scholars suggest that the content of the Hebrew Bible—both the various writings it included and the precise content of each writing—was still quite fluid at the turn of the era, as it probably had been from the beginning. Scholars who hold that view surmise that the entire process of biblical formation involved creative expansion and free-wheeling revisions that went unchecked until the early centuries of the Christian era.[2]

Others, however, properly note that numerous references to the Hebrew Scriptures both in the New Testament and in other ancient writings suggest that there was an early consensus within Judaism as to which writings were deemed sacred and authoritative. By the first century it was widely recognized that the Scriptures consisted of three distinct units: the *law,* the *prophets,* and the *writings.* One of the earliest references to these categories appeared in 130 BCE, in a prologue attached to the Jewish wisdom book Sirach (or Ecclesiasticus). It referred to the practice in Judaism of studying "the Law and the Prophecies and the rest of the books." The Jewish historian Josephus, in *Against Apion* (written in about 90 CE),[3] noted similar biblical categories, as did Jesus in Luke's gospel (24:44).

The extent to which the texts themselves may have been "fluid" also is subject to dispute. It is undeniable that some variations have appeared over the years, either as a result of copying errors or as deliberate redactions. However, as we shall see in Chapter 15, the Dead Sea Scrolls and other ancient manuscripts have shown those changes to have been relatively minor and the text of the Hebrew Bible overall to have remained remarkably stable.

Moreover, ancient written testimony suggests that deliberate redaction of the Scriptures would not have been condoned or widely practiced. As one scholar has noted, the stern injunction of the Bible itself in Deuteronomy 4:2 that "you must neither add anything to the word which I command you, nor take away anything from it," likely would have served to restrain most scribes from engaging in "creative editing."[4] And Josephus asserted of the Hebrew Scriptures that "although such long ages have now gone by, no one has dared to add anything to them, to take away from them, or to change anything in them."[5] Tampering with the Scriptures, it seems certain, would not have been undertaken lightly.

Many scholars conclude that the Hebrew Scriptures of the first century probably were not substantially different from what they are today. The traditional Hebrew Bible as it is now known consists of twenty-four books: the five "books of Moses" (Genesis, Exodus, Leviticus, Numbers, Deuteronomy); the four "former prophets" (Joshua, Judges, Samuel, Kings) and the four "latter prophets" (Isaiah, Jeremiah, Ezekiel, and the "Book of the Twelve" minor prophets); and "the writings"—eleven books including Psalms, Proverbs, Job, Song of Songs, Ruth, Lamentations, Ecclesiastes, Esther, Daniel, Ezra-Nehemiah (considered one book), and Chronicles. One of the earliest references to this precise list appeared in the *baraitha,* a tradition from the period 70–200 CE that is quoted in the Babylonian Talmud.[6]

Even so, the Hebrew canon would not become formally "fixed" in Judaism until sometime after the Jewish War with Rome, which ended with the destruction of Jerusalem and its temple in 70 CE. The five books of Moses, of course, had been long accepted as inspired and authoritative, as had the "former" and "latter" prophets. The precise content of "the writings," however, was still a matter of dispute. It was the subject of a series of discussions by rabbinic councils meeting in Jabneh, or Jamnia, in western Judea beginning around 90 CE.[7] Whether what ensued at Jabneh amounted to an official and authoritative action or was merely part of a longer and more complex process leading toward an eventual consensus is a matter of ongoing debate. Nonetheless, by 135 CE the consensus had emerged, and the twenty-four books of the Hebrew Bible became standard.

Greek-speaking Jews, meanwhile, had long had at their disposal a Greek translation of the Hebrew Scriptures that dated to the third century BCE. It was called the Septuagint, a reference to "the seventy" scribes (it was actually seventy-two) who, legend has it, worked on the translation in Alexandria, Egypt. The language of the Septuagint, however, was not all that differentiated it from the Hebrew Scriptures. The Greek Bible included several books that the Hebrew Bible did not, as well as shorter and longer versions of some of the books in the Hebrew text.

Later, when Christianity arose, Greek-speaking Christians naturally preferred the Scriptures written in their own tongue, and the Septuagint became the version favored by the early church. When the writers of the New Testament quoted the Old Testament, it was usually the Septuagint that they quoted. But as the years passed and the church continued to grow, disagreements arose over which (if any) of the additional books of the Septuagint should be included in the Old Testament canon. Those disagreements would go largely unresolved; they account for the differences that exist today between the Bibles of Protestantism and Roman Catholicism.[8]

## THE NEW TESTAMENT CANON

The formation of Christian Scripture was a slow and gradual process. In the early years of the church, the message of Christianity was transmitted orally. Preachers and evangelists, many of whom had witnessed the events of Jesus' life and had heard his teachings, shared their vivid memories and proclaimed the message of the death, burial, and resurrection of Jesus the Messiah. The teachings of the apostles—those who had been closest to Jesus—were deemed especially authoritative. The oral traditions of the apostles would continue to be recited well into the second century.[9]

As the years rolled on, however, and the church spread into Asia Minor and Rome, written records of the sayings of Jesus and the teachings of the apostles became increasingly important against the fading of memory and the death of the apostles. Eventually, those writings would assume a status equivalent to that of the Hebrew Scriptures.

There is little doubt that the earliest texts in what eventually would become known as the New Testament were letters from the apostle Paul written around 50 CE. It is known from second-century sources that Paul's letters were being copied and widely circulated among the churches of Asia Minor by no later than the early decades of the second century, along with what were described as "memoirs" of the apostles, which later would become known as the "gospels." Paul's letters and the gospels were widely used for study and sometimes were read aloud as liturgy in the churches, along with the Hebrew Bible. That wide usage, many scholars believe, reflected the recognition by the early church of the innate authority of those writings. That authority had not been imparted by decree. The texts conformed to the "rule of faith"—the "Christian truth recognized as normative in the churches."[10]

Still there was no official list of recognized Christian Scriptures. The first step in that direction, most scholars agree, came around 140 CE as a result of what would become known as the "Marcionite Crisis" and disputes over heresies that were springing up in the church.

Marcion was a wealthy shipowner and an influential member of the Roman church who had fallen under the influence of Gnosticism. He also had become obsessed with the apostle Paul's teaching that because of Christ's death and resurrection Christians were no longer "under the law" of Moses. Marcion interpreted the notion as a blanket repudiation of the Hebrew Bible, which he then set out to replace with a more suitable and exclusively Christian Scripture.

Marcion's canon included ten of Paul's letters and an edited version of Luke's gospel—the only gospel Marcion felt accurately reflected Paul's theology—from which Marcion had expurgated all references to Judaism. The official church condemned the move and reaffirmed the normative character of all four gospels as well as all thirteen letters that were ascribed to Paul. Marcion was excommunicated as a heretic. But the incident had prompted church leaders to begin compiling their own larger lists of accepted writings.[11]

The process was hastened as church leaders sought to curb the growing influence of Gnosticism. The Gnostics within the church were teaching that Jesus had not been truly human, that he had been a sort of "spirit person" and therefore had not been crucified in the flesh. Several of the Gnostics' writings had begun circulating among the churches, especially in Egypt. Some purported to be the works of apostles and bore their names—Thomas and Peter, for example. But these documents were widely recognized as having been composed too late to have come from the apostles.

Out of that second-century conflict, scholars say, developed the church's emphasis on authentic apostolic connection as the prime determinant of canonical status. Consequently, some otherwise highly regarded writings—such as First Clement, an early-second-century letter to the church in Corinth from the bishop of Rome, and the Shepherd of Hermas, a second-century Roman Christian's widely circulated account of a vision from the risen Christ—would be excluded from the canon even though they were widely read and were older than some of the canonical books.

Church leaders began circulating lists of books they considered authoritative, and while there was widespread agreement, there also were some minor variations. Early in the fourth century, the church historian Eusebius of Caesarea divided the most widely circulated books into three categories: "recognized" books, "disputed" books, and "heretical" writings. Among those *recognized* were the four gospels (Matthew, Mark, Luke, and John), the Acts of the Apostles, fourteen epistles of Paul (Eusebius included the book of Hebrews), the epistles 1 John and 1 Peter, and the Apocalypse (Revelation). Among the *disputed* books he listed as "generally accepted" James, Jude, 2 Peter, and 2 and 3 John. Thus, all twenty-seven books of what would become the canonical New Testament were listed favorably by Eusebius. The first list to give direct assent to all twenty-seven appeared in the Easter Letter of Athanasius to the Alexandrian church in 367 CE. Under Augustine's influence, the Third Council of Carthage approved the same list in 397 CE, and it was ratified by a papal decree in the year 405.

By the end of the fourth century, then, the New Testament canon for the church in the West was virtually set. Apostolic connection, conformity to the "rule of faith," and acceptance and usage in the churches had been the keys. Conciliar action and papal decree had only ratified what had already become apparent. As scholars Glenn Barker, William Lane, and J. Ramsey Michaels have aptly observed, "The fact that substantially the whole church came to recognize the same twenty-seven books as canonical is remarkable when it is remembered that the result was not contrived."[12] They continue:

> *All that the several churches throughout the Empire could do was to witness to their own experience with the documents and share whatever knowledge they might have about their origin and character. When consideration is given to the diversity of cultural backgrounds and in orientation to the essentials of the Christian faith within the churches, their common agreement about which books belonged to the New Testament serves to suggest that this final decision did not originate solely at the human level.[13]*

Certainly the least that can be said is that the uniformity in the church's recognition of the books of the New Testament canon was an acknowledgment of the power and authority inherent in the writings themselves. And the significance of that nearly universal recognition of the intrinsic authority of the Scriptures went far beyond the mere designation of an approved list of writings. As

Yale University biblical scholar Brevard Childs has noted, the early formation of the New Testament canon also provided a "fixed context" for interpreting the individual Scriptures. It "establish[ed] boundaries inside of which the true witness [of the gospel] was to be found" and functioned as "a check" against misreading texts in isolation from the whole. The Christian canon, says Childs, "marked the arena in which each new generation of believers stood and sought to understand afresh the nature of the faith. It did not establish one doctrinal position, but often balanced several or fixed the limits within which Christians might rightly disagree."[14]

With the questions of canonicity and authorship so closely connected, as we have seen, it is little wonder that biblical scholars and historians through the centuries have focused so much scrutiny on the traditions that identify the writers of Scripture. How reliable have those traditions proven to be? What do we really know about the origins of the books of the biblical canon? And ultimately how important are questions of authorship in assessing the reliability of the Scriptures themselves? We turn to those important questions next.

## CHAPTER 3

# AUTHOR AND AUTHORITY

## WHO WROTE THE BIBLE?

> Since many have undertaken to set down an orderly
> account of the events that have been fulfilled among
> us, just as they were handed on to us by those who
> from the beginning were eyewitnesses and servants
> of the word, I too decided, after investigating
> everything carefully from the very first, to write an
> orderly account for you, most excellent Theophilus,
> so that you may know the truth concerning the
> things about which you have been instructed.
>
> *Luke 1:1–4*

IT IS AN AXIOM OF JOURNALISM THAT A REPORTER IS NO BETTER THAN his or her sources. When it comes to presenting the news, no amount of rhetorical skill can make up for a paucity of facts and pertinent information. Good journalism begins with good reporting, and that means having sources that are credible, reliable, and accurate.

A corollary of that axiom is that all sources are not qualitatively equal. An eyewitness account is almost always better than hearsay, for example. Documented evidence often is to be preferred over the spoken word alone. A source's expertise, biases, and personal agendas all must be taken into account. The accuracy of the story itself ultimately depends on the reporter's correct judgments regarding a source's authority and veracity.

The Bible is not journalism, nor does it purport to be. We will discuss its various literary genres in the next chapter. But like journalism, the Bible operates within the framework of history. It tells stories about people and events that it wants us to believe are true and to which it attaches significance and meaning. Some biblical writers, such as the author of Luke's gospel, are unabashed in disclosing their dependence on external sources, while others declare "that which we have seen and heard" (1 John 1:1) to define the content of their writing. In either case, their methodologies invite attention to legitimate questions of source, authorship, and reportorial accuracy—questions that modern scholars have not been lax in pursuing. Who are the Bible's authors and editors? On what sources of information did they draw? What can we know about the biases and agendas that may have influenced what they wrote? These are questions that have dominated much of modern biblical scholarship.

Some readers of the Bible may think it pointless to ask such questions of a book that claims, after all, to be divinely inspired. If the Bible is God's Word, some aver, then its words are God's; any human involvement in its composition is inconsequential. As the First Vatican Council in the late 1860s expressed it, the Scriptures "have God as their author."[1]

Yet the Bible itself does not spell out precisely how divine inspiration works—whether, as some believe, it is "verbal" and "plenary" (every word and every letter dictated by God), or whether it entails some less imposing form of human-divine collaboration. Theologians have debated these questions since at least the second century. There is little the historian can bring to the discussion other than perhaps proof that the claim itself was made.

The Bible does, on the other hand, call attention to itself in many places as a human witness to historical events. We read about the exodus, for example, in words we are told are those of Moses, who led the Israelites out of Egypt. The ministry of Jesus and his death and resurrection are recounted by men who, according to tradition, were with him in Galilee and Jerusalem. Struggles and successes in the early church are made vivid in letters that are said to have come from the hand of Paul. Questions of author and source, then, are very much on the table for those who would weigh the historical veracity of the Bible.

Many scholars over the years have come to conclude that most of the traditions ascribing biblical authorship simply cannot be substantiated. Most of the books of the Bible, they argue, must be judged as anonymous or even pseudonymous. Yet many others find no compelling reason to reject the long-revered traditions that have attached the authors' names to the biblical books. Which view is correct? Or does the truth lie somewhere in between? And what is at stake in the question? A closer examination of the evidence and arguments perhaps will yield an answer.

## THE OLD TESTAMENT

In the strictest sense, many of the writings of the Hebrew Bible are indeed anonymous. Relatively few make explicit claims as to the identity of their authors. Yet for most of the last two thousand years, there has been very little mystery as to their origins. According to tradition, the prophet Moses, having received a revelation from God on Mount Sinai, wrote the first five books (Genesis through Deuteronomy), a sequence known as the Pentateuch—or the Torah, in Judaism. The writings that followed—the histories and the psalms, the sayings and the prophecies—were the handiwork of such luminaries of ancient Israel's history as the military commander Joshua, kings David and Solomon, the prophets Samuel, Isaiah, Jeremiah, Ezekiel, and Daniel, and a host of others whose names traditionally have been attached to the sacred texts. All of them, it was assumed, had been men "moved by the Holy Spirit [who] spoke from God."[2]

An early intimation that things may not have been quite that simple was whispered early in the second millennium, when the Spanish philosopher and biblical exegete Abraham ibn Ezra (b. 1092, d. 1167) observed somewhat obliquely that the retrospective statement in Genesis 12:6 ("at that time the Canaanites were in the land") could not have been written by Moses; it had to have been a later note. Neither could the great leader of the exodus have recorded his own death in Deuteronomy 34:5. Ezra's observation was a relatively minor annotation, not a full-blown argument. But over the succeeding centuries, others—including the Dutch philosopher Benedict Spinoza and the British philosopher Thomas Hobbes—would expound on the notion that the Bible's origins might had been a bit more complicated than tradition allowed.[3]

### The Books of Moses

With the rise of biblical criticism in the eighteenth and nineteenth centuries, the origins of the Old Testament became a subject of intense scholarly debate. It had become by then the working assumption of Enlightenment thinkers that the Pentateuch could not have been written by one man but was the product of multiple hands and sources. Critical scholars offered up a variety of theories to explain the formation of the "books of Moses."

The most comprehensive and influential of those theories, and one that still carries considerable weight today, is referred to as the "documentary hypothesis." As articulated by the German scholar Julius Wellhausen in 1877, it views the books of Moses as a composite of four primary, distinct, and generally datable documents, each originating in different periods of Israel's history long after Moses' day.

The oldest document, according to this theory, is called *J* after its author, the Jahwist or Yahwist, who uses the name Yahweh for God. Dating to the ninth or tenth century BCE, *J* depicts God in the book of Genesis in anthropomorphic terms—walking with Adam in the Garden of Eden, forming man from the clay of the earth. Next is the *E* document, composed in the eighth century by the Elohist, who refers to God more generically as Elohim and seems more attentive to religious and moral concerns. The *D* document is ascribed to the Deuteronomist, the writer of the book of Deuteronomy, with its extensive explication of legal codes. It is dated to the seventh century, during the time of religious reforms under King Josiah (2 Kings 22–23). And last is *P*, or the Priestly source, so named because of its concern for ritual and worship, chronology, genealogy, and the law. It is said to date between the sixth and fourth centuries—before, during, or after the Babylonian exile.[4]

Wellhausen and others who would come to embrace this theory saw evidence of each of these sources blended and woven together in the "hexateuch"—the first *six* books of the Old Testament (through and including Joshua). Whether any or all of the sources ever actually existed as independent documents could not be affirmed. Some scholars speculated that they were incomplete fragments that had been pulled together by a single postexilic editor. Others suggested that rather than distinct texts that were somehow cut-and-pasted together, the four strands instead reflected a series of redactions over several centuries by editors who amplified and reinterpreted what was an evolving text.

One leading Hebrew Bible scholar, Richard Elliott Friedman of the University of California at San Diego, speculates that the four strands not only existed as separate documents, but that the identities of the authors can be pinpointed—in some instances by name! In his 1987 bestseller *Who Wrote the Bible?*, Friedman weaves a plausible argument from literary and archaeological evidence suggesting that *J* was written in the royal court of Judah (perhaps by a woman) as early as the reign of David or Solomon,[5] that *E* was the work of a Levitical priest in the kingdom of Israel between 922 and 722 BCE,[6] and that *P* was penned in the court of King Hezekiah between 727 and 698 BCE.[7] The Deuteronomist, Friedman speculates, may easily have been the scribe Baruch, a close associate and sometime ghostwriter for the prophet Jeremiah.[8] And the final redactor of the five books of Moses, Friedman avers, was probably Ezra, a postexilic priest in Jerusalem in the middle of the fifth century BCE. "He was in the right priestly family, in the right profession, in the right place, in the right time," says Friedman.[9]

While the documentary hypothesis remains the starting point for most current discussions of the origins of the Pentateuch, it is no longer considered the consensus view.[10] Some scholars who generally accept the notion of separate strands of source material now argue that the dates should be moved a century or two earlier so that the oldest strand, *J*, would be firmly set in the time of King David. Others want to push in the opposite direction—making the first five books of the Bible a product of the exile period just a few hundred years before Christ.[11]

The arguments for the dates and sources of the Pentateuch are varied and complex. But if there is any consensus at all in modern biblical scholarship, among conservatives and liberals alike, it is that the books of Moses do not appear to be the work of a single hand. As Friedman observes: "There is hardly a biblical scholar in the world actively working on the problem who would claim that the Five Books of Moses were written by Moses—or by any one person."[12] One leading conservative, Barry Beitzel of Trinity Evangelical Divinity School in Deerfield, Illinois, acknowledges apparent anachronisms in the books of Moses that clearly seem to postdate Moses' putative lifetime. "That does not mean, however, that Moses wrote no part of the Pentateuch," says Beitzel. "I would argue that there is a Mosaic core there to which other materials were added," perhaps as late as the fourth century BCE.[13]

But that is far from suggesting, as some minimalist scholars do, that the entire Pentateuch originated in that period—that the stories of creation, the flood, the Hebrew patriarchs, the exodus, the giving of the law, the conquest and settlement of Canaan, and the rise and fall of Israel's kingdoms all sprang from the fertile imagination of a postexilic writer in the middle of the first millennium BCE.[14] Archaeological evidence alone would indicate otherwise, as we shall see in Part Two.

What archaeological evidence does suggest is what many of the Hebrew texts themselves make clear: that the compilers of the Pentateuch and other Old Testament writings drew upon ancient sources, both written and oral, as they put the Scriptures into their final form. Scholars note, for example, that Numbers 21:14–15 quotes from the "Book of the Wars of the Lord," a lost document that many scholars think may have originated in the postconquest period as the source of a border description.[15] Other written sources are implied in the indictment of Amalek (Exod. 24:4); the laws of Exodus 20–23, which are described as the "Book of the Covenant" in Exodus 24:7; the cultic laws of Exodus 34 (Exod. 34:27–28); the itinerary of the Israelites as they came out of Egypt (Num. 33:2); the law code in Deuteronomy (Deut. 31:9, 24); and the "Song of Moses" in Deuteronomy 32 (Deut. 31:22). The "Book of the Generations of Adam" in Genesis 5:1 also suggests a preexistence in an earlier written form.[16] Whether they originated with Moses, or were first used by him, or were used by some later redactor, there is no reason to doubt the authenticity or the reliability of these ancient biblical sources.

Ultimately, as many scholars note, the Pentateuch's authority is not dependent upon the claim of Mosaic authorship—a claim, as we have noted, that the books themselves do not make. As Christian and Jewish traditions long have held, they are the "books of Moses" if for no other reason than that Moses is the dominant human figure of the narratives. Even the New Testament, while quoting Moses' words, does not explicitly ascribe to him the books' authorship. Twice the books are referred to simply as "Moses" (Luke 24:27; 1 Cor. 3:15), which can be seen as a title as easily as a designation of authorship.[17] As David J. A. Clines, professor of biblical studies at the University of Sheffield, England, observes, "Whether or not Moses can be called the author in a literal sense of anything in the Pentateuch, it is reasonable to hold that his work and teaching were the initial stimulus for the creation of the Pentateuch."[18]

### The Histories, Prophets, and Writings

For the remainder of the books of the Old Testament, the question of authorship does not get much clearer. As Beitzel notes, "We're dealing with anonymity almost from A to Z."[19] Although Talmudic traditions link some of the books to known biblical figures—the Book of Joshua to Joshua, and the book of Ezra to Ezra, for example[20]—as with the Pentateuch, few books purport to directly identify their writers, and there is no unambiguous external evidence of authorship. Consequently, scholarly attempts to discern their authentic origins have focused instead on questions of source, dating, and literary interdependence.

One prominent theory, for example, supposes that the seven books from Joshua through 2 Kings—often referred to as the "historical books," along with 1 and 2 Chronicles and Ezra-Nehemiah, because of their narrative reconstruction of events—are the work of a single anonymous author writing during the Babylonian exile in the sixth century BCE. The same author, according to this hypothesis, also wrote the book of Deuteronomy—the last book of the Pentateuch. The late date is suggested by the fact that 2 Kings concludes with the release of King Johoiachin of Judah from prison in Babylon, an event generally dated to about 561 BCE. Martin Noth, a German biblical scholar who first proposed this theory in 1943, based his argument for a single author on what he saw as striking similarities in theological themes and in writing styles throughout the books. Noth theorized that the Deuteronomist compiled these books from already existing traditions and put them into a framework that reflected his view of the history of Israel from the time of Moses to the exile.[21]

Many scholars think that the book of Deuteronomy took its basic shape during the reign of Manasseh or early in King Josiah's reign (around 650 to 640 BCE), probably at the hands of a group of priests or prophets in Jerusalem. It is that early form of Deuteronomy, those scholars surmise, that was found in the temple in Jerusalem in the eighteenth year of Josiah's reign (ca. 621 BCE), as described in 2 Kings 22:8.

Others, however, who consider Deuteronomy to be much older and to have been primarily the work of Moses, argue that the later material merely reflects a final redaction in the postexilic period. It must be said, however, that scholars who hold to a purely Mosaic authorship are a distinct minority. Yet even those who reject Moses as the author of Deuteronomy generally agree that ancient Moses traditions (and perhaps even the writings of Moses) lie at the book's core. As Dennis Bratcher of Virginia Union University in Richmond observes:

> The recognition of diverse strands of tradition within the book is no indication that parts of the book should be considered inferior or of less value. The long and complex history of the Mosaic legal traditions and their later incorporation along with commentary into the present setting of Deuteronomy demonstrates an ongoing process of reinterpretation of the old traditions in light of new historical circumstances. The authors, whether prophets or priests, were attempting to revitalize the nation's religion by making the old traditions alive and relevant for their own time.[22]

Whether the work of one author or many, the remaining historical books show clear markings of having drawn upon ancient written sources. Joshua and Samuel, for example, quote from the "Book of Jashar," a poetic collection that has not survived.[23] The books of Kings and Chronicles mention such sources as the "Book of the Acts of Solomon" (1 Kings 11:41), the "Book of the Annals of the Kings of Israel" (1 Kings 14:19), the "Book of the Annals of the Kings of Judah" (1 Kings 14:29), and the written works of various prophets (1 Chron. 29:29; 2 Chron. 9:29). Whether or not the writers considered themselves to be giving purely objective accounts of history—a question we will address in the next chapter—it is clear that they were consulting and quoting historical documents known to their readers. They were not simply making up stories; on the contrary, knowing that their readers had access to the same historical records, they were concerned to get the facts straight.

The books of Esther and Job are anonymous compositions. Some Jewish traditions suggest that Moses wrote or at least edited Job, but there is no convincing evidence. Esther is classified as a historical book because it tells a story of diaspora Jews in Persia (ca. 486–465 BCE) and accounts for the origins of the Jewish festival Purim. Job, on the other hand, is often classified as wisdom literature in that it does not purport to relate historical events but depicts a "wisdom debate" over the question of "the suffering righteous." Many scholars classify both as "historical fiction," although the question of their literary genre is debated in some quarters.[24]

The authorship of the Psalms, the Proverbs, and the other so-called wisdom books is quite a complicated proposition as well. The superscriptions that introduce the 150 psalms contain a variety of names, from David and Solomon, to Asaph, Jeduthun, and even Moses. Scholars debate whether those titles accurately identify the authors and whether they were part of the original compositions or were added later. Some of the titles are problematic. Often, for example, they are stated in the third person while the psalms themselves are written in the first person. In a few cases, the titles seem at odds with the text.[25] Yet even if they were not original, scholars say, the tradition of the titles is an old one. Many find little reason to doubt, for example, that David, whose name appears in seventy-three of the superscriptions, wrote at least some of the psalms ascribed to him.

The book of Proverbs reflects much the same situation. Most scholars consider it to be an anthology from different authors and time periods. Superscriptions indicate authors ranging from Solomon, King Lemuel, Agur, and a group called "the wise." While some take the opening verse to suggest that the entire book was written by Solomon, there is no clear evidence that this is so.[26] Again, the authenticity of the superscriptions must be judged according to the weight one is willing to give the ancient traditions from which they came.

Ecclesiastes also is traditionally ascribed to Solomon, even though it does not make that claim. The writer calls himself the "teacher," in one place saying, "I, the teacher, was king over Israel in Jerusalem" (1:12). Those who doubt that Solomon wrote the book note that there was never a time when he would have spoken in past tense about ruling as king. Similarly, many scholars doubt that Solomon wrote the erotic love poem Song of Songs (even though it claims to be his work) because it seems out of character for the notoriously polygamous king depicted in 1 Kings 11. As Westminster Theological Seminary scholars Raymond Dillard and Tremper Longman have observed, "short of taking the ambiguous superscription as a dogmatic statement of authorship, it is impossible to definitely settle the issue."[27]

The seventeen major and minor prophetic books would seem to lay the strongest claims to definitive authorship. Most internally identify those who were said to have received the divine words or visions that the books convey. Yet as might be expected, some scholars over the years have found an assortment of reasons to doubt the authenticity of most such claims. We will not take the time to go through each one, since the arguments tend to be similar and redundant. In some instances, chronological difficulties are alleged, as in the length of the reigns of kings of Judah mentioned in Hosea. In other instances, evidence of a late redaction is cited, as in the case of Isaiah, suggesting that at least portions of the book could not possibly have come from the historical prophet Isaiah. Some critical scholars theorize that nearly the entire book of Jeremiah, the great preacher of repentance to a nation descending into exile, is the creation of later editors.

In virtually every instance, however, the indictments are refuted by scholars who find no compelling reason to set aside the ancient traditions of authorship and provenance. Indeed, in many cases the evidence and the arguments assailing those traditions prove to be equivocal and tendentious. What often proves most decisive to individual scholars on both sides of the issue, it seems, are their own philosophical presuppositions concerning the possibility of predictive prophecy. If it cannot be true that the prophets of old were "men moved by the Holy Spirit who spoke from God," then another explanation must be in order. We will see in later chapters how the weight of a scholar's predispositions comes into play in other issues as well.

Based on the best tangible evidence, as Beitzel noted, the authors of the Old Testament "almost from A to Z" must continue to be regarded as anonymous—but not as unknown. The integrity of the ancient sources and of the writers and editors who drew upon them to compile the Hebrew Scriptures is not diminished by the formal anonymity that modern scholarship assigns. We may not be certain of their names, but their inspired words resonate no less powerfully as they disclose the sacred history of a covenant people and their self-revealing God.

## THE NEW TESTAMENT

In dramatic contrast to the Old Testament, many of the writings of the New Testament make strong and unambiguous claims as to the identity of their authors. By the early second century CE, as noted in Chapter 2, the question of apostolic origins had become a significant factor in the church's acceptance of texts into the Christian canon. But for many modern scholars, the authorship of much of the New Testament remains a subject of heated debate.

## The Four Gospels

The gospels according to Matthew, Mark, Luke, and John—books that are regarded by many as the most sacred of Christian writings—proclaim through dramatic narrative, recorded sayings, and theological proclamation the story of Jesus of Nazareth and the significance of his life, death, and resurrection. Through most of Christian history, the gospels have been regarded as the only authoritative record of Jesus' words and deeds, in that they are the remembrances either of disciples who sat at Jesus' feet (in the cases of Matthew and John) or of close associates of the apostles (in the cases of Mark and Luke). As we saw in Chapter 2, in large measure it was these apostolic credentials that set the gospels apart from myriad other writings in the early church that claimed to offer divine revelation of Christian truth.

Yet despite early and relatively strong traditions supporting those apostolic connections, most biblical scholars today—from liberal skeptics to conservative traditionalists—agree that there is too little direct evidence to say with certainty that Matthew, Mark, Luke, and John wrote the gospels that bear their names. Nowhere within the texts do the writers identify themselves or claim unambiguously to have witnessed the events they describe. The overwhelming consensus among biblical scholars today is that the gospels must be judged, formally at least, as anonymous.[28]

It is generally agreed, as well, that all four books were composed from a variety of oral and written sources collected over a period of years following Jesus' crucifixion—the very process described in the prologue to Luke's gospel, quoted in the epigraph to this chapter. Once the gospels were written, some experts believe, they were redacted (or edited) as they were copied and circulated among church elders during the late first and early second centuries. At best, those scholars say, the gospels are correctly linked with the names of those early Christian evangelists who originated the oral traditions. At worst, the names of Christ's disciples were attached to the texts later to enhance their authority. "The bottom line," says New Testament scholar Jerome Neyrey of the University of Notre Dame, "is that we really don't know for sure who wrote the gospels."[29]

Yet despite the lack of direct evidence, the early origins and strength of the traditions linking the gospels to the apostles make a strong argument for the soundness of those traditions. The Christian father Justin Martyr, writing in

Rome around 150 CE, referred to the gospels of Matthew and Luke as "memoirs of the Apostles."[30] If nothing else, says Helmut Koester of Harvard Divinity School, that description suggests that the writings were viewed as "reliable historical records."[31]

Writing even earlier, between 100 and 130 CE, Bishop Papias of Hierapolis described Mark as "[the apostle] Peter's interpreter," who "wrote down accurately all that [Peter] remembered, whether the sayings or the doings of the Lord."[32] Papias also mentioned the apostle Matthew as having composed "the sayings of the Lord." However, some scholars suggest that Papias may have referred not to a completed gospel narrative but to an early and separate collection of Jesus' sayings that he ascribed to Matthew and that has not survived.

The first independent evidence that the third gospel was written by Luke—a Greek physician, according to tradition, who was close to the apostle Paul and the only Gentile gospel author—appears in the writings of Irenaeus, bishop of Lyon, in about 180 CE. Irenaeus stated that "Luke, also who was a follower of Paul, put down in a book the Gospel that was preached by him [Paul]." Tertullian, a second-century theologian from Africa, also noted Luke's authorship in his scathing critique of the heretic Marcion (Against Marcion), who had published a distorted version of the third gospel a few decades earlier.

The writer of Luke's gospel also is widely believed to have written the Acts of the Apostles, a detailed chronicle of the development of the young church as it spread from Jerusalem to Rome. It bears the same writing style, begins with a reference to "my former book," and is addressed, as the gospel is, to "Theophilus." His use of the first-person "we" in describing the journeys of Paul suggests to many scholars that Luke accompanied the apostle Paul on some occasions. Other scholars doubt this is so, however, because of apparent disagreements between Acts and Paul's letters regarding some details of the travels.[33]

The tradition attributing the fourth gospel to the apostle John is noted by Irenaeus in 180 CE. "John the disciple of the Lord, who leaned back on his breast, published the Gospel while he was a resident at Ephesus in Asia," Irenaeus wrote,[34] referring to "the disciple whom Jesus loved" as is mentioned in John 13:23. Even earlier, several other Christian writers including Tatian (a student of Justin Martyr), Claudius Apollinaris (bishop of Hierapolis), and the Christian philosopher Athenagoras quoted unambiguously from the fourth gospel as an authoritative source.[35] Eusebius quoted the second-century apologist Clement of Alexandria as declaring that "John, last of all, conscious that the outward facts had been set forth in the Gospels, was urged on by his disciples, and, divinely moved by the Spirit, composed a spiritual Gospel." And two early church writers, Papias and bishop Polycarp of Smyrna, are said to have been personally acquainted with the apostle John and other disciples of Jesus.[36] According to Irenaeus, Polycarp "reported his converse with John and with the others who had seen the Lord, how he remembered their words . . . and reported all things in agreement with the Scriptures."[37]

Those who are skeptical of John's authorship base their objections on modern textual analyses suggesting that the fourth gospel was the work of several writers, perhaps Christians in Asia Minor who were followers of the elderly apostle. Others believe that the writer may have been a different John, a Christian leader in Asia Minor who was known as "the elder."

Even though most scholars today concede the formal anonymity of the gospels based on the absence of direct supporting evidence, many find substantial merit in two arguments that favor the traditional authors:

First, if the names were affixed later to deliberately and deceitfully imbue the writings with authority, as some scholars contend, it makes little sense that Mark and Luke would have been selected, since neither was an apostle. And while Matthew was an apostle, he was certainly not one of the more prominent or, as a tax collector, one of the more esteemed. There were far better candidates than these for the "office" of gospel author.

Second, there is no evidence from the first two Christian centuries that the gospels ever were circulated without the names of the authors attached. Martin Hengel, in a careful study of practices associated with the distribution of literature in the ancient world, has observed that unambiguous titles were considered important in properly identifying widely circulated written works.[38] This expectation, Hengel notes, is apparent in Tertullian's criticism of Marcion for having circulated his own heavily edited version of Luke's gospel without the author's name. "A work ought not to be recognized which holds not its head erect," Tertullian wrote, or which "gives no promise of credibility from the fulness of its title and the just profession of its author."[39]

As soon as two or more versions of the gospel began circulating among the churches—probably no later than 100 CE, according to Hengel—it would have been necessary to differentiate them by title. If the titles had been attached only after decades of circulating in anonymity, he argues, one should expect to find some record of disagreement over authorship. And yet the attribution of the gospels in the second century was unanimous. Hengel concludes that the most plausible explanation is that the four canonical gospels never were circulated without the names of the authors as we know them today.[40]

Even so, while literally thousands of New Testament fragments have survived antiquity, some dating to as early as 125 CE, no original gospel manuscripts are known to exist. Short of the discovery of an autographed original, chances are the question of authorship will never be fully answered to everyone's satisfaction.

The identity of the writers is not the only unsolved mystery concerning the origin of the gospels. For centuries, Bible scholars have puzzled over striking similarities and paradoxical differences in the four separate accounts of Jesus' life and ministry. Some passages are duplicated almost verbatim in Matthew, Mark, and Luke—an agreement that has earned those first three gospels the label "synoptic." Yet in other places the writers disagree, sometimes sharply, in representing the words and deeds of Jesus. Whoever wrote the gospels, scholars say, it seems certain that they drew upon some common sources. But how, then, are the differences to be explained?

The solution that has drawn the widest scholarly acceptance in recent years is called the "two-source hypothesis." In its broadest outlines, it posits that Mark's gospel was the first to be written, probably in Rome between 50 and 70 CE. It drew largely from oral tradition and perhaps also from a written compilation of Jesus' miracles. Sometime later, the writers of Matthew and Luke used copies of Mark as they each set out to write their own versions, which among other things would include more of Jesus' sayings and would address the specific questions and needs of their own Christian communities (perhaps Syria in Matthew's case and Achaia in Luke's).[41]

According to this theory, then, the two writers each used two sources as they performed their work: a copy of Mark and a now-lost collection of Jesus sayings, which scholars refer to as Q or *Quelle*—German for "source." In Matthew, scholars note, the Jesus sayings tend to be clustered into discourses, as they are in the Sermon on the Mount. In Luke, by contrast, the sayings appear in brief anecdotes spread throughout the narrative. Yet both gospels use the sayings in the much the same order, strongly suggesting that both writers were using a common written source. "It is as if they were thumbing through a book and lifting out the sayings in sequence," says Stephen J. Patterson of Eden Theological Seminary in St. Louis.[42]

Some scholars thought they had discovered Q (or something much like it) among a trove of ancient documents unearthed in Nag Hammadi, Egypt, in 1945. The document, a brief Gnostic text known as the Gospel of Thomas, purports to be a collection of Jesus' sayings. Although it remains a subject of debate, many scholars now believe that the Gospel of Thomas is later than Q and probably was derived from the synoptic gospels rather than vice versa. In any event, the sayings in Thomas are substantially different in most cases from those in the canonical gospels.

While many scholars wisely regard the two-source hypothesis more as "a working theory than as a conclusion set in concrete,"[43] it nonetheless provides what most consider to be the best overall explanation for the relationship among the synoptic gospels.

Another theory advanced by the late historian Morton Smith in *The Secret Gospel*—a theory that has tantalized Bible scholars in recent years—suggests that a "secret gospel of Mark" may have been written earlier than the canonical version and that this lost edition contained material that editors deleted from later texts. The theory rests, in large part, on a letter fragment that was discovered by Smith in 1958 in the Mar Saba Monastery, twelve miles southeast of Jerusalem. Allegedly written by Clement of Alexandria between 175 and 200 CE, the fragment purports to reproduce portions of a "secret gospel" that was to be shared only with those "initiated into the great mysteries."[44] Included in the document is a passage absent from all other gospels in which Jesus raises a rich young man from the dead.

Some scholars think that the resuscitated figure may be the same mysterious character who abruptly appears in Mark 14:51 after the arrest of Jesus, casting off a linen cloth of the sort that might have enshrouded a dead body, and running away naked from the Garden of Gethsemane. However, the authenticity of Clement's letter itself is seriously questioned. And if a secret Mark did exist, says Koester, it was probably written after (and as an addition to) the canonical gospel of Mark.[45]

That the gospel tradition developed over time, from a relatively basic oral account of Jesus' sayings and miracles to a written and more detailed biographical and theological treatise, is apparent. But that does not mean, as some like to suggest, that the accounts were embellished with fiction. Rather, as the late scholar Frederick C. Grant of Union Theological Seminary once explained, the development of the gospel tradition reflected the "intense interest" among early Christians in learning more about the historical Jesus. As time passed, "Christians wanted to know how his career began, how his disciples came to believe in him, how his own family understood him," Grant wrote. The result was "not so much creating tradition as sifting, reinterpreting, re-emphasizing and amplifying it."[46]

There are many questions concerning the gospels as history that remain unanswered. We will examine some of them in more detail in Part Four. But it is of no small consequence that these writings that are now the focus of such intense scholarly scrutiny were judged in Christianity's second generation to be a credible witness to the life and ministry of Jesus. The evidence and arguments that persist suggest that the traditional claim of the gospels to apostolic origins is a most plausible one.

### The Letters of Paul

Outside of Jesus himself, no one was more instrumental in the founding of Christianity than the apostle Paul. As a Jewish Pharisee with Roman citizenship, he persecuted Christians in Palestine before his own dramatic conversion in about 34 CE on the road to Damascus, where he is said to have confronted a vision of the risen Christ. As a missionary, he was chiefly responsible for establishing Christianity in the Greco-Roman world. And if tradition is correct, he wrote nearly half of the books of the New Testament: his letters to young churches in Greece, Rome, and Asia Minor are among the earliest and most influential of Christian writings.

For most of Christian history, Paul's authorship of the thirteen letters bearing his name has been widely accepted. But modern scholarship has raised serious questions, based on content as well as writing style, suggesting that at least some of the letters were pseudonymous—written perhaps by close associates of Paul who wanted to continue his legacy.

Paul's authorship of seven of the letters remains virtually undisputed. First Thessalonians, the earliest known Christian text (dating to about 50 CE), is universally ascribed to Paul, along with Galatians, 1 and 2 Corinthians, Romans, Philippians, and Philemon. All but one are epistles addressed to local churches and offering instruction in Christian doctrine and encouragement to "stand firm in the faith." They also contain stern warnings against false teachers who were distorting his message: "I wish those who unsettle you would castrate themselves," he wrote to the Galatians (5:12). Philemon is a brief personal letter written on behalf of a runaway slave to his master.

The letters were held in high regard throughout the growing church. By early in the second century, they had been collected and copied by local church leaders and were being widely circulated together. As early as 96 CE, the Roman bishop Clement was clearly familiar with Paul's letters and wrote to Corinthian churchgoers to remind them of Paul's teaching from forty years before. The oldest surviving copy of the Pauline collection dates to about 200 CE.[47]

However, three letters that Paul allegedly wrote to his friends and former co-workers Timothy and Titus now are often disputed as having come from Paul's hand. Known as the "pastoral letters," they discuss qualifications for the ministry—a sign that the young sect was becoming more formalized in its rules and structure. Some scholars doubt their authenticity because they contain references to bishops and elders in the church, suggesting an organizational structure that, these scholars argue, would not have existed during Paul's time. Prior to Paul's death in about 67 CE, churches are generally thought to have been rather loosely organized and led mostly by itinerant preachers and spirit-filled teachers. In addition, the writing style of the pastorals appears to many scholars to be different from that of the undisputed letters.

Paul's authorship of three other letters also is often contested on grounds of style and content. Ephesians and Colossians, said to have been written from a Roman prison, are broad treatises on doctrine, while 2 Thessalonians suggests that Christ's Second Coming is not at all close at hand, in apparent contradiction to the message of Paul's first letter to the Thessalonians.

Those who doubt that Paul wrote these letters theorize that after Paul died, his followers continued writing in his name, drawing upon his teachings and applying them to new situations. The pseudonymous writings (if that is what they are), scholars say, may accurately reflect Paul's views, perhaps even recalling his very words.

There are many who defend Paul's authorship of the disputed letters. They note that Paul seldom wrote at all, preferring to dictate his letters to an *amanuensis,* or scribe. He might well have granted a trusted scribe considerable freedom in the choice of wording, these scholars surmise, although he certainly would have checked the documents carefully, and sometimes added a personal greeting in his own hand (see 2 Thess. 3:17 and Gal. 6:11). Many scholars think the differences in the linguistic style of some of Paul's letters can be explained by the freedom he granted his amanuenses.[48]

They also note that the letters contain many personal references and greetings that certainly would have been received as having come from Paul. And as he sat in a Roman prison near the end of his life, it should not seem the least improbable that his thoughts would have turned to broader doctrinal concerns rather than to the specific problems and church crises that prompted his earlier letters. Finally, there are no indications from first- or second-century Christian writers that Paul's authorship was doubted. And yet who would have been in a better position than they to judge the authenticity of Paul's work?

Modern scholarship remains divided over these questions. But barring firm proof to the contrary—proof that to date has not been shown to exist—it seems reasonable to take the letters at their word as having come from the hand, or at least the lips, of Paul.

### The "Catholic Letters"

Although Paul was without a doubt the most prolific of New Testament writers, his were not the only letters that circulated among the far-flung churches. As Christianity spread through the Roman Empire, other evangelists found the epistle an effective device for instructing the faithful. Seven letters, each with some claim to apostolic authorship, are included in the New Testament canon as *catholic* (or universal) epistles—so named because they appear to be written for general readership rather than to specific churches or individuals. While they bear the names of such central figures in the early church as James and Jude—believed by some to be brothers of Jesus—and the apostles Peter and John, their authorship has been a subject of debate since the second century.

The epistle of James is a practical book, light on theology and full of advice on ethical behavior. Even so, its place in the Bible has been challenged repeatedly over the years. It is generally believed to have been written near the end of the first century to Jewish Christians—"the twelve tribes dispersed abroad." But scholars are unable to conclusively identify the writer. Five men named James appear in the New Testament: the brother of Jesus, the son of Zebedee (one of the twelve disciples), the son of Alphaeus (also one of the disciples), "James the younger," and the father of the apostle Jude.[49]

Little is known of the last three, and since the son of Zebedee is widely assumed to have been martyred in 44 CE, tradition has leaned toward the brother of Jesus.[50] However, the writer never claims to be Jesus' brother. And some scholars contend that the language is far too erudite for a simple Palestinian. The letter is also disputed on theological grounds. Martin Luther called it "an epistle of straw," claiming that it did not belong in the Bible because it seemed to contradict Paul's teaching that salvation comes by faith as a "gift of God" rather than by good works.[51] Others, however, find the theology of James not at all inconsistent with the more conservative Hebrew Christianity that characterized the Jerusalem church, nor do they find the Greek text to be all that erudite. Even "simple Palestinians" in a city with many Hellenists would likely have been conversant in the language. The tradition that James "the brother of the Lord" is the epistle's author seems reasonably sound.

The two letters of Peter offer encouragement to churches suffering persecution and harassment. Since the second century, Christian tradition has held that the apostle Peter wrote the first epistle, probably in Rome, shortly before his martyrdom in about 65 CE. However, some modern scholars cite the epistle's cultivated language and its references to persecutions that did not occur until the reign of Domitian (81–96 CE) as evidence suggesting that it may have been written by Peter's disciples sometime later.[52] But the letter also indicates that it was written "with the help of Silas" (5:12), also known as the Hellenist Silvanus, which could easily account for the more polished Greek. Scholars also note that the persecutions mentioned might have been those during Nero's time (54–68 CE), or even a more localized harassment. The text does not say.

Second Peter has suffered even harsher scrutiny. Many scholars consider it the latest of all New Testament books, written perhaps as late as 125 CE.[53] Though the writer declares himself to be Peter, he refers to the apostles as "our ancestors" and is clearly familiar with the corpus of Paul's letters. The letter was never mentioned in second-century writings and was excluded from some church canons into the fifth century. Heidelberg University scholar Werner Kümmel concludes, "This letter cannot have been written by Peter."[54] If Peter is not the author, however, the letter is a fraud, because the writer clearly presents himself to be "Simeon Peter, a servant and apostle of Jesus Christ" (1:1). Its defenders note that despite its problems, the letter is better attested than any of the writings that the church ultimately rejected as noncanonical. Again, barring solid evidence to the contrary, they hold that the ancient traditions should be given weight and Peter's authorship should be sustained.[55]

The origins of the three letters of John also are far from certain. The ideas and language of the letters resemble those of the gospel of John, and most scholars think they came from the same source. The first is a sermon restating some basic principles of John's gospel and refuting heretics who "deny that Jesus is the Christ." The others are personal letters in which the author calls himself "the elder" and warns against evildoers. Second-century writers Papias, Irenaeus, and Clement of Alexandria all mention the epistles and attribute them to the apostle John.[56] Some modern scholars, however, detect linguistic and theological differences between the letters and John's gospel, and argue that the self-reference as "the elder" suggests a writer other than the apostle John. These arguments have not proven to be widely convincing.

The letter of Jude is considered by some too late (early in the second century) to have been written by the attested author, the "brother of James" (and thus of Jesus). The letter warns against false teachers and quotes two apocryphal books, the Assumption of Moses and Enoch. Luther refused to include it among the "true, certain chief books" of the New Testament. However, many scholars find the presumption of a second-century provenance to be "largely guesswork" and see little reason to doubt that Jude is its author.[57]

One letter on which there is no longer much dispute is the epistle to the Hebrews. The text itself does not indicate who wrote it. It turned up in some second-century Pauline collections, but many early church leaders doubted its connection to Paul—a view most scholars share today. Still, it was accepted early by the churches as authoritative in depicting Christianity as the fulfillment of Judaism.

### The Apocalypse

Unquestionably the most mysterious of the New Testament writings, the Revelation to John has been embroiled in more controversy than any other book in the Christian canon. Scholars have debated its origins and struggled over its meaning for centuries. Its claim to be a revelation from Jesus Christ of "what must take place soon" (1:1) has invited interpreters in every generation to see in its cryptic signs and symbols a prophetic roadmap through contemporary history, leading to the Second Coming of Christ. The debate over its authorship and its meaning continues.

Most scholars believe it was written toward the end of the reign of the Roman emperor Domitian, around 90 or 95 CE, and was disseminated among Christians in Asia Minor who were confronting official persecution and martyrdom at the time.[58] The writer identifies himself only as Christ's "servant John," who was in exile on the Island of Patmos, a Roman penal colony in the Aegean Sea off Miletus. Most traditions focus on the apostle John, the son of Zebedee, as the probable writer. Several early church fathers—Justin, Irenaeus, Clement of Alexandria, and Tertullian, among others—mentioned him as such. Others, however, disputed the apostle's authorship. Papias thought the style more like that of John the elder, the putative Christian leader in Asia Minor. But all such theories rely heavily on speculation. Ultimately, wrote Kümmel, "we know nothing more than that he was a Jewish-Christian prophet named John."[59]

Despite the unsolved mysteries—or perhaps because of them—the Revelation to John remains one of the most fascinating of religious writings. Its promise of the ultimate victory of good over evil, of God over Satan, has been a source of hope to Christians through the ages. And as with the rest of the New Testament, for those who read with eyes of faith, it is a hope that is not diminished by questions of authorship.

We began this chapter by asking journalistic questions. Who wrote the Bible? How credible and trustworthy are the sources? Simple, straightforward questions. The answers, we have found, are not nearly as simple.

For many reasons, the Bible is quite unlike other books—even the sacred writings of other faiths. It does not claim to be an unmediated message from God or the ciphered etchings of an angel. It is a book that is inseparable from the complexity of its own human history. The story of its origins spans more than a thousand turbulent years in a distant time and cultural setting that, despite our best efforts to comprehend, must remain forever foreign to us. It is a history, therefore, that is nearly impossible to trace with assured accuracy.

And yet it is also a history without a hiatus. Like the Bible itself, the traditions of biblical origins have never been lost or hidden away, but have thrived in living faith communities for over two thousand years, as old as the texts themselves. Nor, as we have seen, are they traditions that have gone unexamined. While scholarly research has illuminated much of the terrain, in some instances it has merely succeeded in bringing into sharper focus questions that cannot be answered to the satisfaction of modern historians. Yet after all the scrutiny, the durability and dependability of those traditions and of the sources they denote have been affirmed to a remarkable degree. The Bible and its sources remain firmly grounded in history.

As we noted at the outset, for those who read the Bible as sacred Scripture, the question of biblical authority ultimately rests not on the scholarly confirmation of its human authors but on the theological assertion of divine inspiration. As James A. Sanders of the Claremont School of Theology observes, if one embraces the very traditional view of the work of God's Spirit as being "far broader than on a canon or only on certain individuals, one can just as faithfully affirm the work of the Spirit all along the path of formation of the Bible, or canon, as on those individuals whose names happen to be recorded."[60]

How the Bible is read and interpreted—as inspired Scripture, as spiritual allegory, as historical text—is dependent in no small measure on a proper understanding of its literary genre. Were the books of the Bible written as history, as we understand history today? What historical demands can and should be placed on these ancient texts? These are the questions we will turn to next.

## CHAPTER 4

# HISTORY AND
# "HIS STORY"

## IS THERE A DIFFERENCE?

> . . . let the wise also hear and gain in learning, and the
> discerning acquire skill, to understand a proverb and
> a figure, the words of the wise and their riddles.
>
> *Proverbs 1:5–6*

THE BIBLE OFTEN IS DESCRIBED AS A TIMELESS BOOK, AS ONE THAT speaks eternal truths to every age and to every generation, its abiding wisdom resonating across centuries and cultures, inspiring hope in those who read it with faith. Given the enduring impact of its universal message on the lives of people and of nations for more than two thousand years, certainly no book can be judged more timeless.

And yet that description can be somewhat misleading. In a very real sense, each of the books in this remarkable ancient library is inextricably bound to a distant time and culture. Each was written, as Raymond Dillard and Tremper Longman remind us, "for people in antiquity in a language and culture and with literary conventions that they understood."[1]

For modern readers who are far removed from the biblical world, it is all too easy to ignore those ancient conventions, attempting to force the Bible into a modern literary mold and reading it accordingly. The danger in such an approach is that it almost inevitably leads to a misapprehension at opposite extremes: either to a hyper-skepticism that faults the Scriptures for failing to meet the tests of modern historiography, or to a totally uncritical literalism that never looks beyond the "plain meaning" of words on a page. That is why it is of utmost importance, scholars tell us, that the Bible be read "in the light of the time period from which it comes"[2]—with recognition not only of its proper historical and cultural contexts but of its varied literary genres as well.

As we have seen already, the Bible is comprised of a rich assortment of literature types—hymns and histories, laws and genealogies, prophecies and proverbs, parables and prayers, epistles and apocalyptic visions. Each employs different literary techniques and is intended to serve different purposes. And each demands to be treated differently. Understanding the story of the Good Samaritan to be a parable, for example, the reader is not concerned to ask, "Did this really happen?" but knows to look instead for the moral lesson embedded in the story (which is, after all, the purpose in its telling). On the other hand, in perusing the historical narrative of the invasion of Judah by the Assyrian king Sennacherib in the book of 2 Kings, the reader rightly expects a much higher degree of historical exactitude from the biblical text. Grasping the differences of literary genre, then, would seem essential to a proper understanding of Scripture.

Yet not all questions of genre are resolved as simply as in the above examples. Indeed, many prove to be as contentious and divisive in modern biblical scholarship as those of authorship and origin. Some twentieth-century scholars, for example, would place the entire book of Genesis into the category of a saga, which they define as a "long, prose, traditional narrative having episodic structure"[3] and "tend[ing] to consist of largely unhistorical accretions upon a possibly historical nucleus."[4] Other scholars have attempted to label Genesis in whole or in part a novella, a legend, a fable, an etiology, or a myth[5]—all of which simply are different ways of asserting that the book contains more fiction than fact. Similar disparaging designations have been assigned to the other "historical books" of the Old Testament, as well as to the gospels of the New Testament, which some scholars argue cannot possibly be regarded as accurate biography. We will examine specific questions raised against the gospels in Part Four.

But as scholars who view the Bible as basically reliable have noted, the attaching of such labels often reflects the modern interpreters' skeptical predisposition toward the historicity of the Bible and the possibility of divine action more than it does any "clear insight into the intention of the text."[6] As the New Testament scholar N. T. Wright observes, "It was not so much that scholars had examined ancient biographies and concluded that the gospels were not that sort of thing at all. It was more that the gospels were believed to be faith-documents; *therefore they could not be about history*."[7]

A classic example of such presuppositions at work in modern scholarship is found in the late G. W. Ahlström's 1986 book *Who Were the Israelites?* Referring to the story of Moses leading the Israelites from Egyptian captivity, Ahlström wrote that "since the biblical text is concerned primarily with divine actions, which are not verifiable, it is impossible to use the exodus story as a source to reconstruct the history [of Israel]." He continued: "The text is concerned with mythology rather than with a detailed reporting of historical facts. As soon as someone 'relates' a god's action or words, mythology has been written."[8]

Whatever disputable merits might exist in Ahlström's argument—"divine actions" indeed are not verifiable—other scholars have been right to point out the double standard implied in his anti-supernaturalist conclusion. Professor Edwin Yamauchi of Miami University in Ohio, for example, observes that supernatural motifs appear in the works of most ancient sources, including the works of the Greek historian Herodotus (ca. 484–425 BCE), who is widely regarded as the "father of history." And yet, as Yamauchi notes,

> *Herodotus's belief in the Delphic Oracle does not disqualify him as an accurate source for Greek history. Persian historians view [the Persian king] Darius's Behistun inscription [from the late sixth century BCE] as the most informative Old Persian text. They do not dismiss it because Darius invokes [the Persian god] Ahura Mazda 69 times in the text. As A. Momigliano comments, "the basic elements of a sacred history are in [the first-century Roman historian] Livy, as much as in the Pentateuch."*[9]

If for no other reason, the anti-supernaturalist argument against the Bible as history is clearly weakened by its uneven application. Whether a writer from antiquity is from the Greco-Roman, Persian, Egyptian, or Hebrew culture, his veracity as a historian should not be impugned solely for having a worldview that is different from that of his twentieth-century critics. Neither should his work be labeled fiction merely for acknowledging the divine. If the anti-supernaturalist argument were evenly applied to all ancient sources, our books of ancient history would become mighty thin indeed.

What, then, can reasonably be said about the literary genre of those books of the Bible that seem to be reporting real events? Did the writers of the Pentateuch, the other so-called historical books of the Old Testament, and the gospels of the New Testament all intend their texts to be read as accurate and objective history? Were the biblical writers good historians?

We would do well to consider some definitions. *History*, as the Dutch scholar Johan Huizinga defined it, "is the intellectual form in which a civilization renders account to itself of its past."[10] It is not a simple recitation of random chronological facts, nor is it like a C-SPAN videotape that plays back everything that was said and done without regard to its relative importance. As Dillard and

Longman note, history "involves a historian, one who must interpret these events for his contemporary audience."[11] *Historiography*, meanwhile, relates to the methods of historical research and presentation. *Webster* defines it as "the writing of history based on the critical examination of sources, the selection of particulars from the authentic materials, and the synthesis of those particulars into a narrative that will stand up to scholarly criticism."[12] In many respects, historiography is a relatively modern concept. It is not one that is readily apparent in the ancient Near East sources, be they biblical or nonbiblical.

It seems clear to many scholars that the biblical writers were indeed interested in history, that they understood themselves to be relating information regarding real people and events. Their concern for accuracy, as we saw in Chapter 3, was demonstrated in their use of historical sources, including some older written records, as they crafted their narratives.

And yet, most scholars concede, they were not interested in relating history merely for history's sake. As Nahum Sarna, professor emeritus of biblical studies at Brandeis University, points out, "The biblical writers were not concerned with the objective recording of details and processes of historical change, as a modern historian would be. The biblical writers were not consciously engaged in what we call historiography. Rather, their concern was with the didactic use of selected historical traditions."[13] The biblical writers, adds William G. Dever, an archaeologist and biblical expert from the University of Arizona, were "concerned not with the question, 'What really happened?' but with the larger question, 'What does it mean?' For them and for their original readers, the Bible is 'His story,' the interpretation of certain happenings as seen through the eyes of faith, the story of the saving acts of God on behalf of his people."[14]

While some scholars would want to argue with Dever over the level of concern the Bible writers exhibited for "what really happened," most no doubt would agree that explaining the eternal significance of the historical events was by far their greater concern. Indeed, traditionalists and skeptics alike judge that the biblical authors were writing not as disinterested historians but as passionate advocates of a particular view that understood God to be working in and through history. It is a genre that Dillard and Longman aptly describe as "theological history"—that is, "history narrated with a divine purpose."[15] The two scholars explain:

> *The author(s) of the Pentateuch believed that God actually created the universe in the past, Abraham migrated from Mesopotamia to Palestine, Moses parted the Red Sea, David ascended the throne of Israel, the kingdom was divided under Solomon's son, the Babylonians defeated the Israelites, Ezra and Nehemiah led a reform in the post-exilic community.*

*However, the historicity of these acts is assumed in that they are stated and not proved. The concern of the text is not to prove the history, but rather to impress the reader with the theological significance of these acts. History and theology are closely connected in the biblical text.[16]*

Recognizing the theological interests and agendas at work in the Scriptures, many biblical scholars, including conservatives, see the Bible's approach to history as something more akin to modern propaganda than to balanced historiography, in that it was consciously written to reflect the views and interests of the writers.[17] As we shall see in Chapter 9, for example, there is no question but that the author of the book of Joshua did *not* intend to give an evenhanded account of the Israelite invasion of Canaan. We never get the Canaanite perspective; there are no sympathetic reports of terrorized refugees being driven from their homes. It is a one-sided story from start to finish. The author's purpose, it seems clear, was to show how God interceded on behalf of the Israelite people by enabling them to vanquish their enemies and take possession of the Promised Land.

Nor, by the same token, were the gospels crafted as an objective summation of the activities of Jesus and his disciples and their reception in Jerusalem and Galilee. They were written to demonstrate that Jesus was indeed Israel's Messiah, who had come proclaiming the kingdom of God, and that "he came to his own and his own received him not."[18] Herod, the priests and Pharisees, Pontius Pilate, and Judas Iscariot do not get full and fair treatment from the gospel writers. They are cast as villains and foils in a compressed narrative plot. Yet neither, for that matter, is Jesus given extensive biographical treatment. The gospels account for little more than the last three years of his life. The selection of historical detail is guided by the theological intent of the authors. As one modern New Testament commentary explains:

*[The gospel writers] wrote with more than (though not less than) historical interest. They were preachers and teachers, concerned to apply the truths of Jesus' life and teachings to specific communities in their own day. This theological purpose of the evangelists has sometimes been lost, with a consequent loss of appreciation for the significance and application of the history that the evangelists narrate.[19]*

The fact, then, that the history reported in the Bible was selected and packaged with a theological purpose does not of necessity make that history less reliable or less true. In some instances, it does make it incomplete, however. But that, as most scholars are aware, is the nature of virtually all historical records from antiquity. The writers of the Bible—like the chroniclers of ancient Egypt,

Mesopotamia, and Greece—did not operate within the meticulous framework of modern historiography. All had agendas, all were selective and interpretive in what they recorded, and, as we have seen, all understood their gods to be actively engaged in history. Relative to other records from the ancient Near East, the Bible certainly should *not* be judged as of lesser value. In many respects, in fact, as we shall see in Part Two, it stands head and shoulders above the others.

Even though the biblical writers may not have employed all the techniques of modern historiography, neither were they entirely "precritical" in their assessment and selection of historical material, as is sometimes suggested.[20] Some scholars, for example, attempt to juxtapose the writers of the Old Testament unfavorably against Herodotus, who is regarded as the early exemplar of the critical evaluation of sources. The Greek historian, it is noted, typically demonstrated his critical approach by reporting things he had heard and then adding an often skeptical concluding comment. So, for example, after repeating a Scythian tale about members of a tribe who were said to turn themselves into wolves once a year, Herodotus added, "For myself, I cannot believe this tale."[21] In other instances, however, as A. R. Millard of Liverpool University observes, Herodotus "reports without comment many things that are recognized today as untrue (e.g., that the semen of Indians and Ethiopians is black) and takes some incidents as 'clear evidence of divine intervention.' "[22]

On that score, as Millard argues, the biblical writers compare quite favorably to Herodotus. Their presentation of history also involved critical judgment, in that it included only material that the authors believed to be pertinent and true. He explains:

> *These writers were not jackdaw historians, like Herodotus who relayed any piece of information brought to his attention, whether he believed it or not, as a means of preserving the memory of the past. The Israelite historians had definite purpose in their writing and rejected the irrelevant, informing the inquisitive that there were sources containing other material that they could consult if they wished (e.g., "the book of the annals of the kings of Israel," 2 Kings 1:18).*[23]

So the history in the Bible, then, should not be judged deficient merely because it is found in some instances to be limited in breadth and detail in comparison to the more expansive Greek and modern historiographies. The biblical authors, as we have seen, were writing with purpose and focus. They demonstrated themselves to be as attentive to accuracy as could reasonably be expected of any writer from antiquity. They wrote not to convince skeptics of the historicity of certain past events, but rather to explain and expound upon the significance of those events that formed the shared historical tradition of Israel as the people of God. And they wrote from within their own time and culture to an audience whose worldview they shared, employing literary conventions that would have been familiar to all. They wrote sacred history—"theological" history, if you will. But history nonetheless. And it is history that for the most part is subject to testing and verification. There are sources that can be examined, and other ancient writings and archaeological discoveries that can be consulted. It is precisely that process that will occupy the remainder of this investigation.

But before we leave the discussion of literary genre and of what legitimately constitutes historical writing, we must briefly acknowledge a long and divisive dispute that, for many Bible readers, has proved to be something of a litmus test for biblical fidelity. Nowhere has the question of literary genre been more central in the wrangling over the Bible's veracity than in regard to what many scholars refer to as the "primordial history" in the opening chapters of Genesis. What are we to make of the stories of creation and of Noah's ark and the worldwide flood? Should they be taken as literal history, as religious myth, or perhaps as some literary hybrid that combines features of both?

The books and articles generated in the emotionally charged creation-versus-evolution debates of the past century would easily fill a small library. It would serve no productive purpose for us to try to replicate or adjudicate all of the arguments and evidence here. We have neither the space to do that task justice nor any reasonable prospect of settling a dispute so couched in fundamental differences of viewpoint. It may be helpful, though, to consider in somewhat broad strokes the nature and development of the debate in order to discern the extent to which it ultimately hinges on a proper understanding of biblical genre.

The story of creation—whether it is told through the imagery of ancient myth, the words of divine revelation, or the theories of modern physics and biology—is the story of what it means to be human. And it is a story over which religion and science have been at odds for centuries. Ever since Copernicus overturned the church-sanctioned view of earth as the center of the universe and Charles Darwin posited random mutation and natural selection as the real creators of human life, the biblical view that "in the beginning God created the heavens and the earth" has found itself increasingly on the defensive in modern Western thought.

Despite the dominance of Darwin's theory—that human beings evolved from lower life-forms over millions of years—theologians and biblical scholars have yielded relatively little ground on what for them is a fundamental doctrine of faith. The three major Western religions—Christianity, Judaism, and Islam—all teach that the universe is the handiwork of a divine creator who has given humanity a special place in that creation. This view of human origins is shared by most Americans as well. A 1997 poll by the Gallup Organization found that about 44 percent of Americans, including 31 percent of college graduates, subscribed to a fairly literal reading of the Genesis creation account, while another 39 percent (53 percent of college grads) believed God played at least some creative role in the universe. Only 10 percent (17 percent of college grads) embraced a purely natural evolutionary process with no divine involvement.[24]

The apparent conflict between religious and scientific explanations of creation has left a centuries-old legacy of suspicion and outright acrimony that in modern times has erupted in open warfare in the nation's courtrooms and classrooms. Often the modern debate has amounted to little more than a shouting match between extremists on both sides—fundamentalists who dismiss evolution as a satanic deception, and atheistic naturalists who assert that science offers the only window on reality and who seek to discredit religious belief as ignorant superstition.

In more recent years, a move to soften the rhetoric and perhaps even to bridge the historical gap between religion and science has gained momentum. While few experts suggest that an actual convergence of the two is possible (and some question whether convergence would even be desirable),[25] creative dialogue is on the upswing. Books and scholarly articles by scientists and theologians exploring the possibilities of rapprochement are appearing with increasing regularity. At least seventy-two organizations worldwide, many in the United States, now provide forums for creative exchange of religious and scientific perspectives.[26] Pope John Paul II, in a 1988 message, heartily endorsed such interaction. Science, said the pontiff, "can purify religion from error and superstition," while religion "can purify science from idolatry and false absolutes."[27]

Although religion and science have a long history of conflict, they have not always been at odds. In the West, early science grew out of a decidedly religious impulse: to understand God and his relationship with humanity. The biblical picture of an orderly creation by a dependable God gave impetus to scientific inquiry. The universe "made sense" because it was overseen by a Supreme Intelligence who made mathematical description and prediction possible. Throughout Christianity's early history, theologians such as Augustine and Thomas Aquinas did most of the scientific pondering, and their inquiries were seen as a religious quest.

Not until the fifteenth century did the relationship between science and religion begin to seriously fray. When Copernicus, who besides being an astronomer also was the canon of his local cathedral, put forth his notion that the earth revolved around the sun rather than vice versa, he was so fearful of the church's reaction that he passed his results around anonymously. Only on his deathbed did Copernicus dare sign his name to the astonishing finding. It was the Italian astronomer Galileo, building upon Copernicus's work, who argued in the seventeenth century that scientific inquiry should be free from the restraints of church authority. The church responded by putting him under house arrest and forbidding him to write or speak of Copernicus's theory.

Other scientists of Galileo's day struggled privately with conflicts between religious belief and science. But by the eighteenth century, Enlightenment thinkers were arguing that human reason and scientific empiricism, rather than religious belief, were best equipped to explain human existence. A century later Darwin, a lifelong member of the Church of England, published *Origin of Species,* detailing his theory of evolution. But it was Thomas Huxley, an associate of Darwin's, who expounded on the theological implications of evolution—that human beings were not a unique creation of God at all but were derived from animal ancestors.

Church reaction against such thinking was strong from the start, but nowhere so strong as in the United States. Fundamentalists pressed for state laws banning the teaching of evolution in public schools. Literal creationists reached their zenith with their victory in the famous Scopes "monkey trial" in Tennessee in 1925, and evolution almost disappeared from high-school textbooks for a quarter-century. In the 1950s, however, Darwin's theory began once again to be incorporated into some biology studies, and by the end of the 1960s, state laws banning evolution texts had disappeared. More recently, court battles have been fought in Arkansas, Louisiana, Michigan, and elsewhere over whether the public schools ought to teach "creation science," which argues that geological and fossil evidence is consistent with the book of Genesis. So far, courts have turned back all such moves.

Today, while some scientists and theologians are sending out peace feelers, literal creationists continue to draw battle lines. For fundamentalists and some evangelical Christians, a literal interpretation of creation in Genesis rules out any chance of rapprochement with science—at least on questions of human origins. "Anyone who believes in evolution cannot accept the biblical record of creation," insists Duane Gish of the Institute for Creation Research in San Diego, a group that espouses creation science.[28]

Under their theory of "recent special creation," believers in creation science hold that God created the universe *ex nihilo* ("out of nothing") in six days as described in the first two chapters of Genesis. By tracing the biblical genealogies, they estimate that the earth came into being just ten thousand years ago. The vast fossil and geological evidence of an earth millions if not billions of years old, they explain, is the result of Noah's flood or, alternatively, is simply part of an "appearance of age" that God intentionally built into the universe. That presumably also would explain how stars millions of light-years away could be visible on earth if the universe had been created so recently. Not the least of the problems with that view is the theological dilemma it poses: that of a God who engages in deception.

Many Bible scholars and most scientists—including many who are devoutly religious—dismiss creation science as engaging more in polemics than in rigorous scientific inquiry. Among groups that reject literal creationism is the American Scientific Affiliation (ASA), an organization of some 2,300 scientists who identify themselves as evangelical Christians. They support a more conventionally scientific approach to the question of origins, acknowledging evidence for natural processes at work in the universe, yet affirming a belief in God as the creator and sustainer of life. "A lot of educated people in the sciences see the two as perfectly compatible," says Robert L. Herrmann, a molecular biologist and ASA's former executive director.[29]

In fact, many religious scientists are convinced that there should be no conflict at all between science and religion. "We have two databases: Scripture and nature," says Dorothy Chappell, a biologist and academic dean at Gordon College, a Christian liberal-arts school in Wenham, Massachusetts. "Many of us believe God has revealed himself in both." Thus, when science and theology seem to conflict, both should be open to testing and revision. An apparent conflict with science certainly does not mean Scripture is wrong, says Chappell, but it may well mean that interpretation is faulty.[30]

Listening to some of the rhetoric today, one might easily assume that the views espoused by creation science represent the historic position of Christianity and of the Bible, and that it is only in modern times—with the rise of philosophically tainted theories of evolution—that creationism has come under siege. Yet this is not the case.

As early as the fifth century, the great Christian theologian Augustine warned against taking the six days of Genesis literally. Writing on *The Literal Meaning of Genesis,*[31] Augustine argued that the days of creation were not successive ordinary days—the sun, after all, according to Genesis, was not created until the fourth "day"—and had nothing to do with time. Rather, the six days occurred "in a form unfamiliar to us as intrinsic principles within things created" (125). He continued: "We should not think of those days as solar days. . . . He made that which gave time its beginning, as He made all things together, disposing them in an order based not on intervals of time but on causal connections" (154). Why, then, does the narrative use the device of the six days? "The reason," said Augustine, "is that those who cannot understand the meaning of the text, He created all things together, cannot arrive at the meaning of Scripture unless the narrative proceeds slowly step by step" (142). The sacred writer, he said, "was able to separate in the time of his narrative what God did not separate in time in His creative act" (36).

Augustine also sounded like an evolutionist when he claimed that while God created everything in the beginning, some things were made in fully developed form and others were made in "potential form" that developed over time to the condition in which they are seen today. Saint Basil, the fourth-century bishop of Caesarea, made a similar argument in his *Nine Homilies of the Hexaemeron*.[32] Yet neither Basil nor Augustine ever was accused of being a heretic for espousing such views. To the contrary, Augustine spoke contemptuously of Christians who he said exposed the church to ridicule by interpreting Scripture in ways that flatly contradicted the evidence in nature. "The shame," wrote Augustine, "is not so much that an ignorant individual is derided but that people outside the household of faith think our sacred writers held such opinions . . . and are criticized and rejected as unlearned men" (42–43).

It is simply historically inaccurate, then, as many scholars note, to contend that the church was solid on literal creationism prior to the rise of modern evolutionist theories. As Davis A. Young, a geology professor at Calvin College in Grand Rapids, Michigan, has written:

> *Given that a theological thinker of Augustine's genius arrived at the views he did after years of careful study of the text, it is incumbent upon us to approach the early chapters of Genesis with far less dogmatism and far more humility and caution than we often do. . . . Not that we should adopt Augustine's specific interpretations . . . but that we should recognize what Augustine recognized: namely, the early chapters of Genesis are in fact complex and do not render easy, pat answers.[33]*

Today, a growing number of conservative scholars, harking back to Augustine, are convinced that more nuanced views of the biblical creation account are required to accommodate the knowledge revealed in science. Some nonetheless attempt to adhere as closely to a literal interpretation of Genesis as the scientific evidence will allow. One view to emerge as a result is the "day-age theory"—the idea that creation was gradual, occurring perhaps over millions of years, and that the "days" of Genesis actually were geological increments. Proponents of this view find support in words of the New Testament: "With the Lord, one day is like a thousand years" (2 Pet. 3:8). But some strict biblicists object to this interpretation, saying that references in Genesis to "evening and morning" in each of the six days of creation clearly connote twenty-four-hour days.

A similar approach is the "multiple-gap theory," which suggests that creation was a series of instantaneous acts occurring over six twenty-four-hour days, but that each day was separated by eons of time. Proponents of this view say it helps to account for the sudden appearance of new life-forms, some of which are found in the fossil record. However, some text experts see no scriptural basis for long lapses between the six days of Genesis.

Another proposal, the "gap and restitution theory," postulates that the passage of an indeterminate but presumably very long period of time is implied between the first and second verses of Genesis:

1. In the beginning God created the heavens and the earth.
2. And the earth was formless and void, and darkness was over the surface of the deep.

This view assumes that there was an initial creation as described in the first verse, followed by destruction and chaos in the second verse—all of which preceded the "recreation" of an inhabitable earth as spelled out in the succeeding verses. This scenario, its proponents argue, could account for geological evidence of an ancient earth. It finds little support outside of fundamentalist circles, however.[34]

More prevalent among religious scientists is "theistic evolution"—the view that evolutionary theory is basically correct and that life on earth, including humanity, evolved over millions of years. But unlike traditional Darwinists, those who espouse theistic evolution consider the evolutionary process, like all other physical processes known to science, to be divinely designed and governed. In this view, held by much of mainline Protestantism, Reform and Conservative Judaism, and Roman Catholicism, the Genesis account is understood as speaking allegorically of the relationship between God and creation, rather than presenting a scientific or historical account of how and when creation occurred. "Creation and evolution are not contradictory," explains Howard Van Till, a professor of physics and astronomy at Calvin College. "They provide different answers to a different set of questions."[35] To that way of thinking, adds Ian Barbour, professor emeritus of science and religion at Carleton College in Minnesota, "we can look at the Big Bang and subsequent evolution as God's way of creating."[36]

In large measure, then, the creation-evolution debate hinges on a proper understanding of the genre and purpose of the Genesis creation story. Should it be read as if it were a modern chronicle of "what really happened" in primordial times? Or should it be understood, as it has been through most of Christian history, as an ancient and inspired literary affirmation of the relationship between God and humanity as that of creator and creation? It is a question that no doubt will continue to divide Bible believers, as it has for centuries. For those who hold to a literalist position, the daunting challenge must remain one of reconciling their interpretation of Scripture with the evidence from creation itself.

Attempts to do so to date have not proven particularly persuasive beyond fundamentalist circles. Meanwhile, those who read the creation account allegorically must delineate more convincingly for the benefit of their more conservative colleagues precisely where in the Bible they suppose the allegory ends and authentic history begins. It is a problem with no easy solution.

Much the same may be said of disputes over the meaning and intent of the biblical story of the flood. Those who take it as literal history believe that in divine judgment against a creation gone bad, God unleashed a worldwide deluge that destroyed all air-breathing life on earth except for those creatures taken aboard the ark. When God finally allowed the waters to recede, the ark was emptied and the world was repopulated by the creatures that disembarked. Based on biblical genealogies, all of this would have transpired less than ten thousand years ago—in fact, according to some readings, as late as 2300 BCE.[37]

While most biblical scholars consider the story of the flood a myth or a folktale or assign it to some other category of literature that allows for an allegorical interpretation, many conservatives have little difficulty imagining that an omnipotent God could pull off precisely what the Genesis story describes. As with the creation narrative, however, the evidence and arguments from science stack up overwhelmingly against a literal interpretation of the flood story. Where, for example, it is often argued, would such a volume of water have come from, and where would it have gone afterward? How would mammalian life have reemerged on isolated islands and land-masses that emerged from the receding flood waters? As with proponents of creation science, some conservatives argue that there is, indeed, geological evidence consistent with a universal deluge.[38] But such arguments have found little support within the scientific mainstream.

Moreover, many scholars note that the biblical story seems to borrow directly from the flood myths of other civilizations in the ancient Near East. In both the Sumerian *Gilgamesh* epic, believed to have originated in the third millennium BCE, and the Old Babylonian myth of *Atrahasis,* a god warns the hero of an impending deluge. The hero responds by building a boat and bringing his family and an assortment of animals aboard. They ride out the flood, and the boat comes to rest on a mountain. In *Gilgamesh,* as in Genesis, the hero releases three birds on three different occasions, and when the third bird does not return, it is seen as a sign that the waters have receded.[39] And as in Genesis, the *Sumerian King List* and other Mesopotamian traditions divide primeval history into antediluvian and postdiluvian periods, with extraordinarily long lifespans being common prior to the flood and shorter ones becoming the norm afterward.[40] There are some significant differences in the accounts as well. But the fact that the biblical story tracks these others so closely, says Professor Michael

D. Coogan of the Harvard Semitic Museum, suggests that the Genesis flood is "the clearest example of direct dependence on other ancient myths."[41]

Some conservative scholars, on the other hand, read the same ancient writings and draw exactly the opposite conclusion. They argue that Genesis and the Sumerian and Babylonian writings are independent and indicate a shared memory of an actual event that came to be recounted in somewhat different terms as it passed through the divergent civilizations.[42]

As with the creation account, adherence to an understanding of the flood story as literal history has become for many a test of biblical orthodoxy. That being so, there is little likelihood that disputes over the genre of the narrative (history? mythology? spiritual allegory?) will be settled anytime soon. Yet there is little doubt that a lack of compelling evidence makes a purely literal reading of the Bible's primordial history a most difficult position to sustain.

The emotional intensity that has often characterized debates over biblical genre and history is certainly understandable. It reflects the profoundly important role the Bible continues to play in the lives of individuals, faith communities, and a broader culture that regards it with high esteem. For many who revere the Scriptures as the inspired Word of God, affirming the accuracy of biblical history is far more than an academic exercise. A challenge to the factuality of one passage is often seen as a challenge to the integrity of the Bible as a whole. If the story of creation is declared a myth, it is argued, then what prevents the same label being attached to the accounts of the exodus from Egypt, the battle of Jericho, and the resurrection of Christ? As one scholar wryly asks, "If Jericho is not razed, is our faith in vain?"[43]

Such concerns are legitimate (if perhaps overstated). In the extreme, they reflect a misapprehension of the Scriptures as a monolithic literary entity rather than the complex array of writings that their own history has shown them to be. Sufficient interpretive leeway, it seems, must be granted to accommodate the demonstrable differences in literary genre.

Yet it is no less important to attempt to ascertain as objectively as possible exactly what is historical in the Scriptures and what is not. As William Dever observes, whether the biblical texts are truly historical or "merely possess an essential 'historicality,' it really does matter what actually happened in the past, not just how the religious community came to interpret the supposed events for its own needs in its own time and circumstance."[44] And when biblical writings that are unambiguously historical in their *intent* are critically examined, they consistently show themselves to be remarkably dependable. As the American archaeologist Siegfried H. Horn, former director of the American Center of Oriental Research in Amman, Jordan, has written regarding one era of biblical history—the period of the divided monarchy:

*The factual information contained in the historical books of the Bible has generally proved to be trustworthy and accurate insofar as this can be determined from contemporary cuneiform records that have turned up in Assyrian and Babylonian archives. Wherever events recorded in the Bible for this period are mentioned in such secular documents, they either corroborate or supplement the biblical information.*[45]

Archaeological discoveries, as Horn observes, often have been an important source of pertinent data in evaluating the historicity of the Bible. These discoveries have not always been supportive of traditional views, but they have always proved illuminating. We turn next to a detailed survey of the fascinating and compelling evidence concerning the Bible from the field of archaeology.

# PART TWO

# THE BIBLE
# AND
# ARCHAEOLOGY

## CHAPTER 5

# THE STONES
# CRY OUT

## A DISCOVERY AT DAN

*Truth shall spring out of the earth.*

*Psalm 85:11*

IT WAS JULY 21, 1993, AND THE WORKDAY WAS NEARLY OVER FOR THE team of Israeli archaeologists excavating the ruins of the ancient Israelite city of Dan in upper Galilee. The team, led by Avraham Biran of Hebrew Union College in Jerusalem, had been toiling since early morning, sifting debris in a stone-paved plaza outside what had been the city's main gate. Now the fierce afternoon sun was turning the stoneworks into a reflective oven. Gila Cook, the team's surveyor, was about to take a water break when something caught her eye—an unusual shadow in a portion of recently exposed wall along the east side of the plaza. Moving closer, she discovered a flattened basalt stone protruding from the ground with what appeared to be Aramaic letters etched into its smooth surface. She called Biran over for a look. As the veteran archaeologist knelt to examine the stone, his eyes widened. "Oh, my God!" he exclaimed. "We have an inscription!"[1]

In an instant, Biran knew that they had stumbled upon a rare treasure. Unlike pottery and other "mute" artifacts commonly found at archaeological excavations, an inscription, it is said, speaks in a voice from the past. In his twenty-seven years at the site, Biran had found other inscriptions, but none like this one. Most consisted of a few letters in Aramaic, Hebrew, or Greek etched onto tiny potsherds, the popular "notepads" of the ancient Near East. One important fragment unearthed in 1976 identified the site as the biblical city of Dan, the strategic northern outpost mentioned prominently in the books of 1 and 2 Samuel, 1 and 2 Kings, and 1 and 2 Chronicles.

But this discovery, as Biran suspected when he first saw it, would prove to be far more significant. It would make the front page of the *New York Times* and touch off a heated debate in the often arcane world of biblical scholarship. The basalt stone was quickly identified as part of a shattered monument, or *stele,* from the ninth century BCE, apparently commemorating a military victory of the king of Damascus over two ancient enemies: the king of Israel and the house of David. As it would be translated later, the twelve partial lines of inscription read:

> . . . *my father went up* . . .
> . . . *and my father died, he went to [his fate . . . Is-]*
> *rael formerly in my father's land* . . .
> *I [fought against Israel?] and Hadad went in front of me* . . .
> . . . *my king. And I slew of [them X footmen, Y cha-]*
> *riots and two thousand horsemen* . . .
> *the king of Israel. And [I] slew [. . . the kin-]*
> *g of the House of David. And I put* . . .
> *their land* . . .
> *other . . . [. . . ru-]*
> *led over Is[rael . . . ]*
> *siege upon . . .*[2]

The fragmentary reference to David was a historical bombshell. Never before had the familiar name of Judah's ancient warrior king, a central figure of the Hebrew Bible and, according to Christian Scripture, an ancestor of Jesus, been found in the records of antiquity outside the pages of the Bible. Skeptical scholars had long seized upon that fact to argue rather persuasively within the biblical academy that David was a mere legend, invented, they said, like much of Israel's biblical history, by Hebrew scribes during or shortly after Israel's Babylonian exile (roughly five hundred years before the start of the common era). David and presumably other heroes of the Hebrew Bible, the skeptics argued, were about as historical as King Arthur.[3] "There are no literary criteria for believing David to be more historical than Joshua, Joshua more historical than Abraham, and Abraham more historical than Adam," British biblical scholar Philip R. Davies had argued just a year before the discovery at Dan. "There is

no non-literary way of making this judgment either, since none of these characters has left a trace outside the biblical text!"[4]

But with Biran's startling discovery, the skeptics' argument had suffered a
serious blow. Now, at last, there was material evidence, an inscription written
not by Hebrew scribes but by an enemy of the Israelites a little more than a century after David's presumptive lifetime. It seemed to be a clear corroboration of
the existence of King David's dynasty and, by implication, of David himself.

Conservative scholars, whose high view of biblical history had long been
relegated to a minority position within the biblical academy, felt rightfully vin-
dicated. At evangelical Wheaton College in Illinois, James K. Hoffmeier, chairman of archaeology and biblical studies, declared the King David inscription a
"tremendously important find" that would "certainly cause anxiety for the
skeptics."[5] Others were more exuberant, hailing the discovery as the beginning
of a new golden age of biblical archaeology that was certain to unearth even
more dramatic evidence of the Bible's historical veracity. Some believers went so
far as to exult that the inscription at Dan had confirmed not only David's existence but, by implication, the historical accuracy of the entire biblical narrative
about him, from his slaying of the giant Goliath to his adulterous affair with
Bathsheba, his murderous cover-up, and his subsequent redemption.[6] There
was, of course, nothing in the appearance of the name alone in the inscription
to warrant such a broad conclusion. Yet for those already convinced of the
Bible's reliability as a source of historical information, the David inscription was
one more important reason to believe.

While some, indeed, were reading more into the David inscription than the
evidence warranted, others at the opposite extreme questioned whether it had
changed anything at all. A handful of minimalist Bible scholars contended that
Biran and his colleague Joseph Naveh, a paleographer at the Hebrew University
in Jerusalem who had helped decipher the inscription, had badly botched the
translation. The stele, one prominent skeptic argued, referred not to David or
to his dynasty but to the house of Dod—probably a Canaanite god, although
no one had ever heard of one by that name. Or perhaps it was intended to signify a place rather than a person or a dynasty—a place that was inscrutably
named house of beloved, or house of uncle, or even house of kettle.[7] A few even
suggested, without offering a shred of evidence, that the inscriptions were modern forgeries that had been planted at the Dan site.[8] Not surprisingly, the minimalists' arguments fell flat. Among biblical scholars and archaeologists alike,
Biran's discovery was overwhelmingly accepted for what it appeared at first to
be: an extraordinary extrabiblical testimony to the existence of David and his
monarchy.

The discovery a year later of two additional fragments of the stele added further weight to Biran's initial interpretation. Those pieces contained what appeared to be the names of the two defeated monarchs: Jehoram, king of Israel, and Ahaziah, king of Judah, both of whom ruled in the middle of the ninth century BCE.[9] The battle commemorated on the stele, some scholars now believe, may have been the one described in 2 Chronicles 22:5, in which Ahaziah "went with Jehoram son of King Ahab of Israel to make war against King Hazael of Aram."

Beyond their weighty impact on the question of David's existence, the discoveries at Dan had other major repercussions. They provided a dramatic illustration of both the promise and the peril that come into play whenever the Bible is weighed on the scales of modern archaeology. They showed how, in one serendipitous moment, the unearthing of an inscription or artifact can shed bold new light, or cast an ominous shadow, on a passage of Scripture, in the process obliterating the confident presuppositions and conventional wisdom of modern biblical scholarship.

Over and over again in this century, archaeological discoveries have helped illuminate biblical texts and their cultural and historical settings. But illumination of Scripture has not always meant corroboration. In some important instances, as we shall see, archaeological and biblical data simply have not matched. While the David inscription and other recent discoveries may well have pushed the pendulum of scholarly opinion back in a "pro-Bible" direction, some modern finds have raised difficult questions about the Bible's reliability as a historical record. These are the subjects of vigorous debate.

Perhaps more than anything else, the discovery at Dan served as a powerful reminder that archaeology—as useful as it may be in illuminating biblical history—is an evolving discipline, as much art as science, and its capabilities are limited. Its evidence is all too often equivocal and easily subjected to unwarranted interpretation. Few reputable scholars today would venture to claim, on the basis of archaeological data alone, that the Bible is accurate in its representation of events—or that it is not. Archaeology is, after all, just one source of historical information, albeit an important one.

Just how far can archaeology reasonably be expected to go in proving or disproving the Bible? And to what extent can, and should, Bible texts be used to interpret archaeological data? These are questions that archaeologists, historians, and biblical scholars have wrestled with for decades. Most in the field today would agree with archaeologist Kenneth Holum of the University of Maryland: "The point of our work is not to try to prove or disprove the Bible. It is to help scientists understand the ancient cultures."[10]

Yet without question, archaeology has influenced modern conceptions about the Bible, its nature, and its origins. In some cases, it has profoundly and literally changed how we read and understand the biblical text. Before we examine some of those changes, it is important to first consider, at least briefly, how archaeology itself has evolved during the past century to become an important and useful tool in interpreting and understanding the Scriptures.

## CHAPTER 6

# BIBLES AND SPADES

## THE BIRTH OF BIBLICAL ARCHAEOLOGY

I believe in the spade. It has fed the tribes of mankind.
It has furnished them water, coal, iron, and gold. And
now it is giving them truth—historic truth, the
mines of which have never been opened till our time.

*Oliver Wendell Holmes[1]*

ARCHAEOLOGY AS IT IS COMMONLY THOUGHT OF TODAY—THE CAREFUL recovery and systematic study of the material remains of the past—is a relatively young science. While the relics and ruins of ancient civilizations have long been a source of popular fascination, they have not always been prized for their scientific value. Prior to the mid–nineteenth century, archaeological expeditions seldom amounted to much more than treasure hunts. Priceless statues, coins, jewelry, and other artifacts from the ancient Near East often were plundered and sold to collectors and museums as historical trophies or exotic *objets d'art*. Because excavations tended to be haphazard, important discoveries were largely accidental.

Not until the mid-1800s, when archaeological methods slowly became more organized and systematic, did the search for ancient artifacts begin to evolve into a disciplined field of scientific exploration. This powerful new tool for historical research was quickly drafted into the service of biblical scholarship.

Among the first of the more systematic expeditions in Palestine were those conducted in 1838 by Americans Edward Robinson, a noted geographer and Bible scholar, and Eli Smith, a Yale-educated Congregational minister who was fluent in Arabic. The two set out to rediscover significant sites mentioned in the Bible and, by doing so, to confirm at least the geographical accuracy of the Holy Scriptures. They succeeded on both scores. Making systematic use of topological surveys and excavations, the two Americans found and correctly identified over a hundred biblical locations—from Bethsaida to Beersheba.

What is widely viewed as Robinson's most noteworthy achievement, however, occurred in Jerusalem. Excavating at the southwest corner of the Temple Mount, Robinson unearthed the broken stub of what once had been a massive stone arch affixed to the exterior of the mammoth retaining wall. The arch, it was believed, had supported a major entryway to the temple in the days of Jesus and Herod. The discovery ignited a new spark of excitement among biblical scholars and ordinary believers, who could now behold the ancient stonework and proclaim with a degree of confidence greater than before, "Here is where Jesus walked."

The publicity generated by Robinson's work, coupled with his relatively careful and studied approach to exploration, soon spurred others to take up the Bible and the spade and venture to the Holy Land. In the decades that followed, this new wave of exploration would give rise to a popular new field of study that would become known as biblical archaeology.

As important as Robinson's work was in advancing archaeology as a science, and in using archaeology to explore biblical history, his methods were quite crude when judged by today's standards. The birth of what we might call *modern* archaeology in Palestine generally is linked to the work of Sir William M. F. Petrie, a British archaeologist and Egyptologist who worked at Tel el-Hasi, in the Negev Desert south of Jerusalem, in the early 1890s.[2] Petrie is widely credited with having pioneered the use of stratigraphy and ceramic typology—two important methods of sequence dating that would enable archaeologists to more accurately reconstruct the chronology of biblical sites.

Stratigraphy is the process of systematically excavating and analyzing the layers of man-made and natural debris that accumulates at inhabited sites over the centuries. In modern times, these layers often appear as an artificial mound, or *tell*. At some tells in modern Israel and the West Bank, as many as thirty different strata have been discovered, containing the debris of successive cities over a period of three thousand years or more. Previously, archaeologists might have slashed through the strata haphazardly in search of buried treasure. But Petrie understood the importance of carefully removing and sifting through each successive layer and analyzing the artifacts and ruins that were revealed. He believed that archaeologists, in that process, could uncover and document the material evidence of battles and conflicts, the settlement and destruction of cities, the rise and fall of kings and kingdoms, and other major "political" events chronicled in the Bible.

While stratigraphy proved helpful in reconstructing a relative sequence of events, it was of little use in determining dates. That's where ceramic typology came in. Shards of broken pottery are, without a doubt, the most common artifacts recovered at Near Eastern archaeological sites. Sometimes the discarded earthen vessels are found nearly intact or in pieces that are easily reassembled. Even in Petrie's time, such a wealth of ancient pottery was available from sites throughout the region that scholars were beginning to become rather adept at identifying, classifying, and dating the earthenware.

For archaeologists, the implications of this advance were nothing short of revolutionary. Armed with a knowledge of ceramic typologies, an archaeologist could sift a layer of debris and, finding shards of a pottery type known to be popular during a particular period, confidently date the debris layer to that timeframe. Today, the development of this technique is considered one of the greatest achievements of the early biblical archaeologists.[3]

From Petrie's time onward, archaeological work in Palestine began to grow more sophisticated. It was also increasingly better financed, thanks mainly to the formation of an assortment of new international sponsoring agencies. The growth was further enhanced in 1919 by the promulgation of new antiquities laws in Palestine under the British Mandate Department of Antiquities. That action gave rise to a host of new foreign schools in Palestine that combined archaeological research with academic field instruction. Among the more prominent of these was the American School of Oriental Research in Jerusalem, under the direction first of William Foxwell Albright, a professor of Semitic languages at Johns Hopkins University, and then of Nelson Gleuck, a rabbi and biblical scholar.

The son of Methodist missionaries, Albright would become the most respected and renowned of the new breed of biblical archaeologists. Working at sites in Palestine and in Jordan during the years following World War I, he refined Petrie's pioneer efforts in pottery-dating techniques and contributed mightily to the understanding of Bronze and Iron Age pottery types.

Although Albright was no biblical literalist, he held a generally high view of the historicity of Scripture. And he was confident that archaeology, properly conducted, would contribute to a better understanding and appreciation of the Bible. Archaeology, he was convinced, would help fill a troublesome void in biblical knowledge—a void that had been exploited for years by skeptical scholars who saw the Bible as little more than a book of fables. "From the chaos of prehistory," Albright wrote at mid-century, "the Bible projected as though it were a monstrous fossil, with no contemporary evidence to demonstrate its authenticity and its origin in a human world like ours."[4]

Through his own work at Tell Beitin, which he identified as biblical Bethel, and the work of other well-financed teams at biblical sites such as Beth-Shan, Jericho, Samaria, and Shechem, Albright saw the Bible taking on a new measure of connectedness with the material history of the region. "Discovery after discovery," Albright noted, "has established the accuracy of innumerable details, and has brought increased recognition of the value of the Bible as a source of history."[5]

Interest among religious groups was so high that Albright soon had working with him a consortium of church-sponsored and church-related schools that were eager to provide staff and financial support for digs in the Holy Land. Although Albright was no fundamentalist, many of his supporters were. His work had heightened their expectations that science, at last, was coming down on the side of biblical literalism. Their exuberance quickly gave rise to the popular but mistaken notion that biblical archaeology would "prove the Bible true." It was a seductive notion that relatively few in this burgeoning new field of research ever embraced but that nonetheless would take decades to fully dispel.

Without question, the early decades of biblical archaeology had produced some sensational discoveries that enhanced the image of biblical history. Famous people and places in the Bible that had long seemed ghostlike and legendary suddenly became more tangible as material traces of their existence turned up under the archaeologist's spade. "By the aid of archaeology," Millar Burrows, an eminent archaeologist and biblical scholar, wrote in 1941, "the study of the Bible ceases to be, as it were, suspended in the air, and gets its feet upon the ground."[6]

Yet it soon became apparent, for some scholars at least, that a far too ambitious agenda had been set for biblical archaeology: the discovery of physical "proof" of the truth of the Bible itself. While archaeologists could reasonably look for traces of a forty-year nomadic sojourn in the Sinai desert (traces that so far have not been found), what type of evidence could they hope to find that would verify the Bible's assertions that God went before the Israelites in a pillar of fire, fed them with manna from heaven, and ultimately led them to the Promised Land? Archaeologists could sift the Judean desert for relics of a first-century religious sect that believed in a Messiah who was crucified in Jerusalem under a Roman prefect. But what material evidence could even begin to assess the factuality of that sect's central theological assertion that Jesus of Nazareth arose from the dead on the third day? "The truth of the Bible," the eminent French archaeologist Roland de Vaux wrote, "is of a religious order. It speaks of

God and man and their mutual relations. This spiritual truth can neither be proven nor contradicted . . . by the material discoveries of archaeology." What archaeology *could* do for biblical study, wrote G. Ernest Wright, a distinguished student of Albright's who worked at biblical Shechem in the 1960s, was "to provide a physical context in time and place which was the environment of the people who produced the Bible or who are mentioned in it."[7]

Out of that more moderate response to the faith-driven exuberance that seemed to characterize at least some biblical archaeologists, there arose in the decades after World War II a parallel "secular" tradition in Middle Eastern archaeology. It was led mainly by British scholars but included American teams from the University of Chicago, the University of Pennsylvania, and a handful of other schools. Even though they worked at biblical sites such as Megiddo (an ancient city smote by Joshua and later fortified by King Solomon) and Beth-Shan (where the body of King Saul was said to have been hanged), their task was more than a quest to affirm or to challenge the Bible. They emphasized remaining true to the scientific method, allowing ancient evidence to speak for itself rather than judging its worth by the degree of light it shed on biblical texts.[8]

Further evolution of the field of biblical archaeology resulted during those post–World War II years from important new refinements in some of the techniques employed by archaeologists. Serious shortcomings in the stratigraphic method had become evident. Even though biblical archaeologists had uncovered huge amounts of material, in many cases the material was found to have been so poorly excavated that it was impossible to accurately date.

Working in Jericho in the 1950s, the British archaeologist Kathleen Kenyon adapted a more precise stratigraphic technique. Called the "balk-debris layer method," it involved carefully sifting through the strata in a series of five-meter-square grids with "balks" of undisturbed debris, one meter wide, in between. The emphasis of this method was not on architecture but on the discovery of smaller debris in each layer—everything from a blade or a shard of pottery to a fish hook. Archaeologists looked upon these items not as confirming or denying biblical stories or major events in history but as telling their own story about the everyday human activity of the time. The method was widely adopted by other schools of archaeology.[9]

By the early 1970s, Near Eastern archaeology had entered an important new phase that has been described as the "new archaeology." It grew in part out of the new and more efficient methodologies, but also out of a growing sense of frustration over the many important questions biblical archaeology seemed to leave unanswered. Archaeologists now could accurately date strata by using pottery and other evidence and could compare ancient Palestinian culture to other cultures of the era. But what could the material data tell about how people really lived, what they believed, and how they worshiped? What could the data explain that the Bible and other ancient texts could not?

William Dever, professor of the University of Arizona, observed that after nearly a hundred years of active research on early Israelite origins, scholars were "further than ever from a consensus" on such important basics as the historical origins of Yahweh worship in ancient Canaan, whether the biblical patriarchs ever truly existed, and whether there was an Egyptian captivity and exodus of the Israelites. "If the 'biblical archaeology' movement had as its aim a convincing reconstruction of an actual historical setting for these events," Dever noted, "then it must be confessed that it failed. Perhaps the failure was the result of unrealistic expectations. Archaeology can answer such questions as 'what,' 'who,' 'when,' and 'how'—but not 'why.'"[10]

Many scholars attempting to shape the "new archaeology" realized that the earlier, more parochial approach to archaeology—focused mainly on the Bible and biblical history—had resulted in much historical evidence being overlooked, discarded, or even destroyed. "Archaeologists began to see," says Dever of that decade, "that if total retrieval of the material remains were possible, and if they were studied in both natural and cultural context, they could begin to discern social, economic, ethnic and perhaps even religious groupings. Moreover, they might then get at what they had really sought all along (now defined as the true objective of archaeology): an understanding of the phenomenon of cultural process and change."[11]

As a result, during the 1970s archaeologists began adding to their excavation staffs experts in other fields—geologists, climatologists, zoologists, cultural anthropologists, and even statisticians and computer experts—in order to identify and analyze data in a way that would address questions that previously had not been asked of archaeological evidence. It was obviously a more expensive and detailed task, and so novel that results from such comprehensive studies were slow to be published. Even so, the multidisciplinary approach has become standard procedure in what some now refer to ecumenically as "Syro-Palestinian archaeology."[12]

The considerable costs of this new, more sophisticated endeavor have further embedded archaeology in the domain of publicly funded schools and institutions. And even though biblical archaeology is, as a result, more "secular" than the old religion-based study, it has produced a dizzying array of discoveries in recent years that have had a direct bearing on the Bible and its times. In that respect, secular archaeology is succeeding in ways that biblical archaeology did not (and perhaps *could* not). Some of these important findings, such as the

David inscription, have tended to affirm the substantial historicity of Scripture. But others have raised serious questions, sufficient to make untenable an entirely literal reading of the Bible as an objectively factual and chronologically correct historical text. Yet whether confirming or contradicting traditional views, modern archaeology is constantly illuminating the distant times and places that shaped Judaism and early Christianity.

In the following pages, we will examine some of the archaeological evidence regarding the major epochs of biblical history: the age of the patriarchs, the captivity in and exodus from Egypt, the conquest of Canaan, the Israelite monarchy, and the days of Jesus.

## CHAPTER 7

# THE PATRIARCHS

## IN SEARCH OF

## ISRAEL'S ORIGINS

> Now the Lord said to Abram, "Go from your
> country and your kindred and your father's house
> to the land that I will show you. I will make of
> you a great nation, and I will bless you, and make
> your name great, so that you will be a blessing."
>
> *Genesis 12:1–2*

WHO WERE THE ANCIENT ISRAELITES? WHAT WERE THEIR ETHNIC origins? How did they come to possess a land torn, then as now, by territorial conflict? For more than a century, historians and Bible scholars have debated the veracity of the biblical account of Israel's beginnings. While minimalist scholars long have argued that there is far more mythology than history in the Old Testament stories of the ancient Hebrew patriarchs, many others remain convinced that there is a solid historical core behind the biblical record.

The book of Genesis traces Israel's ancestry to Abraham (Abram), a monotheistic nomad who God promises will be "ancestor of a multitude of nations" and whose children will inherit the land of Canaan as "a perpetual holding."[1] God's promise and Israel's ethnic identity are passed from generation to generation—from Abraham to Isaac to Jacob, whose name is changed to Israel ("contender with God") after he engages in a wrestling match with an angel of the Lord. Then Jacob and his sons—the progenitors of Israel's twelve ancient tribes—are forced by famine to leave Canaan and migrate to Egypt, where the Israelite people emerge over a period of some four hundred years.

But modern archaeology has found no direct evidence from the Middle Bronze Age (2000–1500 BCE)—roughly the period many scholars believe to be the patriarchal era—to corroborate the biblical account. No inscriptions or artifacts relating to Israel's first biblical ancestors have been recovered. Nor are there references in other ancient records, outside of the Bible, to the early battles and conflicts that are reported in some detail in Genesis, as Abraham and his descendants claim their inheritance.

## MYTHICAL FIGURES?

This lack of corroborating evidence, along with their own critical analysis of the text, has prompted biblical scholars such as Robert Coote, of San Francisco Theological Seminary, to assert that "the period of the patriarchs . . . as devised by the writers of Scriptures . . . never existed."[2] Niels Peter Lemche, a professor at the University of Copenhagen and a leading voice among the biblical minimalists, flatly categorizes the stories of the patriarchs as "fiction written around the middle of the first millennium" BCE to help establish a historical pedigree for Israel after the Babylonian exile.[3] Archaeological data from the second and third millennia, says Lemche, "do not contain a single direct reference to any of the features mentioned in the Old Testament narrative."[4] Even the evangelical magazine *Christianity Today*, in a 1998 cover story on archaeology and the Bible, had to concede that "not one shred of direct archaeological evidence has been found for Abraham, Isaac, or Jacob or the 400-plus years the children of Israel sojourned in Egypt."[5]

Moreover, some scholars contend that the patriarch stories contain glaring anachronisms that suggest that they were written many centuries after the events they purport to portray. Abraham, for example, is described in the eleventh and fifteenth chapters of Genesis as coming from "Ur of the Chaldeans"—a city in southern Mesopotamia, or modern-day Iraq. But the Chaldeans settled in southern Mesopotamia "not earlier than the ninth or eighth centuries" BCE, according to Lemche. That, he says, is more than a thousand years after Abraham's time and at least four hundred years after the time of Moses, who tradition says wrote the book of Genesis.[6]

Yet despite what seem to be powerful arguments challenging the Bible's account of Israel's origins, the case against the patriarchs is far from airtight.

Many scholars find no reason to doubt the substantial accuracy of the patriarch tradition. Some, like Barry Beitzel, professor of Old Testament and Semitic languages at Trinity Evangelical Divinity School in Deerfield, Illinois, are neither surprised nor troubled by the apparent lack of direct archaeological evidence for Abraham's existence. Why, they argue, should one expect to find the names of an obscure nomad and his descendants in the official archives of the rulers of Mesopotamia? The Genesis narratives, says Beitzel, "talk about men getting wives, wives getting babies and babies getting inheritances." These are "family stories," he says, and not geopolitical history of the type one might expect to find preserved in the annals of kings.[7]

Nor do traditionalists find the apparent anachronisms in the patriarch stories to be particularly problematic. For a later redactor of the biblical narratives to have identified Ur with the Chaldeans, they argue, is not much different than for historians today to speak of Columbus landing in the Dominican Republic. In both cases, the anachronism is a rhetorical device employed to help a "modern" audience visualize a historical setting. It hardly amounts to evidence of fakery or of garbled history, and it certainly does not mean there is no historical core behind the stories themselves.

## A CREDIBLE SETTING

While there may, indeed, be no direct material evidence relating to the biblical patriarchs, archaeology has not been altogether silent on the subject and its background. Some scholars now are reexamining the archaeological record and are finding some compelling evidence of a more circumstantial nature.

One of those is Kenneth A. Kitchen, an Egyptologist now retired from the University of Liverpool in England, who argues that archaeology and the Bible "match remarkably well" in depicting the historical context of the patriarch narratives. In Genesis 37:28, for example, Joseph, a son of Jacob, is sold by his brothers into slavery for twenty silver shekels. That, notes Kitchen, matches precisely the going price of slaves in the region during the eighteenth and nineteenth centuries BCE, as affirmed by documents recovered from ancient Mesopotamia and from Mari, in what is now modern Syria.[8] Other documents show the price of slaves rising steadily during later centuries. By the eighth century BCE, the price of slaves, as attested in ancient Assyrian records, had risen to fifty or sixty shekels, and to ninety to 120 shekels during the Persian Empire in the fifth and fourth centuries BCE. If the story of Joseph had been dreamed up by a Jewish scribe in the sixth century, as some skeptics have suggested, argues

Kitchen, "why isn't the price in Exodus also ninety to one hundred shekels? It's more reasonable to assume that the biblical data reflect reality."[9]

The circumstantial evidence favoring the biblical patriarchs does not stop there. The stories of Abraham and his progeny also seem generally consistent with what historians now know about the form of treaties, contracts, and other social conventions of the ancient world.

Archaeologists have turned up close to one hundred legal documents from ancient Mesopotamia representing five distinct periods over a course of more than two thousand years. As a result, says Kitchen, "we can now construct a typology of treaties that allows us to date them by their essential form and structure, which vary from time to time and from place to place." One group of treaties, discovered at Mari and at Tell Leilan in northern Syria, date from the early second millennium BCE—roughly the period of the patriarchs. Those documents, says Kitchen, with their invocation of witnesses, oaths, curses, and stipulations fashioned in a distinctive style and pattern, match almost exactly the form and structure of treaties that Abraham, Isaac, and Jacob entered into with their neighbors, as described in Genesis 21, 26, and 31. Yet treaties from Mesopotamia that were written a few centuries to either side of the patriarchal period do not match the biblical treaties at all.[10]

Interestingly, notes Kitchen, the Sinai Covenant (Exod. 20–31, 34–35; Lev. 1–7, 11–26), which contains the Ten Commandments and other Mosaic laws, is dated in traditional biblical chronologies some five hundred years after the patriarchs, in the fourteenth or thirteenth centuries BCE. It is composed in a much more elaborate sevenfold structure—the exact structure found in Hittite imperial treaties from that same later period. In both cases—the patriarch treaties and the Sinai Covenant—says Kitchen, "the treaty forms fit the times when the Bible places the narratives."[11]

Another point of convergence is found in ancient laws regarding inheritance. In the Bible, Jacob had four sons by two wives and two concubines, and he bequeathed equal portions to each of them (Gen. 49). But by the time of the exodus from Egypt, Hebrew law provided that the eldest son receive a double portion of the inheritance (Deut. 21:15–17). That correlates precisely with what is now known of the evolution of inheritance laws in ancient Mesopotamia. Under the laws of the Amorite king Lipit-Ishtar during the early twentieth century BCE—roughly concurrent with the biblical patriarchy—all children were to receive an equal share of an inheritance. Two hundred years later, the Code of Hammurabi gave first choice of any inheritance to the first son of a man's first wife. Then, from the eighteenth to the fifteenth centuries, under the laws of ancient Mari and Nuzi (in modern Iraq) during the years leading up to the exodus from Egypt, the natural firstborn son was entitled to a double share of his father's wealth. Later, under neo-Babylonian laws in the first millennium BCE, the sons of a first wife would get a double portion while sons of a second wife received a single share.[12] Once again, the biblical scenario fits comfortably within its historical setting.

Recent archaeological work also has made more plausible the geographical backdrop of the patriarch stories. The ruins of a number of important biblical sites—including Ur, Shechem, and Hebron—have been clearly identified and studied. One ancient city, Haran in upper Mesopotamia, appears to have been a major commercial hub in the period when Abraham and his father would have arrived there after leaving Ur. The site, which was excavated by archaeologists from the University of Chicago, was abandoned shortly after the patriarchal period in about 1800 BCE and remained unoccupied until about the seventh century BCE, experts say. "It's highly improbable," says Barry Beitzel, that someone inventing the story later "would have chosen Haran as a key location when the town hadn't existed for hundreds of years."[13]

Meanwhile, the story of Jacob and his sons migrating into Egypt—where their progeny would emerge later as the Israelite people in the exodus—also fits reasonably well in its historical and archaeological context. In the biblical narrative, Jacob's youngest son, Joseph, is sold to slave traders by his jealous brothers and taken into Egypt. There he eventually finds favor with the Egyptian king and rises to a position of power. Later, when his father and brothers seek refuge in Egypt to escape famine at home, the magnanimous Joseph helps them to settle in Goshen, in the eastern portion of the fertile Nile delta.

Because the Joseph story contains some apparent anachronisms—names and titles, for example, that are more at home in the thirteenth century BCE or later—many scholars believe that the narrative is mainly fiction and probably was not composed prior to the establishment of the united monarchy—around 1000 BCE. Yet, argues P. Kyle McCarter, Jr., chairman of biblical and Near Eastern studies at Johns Hopkins University in Baltimore, "it does not follow from this . . . that the tradition upon which the story is based is unhistorical." Many scholars, he says, believe that the events described in the Joseph narrative "have an ultimate basis in historical fact."[14]

If Joseph lived during the Middle Bronze Age (about 2000–1550 BCE), as some suppose, his lifetime would have fallen within Egypt's so-called Hyksos period. That was a turbulent era that lasted roughly two centuries, ending in about 1542 BCE, during which northern Egypt was ruled by foreign Asiatic people who had settled in the eastern delta—the biblical "land of Goshen."[15] Writing in the first century CE, the Jewish historian Josephus described the

Hyksos as a nomadic people, possibly from Canaan, who were despised by native Egyptians as "men of ignoble birth." Citing Egyptian sources, he translated their name as meaning "king-shepherds" or "captive shepherds."[16]

Could the Hyksos have been the Hebrews of the Old Testament? Josephus seemed to think so, but few historians today agree with him. They see far too many historical divergences to make such a connection. Some scholars do believe it is possible, however, that the Hebrews arrived in Egypt during the Hyksos period. They surmise that Joseph, a Semitic-speaking Asiatic, would likely have found a favorable reception among the Hyksos rulers. Egyptian records from the Middle Kingdom (before 1786 BCE) and the Roman era (after 30 BCE) contain numerous examples of persons of Syrian or Canaanite origin rising to powerful positions in the Egyptian government. One account, with interesting parallels to the Joseph story, involves an Asiatic named Irsu who came to power in Egypt during a period of hardship—possibly famine—around 1200 BCE.[17] "Clearly," says McCarter, "the biblical description of Joseph's career is historically plausible in its general outline."[18]

What follows in the biblical narrative also seems historically plausible. The Hyksos dynasty is known to have ended rather abruptly and violently in the middle of the sixteenth century BCE, when Egyptian rulers in Thebes waged war against the Asiatic interlopers and ran the Hyksos leaders out of Egypt. That episode is commemorated on an ancient stele at the Karnak temple in Luxor.[19] With the overthrow of the Hyksos dynasty, the political environment in Egypt would have turned decidedly unfriendly against any Semitic people who remained in the eastern delta. This sudden turn of events seems quite compatible with the biblical scenario leading up to the exodus—that "a new king arose over Egypt who did not know Joseph" (Exod. 1:8) and who conscripted the Hebrew people into forced labor.

All of this, of course, hardly amounts to proof that the biblical patriarchs—Abraham, Isaac, Jacob, and Joseph—ever truly walked the earth or that the dramatic Bible stories about the origins of Israel are good history. But the circumstantial evidence argues strongly for their plausibility. The patriarch narratives fit comfortably in the historical context that modern archaeology has helped to reconstruct. And that context places the patriarchs precisely where the book of Genesis suggests they should be—in the early second millennium BCE—rather than in the hands of a postexilic fiction writer.

## CHAPTER 8

# THE EXODUS

## OUT OF EGYPT

> Moses said to the people, "Remember this
> day on which you came out of Egypt, out of
> the house of slavery, because the Lord brought
> you out from there by strength of hand."
>
> *Exodus 13:3*

THE DRAMATIC STORY OF THE EXODUS—OF GOD DELIVERING MOSES and the Israelite people from Egyptian bondage and leading them to the Promised Land of Canaan—has been called the "central proclamation of the Hebrew Bible."[1] Yet, as with the patriarch narratives in the book of Genesis, archaeologists to date have found no direct evidence to corroborate the biblical story. Inscriptions from ancient Egypt contain no mention of Hebrew slaves, of the devastating plagues that the Bible says preceded their release, or of the destruction of the pharaoh's army during the Israelites' miraculous crossing of the Red Sea (or perhaps the Sea of Reeds). No physical trace has been found of the Israelites' forty-year nomadic sojourn in the Sinai wilderness. There is not even any indication, outside of the Bible, that Moses existed.

This lack of extrabiblical evidence, coupled with certain apparent inconsistencies in the Bible's own chronology, has prompted some biblical scholars to conclude that the exodus story is pure legend. "The actual evidence concerning the Exodus," writes Baruch Halpern, professor of ancient history at Pennsylvania State University, "resembles the evidence for the unicorn."[2]

Yet as with the patriarch narratives, many scholars argue that a lack of direct evidence is insufficient reason to reject the core historicity of the exodus event. "Absence of evidence," observes Egyptologist Kenneth Kitchen, "is *not* evidence of absence."[3] Nahum Sarna, professor emeritus of biblical studies at Brandeis University, argues that the exodus story—tracing, as it does, a nation's origins to slavery and oppression—"cannot possibly be fictional. No nation would be likely to invent for itself, and faithfully transmit century after century and millennium after millennium, an inglorious and inconvenient tradition of this nature," unless it had an authentic core.[4] "If you're making up history," adds Richard Elliott Friedman, professor at the University of California at San Diego, "it's that you were descended from gods or kings, not from slaves."[5]

Indeed, the absence of direct material evidence of an Israelite sojourn in Egypt is not as surprising, or as damaging to the Bible's credibility, as it first might seem. What type of material evidence, after all, would one expect to find that could corroborate the biblical story? "Slaves, serfs and nomads leave few traces in the archaeological record," notes William Dever.[6] And since official records and inscriptions in the ancient Near East often were written to impress gods and potential enemies, it would be quite surprising to find an account of the destruction of the pharaoh's army immortalized on the walls of an Egyptian temple. Perhaps we should have expected, as a writer in the popular magazine *Bible Review* playfully imagined, a dispatch such as this from the pharaoh's court:

> *A spokesman for Ramesses the great, Pharaoh of Pharaohs, supreme ruler of Egypt, son of Ra, before whom all tremble in awe blinded by his brilliance, today announced that the man Moses had kicked his royal butt for all the world to see, thus proving that God is Yahweh and the 2,000-year-old culture of Egypt is a lie. Film at 11:00.*[7]

If the exodus happened as reported in the Bible, the pharaoh's silence is certainly understandable. And so is the absence of temple inscriptions. But faced with that deafening void in the archaeological record, how could anyone reasonably maintain that there is history behind the exodus story?

While direct evidence may, indeed, be lacking, many scholars again see strong circumstantial evidence supporting the notion that something like the biblical exodus occurred. A portion of that evidence relates to the long-standing problem of accurately dating the exodus.

Internal conflicts in the Bible's own chronology long have been a popular target of biblical skeptics. The book of 1 Kings (6:1) gives what appears to be a clear-cut historical marker for the end of the Israelite sojourn in Egypt: "In the four hundred eightieth year after the Israelites came out of the land of Egypt, in the fourth year of Solomon's reign over Israel, in the month of Ziv, which is the second month, he began to build the house of the Lord." Biblical historians (at least those who consider Solomon to be a real, historical person) generally agree that the son and successor of David (and the builder of Israel's first great temple) came to the throne in about 962 BCE.[8] If this is so, then the exodus would have occurred in about 1438 BCE, based on the chronology of the 1 Kings passage.

However, that date does not fit at all with other biblical texts and with what is known of ancient Egyptian history. The book of Exodus (1:11), for example, notes that Hebrew slaves were building "supply cities, Pithom and Rameses," for the Egyptian pharaoh. Many scholars now think Rameses was Pi-Ramesse, a Nile delta city that was built by Ramesses II, the third king of the nineteenth dynasty of Egypt, in the late thirteenth century BCE—some two hundred years *after* the exodus date extrapolated from 1 Kings. That apparent discrepancy is often cited by skeptics as one important reason to dismiss the entire exodus event as legend.

But the chronological flaw is far from fatal. Nahum Sarna and others argue that the timespan cited in 1 Kings—480 years—bears the marks of a symbolic number and should not be taken literally. "It is 12 generations of 40 years each," notes Sarna—forty being "a rather conventional figure in the Bible," frequently used to connote a long period of time.[9] The Israelites' wanderings through the wilderness, for example, are said to have lasted forty years (Num. 14:33, Josh. 5:6, etc.), as are the tenure of Eli the priest (1 Sam. 4:18), the reigns of David (2 Sam. 5:4) and Solomon (1 Kings 11:42), and several eras of peace and conflict mentioned in the book of Judges (3:11, 5:31, 8:28, 13:1). And based on data in the books of 1 and 2 Kings, says Sarna, another 480 years elapsed from the commencement of temple construction under Solomon to the end of Israel's exile in Babylon. All of this, says Sarna, suggests a "schematized chronology" rather than a literal historical recollection. "The biblical writer wanted to place the Temple at the center of biblical history."[10]

Viewing the 1 Kings chronology in that light—as a primarily theological statement rather than as "pure" history in the modern sense—the exodus can be more comfortably placed in the thirteenth century, in the days of Ramesses II, where it finds strong circumstantial support in the archaeological record.

Even though there are no specific references in nonbiblical writings to Israelites living in Egypt, there are plenty of inscriptions that support a strong Syro-Palestinian presence there during the fourteenth and fifteenth centuries BCE. After the Hyksos dynasty was overthrown in the mid–sixteenth century BCE, says James Hoffmeier of Wheaton College, "Egypt was teeming with Semitic-speaking peoples," many of whom were treated as prisoners of war. The presence of Israelites in this mix, notes Hoffmeier, "is very plausible."[11]

Inscriptions at the tomb of Rekhmire, vizier of the Egyptian pharaoh Thutmose III in the mid–fifteenth century BCE, for example, depict prisoners from Canaan and Syria making mud bricks, with stick-wielding taskmasters overseeing their forced labor, during the construction of the temple at Karnak. It is a scene that vividly evokes the plight of the Israelites described in the book of Exodus. "It is worth noting," says Hoffmeier, "that the practice of using forced labor for building projects is only documented for the period 1450 to 1200, the very time most biblical historians place the Israelites in Egypt."[12]

Even more tantalizing is a line in a surviving Egyptian document called the Leiden Papyrus 348, dating from the reign of Ramesses II. It contains orders that food be distributed to "the Apiru who are dragging stones to the great pylon" of some unidentified construction project.[13] Although the meaning of the Egyptian word "Apiru" is hotly debated, some scholars believe it may refer to the Hebrews, or the Ivri, a term used in the Bible to describe Israelite ethnicity.[14] Others contend it is a more generic term that was often used to describe Semitic people hired to perform work. In any event, these (and other) Egyptian sources seem to clearly attest that Asiatic people of varied ethnicity were drafted to work on construction projects for the pharaohs. That there was a variety of people so engaged, says Hoffmeier, also may help explain the "mixed multitude" of Exodus 12:38, who accompanied the liberated Israelites as they fled from Egypt.

Perhaps the most dramatic circumstantial evidence for a thirteenth-century exodus is a line of hieroglyphics in what has become known as the Merneptah Stele, commemorating the military conquests of Pharaoh Merneptah, son of Ramesses II. The granite monument, found in the ruins of Merneptah's funerary temple in Thebes, contains the earliest known reference to Israel outside of the Bible. It boastfully lists the enemies vanquished by the pharaoh during a campaign in the central highlands of Canaan around 1207 BCE:

> The princes are prostrate, saying "Peace!"
> Not one raises his head among the Nine Bows.
> Desolate is Tehenu; Hatti is pacified;
> Plundered is Canaan with every evil;
> Carried off is Ashkelon; seized upon is Gezer;
> Yanoam is made as that which does not exist;
> Israel is laid waste, his seed is not.[15]

The hyperbole of the pharaoh's chronicler aside—the pharaoh's army obviously had not been quite as thorough as advertised in wiping out its enemies—the reference to Israel as a people is both clear and striking. Without question, it establishes the Israelites' presence in Canaan by the end of the thirteenth century as a people known to Egypt's rulers. Nahum Sarna argues that the exodus "would therefore have taken place about half a century earlier."[16]

Recent archaeological data are consistent with the Bible's explanation in Exodus 13:17 of why Moses and the Israelites took the long way to Canaan through the desolate Sinai wilderness rather than following the shorter coastal route: enemy military posts lay on that path. Egyptian hieroglyphics from about 1300 BCE at the temple of Amun in Karnak depict a series of Egyptian installations along the coastal route. And modern excavations have uncovered a string of Egyptian citadels strikingly similar to those in the Amun relief, stretching from the Nile delta to Gaza. The presence of the forts "is perfectly compatible with the Exodus," says Trude Dothan, an archaeologist at Hebrew University in Jerusalem, who excavated there.[17]

And although the biblical Moses has not turned up in other ancient sources, many scholars find his depiction in the Bible to be consistent with what is known of Egypt in the thirteenth century BCE. His name fits with Egyptian etymology from the exodus era, suggesting to some that the Moses tradition has its roots in Egypt and not in postexilic Palestine. The name is derived from the Egyptian *mose* ("is born"), a term that often was combined—sometimes in modified form—with the name of a deity, as in the names of the pharaohs Thut*mose* ("Thoth is born") and Ra*messes* ("Ra is born"). Some scholars theorize that in the earliest traditions, Moses' name also may have been linked with a deity. Or it simply may have stood alone in its original form as if to signify the one who gave birth to Israel as a covenant nation.[18] And the story of his growing up in the court of the pharaoh, notes Baruch Halpern, "mirrors the practice of Egyptian kings raising the children of their Semitic vassals as hostages in the court."[19]

Yet many scholars still find it unlikely that a group described in the Bible as numbering as many as three million[20]—or even a much smaller group of eighty thousand, as has been estimated by other sources—left Egypt en masse and "went rattling around in the Sinai Peninsula or the Negev for any length of time"[21] without leaving a trace. Direct material evidence for such an undertaking simply is not there.

But the weight of circumstantial evidence is far too strong to dismiss the exodus as mere theological fiction. Many scholars find it much more reasonable to conclude, along with Halpern, that the exodus story is at least "typologically true." In other words, although the indirect external evidence that we now have may not allow us to say with certainty that the events of the exodus occurred exactly as described, or even that they occurred as a singular event involving a single group, circumstantial evidence sketches in the contours of the event.

The biblical details do "conform to the Canaanite experience of Late Bronze Age Egypt," notes Halpern. "There were Semites there, there was forced labor, there was brick-making, there was intense building activity under Ramesses II, including the city of Rameses."[22] There were even reports in ancient Egyptian papyri of small numbers of runaway slaves from the city of Rameses fleeing into the Sinai desert, just as the Israelites fled in the book of Exodus.[23] At its basis, then, the exodus story has the ring of truth.

According to Halpern, it is "historically imaginable," based on current evidence, that there were "repeated incidents of this stripe . . . that would be invisible to us archaeologically and historically—as the Exodus is."[24] Does that suggest a smaller, less dramatic exodus—or multiple exoduses? Perhaps. Abraham Malamat, a biblical historian at Hebrew University in Jerusalem, similarly suggests that the exodus story is the result of a "telescoping process—the compression of a chain of historical events into a simplified and brief account . . . by later editors viewing the events in retrospect." There could conceivably have been two or more exoduses, agrees Malamat, "or even a steady flow of Israelites from Egypt over hundreds of years."[25] It is certainly conceivable that when the famine that initially brought the descendants of Abraham to Egypt finally ended, many Israelites returned to Canaan while they were still free to do so. When the exodus, however large or small, did occur decades or perhaps centuries later, it need not have involved such a magnitude of people as to account for all of the Israelites who would subsequently be found settled in the Promised Land. (We will visit that subject in much more detail in Chapter 9.)

Theories suggesting that the exodus may have been a smaller or perhaps a serial event resonate with many scholars who see the exodus tradition as rooted in real Egyptian history and not in the imagination of a fourth century BCE writer. But if the book of Exodus is *merely* typologically true—that is, if it reflects the recollection of a *type* of historical experience rather than of a specific historical event—it raises another set of problems for historians. It implies, as Hoffmeier points out, that the Israelites "knew more about Egypt's history than their own" and were "incapable of preserving their early history, in either oral or written form, from the second half of the second millennium [BCE] onward." As such, they would have been the only nation in the region in the Late Bronze Age lacking that capability. To attempt to explain the origins of the exodus narratives that way, notes Hoffmeier, "requires a greater leap of faith than to believe the narratives are historical in nature," were preserved by Hebrew scribes, and perhaps even have their origin in the recorded memory of a man named Moses.[26]

It may well be that we have not yet heard the last word or seen the last piece of evidence regarding this definitive event in Israel's history. Who knows what secrets still lie buried in the sands of Egypt and the Transjordan? Archaeology could break its silence on the exodus at any moment.

Yet whatever the event's origin and magnitude, and however elusive the historical details, it is clear that the story of the exodus became etched into the memory and tradition of the Hebrew people as they emerged in Canaan late in the second millennium BCE. The deliverance from Egypt would come to define both the identity and the ideology of the Israelite nation as a people led by God to inhabit the Promised Land.

## CHAPTER 9

# THE CONQUEST

## SETTLING THE

## PROMISED LAND

So Joshua defeated the whole land, the hill country and
the Negeb and the lowland and the slopes, and all their
kings; he left no one remaining, but utterly destroyed all
that breathed, as the Lord God of Israel commanded.

*Joshua 10:40*

AFTER WANDERING FORTY YEARS IN THE SINAI WILDERNESS, ACCORDING
to the book of Joshua, the Israelites crossed the Jordan River from the east and
invaded Canaan. Swiftly and relentlessly under Joshua's command, they
launched military attacks on city after city until the Promised Land was theirs.
It is a story amplified—some say contradicted—in the book of Judges, where
the settlement of Canaan is depicted as a long and arduous struggle marked by
military and moral setbacks for the Israelite people. Throughout both accounts,
the overarching theme is the same, however: the God who delivered the Israelites from Egyptian bondage now had given them a homeland.

But citing a lack of archaeological evidence of sudden destruction at several
key sites, many scholars now flatly reject the biblical description of a military
conquest of Canaan. Instead, some argue that ancient Israel more likely arose
out of a gradual and generally peaceful infiltration, or as a result of an internal
social rebellion among people already present in the land. Whatever the explanation, says Israel Finkelstein, a prominent archaeologist at Tel Aviv University,

"archaeology has pushed aside a military conquest. It's not a possibility. It's over."[1]

Not everyone agrees, of course, and with good reason. But even those who regard a military conquest as historical concede that the archaeological record has raised a serious challenge. The book of Joshua, for example, describes an early and important battle at the fortified city of Jericho in the southern Jordan River valley. There, according to the Bible, the Israelites marched around the walled city for seven days and sounded their trumpets at God's command, and the walls came tumbling down. Joshua and his army then rushed into the city and destroyed every living thing in it.[2]

The historicity of that account received a strong boost in the 1930s, when the British archaeologist John Garstang found evidence of a collapsed mud-brick wall and fiery destruction at Jericho—evidence that he dated to about 1400 BCE. Although that date was nearly two centuries too early to coincide with a now more commonly posited thirteenth-century exodus, it fit neatly with the Bible's internal chronology and thus was hailed at the time in conservative religious quarters as dramatic confirmation of biblical history.[3]

But Garstang's findings did not hold up for long. In the 1950s, another eminent British archaeologist, Kathleen Kenyon, returned to Jericho with more accurate excavation and dating methods and retraced some of Garstang's steps. Kenyon concluded that the mud-brick wall had collapsed in about 2400 BCE—a thousand years earlier than Garstang's estimate. Even more devastating to the biblical scenario, Kenyon found that there was no occupied city at Jericho for Joshua to attack during the period many scholars associate with the Israelite conquest—the Late Bronze Age (1300–1200 BCE). She found that Garstang's city and wall were from two separate periods, and that the city had been destroyed at the end of the Middle Bronze Age, about 1550 BCE. After that, she concluded, it remained largely uninhabited until the ninth century BCE.[4] Some experts, as we will see later, suggest that Kenyon might have misdated the debris. Nonetheless, hers is still the accepted interpretation in most archaeological circles.

After the defeat of Jericho, Joshua is depicted as turning to Ai, a Canaanite stronghold some ten miles to the west. There the Israelites "utterly destroyed all the inhabitants" and "burned Ai, and made it forever a heap of ruins, as it is to this day."[5] But, just as with Jericho, archaeologists have found no evidence of a Late Bronze Age occupation at Ai.

The French archaeologist Judith Marquet-Krause, excavating in the mid-1930s, concluded that the walled city was destroyed and abandoned in about 2400 BCE—more than a thousand years before the Israelites arrived—and was not resettled until about 1200 BCE, when a small unfortified village was built on part of the ruins. Later excavations confirmed Krause's findings and also determined that the tiny village, hardly the gated city of some twelve thousand inhabitants described in Joshua, was abandoned in about 1050 BCE, prior to the rise of the Israelite monarchy—the period in Israel's history when many scholars believe the book of Joshua took shape.[6]

Consequently, some prominent scholars have theorized that the account of the Israelites' destruction of Ai is an etiology—a story concocted to account for the imposing ruins that were visible "to this day" to the writer of Joshua. It is clear, says the American archaeologist Joseph A. Callaway, a Southern Baptist who excavated Ai for many years, that the biblical story "reflects a time when the site of Ai was a ruin, after 1050 BCE . . . not the time of the conquest some centuries earlier."[7] The noted biblical archaeologist William Albright sought to further explain the discrepancy by suggesting that the battle described in Joshua may have actually occurred at Bethel, an important crossroads city less than two miles to the west, where evidence of fiery destruction has been found. Albright theorized that later tradition came to associate the story with Ai, whose name in Hebrew means "ruin" or "heap."[8]

There are other apparent mismatches in the biblical and archaeological records regarding the Israelite conquest. William Dever argues that of a total of sixteen sites said in the Bible to have been destroyed by the invading Israelites, evidence of Late Bronze Age destruction has turned up at just three—Lachish, a fortified town in the lowlands southwest of Jerusalem; Hazor, the chief Canaanite city-state in upper Galilee; and Bethel. Of the remaining thirteen sites, says Dever, seven "were not even occupied in the period or show no trace of a destruction." Those include Zephath, Makkedah, and Eglon, all in southern Judah, and Heshbon and Dibon in the Transjordan—in addition to Jericho and Ai. At the other six sites, "archaeology is simply silent"—either the sites have not been identified or they have not been sufficiently excavated. Consequently, says Dever, "it may be stated confidently that the archaeological evidence is overwhelmingly against the classic conquest model of Israelite origins" as depicted in the book of Joshua.[9]

## REASSESSING THE CONQUEST MODEL

As confident as Dever and others may be, not all scholars are ready to toss aside the Bible's depiction of military campaigns in the settlement of the Promised Land. A close examination of the evidence suggests that there is plenty of history to be found in the biblical narratives. Some scholars, including Wheaton's

James Hoffmeier, argue that the "conquest model" to which Dever refers has become something of a straw man for skeptics who improperly equate it with the biblical record.[10] More often than not, it is the model—an explanatory summary of biblical and physical data assembled by Bible scholars and archaeologists—rather than the Bible itself that conflicts with the archaeological evidence.

A case in point: In an unsuccessful attempt during the 1950s to show how modern archaeology confirms the Israelite conquest, G. Ernest Wright, a protégé of William Albright, overstated what the Bible actually claims concerning the military exploits of the Israelites: "The books of Joshua, Judges, and Samuel carry the story from triumph to triumph, until even the greatest of Canaanite walled fortresses were destroyed (Lachish about 1220 B.C., Megiddo, Beth-Shan, Jerusalem and finally Gezer shortly after 1000)."[11]

Yet nowhere in Joshua or Judges are Megiddo or Beth-Shan listed among the cities devastated, or even conquered, by Israel. Wright also ascribed the destruction of Beitin, which he believed to be biblical Bethel, to the Israelites even though the Bible does not make that claim.[12] Nonetheless, when some of Wright's archaeological evidence later came into question, weaknesses in his argument were widely represented as weaknesses in the biblical record. In the collective mind of biblical and archaeological academia, the "conquest model" and the Bible had become synonymous, and the historical veracity of both had been eroded.

However, a careful reading of Joshua suggests a far more modest military outcome than the blitzkrieg scenario some critical scholars are so fond of challenging. The Bible does not explicitly say, for example, that the Israelites demolished the cities enumerated in Joshua 10—several of which appear on Dever's list of unattested sites. Instead, in describing what happened at those cities, the text uses terms that some biblical scholars say are more accurately translated as "smote," "laid siege," or "captured."[13] While the inhabitants of those cities may indeed have been annihilated, as the Bible says, the cities themselves presumably were left standing.

Seldom, in fact, does the Bible depict the Israelites as even directly attacking the cities of their adversaries. More often, notes Abraham Malamat of Hebrew University, Joshua and his men are seen employing an "indirect military approach"—either covert infiltration to neutralize a city's defenses, or enticement to draw the defenders out into the open.[14] Battles fought in that manner likely would have left little or no evidence of catastrophic destruction for archaeologists to uncover.

Furthermore, some conservative scholars allow that the writer of Joshua probably engaged in a bit of bravado from time to time, using a type of rhetorical hyperbole that was common among the chroniclers of warfare in the ancient

Near East. In Joshua 10:20, for example, the writer proclaims that the Israelite army "wiped out" its enemy during a campaign in southern Judah, but in the very next phrase he describes what became of "the survivors." Moreover, Joshua 13:1 says that when Joshua was "very old" there were "still very large areas of the land to be taken." The following verses then go on to list the vast areas that the Israelites had not yet occupied. It seems clear that despite a few statements of bravado, the book of Joshua, taken as a whole, points to something other than a lightning-fast military conquest of the Promised Land.

The type of hyperbole found in Joshua also is evident in ancient Egyptian, Assyrian, and Hittite military inscriptions describing the magnitude of enemy defeats.[15] One Egyptian stele from the fifteenth century BCE, commemorating the exploits of Thutmose III in the Euphrates, makes the grandiose claim that "the heads of the Asiatics are severed, none escape (death)." However, a few lines later it brags that thousands of prisoners were captured.[16] That the inscription "is describing real events, albeit with rhetorical flourishes and propaganda, is undeniable," says Hoffmeier.[17]

Despite such exaggerations, most scholars view inscriptions from the Egyptians, Assyrians, and Hittites as invaluable sources of historical information. The book of Joshua, Hoffmeier rightly argues, should be judged no less valuable.[18] Nor should its core historicity be considered diminished if its sometimes hyperbolic rhetoric does not stand up to archaeological scrutiny.

On the other hand, where the Bible specifies that a city was burned to a heap of ruins, one should reasonably expect to find some evidence of fiery destruction in an archaeological excavation. But the book of Joshua describes only three such cases: Jericho (Josh. 6:24), Ai (Josh. 8:19–20, 28), and Hazor (Josh. 11:11). What have archaeologists found at those sites?

At Hazor, in upper Galilee, the physical evidence is strikingly consistent with the book of Joshua. Excavations in the 1950s turned up the ruins of a heavily fortified Late Bronze Age citadel that had been destroyed in a terrible inferno no later than 1230 BCE. The devastation was so complete that the 180-acre lower city was never resettled. The famous Israeli archaeologist Yigael Yadin, who directed the dig, was confident that he had discovered physical evidence of the Israelites' victory over Jabin, the king of Hazor, as recounted in Joshua 11:10–13.[19]

More recent digging at Hazor has uncovered even more dramatic parallels to the Joshua account. In 1996, for example, an Israeli team led by Hebrew University professor Amnon Ben Tor found the charred remains of a Canaanite palace and a small chapel. The conflagration had been so intense that clay vessels were melted and mud bricks were turned into glass. Scattered about the floor of the chapel were the heads of decapitated statues of Canaanite deities and an Egyptian sphinx with the name of the pharaoh chiseled away. As he surveyed the grim scene, Ben Tor was reminded of Moses' instructions to the Israelite warriors in Deuteronomy 7:5: to "break down their altars, smash their pillars, hew down their sacred poles, and burn their idols with fire."[20]

So far, Ben Tor has been unable to pinpoint a precise date for the destruction or to conclusively link it to the Israelites. Some scholars have suggested that the debris may instead be evidence of internecine warfare between Canaanite kings, or of Egyptian invaders whose late-thirteenth-century incursion into the Levant is commemorated in the Merneptah Stele. But would Canaanites or Egyptians have defaced their own deities? The biblical notation in Joshua 11:11 that the Israelites "burned up Hazor itself" fits far more comfortably with the archaeological record.

## KEEPING THE CASE FILE OPEN

At Ai and Jericho, the final verdict of archaeology has not been heard. As noted earlier, the evidence in hand seems to indicate that Ai was uninhabited in Joshua's time and was not destroyed by fire. But could it be, as Albright suggested, that archaeologists have been looking in the wrong place? Could the events associated with Ai actually have occurred at nearby Beitin (thought by some to be the biblical Bethel, as noted earlier), where there is, in fact, evidence of fiery destruction in the Late Bronze Age? Or is it possible that neither site is correct? The location of Ai—the archaeological mound now known as Et Tell—has always been contingent upon the correct identification of Bethel, and not everyone is satisfied that Beitin is it. Some scholars think the village of el-Birah, a few miles southwest of Tell Beitin, is a more likely site of the biblical Bethel— though no one so far has made a convincing case. Perhaps additional research will resolve these questions.

At Jericho the situation is murky, but the question nonetheless remains open. While archaeological remains seem to suggest a chronology of warfare different from that presented in the book of Joshua, notes Hershel Shanks, editor of the *Biblical Archaeology Review,* a recent reexamination of the evidence has shown that fiery destruction did occur at Jericho "in uncanny detail just as the Bible describes it." The upper mud-brick wall of the city collapsed outward, piling up at the base of a lower wall to form a narrow ramp of debris large enough to allow an invading army to clamber into the breach. "And sure enough," notes Shanks, "the Bible tells us that the Israelites who encircled the city 'went up into the city, every man straight before him' (Joshua 6:20)." Inside, the walls and floors appeared to have been blackened by fire *after* the collapse—precisely the sequence of the biblical account. Heaps of burned grain discovered inside the houses suggest a sudden conquest rather than a lengthy siege. They suggest, too, that the attack occurred shortly after spring harvest, exactly when the Bible says it did. And the fact that the grain was burned instead of plundered also fits the biblical scenario. "The Bible tells us," notes Shanks, "that the Lord commanded that everything from Jericho was to be destroyed; they were to take no plunder."[21]

Everything seems to fit except the timing. Jericho's famous wall, according to Kathleen Kenyon, collapsed nearly a thousand years before the Israelites arrived. And the city itself was destroyed at least three hundred years too soon. Or was it?

One scholar who has reexamined Kenyon's evidence now argues that the famous British archaeologist may have misread some of her own data. Bryant Wood, a former professor of Near Eastern studies at the University of Toronto and director of the Associates for Biblical Research, believes that some of Kenyon's own findings suggest that Jericho fell much later—and much closer to the biblical chronology—than Kenyon reported.

Writing in the *Biblical Archaeology Review*, Wood notes that Kenyon unearthed a type of pottery in the city ruins that appeared for only a limited time in the late fifteenth century BCE—some 150 years *after* her 1550 destruction date. She apparently overlooked this evidence, Wood says, and based her conclusions instead on the *absence* at Jericho of another type of imported pottery that is commonly found at important trade cities of the Late Bronze Age.

Kenyon also apparently was unimpressed by Garstang's earlier discovery of a series of tiny Egyptian amulets, called "scarabs," in a cemetery northwest of the city. The scarabs, notes Wood, were inscribed with the names of pharaohs beginning with Hatshepsut (ca. 1503–1483 BCE) and ending with Amenhotep III (ca. 1386–1349 BCE). "The continuous nature of the scarab series," he says, "suggests that the cemetery was in active use up to the end of the Late Bronze I period."[22] An active cemetery would indicate an active population at Jericho precisely at the time when the Bible says the Israelites were arriving in Canaan.

And Kenyon's own carbon-14 analysis of a piece of charcoal found in the destruction debris dated the residue to about 1410 BCE, says Wood, providing further evidence—apparently overlooked or disregarded by Kenyon—that the conflagration occurred in the Late Bronze Age. All of this suggests to Wood that Jericho "was destroyed in about 1400 BCE, *not* 1550 BCE as Kenyon maintained."[23] Garstang, he says, was right.

While Wood is in the minority among biblical scholars and archaeologists in his reassessment of Kenyon's work, his argument has reopened the question of the cause and chronology of Jericho's demise. Even if he is correct, and the fall of Jericho can be ascribed to an Israelite invasion in the late fourteenth or early fifteenth century BCE, Wood acknowledges that the new dating would place the Israelites in Canaan almost two hundred years too soon for most historians. Nonetheless, he is convinced that "as new data emerges and old data is reevaluated," scholars will be forced to reconsider their broader assumptions about how and when Israel emerged in the Promised Land.

For now, however, the evidence remains far too ambiguous. Barring some startling new archaeological discoveries, the case for the fall of Jericho and for a military conquest of Canaan simply cannot be sustained with material evidence. Yet there is plenty about the larger biblical story of the Israelite possession of the Promised Land that *is* consistent with the archaeological record.

## SEARCHING FOR ISRAELITE FOOTPRINTS

During the past two decades, archaeologists have found what some think may be the figurative footprints of the early Israelite settlers—evidence of hundreds of small villages suddenly appearing in the hill country west of the Jordan River during the twelfth century BCE. Lawrence Stager of Harvard University found that in about a century's time the number of villages between Hebron and Shechem, an area of some 2,600 square miles, had increased from 23 to 114, and the population in the region had mushroomed from about 14,000 to more than 38,000.[24] Such a sudden population boom, most scholars agree, could not possibly be accounted for by birthrate alone. Clearly, a significant influx of newcomers had arrived.[25]

Moreover, the characteristics and location of those villages, along with artifactual evidence, says William Dever, "provide an archaeological assemblage that agrees remarkably well" with the conditions and cultural setting described in the conquest and settlement narratives.[26] The settlers apparently were farmers and herders of sheep and goats who terraced the hillsides and carved bell-shaped cisterns to provide household water supplies. Their houses generally were simple four-pillared structures with courtyards and sometimes silos. The hilltop villages were unfortified and appeared to follow a general migration pattern from the northeast to the southwest.[27]

Yet whether or not these settlements are Israelite is still hotly debated. And even if they are, scholars say it is impossible from the archaeological evidence now in hand to confidently link their sudden appearance either to a sweeping military invasion or to one of the alternative scenarios that some modern scholars have proposed: a gradual and generally peaceful infiltration or an internal social rebellion.

The notion of a peaceful infiltration of Israelite settlers during the Late Bronze and Early Iron Ages has commanded serious attention since the German scholar Albrecht Alt first proposed it in 1925. Basing his arguments on texts rather than archaeology, Alt concluded that the early Israelites were pastoral nomads who migrated from the east into Canaan's thinly populated hill country, where they gradually settled down and took up farming. This first phase of Israelite settlement was generally peaceful, Alt surmised, because there would have been relatively little contact with the Canaanite population, still largely urban and concentrated in a handful of powerful city-states.[28]

Later, during a second phase of territorial expansion, military confrontations occurred as the Israelite settlers collided with groups of Canaanites who occupied the plains and valleys of the region. This phase, Alt supposed, was rather lengthy, extending from late in the period of the judges to the early monarchy, and was marked by seesaw battles for possession of fortified Canaanite cities. Some scholars suggest that it may have been the memory of these battles, which would have occurred at the end of the eleventh century BCE, that lay behind the biblical tradition of a military takeover of Canaan. It is a scenario that also seems to accommodate the prolonged and complex settlement process depicted in the book of Judges.

But there is little archaeological evidence to support Alt's contention that the early Israelites were pastoral nomads. An increasing volume of data indicates that the earliest settlers were primarily farmers; they were herdsmen only secondarily.[29] Consequently, some scholars, such as Lawrence Stager, have found it unreasonable to attribute all of the hundreds of new Early Iron Age settlements to a single source—nomadic shepherds and goatherds—let alone to Israelite immigrants.[30]

Instead, some have speculated that the settlers were Canaanite peasants who revolted against their urban masters and fled to the hill country. This "peasant revolt" model was first formulated in the early 1960s by University of Michigan scholar George E. Mendenhall and then elaborated by Norman Gottwald, a New York Theological Seminary professor. Arguing mostly on sociological and anthropological grounds, both scholars contended that the Israelite culture arose out of what was chiefly a social and economic struggle of oppressed indigenous people who forged their own egalitarian society and religious identity. Archaeological support for their thesis, they argued, could be found in the pottery and architecture of the highland settlements, which they noted shared some common features with those of the Canaanite culture.[31]

Provocative though it may be, the peasant revolt model has not caught on in a big way among mainstream historians. Some critics have simply dismissed it as an ideologically driven effort to impose a modern Marxist sociopolitical paradigm on biblical history.[32] Others have pointed to an absence of inscriptions corroborating what surely would have been a major social upheaval in the major Canaanite urban centers.[33] And archaeological surveys of biblical Ephraim and Manassah in the central portion of the modern-day West Bank have shown that there was a general population decline in those regions during the two centuries preceding the new settlement pattern. That suggests to some scholars that there would have been too few people in the region to carry out a peasant revolt sufficient to account for such widespread changes in the occupation of Canaan's highlands.[34] "The archaeological evidence from these central hills alone," says biblical scholar Thomas Thompson of the University of Copenhagen, "makes it categorically impossible to assert . . . that the villages of Israel emerged out of oppressed Late Bronze Age peasantry."[35]

So where does all of this leave the Bible's account of the Israelite settlement of Canaan? What can be reasonably concluded from the evidence? It is clear that gaping holes in the archaeological record currently make it impossible to sustain a case for a purely military conquest. Yet there is little question, after examining all the evidence, that there was some military component to Israel's emergence in Canaan. So far, all of the alternative explanations to a military conquest have come up short as well. Perhaps the most that can be said for now is that the final and definitive word, from an archaeological standpoint, has yet to be heard. It may well take some dramatic new discovery and additional research to finally resolve the debate.

Despite all the remaining uncertainties, however, most scholars would agree that there is a historical core behind the biblical stories of Israel's emergence in Canaan. What is disputed is the extent to which that history is discernible in the redacted theological narrative that we read today. The real history of Israel's origins is, no doubt, much more complicated—as most histories are—than its narrative form. That does not make the biblical narrative, in its broad outline, less true. It does, however, make the modern historian's task more daunting.

The respected Israeli archaeologist Yigael Yadin, who held a generally high view of the Bible as history, wisely cautioned against dogmatism on either side of the debate. "It is not necessary either to accept each detail of the biblical account, on the one hand, or to reject the basic historicity of the Conquest, on the other," he wrote. Archaeology, in his view, "broadly confirms that at the end of the Late Bronze Age, semi-nomadic Israelites destroyed a number of major Canaanite cities; then gradually and slowly, they built their own sedentary settlements on the ruins, and occupied the remainder of the country."[36]

While the debate over Israel's emergence in Canaan continues, there is nothing in the archaeological record to dispute the central proclamation of the

Bible concerning this period: "Thus the Lord gave to Israel all the land that he swore to their ancestors that he would give them; and having taken possession of it, they settled there" (Josh. 21:43). The significant message of the Hebrew Bible, after all—as Dever notes—is not the historical claim that the Israelites "took Canaan by military might" but rather the theological claim "that God miraculously gave them the land as an unforgettable sign that he had chosen Israel as his own special people."[37] That is an assertion of biblical truth that archaeology simply cannot address.

## CHAPTER 10

# ISRAEL'S
# MONARCHY

## THE UNITED AND
## DIVIDED KINGDOMS

> Then all the tribes of Israel came to David at Hebron, and
> said, "Look, we are your bone and flesh. . . . The Lord said
> to you: 'It is you who shall be shepherd of my people
> Israel, you who shall be ruler over Israel.'" . . . [A]nd they
> anointed David king over Israel. David was thirty years old
> when he began to reign, and he reigned forty years.
>
> *2 Samuel 5:1–4*

FACED WITH A GROWING MILITARY THREAT FROM PHILISTINE WARRIORS
and filled with a renewed resolve to follow Yahweh, the independent-minded Israelite tribes began to unite, according to the Bible—first under Saul and then
David, who forged the scattered tribes into a powerful nation with Jerusalem as
its capital. The reigns of King David and his son Solomon over a united monarchy mark the glory years of ancient Israel. That period (roughly 1000 BCE to
920 BCE)—described in detail in the books of 1 and 2 Samuel, 1 and 2 Kings,
and 1 and 2 Chronicles—marks the beginning of an era of stronger links between biblical history and modern archaeological evidence.

As noted earlier, prior to the discovery of the "house of David" inscription
at Tell Dan in 1993, it had become fashionable in some academic circles to dismiss the David stories as an invention of priestly propagandists who were trying

to dignify Israel's past after the Babylonian exile. Given his amazing deeds and his complete absence from nonbiblical sources, King David was considered by modern biblical nihilists—a cadre of scholars who find little of historical value in the entire Hebrew Bible—to be nothing more than a figure of religious and political mythology. But as Tel Aviv University archaeologist Israel Finkelstein observes, "Biblical nihilism collapsed overnight with the discovery of the David inscription."[1] With his name found etched in a monument to a ninth-century BCE king of Damascus, David and his dynasty could no longer be denied their rightful place in Israel's ancient history.

## ANOTHER DAVID INSCRIPTION?

In the aftermath of the dramatic discovery at Dan, another famous ancient inscription—one found more than a century ago—has attracted renewed scholarly interest. Now some experts believe that it, too, mentions the house of David. The so-called Mesha Stele, like the stele on which the Dan inscription is etched, is a basalt monument from the ninth century BCE that commemorates a military victory over Israel—this one by the Moabite king Mesha. The lengthy Tyrian text describes how the kingdom of Moab, a land east of the Jordan River, had been oppressed by "Omri, king of Israel" (whose reign is summarized in 1 Kings 16:21–27) and by Omri's successors, and how Mesha threw off the Israelites in a glorious military campaign.

But the name of another of Mesha's conquered foes may lie hidden in a partially obliterated line of text that reads b[—]wd; the remainder of the inscription is missing. The French scholar Andre LeMaire, after carefully reexamining the damaged inscription, has suggested that the incomplete line should be filled in to read bt dwd—"Beit David," or "house of David"—a reference to the kingdom of Judah.[2] "No doubt," says LeMaire, "the missing part of the inscription described how Mesha also threw off the yoke of Judah and conquered the territory southeast of the Dead Sea controlled by the House of David." The fragment from Tell Dan, he says, "helps to confirm the reading of the Mesha stele. . . . Indeed, both inscriptions may reflect more or less the same historical context."[3]

As significant as they are, these two inscriptions—both still contested in some quarters—remain for now the only extrabiblical references to David's dynasty. And both were written more than a century after the reigns of David and Solomon. Given the grandeur of the Israelite monarchy under the two kings as described in the Bible, some scholars understandably wonder how such an influential and popular regime could have attracted so little notice in ancient Near Eastern documents from the eleventh and tenth centuries BCE.

The answer, suggests Carol Meyers, professor of biblical studies and archaeology at Duke University, may lie in the unique political climate in the region at
the time. "During precisely these years," she says, "a power vacuum existed in
the eastern Mediterranean." The collapse of Egypt's twentieth dynasty around
1069 BCE led to a lengthy period of economic and political decline for a nation
that had exerted powerful influence over the city-states of Palestine during the
Late Bronze Age. This period of Egyptian weakness, which lasted for over a
century (until around 945 BCE), saw a "relative paucity of monumental inscriptions," says Meyers. "The kings had nothing to boast about in the usual fashion
of royal texts; none would have reported Egypt's loss of its long-standing control over parts of the Palestinian corridor to Asia."4

Similarly, the Assyrian empire to the east was unusually silent from the late
eleventh to the early ninth centuries BCE regarding the western lands it once
had dominated. During those years, notes Meyers, Assyria was preoccupied
with its own internal turmoil following the death of Tiglath-pileser I (ca. 1076),
one of the greatest of its early kings, and more or less remained that way until
the Neo-Assyrian empire arose under Ashur-dan II (934–912). Whether the
Assyrians ever ventured into Palestine or tried to reassert themselves in the region during the intervening years is unclear, says Meyers, but also unlikely.5

Another major power in the region, Babylonia, also was uncharacteristi-
cally quiet at the time. For centuries following a raid on Assyria in 1081 BCE, it
seldom ventured beyond its own borders, says Meyers, "and thus its records
would hardly have mentioned a new dynastic state to the west."6 The emergence of a national monarchy in Palestine, then, unheralded and largely unmo-
lested by its militaristic and normally prolific neighbors, says Meyers, "is related
to the weaknesses in the traditional centers of power in the Near East at the end
of the second millennium BCE."7

While the inscriptional evidence is rather meager, other archaeological evidence has provided important information concerning the life and times of Israel's early monarchy.

About fourteen miles south of the Sea of Galilee, at the strategic junction
of the fertile Jezreel and Jordan valleys, lies one of Israel's largest and most fascinating archaeological sites—Tell el-Husn, the biblical Beth-Shan. Founded as a
Canaanite city before 3000 BCE, it was the site of an Egyptian garrison from
the fifteenth to the twelfth centuries BCE, and was occupied by the Philistines
during the early Israelite monarchy. Along with thirteen inscribed monuments
and carved reliefs from the time of the Egyptian occupation, two temples from
the eleventh century BCE have been uncovered there. One was dedicated to
Ashtaroth, a Canaanite goddess of fertility, love, and war. Archaeologists say
that this is almost certainly the temple referred to in 1 Samuel 31:10. According

to that passage, after King Saul's death in the battle at nearby Mt. Gilboa, enemy soldiers "put his armor in the temple of Ashtaroth and fastened his body to the wall of Beth-Shan."[8]

## IN SEARCH OF THE PHILISTINES

The reign of David, Saul's successor, was a time of territorial expansion for the united Israelite kingdom and was marked, according to the Bible, by a series of military victories over a variety of foes. Twice the Israelite armies repulsed invasions by the Philistines, a belligerent horde of pagan marauders who occupied Canaan's Mediterranean coastal plains. While the Bible depicts the Philistines as a frequent nemesis of the Israelites, their name does not appear in ancient non-biblical sources before 1200 BCE. Some minimalist scholars have suggested that the biblical stories of run-ins with the dreaded Philistines were invented by priestly scribes in the middle of the first millennium BCE to dramatize the military prowess of the mythical Davidic dynasty.

But modern archaeology has uncovered a wealth of information regarding the Philistines—a notorious militant group known as the Sea People—that is thoroughly consistent with their portrayal in the Bible. External sources, including numerous Egyptian inscriptions, indicate that the Philistines most likely originated in the Aegean area, probably on the island of Crete. That fits with biblical passages (Jer. 47:4 and Deut. 2:23, for example) linking them with Caphtor, a location most scholars identify with Crete.[9] After battling Egypt and others for a piece of the Levant, the Philistines established a confederation of five powerful city-states on Canaan's coastal plain and foothills. Those cities are prominently mentioned in the Bible (1 Sam. 6:17) in connection with the Philistines. The locations of four of the cities have been positively identified and excavated—Gaza, Ashkelon, Ashdod, and Ekron—and artifacts clearly associated with the Philistines have been uncovered. The whereabouts of the fifth city, Gath, remains uncertain.[10]

The Bible depicts the Philistines as expert metallurgists, possessing skills vastly superior to those of their Israelite neighbors and dominating the metal-working trade during the time of the early monarchy, as suggested in 1 Samuel 13:19: "Now there was no smith to be found throughout all the land of Israel; for the Philistines said, 'The Hebrews must not make swords or spears for themselves.' "

Archaeologists have found material evidence that the Philistines were, indeed, expert metal-workers. Numerous bronze implements and artifacts have been uncovered at Ekron, Ashdod, and other sites. Trude Dothan, a Hebrew University archaeologist who has excavated many of the Philistine sites, says their superior knowledge of metal-working no doubt gave them a military advantage in their early battles with the Israelites. She notes that in the famous story of the duel between David and Goliath in 1 Samuel 17, the giant Philistine warrior is described as wearing a bronze helmet and bronze body-armor and carrying a spear with a shaft "like a weaver's beam" and with a head of iron. "The Bible compares Goliath's spear to a weaver's beam," Dothan says, "because this type of weapon was new to Canaan and had no Hebrew name."[11] Once again, the Bible and archaeology have been found to be in agreement.

The extensive work of Dothan and others has produced a detailed record of the presence and influence of Philistine culture in Canaan during the Late Bronze and Early Iron Ages. The Bible, says Dothan, played an important role in their work:

> When we went to the Philistine sites, we were not looking to prove the Bible or to find where David fought Goliath. Our aim was to bring to light this ancient civilization, to learn how the people lived, how they built their cities, what their culture was like. The Bible was an important ingredient in helping us understand what we were seeing.[12]

The information Dothan and her colleagues gleaned from their excavations goes far beyond the Bible's descriptions of Israel's ancient foe—shedding light, for example, on the Philistines' religion, their burial customs, and even, to a small extent, their language. Yet in every instance, the researchers found the archaeological data regarding the Philistines to be consistent with the biblical record. "That all this 'fits' the many biblical allusions so well," notes William Dever of the University of Arizona, "shows that a post-Exilic editor cannot simply have invented these passages, that they are genuinely archaic."[13]

## SOLOMON'S LEGACY

The reign of David's successor, Solomon, has proven to be even more tantalizing to modern archaeologists. According to the Bible, Solomon's reign (ca. 960–920 BCE) was a time of peace and tremendous prosperity for the Israelite nation as Solomon consolidated the young monarchy into a strong central government and expanded its foreign trade (1 Kings 4). The vast wealth pouring into Jerusalem enabled Solomon to launch ambitious building projects in the capital city and throughout the kingdom. The remains of some of those build-ings, says Dever, "are not only the earliest evidence we possess of monumental architecture in ancient Israel but are among the most impressive."[14]

No doubt the most famous of Solomon's buildings was the temple in Jeru-salem—a mammoth, elaborately adorned edifice of quarried stone and cedar that would become the "House of Yahweh" and the focal point of the Israelite religion. According to the Bible, it took more than seven years and thousands of laborers and skilled artisans under the direction of Phoenician craftsmen to complete the project, which is described in detail in 1 Kings 5–8. Built on Mount Moriah—known today as the Temple Mount—Solomon's temple stood for more than 360 years, until it was pillaged and destroyed by the Babylonians in 587 BCE. A second, more modest temple built on the same site after the Babylonian exile late in the sixth century BCE was massively renovated and ex-panded by Herod the Great in 18 BCE. Herod's temple was destroyed by the Romans in 70 CE. However, what some experts believe to be a small portion of the retaining wall of Solomon's temple can still be seen on the eastern side of the Temple Mount, about 105 feet north of its southeast corner.[15]

While Solomon's temple was the most famous of his building projects, it was by no means the only one. The temple complex in Jerusalem was composed of several impressive structures, including Solomon's palace—the Palace of the Forest of Lebanon—a colonnade, a "hall of justice," and a palace for one of his wives, the daughter of the pharaoh of Egypt (1 Kings 7). Few traces of any of those structures have been found. However, archaeologists have discovered key elements of the design and architecture of Solomon's buildings reflected at other Bronze and Iron Age sites in the Levant. Assyrian palaces from the ninth and eighth centuries BCE at Zinjirli (ancient Samal) in south-central Turkey, Tell Tayinat in Syria, and Tell Halaf (ancient Gozan) in Mesopotamia are re-markably similar in design and furnishings to the biblical descriptions of Solomon's royal complex.[16] As Dever observes:

> Here we see all the elements of Solomon's "Royal Quarter" in Jerusalem. We can even illustrate details of the individual buildings and their furnishings with findings from archaeology: the ashlar masonry (1 Kings 7:9–10), the alternating stone and wood courses and the cedar paneling (1 Kings 7:11–12), the throne borne on the wings of lion-cherubim (cf. 1 Kings 6:23–28), and the portable braziers.[17]

The existence of such close architectural parallels, says Dever, "reinforces the unanimous biblical witness that Solomon, having no native Israelite tradi-tion in art and architecture to draw on, employed artisans and architects from

Phoenicia,"[18] as is suggested in 1 Kings 5 and in 2 Chronicles 3. And "almost every detail of the sometimes enigmatic descriptions" of Solomon's temple in the Bible, says Dever, can be illustrated by viewing the remains of Phoenician-built temples found at other Near Eastern sites. "A later writer who had never seen the temple," he concludes, "could not possibly have given such accurate, detailed descriptions."[19]

Solomon's building campaign also included new fortifications at the strategic cities of Hazor, Megiddo, and Gezer, the construction of "store cities" to stockpile material important to his kingdom, and the building of numerous military bases for his charioteers (1 Kings 9:15–19). Archaeologists have found dramatic evidence of Solomon's handiwork at several of these sites. Fortifications of almost identical design and material have been discovered at Hazor, Megiddo, and Gezer, dating to the middle of the tenth century BCE—precisely the time of Solomon's reign. At each location, the rebuilt city walls were of casement construction (having two parallel walls with narrow storage chambers in between), and the gates were built of fine ashlar stonework with four chambered entryways of nearly identical dimensions.[20] Yigael Yadin, the Israeli archaeologist who worked at Hazor in the 1950s, was convinced that the gates of all three cities "were in fact built by Solomon's architects from identical blueprints."[21] Some recent excavators at Megiddo have proposed that the gates of that city may have been built a century later, perhaps during the dynasty of King Omri. But Hebrew University's Amnon Ben Tor, the current excavator at Hazor, and Dever, who excavated Gezer, remain convinced of the tenth-century origin of those cities' fortifications. "Here," says Dever, "is a dramatic instance of archaeology turning up actual structures mentioned specifically in the Bible."[22]

## DIGGING THE DIVIDED KINGDOM

At the end of Solomon's reign in about 920 BCE, the national unity forged by David and Solomon failed to hold, and Israel split into rival northern and southern kingdoms. Israel, the northern kingdom, came to an end with an Assyrian invasion in 722 BCE. The southern kingdom, Judah, survived until the Babylonian exile in about 540 BCE. This turbulent era of almost four hundred years is thoroughly outlined in the books of 1 and 2 Kings and 1 and 2 Chronicles. It is a period of biblical history supported as well by numerous inscriptions and other archaeological evidence.

Several of the kings of Judah and Israel—from Omri and Ahab to Hezekiah and Manasseh—are mentioned in Assyrian and Babylonian inscriptions from the period, although there are some apparent disagreements in chronology. Ancient records from Egypt, as well as from Assyria and Babylonia, also corroborate some of the key events described in the Bible.

Late in the reign of King Solomon, for example, Jeroboam—Solomon's construction manager, who soon would become king of the northern kingdom—rebelled against the king, according to the Bible, and fled to Egypt, where he sought out the protection of the pharaoh Shishak (1 Kings 11:40). Egyptologists now identify this pharaoh as Sheshonq, or Shoshenq, ruler of Egypt's twenty-second dynasty (945–924 BCE). The biblical text goes on to say that after Solomon's death, in the fifth year of the reign of Solomon's son Rehoboam as king of Judah, Shishak "came up against Jerusalem" and "took away the treasures" of the temple and the palace. The episode is expanded upon in 2 Chronicles 12, which notes that Shishak came with a large army and "took the fortified cities of Judah."

Now we have corroboration from Egyptian records and from archaeological remains as well. At the south entrance to the Amun temple at Karnak, on the banks of the Nile, a bas relief from the tenth century BCE carved into a stone pylon depicts Shishak and his army slaying Asiatic enemies during an invasion of Palestine. The damaged relief also lists more than 150 cities the pharaoh boasted of having conquered in the lightning-swift invasion. Piecing together the data from that ancient inscription, Professor Harry T. Frank reconstructs the route of Shishak's destructive expedition:

> *Judging from the Karnak list, all the fortified towns along this route fell to Egyptian arms. Jerusalem alone was spared but only at the cost of much of the gold that had adorned Solomon's capital. Shishak's army now moved northward along the mountain highway in order to reduce his principal target: Israel, which still exercised control over the trade routes. Ancient Shechem felt the Egyptian battering ram once more, and succumbed. By way of the Wadi Farah, Shishak descended eastward into the valley of the Jordan, capturing Tirzah along the way. . . . Penuel, Mahanaim, and other cities of Transjordan fell before the relentless Egyptians as they wrested control of The King's Highway from Israelite hands. The Way of the Sea, the other principal commercial avenue, passed through the Plain of Esdraelon in Israel. Here the Egyptians now proceeded laying waste the great cities of the Plain, Beth-shan, Shunem, Taanach, and Megiddo among them.*[23]

Archaeology confirms that a number of the sites mentioned in Shishak's carvings were indeed attacked during this period. Modern excavations have turned up destruction layers dating from the tenth century BCE at ancient military outposts in the Negev, at the biblical cities of Timnah, Gezer, and Megiddo, and at numerous other sites in both the northern and southern kingdoms. In addition, a fragment of an Egyptian stele erected to commemorate Shishak's conquest has been discovered in the ruins at Megiddo.[24] Without question, this remarkable convergence of evidence bears strong witness to the veracity of this chapter of biblical history. It also strikes a powerful blow against the argument of biblical minimalists that the history of ancient Israel, as recorded in the Bible, is a later invention. Professor Michael D. Coogan of the Harvard Semitic Museum explains:

> It is the first direct correlation between an individual and an event mentioned in the Bible in contemporaneous nonbiblical sources. Moreover, Shishak is the first Egyptian Pharaoh named in the Bible. Prior to this, significantly, not one is named—none of the Pharaohs with whom Abraham, Joseph, the Israelites in Egypt, and Moses has dealings are identified in biblical tradition. If the biblical writers wanted to be vague here, they had ample precedent.[25]

Instead, they chose to report the history that was known to them, drawing on real memory of real events preserved, if not recorded, from the time the events transpired. Might Hebrew writers from the Persian period (540–330 BCE)—the era in which some critics suggest the narratives originated—simply have known their Egyptian history and been careful to weave the right pharaoh into their historical "novel," in order to make it more believable? It is certainly possible. But why would they have gone to the trouble when, as Coogan notes, "they don't show the same concern for historical verisimilitude" in the books of Jonah or Judith (which the critics would assign the same late date of origin)?[26] Given the strong corroboration both from Egyptian records and from archaeological evidence, it seems far more reasonable to conclude that the people and events in the Shishak episode, as recorded in the Bible, are authentic.

Inscriptions from the Assyrian empire have added further support to the Bible's account of the history of Israel's divided kingdom. Archaeologists working south of Mosul in Iraq during the mid–nineteenth century uncovered a stone monument from the ninth century BCE that has become known as the "Black Obelisk." Its carved cuneiform inscriptions and graphic reliefs show the leaders of vassal states paying tribute to the Assyrian king Shalmaneser III, who reigned from 858 to 824 BCE. Among those depicted on the obelisk is a figure identified as "Jehu, son of Omri"—a reference to the tenth king of Israel, whose turbulent reign is described in 2 Kings 9–10. This carving is the earliest known graphic representation of an Israelite monarch. Some scholars see the reference to Jehu's being "son of Omri" as something of a problem, since the Bible identifies him as the son of the Judahite king Jehoshaphat (2 Kings 9:2). Most, however, see the designation "son of" merely as an acknowledgment by the Assyrians that Jehu was a successor to the powerful Omride dynasty, which apparently had left quite an impression on the Assyrians, considering that other Assyrian records refer to Israel as "the land of Omri."[27]

Perhaps the most thoroughly documented biblical figure from the period of the divided monarchy is King Hezekiah, of whom the Bible says, "There was no one like him among all the kings of Judah . . . for he held fast to the Lord" (2 Kings 18:5–6). The son of King Ahaz, Hezekiah ruled Judah from 727–698 BCE as a vassal of the mighty Assyrian empire, which had recently defeated and dismantled the northern kingdom of Israel.

But after the death of Assyria's powerful King Sargon (another figure mentioned in the Bible whose existence was doubted until modern archaeology "discovered" him), Hezekiah "rebelled against the king of Assyria and would not serve him" (2 Kings 18:7). Wisely anticipating reprisals from the new Assyrian king, Sennacherib, Hezekiah prepared Jerusalem for an Assyrian attack. First, he buttressed its fortifications (2 Chron. 32:5) by dismantling houses that had recently appeared on the city's western hill and using the masonry to reinforce the city's wall (Isa. 22:10). What is believed to be a small portion of that massive wall, some twenty-three feet wide, has been found in modern excavations in the Old City of Jerusalem.[28]

Next, Hezekiah secured Jerusalem's water supply (2 Kings 20:20; 2 Chron. 32:30). His workers carved a winding tunnel some 1,750 feet through limestone bedrock, creating an underground conduit to the Gihon Spring in the Kidron Valley and diverting the water into the city. The Siloam Tunnel, also called Hezekiah's Tunnel, is well known in modern times. An inscription chiseled into its wall was discovered in 1880 by two young boys who were wading inside the carved passageway near the city's western reservoir. Written in ancient Hebrew script, it describes the final stages of the tunnel's construction:

> The [ . . . ] of the penetration. This is how the penetration took place. While [the diggers were] still [wielding] their axes towards each other, with three cubits still to be pen[etrated, they could he]ar each other shouting, for there was a fissure in the rock running to the south [and to the nor]th. So at the moment of penetration, the diggers struck towards each other, axe against axe. Then the waters flowed from the spring to the pool—one thousand two hundred cubits. And one h[un]dred cubits was the height of the rock above the heads of the digger[s].[29]

As Hezekiah had expected, Sennacherib attacked—first striking and defeating Judah's Phoenician, Philistine, and Egyptian allies to the west and then advancing on Judah itself. The Bible describes the grim outcome: "Sennacherib king of Assyria came up against all the fortified cities of Judah and took them" (2 Kings 18:13). The report of the defeat of Judah is confirmed in much more detail in the Annals of Sennacherib, Assyrian royal inscriptions from the eighth century BCE:

> As for Hezekiah of Judah, who did not submit to my yoke, I laid siege to 46 of his strong cities, walled forts and to the countless small villages in their vicinity, and conquered them. . . . I drove out 200,150 people, young and old, male and female, horses, mules, donkeys, camels, big and small cattle, beyond counting and considered them booty.[30]

One of the cities conquered by the Assyrians was Lachish, a heavily fortified outpost some thirty-five miles southwest of Jerusalem (2 Kings 18:14). The siege of Lachish is depicted in graphic detail in a magnificent wall relief discovered in the mid–nineteenth century at Sennacherib's palace at Kuyunjik (ancient Nineveh) opposite modern Mosul in northern Iraq. It now hangs in the British Museum in London.[31] Among other things, the carved relief shows a line of conquered Judahites filing out of the city gates and passing before the Assyrian king. Sennacherib's presence at the battle of Lachish also is noted in 2 Kings 18:14.

According to the Bible, Hezekiah—hearing of the fall of Lachish and hoping to save Jerusalem from a similar fate—paid the Assyrian king a heavy tribute of gold and silver (2 Kings 18:15–16). That payment is confirmed in Sennacherib's records. The two accounts differ only in the amount of silver Hezekiah paid. The Bible reports the tribute as thirty talents of gold and three hundred talents of silver, and the Annals of Sennacherib have it as thirty talents of gold and eight hundred talents of silver.[32]

But the Assyrian king was not easily bought off. Sennacherib sent his army to lay siege against Jerusalem, but rather than attack the heavily fortified capital, he dispatched two high-ranking officers to try to coax Hezekiah into surrendering (2 Kings 18:17). Judah's king refused to yield, obeying instead the admonition of the prophet Isaiah, a compatriot, who assured him that the Lord "will defend this city to save it" (2 Kings 19:34). The siege ended, according to the next verse, when "the angel of the Lord set out and struck down one hundred eighty-five thousand in the camp of the Assyrians; when morning dawned, they were all dead bodies. Then King Sennacherib of Assyria left, went home, and lived at Nineveh."

Not surprisingly, there is no mention of such a catastrophe in Assyrian records, although some scholars see an echo of Sennacherib's failure to capture Jerusalem in the writings of the Greek historian Herodotus (ca. 484–420 BCE) and the Jewish historian Josephus (ca. 37–100 CE). Herodotus relates a story, one he claims to have heard while visiting Egypt, concerning a military catastrophe that befell the Assyrians after a plague of mice gnawed away their bow strings. Josephus, citing Herodotus, suggests instead that it was a "pestilential distemper" that decimated the Assyrians.[33] Sennacherib's only final notation on the episode is his boastful claim to have neutralized Hezekiah's rebellion: "As for Hezekiah the Judean . . . I locked him up within Jerusalem, his royal city, like a bird in a cage."[34]

With the Assyrian army withdrawn, Hezekiah retained his throne and Judah resumed its status as an Assyrian vassal state. Back in Nineveh, Sennacherib was assassinated by two of his sons while worshiping in the temple of his god Nisroch. The incident is recorded both in the Bible (1 Kings 2:37; 2 Chron. 32:20–21; Isa. 37:21–38) and in the Annals of Esarhaddon, the inscriptional records of a third son of Sennacherib, who succeeded him as king:

> *A firm determination fell upon my brothers. They forsook the gods and turned to their deeds of violence, plotting evil. . . . Evil words and deeds contrary to the will of the gods they perpetrated against me. Unholy hostility they planned behind my back. My brothers . . . trusting in their own counsel . . . committed unwarranted acts. . . . To gain the kingship, they slew Sennacherib their father.*[35]

The ancient Babylonians also left behind an impressive archive that attests to the kings and events of the divided Israelite monarchy. Among some three hundred cuneiform tablets from the sixth century BCE that were unearthed near the Ishtar Gate near modern-day Baghdad, for example, are lists of ration allowances granted by the Babylonian king Nebuchadnezzar to captives living in or near the capital city. Included in the list is an allotment for "Yaukin, king of Judah."[36] Most scholars recognize this as a reference to Jehoiachim, who, according to the Bible, was taken captive to Babylon after Nebuchadnezzar's first conquest of Jerusalem in 597 BCE. His release by Nebuchadnezzar's successor is recorded in 2 Kings 25:

> *In the thirty-seventh year of the exile of King Jehoiachim of Judah, in the twelfth month, on the twenty-seventh day of the month, King Evil-merodach of Babylon, in the year that he began to reign, released King*

*Jehoiachim of Judah from prison; he spoke kindly to him, and gave him a seat above the other seats of the kings who were with him in Babylon. So Jehoiachim put aside his prison clothes. Every day of his life he dined regularly in the king's presence. For his allowance, a regular allowance was given him by the king, a portion every day, as long as he lived.*

A parallel of the biblical account of Nebuchadnezzar's sacking of Jerusalem and capture of its monarch in 2 Kings 24:10–17 has been found in another cuneiform tablet found among the Babylonian chronicles. The two accounts are remarkably similar. Here is how the Bible describes it:

*King Nebuchadnezzar of Babylon came to the city, while his servants were besieging it; King Jehoiachim of Judah gave himself up to the king of Babylon, himself, his mother, his servants, his officers, and his palace officials. The king of Babylon took him prisoner in the eighth year of his reign. He carried off all the treasures of the house of the Lord, and the treasures of the king's house. . . . The king of Babylon made Mattaniah, Jehoiachim's uncle, king in his place, and changed his name to Zedekiah.*

And here is the Babylonian version:

*Year 7 [of Nebuchadnezzar]. In the month of Kislev [December 598], the king of Babylonia mobilized his troops and marched to the west. He encamped against the city of Judah [Jerusalem], and on the second of Adar [March 16, 597], he captured the city and he seized [its] king. A king of his choice he appointed there; he to[ok] its heavy tribute and carried it off to Babylon.*[37]

The corroboration of the biblical text by the records of Israel's ancient foe is unmistakable, and a bit ironic. Until a century ago, it was commonly claimed by skeptics in the biblical academy that Nebuchadnezzar had never existed—that he was yet another of the Bible's legendary figures invented for propaganda purposes. But then the German archaeologist Robert Koldewey, excavating in Iraq beginning in 1899, came upon the ruins of Nebuchadnezzar's magnificent palace complex, the famed temple of Marduk, and the remains of the Ishtar Gate—as well as numerous inscriptions, statues, and stelae from the ancient Babylonian empire.[38] At once, Nebuchadnezzar ceased to be a fictional foil in a supposed Hebrew mythology; archaeology had affirmed him as a true historical figure. And now the royal records of this ancient enemy of the Israelites are adding testimony to the accuracy of the Bible as it relates this important chapter of Israel's history. This reversal once again shows the capacity of archaeology to turn the skeptical suppositions of biblical scholarship upside down.


## MYSTERIES SOLVED

Besides helping to set the historical record straight, archaeological discoveries from Israel's kingdom era also have solved long-standing mysteries regarding some previously unintelligible biblical texts. Modern excavations at David's City outside the present Old City of Jerusalem, for example, have helped to clarify the meaning of the word *millo* in 2 Samuel 5:9 and 1 Kings 9:15. Most English translations simply transliterate the Hebrew word, which means "filling," without explanation or clarification. In the King James Version, for example, 2 Samuel 5:9 reads, "So David dwelt in the fort, and called it the city of David. And David built round about from Millo and inward." Modern excavations in Jerusalem have revealed a large stepped-stone structure that probably served as a retaining wall supporting a large building, perhaps a citadel. These stones are now widely believed to be the *millo* mentioned in the Bible.

Another mystery was solved in the book of 1 Samuel, where 13:20 tells of Israelites going down to the Philistines to sharpen their tools. In modern translations, verse 21 reads, "And the charge was a pim," or two-thirds of a shekel. But for centuries, no one knew for sure how to translate the word *pim*. In some translations it was rendered as "mouths" or "cutting edges." The King James Version had it as "file," so that rather than describing the price charged by the Philistines, the verse described the tool used to sharpen the implements. One guess, it seemed, was as good as another. Biblical scholars were able to arrive at the correct translation after archaeologists, working at the fortress city of Lachish and at other sites, discovered stone counterweights with the word *pym* carved into them. The stones weighed about a quarter-ounce (or about two-thirds of a shekel) and were used, prior to the minting of coins, to measure out silver and gold. The discovery also added further weight to the argument against a late date for the composition of the Bible. Dever poses this question: "Is it possible that a writer in the second century BCE could have known of the existence of these pym weights, which occur only in the ninth to seventh century BCE and would have disappeared for five centuries before his time? It is not possible."[39]

Meanwhile, archaeologists recently have raised an intriguing question concerning ancient conceptions of the Hebrew God, Yahweh. Two storage jars with inscriptions and drawings were found at Kuntillet Ajrud, a desert way-station halfway between Beersheba and Elat in southern Judah. One inscription, believed to date from the late ninth or early eighth century BCE, reads, "May you be blessed by Yahweh and his Asherah." (Asherah has long been known as a female deity of Canaan.) Below the inscription is a drawing of three figures, two of which are assumed to represent Yahweh and Asherah. This discovery, says Leslie Hoppe of Catholic Theological Union, "has opened for study and discussion an issue never raised by the biblical text: Did ancient Israel, at one point in its religious quest, believe that Yahweh had a consort?"[40] At the least, it suggests that there was a diversity of views among the Israelites concerning their God— an outlook that fits well with the Bible's depiction of an Israelite people frequently getting into trouble by mixing their Yahwistic faith with local Canaanite religion (1 Kings 18:19; 2 Kings 11:18).

Without question, the Scriptures' portrayal of ancient Israel's kingdom era is remarkably well attested by the weight of modern archaeological evidence. In broad and colorful strokes, the amazing abundance of inscriptions, artifacts, and ruins from that pivotal period unearthed during the last century has both corroborated and amplified the Bible's accounts of history. And as the turbulent years of Israel's exile and return gave way to the turn of the era and the seminal years of the Christian movement, the historical data transmitted through both the scriptural and the material records would prove to be no less abundant or compatible. What has modern archaeology disclosed about the life and times of Jesus as recorded in the gospels? We turn to that important subject next.

## CHAPTER 11

# A NEW ERA

## THE DAYS OF JESUS

Five gospels record the life of Jesus. Four
you will find in books and one you will find
in the Land they call Holy. Read the fifth gospel
and the world of the four will open to you.

*Bargil Pixner, archaeologist*[1]

COMPARED TO THE EARLIER EXTENDED ERAS OF BIBLICAL HISTORY, THE days of Jesus are a fleeting moment. A lifespan of just three short decades and a public career of only two or three years leave a dauntingly narrow target for archaeological exploration. One might reasonably expect the volume of recovered evidence relevant to Jesus' life and times to be rather meager. But in fact, quite the opposite has proven to be true. During the past four decades, spectacular discoveries have produced a wealth of archaeological data illuminating the story of Jesus and the birth of Christianity. The picture that has emerged overall is one that closely matches the historical backdrop of the gospels.

In 1968, for example, explorers found the skeletal remains of a crucified man in a burial cave at Giva'at ha-Mitvar, near the Nablus road outside of Jerusalem. It was a momentous discovery: while the Romans were known to have crucified thousands of alleged traitors, rebels, robbers, and deserters in the two centuries straddling the turn of the era, never before had the remains of a crucifixion victim been recovered. The condition of the remains unearthed at the necropolis dramatically corroborated the Bible's description of the horrendous Roman method of execution.

The bones were preserved in a stone burial box called an *ossuary* that was etched with the name *Yhohnn Yehohanan*. The remains appeared to be those of a man who was about five feet five inches tall and between twenty-four and twenty-eight years old. His open arms had been nailed to the crossbar, in the manner typically shown in crucifixion paintings. The knees had been doubled up and turned sideways, and a single large iron nail had been driven through both heels.[2] The nail—still lodged in the heel bone of one foot, though the executioners had removed the body from the cross after death—was found bent, apparently having hit a knot in the wood. The shin bones appeared to have been broken, corroborating what the gospel of John seems to suggest was the normal practice in Roman crucifixions: "Then the soldiers came and broke the legs of the first and of the other who had been crucified with him. But when they came to Jesus and saw that he was already dead, they did not break his legs" (19:32–33). In other respects, too, the physical evidence from the bones of Yehohanan matches the type of execution described by the writers of the gospels.

The discovery also posed a powerful counterargument to the objections some scholars have raised against the gospels' description of Jesus' burial. It has sometimes been argued that the common practice of Roman executioners was to toss the corpses of crucified criminals into a common grave, or to leave them on the cross to be devoured by scavenging birds and animals. It hardly seems feasible, therefore, the argument goes, that the Roman authorities would have permitted Jesus to undergo the type of burial described in the gospels. But now, with the remains of a crucified contemporary of Jesus found buried in a family grave, we know that at least on some occasions the Romans permitted proper interment consistent with the biblical account.

A more recent and equally dramatic find at another Jerusalem grave site has added to the list of important gospel figures whose historical existence has been verified by archaeological evidence. Workers building a water park in an area called the Peace Forest some two miles south of the Temple Mount in 1990 inadvertently broke through the ceiling of a hidden burial chamber dating to the first century CE. Inside the chamber, archaeologists found twelve limestone ossuaries. One of the boxes, elaborately decorated with six-petaled rosettes, contained the bones of a sixty-year-old man and bore the inscription *Yehosef bar Qayafa*—"Joseph, son of Caiaphas." Experts identified the remains as almost certainly those of Caiaphas the high priest of Jerusalem,[3] who according to the gospels ordered the arrest of Jesus, interrogated him, and handed him over to Pontius Pilate for execution. While the gospels refer to him merely as Caiaphas, the historian Josephus gives his complete name as "Joseph, who was called Caiaphas"[4]—similar to the wording of the ossuary inscription. Never before had archaeologists recovered the actual remains of a New Testament figure. The bones were subsequently reburied on the Mount of Olives, and the ornate ossuary now resides in the Israel Museum in Jerusalem.

A few decades earlier, another key figure in the arrest and crucifixion of Jesus had turned up in the archaeological record—but in name only. During excavations in 1961 at the seaside ruins of Caesarea Maritima, the ancient seat of Roman government in the Judean province, a first-century inscription was uncovered confirming that Pilate had been the Roman ruler of the region at the time of Jesus' crucifixion. Italian archaeologists working at the city's magnificent Herodian theater found the inscribed stone slab in secondary use in the theater's steps. Though it is believed to have been placed there during fourth-century renovations, experts say it originally was a first-century dedicatory plaque at a nearby temple honoring the emperor Tiberius. The badly damaged Latin inscription reads in part, *Tiberieum . . . [Pon]tius Pilatus . . . [Praef]ectus Juda[ea]e*. According to experts, the complete inscription, when fully reconstructed and translated, reads, "Pontius Pilate, the Prefect of Judea, has dedicated to the people of Caesarea a temple in honor of Tiberius."[5]

The discovery of the so-called Pilate Stone has been widely acclaimed as a truly significant affirmation of biblical history. Although the writings of Josephus and Philo late in the first century have also attested to the existence of Pilate as procurator of Judea between 26 and 36 CE,[6] this is the first contemporary witness, and the only lithic inscription that bears his name and title. As archaeologists John Rousseau and Rami Arav observe:

> *The inscription indisputably establishes Pilate's title, which has long been debated (was he a governor, a procurator or a prefect?). The prefect had administrative, financial, military, and judicial functions. As supreme penal judge in his territory—except for recourse to the emperor himself in the case of a Roman citizen—he had the power to pronounce death sentences as he did for Jesus, and to pardon as he did for Barabbas.[7]*

In short, it is now confirmed by nonbiblical evidence that the man depicted in the gospels as Judea's Roman governor had precisely the responsibilities and authority that the gospel writers ascribed to him. The evidence suggests that the gospel writers were thoroughly familiar with the form and function of the governmental structure in place at the time of the events they described.

Archaeology also has revealed that the writer of John's gospel knew more about the topography of Jerusalem in Jesus' time than some scholars have thought. John 5:2, for example, describes the five-sided pool of Bethsaida just inside the Sheep Gate, where the sick and lame came to be healed. The pool of such unusual design is mentioned nowhere else—not in the Old Testament, not by Josephus, not by any other ancient source. Consequently, it had long been regarded as an invention of the gospel writer. But when modern archaeologists decided to dig precisely where John claimed the pool was located, they found an ancient pool with shrines dedicated to the Greek god of healing. The pool had five porticoes: one to the north, one to the south, one to the east, one to the west, and one transecting the rectangular structure. In other words, it was a pool dedicated to healing with five porticoes, just as the gospel of John describes it.[8]

## Holy Sites?

Pilgrims and tourists in the Holy Land today are shown scores of sites said to be significant in the life of Jesus—sites where "tradition says" Jesus preached a sermon, performed a miracle, met with his disciples, was born, crucified, and buried. Few venerated sites have been verified with solid physical evidence, however. In many cases, the sites are covered over by churches or shrines, some dating to the Byzantine or Crusader era and some much more modern—structures that obscure any archaeological evidence that might exist from the first century. It can be frustrating indeed for visitors expecting to catch a glimpse of, say, the rock-hewn tomb of Jesus to instead find their attention directed to a garishly ornamented nineteenth-century edicule, a small stone building said to encase the tomb in Jerusalem's cavernous Church of the Holy Sepulchre. Yet even though there may be nothing visually evocative of a first-century grave (or, at the Church of the Nativity in Bethlehem, of a rustic cave where "tradition says" Jesus was born), in some instances there are sound reasons to believe that the ancient traditions are accurate.

From the earliest centuries, no piece of real estate has been venerated more by Christians than the traditional site of the burial and resurrection of Jesus inside the Church of the Holy Sepulchre. For more than 1,600 years, devout pilgrims from throughout the world have gathered at the historic basilica, located some five hundred meters west of the Temple Mount, to worship and to commemorate Christianity's most central event. Until the nineteenth century, there was little question but that this was the authentic location of the garden tomb described in the Scriptures. Few scholars doubted that the first Christians in Jerusalem would have known and revered the place where, according to the gospels, the crucified Jesus was laid to rest and from which he emerged on Easter morning. Surely they would have preserved such a significant memory.

But modern scholars note that it was not until the fourth century, when Emperor Constantine ordered the construction of a church edifice at the site, that any lasting commemorative markers were set in place. Many question whether an accurate memory of the precise location of the tomb could have survived that lapse of nearly three hundred years—a period marked by violent upheaval in Jerusalem.

At the outbreak of the First Jewish Revolt in 66 CE, Jewish Christians fled the city and settled in Pella, across the Jordan—although some historians say it is likely that Gentile Christians stayed behind.[9] The Romans destroyed Jerusalem and its temple in 70 CE. After the Second Jewish Revolt of 132–135 CE, Emperor Hadrian razed Jerusalem again and on its ruins built a new Roman city, Aelia Capitolina, from which Jews were banned. On the spot where Constantine later would build his church, Hadrian erected a temple to the love goddess Venus/Aphrodite. During its construction, the Romans filled in and paved over an old abandoned limestone quarry that in later years had become honeycombed with burial grottoes and had sprouted trees and other vegetation.[10] Might Hadrian have deliberately selected the site for the pagan temple knowing of its veneration by Christian locals? That certainly appears to have been his modus operandi. The third-century Roman historian Dio Cassius tells us that Hadrian also erected a shrine to Jupiter on the Temple Mount on the very spot where the Jewish temple had stood.[11]

Roughly two centuries later, Constantine ordered what remained of Hadrian's Venus temple removed and an edifice honoring the resurrection built in its place. It is clear from the writings of Eusebius, the bishop of Caesarea (ca. 260–340 CE), that by then the tradition identifying the site as that of Jesus' tomb was well established. Eusebius described what happened next:

> As soon as [Constantine] had issued his order, this false device [Venus's shrine] was cast to the ground with its images and gods. The Emperor also commanded that . . . a large area of the foundation soil, defiled as it was by devil worship, should be dug away to a considerable depth and removed. . . . As layer after layer of the subsoil came into view, the venerable and holy memorial of the Savior's resurrection, beyond all our hopes, came into view. Thereupon the Emperor . . . gave orders that a house of prayer should be built in the precincts of the Saving Cave, rich, royal, and magnificent.[12]

The church that Constantine built was magnificent indeed. According to literary sources, part of the limestone that surrounded the burial cave was trimmed away so that the tomb itself was standing free, and a massive rotunda was erected around it. Then, according to Eusebius, the emperor "adorned the sacred cave itself, as the chief part of the whole work . . . with rare columns and profusely enriched with the most splendid decorations of every kind."[13] In front of the rotunda, off to the right and just a stone's throw away, was a rocky hillock identified as Golgotha, the site of the crucifixion, enclosed in a court-yard described in literary sources as the Holy Garden. Beyond the garden and facing the tomb, Constantine built a magnificent basilica with polished marble floors and a gilded ceiling where the faithful could gather and pray.[14]

What is described by Eusebius as "the Church of Our Savior" was dedi-cated in 335 CE, the thirtieth year of Constantine's reign. But the church and the sepulchre itself were in for a turbulent future. They were badly damaged when the Persians conquered Jerusalem in 614, and were destroyed by the Fa-timid Caliph al-Hakim in 1009. The Crusaders rebuilt and expanded the church in 1099, enclosing both Golgotha and the garden under roofing for the first time. With some modifications over the years—including repairs after a devastating fire in 1808—it is essentially the Crusader church that exists today.

The ornate marble edicule now standing in the church's rotunda is the fourth version of the tomb. Just how much, if any, of the actual burial cave is encased inside the polished honey-colored stonework is unknown. The last time anyone peered beneath the marble was in 1809, when the Greek Ortho-dox Church erected the current structure after the fire.

However, a British archaeologist who recently completed a ten-year survey of the site believes that much of the tomb is intact. Martin Biddle, a senior research fellow at Hertford College, Oxford, used a process called *photogrammetry*—a camera technology that produces computer-enhanced, three-dimensional im-ages—to examine the edicule. He contends that if the outer skin could be re-moved, it would reveal three other layers of construction and adornment going back to Constantine's time. Beneath that, he says, "we are now sure there are sub-stantial remains of a tomb that stands higher than a man cut into the living rock."[15] Restoration of the edicule is expected within a few years, says Biddle. That may give experts a chance to see the actual tomb for the first time in nearly two hundred years.

Other archaeological evidence supports the authenticity of the tomb tradi-tion. Soundings and excavations beneath the church were conducted during restoration work between 1961 and 1981. Those investigations confirmed that an ancient limestone quarry lies below the church. They also exposed several other rock-hewn tombs, portions of a retaining wall believed to be part of Hadrian's temple, and several wall segments from Constantine's original basil-ica.[16] Significantly, archaeologists in the late 1960s also found evidence nearby of a portion of city wall—described by Josephus as the "third wall"—built by Herod Agrippa between 41 and 44 CE,[17] some ten or fifteen years after the crucifixion of Jesus. The wall extended the city's boundaries well beyond the sepulchre. Its discovery provided substantial proof that when Jesus was crucified, the site of his death and burial would have been "outside the walls," just as John's gospel and the book of Hebrews describe it.[18]

For most scholars, the literary and archaeological evidence makes a strong case for the accuracy of the tradition identifying the Church of the Holy Sepulchre as the site of Jesus' tomb. As Israeli archaeologist Dan Bahat observes, "We may not be absolutely certain that the site of the Holy Sepulchre is the site of Jesus' burial, but we certainly have no other site that can lay a claim nearly as weighty, and we really have no reason to reject the authenticity of the site."[19]

The only other site that has been suggested is the so-called Garden Tomb identified in 1883 by a British general, Charles G. Gordon. Located north of the Church of the Holy Sepulchre and outside the present walls of the Old City, it is a carved tomb on which are painted two red Byzantine crosses. While exploring the tomb, Gordon saw a nearby stone outcropping that he thought resembled a human skull, symbolic of the biblical Golgotha. He concluded that this was the true site of Jesus' crucifixion and burial, as opposed to the Holy Sepulchre (which he regarded, understandably at the time, to have been inside the ancient city walls). However, there is no archaeological evidence to support the authenticity of Gordon's tomb. Subsequent discoveries have dated the site and other nearby tombs to the seventh or eighth century BCE, which conflicts with the notation in John's gospel that Jesus was placed in a "new tomb in which no one had ever been laid" (19:41).

A similar tradition, but one less substantiated by archaeology, identifies Bethlehem's Church of the Nativity as the site of Jesus' birth. The first recorded tradition locating the site appears in the writings of Justin Martyr from the middle of the second century:

> But when the Child was born in Bethlehem, since Joseph could not find a lodging in that village, he took up his quarters in a certain cave near the village; and while they were there Mary brought forth the Christ and placed him in a manger, and here the Magi who came from Arabia found him.[20]

Origen, a frequent visitor to Palestine, wrote about one hundred years later that "there is pointed out at Bethlehem the cave where [Jesus] was born."[21] And in the fourth century, both saints Jerome and Paulinus of Nola wrote that Emperor Hadrian had deliberately profaned the nativity grotto in the second century by dedicating a grove there in honor of Adonis, the lover of Venus/

Aphrodite whose temple Hadrian had erected in Jerusalem at the site of Jesus' tomb.[22] If their recollection is correct, then the identification of the Bethlehem cave goes back before Hadrian's time, perhaps into the first century.

As he had done in Jerusalem at the site of the Holy Sepulchre, Emperor Constantine early in the fourth century erected an elaborate basilica on what he believed to be the site of the birth grotto. That church was substantially rebuilt in the sixth century, essentially to its present form. Limited excavations during the 1930s and again in the late 1940s revealed the elaborate mosaic floor of the Constantinian church. But the grotto itself remains closed off to archaeological inspection, buried beneath marble slabs and religious ornamentation.[23] Ongoing debates over whether Jesus was born in a cave, a stable, or a house—or whether he was born in Bethlehem at all—will be explored in Chapter 20.

There are numerous other sites throughout modern-day Israel and the West Bank that lay somewhat dubious claims to Jesus traditions. The village of Chorazin, for example, which Jesus condemned for refusing to repent,[24] is identified as the popular archaeological park at Khirbet Karaze, located some three miles north of the Sea of Galilee. The volcanic basalt ruins include a majestic synagogue and numerous houses, cisterns, and ritual baths. But scholars assert that artifacts found at the site indicate it is a third- or fourth-century city and probably was not inhabited during Jesus' time.[25]

The modern town of Kefr Kenna, some five miles northeast of Nazareth, also claims a link to Jesus. This is the town that tourists and pilgrims are generally told is "Cana in Galilee," where Jesus turned water into wine. However, most archaeological evidence found in Kefr Kenna does not predate the Byzantine era. Many scholars now believe that Khirbet Qana, some nine miles north of Nazareth in the Netofa Valley (where ruins of a first-century village have been found), is more likely the biblical Cana.[26]

However, one ancient town whose authentic connections to Jesus are widely acknowledged today is Capernaum, an impressive archaeological complex known as Tell Hum on the northwest shore of the Sea of Galilee. Discovered in 1838 by the American archaeologist Edward Robinson, it was later identified as the city where the gospels say Jesus lived for a time; it also was home to the apostles Peter, Andrew, and Matthew. Among the ruins that Robinson discovered was a magnificent limestone synagogue believed then to have been the place where Jesus taught and performed at least one miracle. Later examination of the site, however, determined that the synagogue probably dated to the third or fourth century CE—much too late to have had any connection to Jesus or his disciples. But still further exploration beginning in the 1960s revealed that underneath the limestone structure were the ruins of an older building of almost the same dimensions, but constructed of the same basalt rock as the surrounding houses. Most scholars now believe this to be a first-century synagogue, and almost certainly the one visited by Jesus.[27]

Nearby, an even more breathtaking discovery occurred. Italian archaeologists in the late 1960s began excavating at the site of an unusual octagonal structure that had been identified earlier as a Byzantine-era church (ca. 400–500 CE). But underneath the church they found the ruins of another, older building that was heavily marked with Christian graffiti. Pottery shards and other artifacts indicated that it originally had been a house, probably built around 63 BCE, that had been renovated sometime around the middle of the first century CE. Its walls and floors were plastered—an unusual feature in ordinary houses of the era, but common in buildings used for large gatherings and for study. Experts concluded that the building had been turned into a "house church" and that it was used as such until the middle of the fifth century.[28]

But that was not its only significance. Included among the graffiti were at least two references to Peter (although some scholars contest the inscriptions). Moreover, fourth-century pilgrims to Capernaum reported that they had seen Peter's house, which they said had been turned into a church.[29] While the case is far from airtight, many scholars now conclude that this was indeed the house of Peter, and if so, the house where Jesus stayed and perhaps lived at the beginning of his ministry. In the mid-1980s, the Franciscans (who had bought the property decades earlier) erected a modern sanctuary shaped like a flying saucer directly over the site. It hovers a few feet off the ground, blocking a clear view of the octagonal church and the "house of Peter" that lies beneath it.

Current excavations at other ancient cities in Galilee, Judea, and elsewhere are casting new light on everyday life in the Roman-occupied land of Jesus' time. At Sepphoris, an ancient capital just an hour's walk from Jesus' boyhood home of Nazareth, experts have found evidence of a cosmopolitan city, suggesting that Jesus did not grow up in rustic surroundings, as is often thought, but would have been exposed to Greek and other cultures.

Meanwhile, numerous artifacts recovered from New Testament times have helped paint a colorful backdrop for the gospel stories—a backdrop that matches the biblical text remarkably well. The gospel of Mark (14:3), for example, tells of a woman who broke an alabaster jar and poured expensive perfume over Jesus' head. The anecdote creates a rather puzzling picture, since breaking a sturdy alabaster container would be akin to cracking open a rock. But archaeological and literary evidence has revealed that sometime during the Hellenistic period—the end of the fourth century to the end of the first century BCE—alabaster jars were replaced by glass vessels as containers of rare perfume, though they continued to be called "alabasters." The sealed glass containers were opened by breaking.[30] So the writer of Mark no doubt got it exactly right when he said that the woman broke open the jar.

The archaeology of the New Testament paints a vivid picture indeed of the dramatic era of Christian origins. While the exact footprints of Jesus may not be discernible in the archaeological record, the wealth of material data clearly affirms the historical background of the gospels and lends weight to many of the sacred traditions that look to the ancient sites and proclaim, "Here is where Jesus walked!"

## CHAPTER 12

# INTO THE
# FUTURE

## THE PROMISE OF

## BIBLICAL ARCHAEOLOGY

> Every area on the face of the earth, be it seemingly ever so
> waste and empty, has a story behind it which the
> inquisitive sooner or later will attempt to obtain.
>
> *Nelson Glueck*[1]

MODERN ARCHAEOLOGY MAY NOT HAVE FULFILLED ALL OF THE EXPECTATIONS
of the early biblical archaeologists, but it has accomplished much. Because of
archaeology, as William Albright reminds us, the Bible "no longer appears as an
absolutely isolated monument of the past, as a phenomenon without relation to
its environment."[2] Instead, it has been firmly fixed in a context of knowable history, linked to the present by discernible footprints across the archaeological
record.

Just as archaeology has shed new light on the Bible, the Bible in turn has
often proved to be a useful tool for archaeologists. Yigael Yadin, who directed
the excavation at Hazor in the 1950s, relied heavily on its guidance in finding
the great gate of Solomon at the famous upper Galilee site: "We went about discovering [the gate] with Bible in one hand and spade in the other."[3] Trude
Dothan, whose work centers on the Philistines, notes that "without the Bible,
we wouldn't even have known there *were* Philistines."[4] And William Dever, who

argued earlier in his career that archaeology and the Bible each should keep a safe distance from the other, now firmly believes that "all archaeologists working in Israel must have sound training in biblical studies" in order to properly understand the context of their work.[5]

That openness of attitude toward the Bible on the part of today's archaeologists bodes well for the future of the field. As recent history has shown, both extremes of the swinging pendulum—from the fundamentalist search for scientific evidence of biblical truth to the unwarranted presumption of some secularists that nothing biblical can possibly be historical—stand only to obstruct progress in both fields. Indeed, there are encouraging signs that within the new archaeology, discoveries of historical and social significance often are recognized as having biblical significance as well.

There still are those, of course, who assume that the story of ancient Israel—from the patriarchs and the exodus to the conquest of Canaan and beyond—is merely a well-crafted tale placed, like a good historical novel, in a credible setting by an author who had done his or her homework. Yet for many scholars, to assume such a depth and breadth of knowledge on the part of a "biblical novelist"—down to the arcane details of the economic and social milieu of distant times and places—takes a far greater leap of faith than to believe that the Bible contains history remembered and recorded. Few in biblical academia today doubt that the stories in the Bible were compiled and edited over time. It even makes sense, as many scholars have argued, that at least portions of the first books of the Bible would have been written in the form we know them no earlier than the days of David and Solomon. That, after all, is when the divided and disorganized tribes of Israel—each with its own oral, and perhaps written, traditions—first became a united people. Only then, it is argued, could their separate threads of memory have been woven into a unified story of the God of Abraham working through the history and people of Israel.

But accepting a relatively late compilation of biblical material—during the time of Solomon, or even later—does not require negating its authenticity or its historical accuracy. Archaeology has shown us otherwise. As Kenneth Kitchen points out, "There is quietly mounting evidence that the basic inherited outline" of biblical history "is essentially sound." Instead of casting the Bible aside if it seems at times to fail to measure up to modern standards of historical reporting, says Kitchen, "we should seek to revise our knowledge of what is a basically sound historical outline, and work to fill it in from the massive wealth of external data archaeology has uncovered."[6]

It is important to remember, too, when pondering holes in the archaeological record, that arguing from an absence of evidence is always a tenuous proposition. "Archaeology," after all, writes Leslie Hoppe, "can uncover only what has survived, and what has survived and has been discovered is the result of sheer accident."[7] Who can say what archaeological bombshells of the mind-changing magnitude of the King David inscription lie hidden in the sands of Egypt or the hills and caves of the Levant? At many important tells, even some that have been excavated for decades, only a small fraction of the ground has been explored. Dozens of recently discovered sites have undergone little more than a superficial survey.

Much work remains for the archaeological explorers of the next century, and many more mysteries of the Bible wait to be solved. Where, for example, are the lost "Annals of the Kings" of Israel and Judah cited as literary sources in the Old Testament book of 1 Kings, and the five books of Papias mentioned in early church writings as a collection of the sayings of Jesus? Where is the tomb of Herod the Great, the imperious ruler of Palestine at the time of Jesus' birth? "There's so much out there, waiting to be found," says James Hoffmeier. "It's just a matter of time."[8]

If indeed a new golden age of biblical archaeology awaits, scholars say that it will be helped along by long-term peace in the Middle East, which will preserve access to lands long closed to modern international explorers. New technologies will also be important. Radar and sound-wave imaging, for example, already show promise in scanning beneath the earth's surface for buried ruins and artifacts.[9] But the key lies in commitment: vast new resources—human and financial—will be needed to excavate and analyze the historical treasures that still lay hidden.

Perhaps new resources also will help scholars expedite their work and avoid the frustrating delays in reporting findings that too often have plagued them in the past, sometimes with deleterious results. Nowhere have such daunting delays been more frustrating or stirred more controversy and rancor in the world of biblical scholarship than in the discovery of the Dead Sea Scrolls. After fifty years of research, this huge cache of ancient documents from the Judean desert still is revealing its secrets. What these mysterious texts divulge about the Bible and its accuracy, about the birth of Christianity and the rise of modern Judaism, is the subject of the next section.

# PART THREE

# THE BIBLE AND THE DEAD SEA SCROLLS

*"Hurry! There's no time!" the old man shouted at his young companion, who stood dazed, staring over the edge of the sheer cliff at the shattered clay jar that littered the rocks below.*

*"Take this one," he said, thrusting another heavy jar into the young man's sweaty arms. "It's the last. And be more careful!"*

*Unsteadily, the young man clambered down the rocky slope toward a dark sliver of a hole in the side of the chalky limestone cliff, half-hidden by a flat, oblong boulder. Cradling the jar in one arm, he dropped to his knees and squeezed through the narrow opening.*

*The dry air inside felt cool compared to the blistering heat of the Judean desert sun. But the cave was cramped and dark, and he hurried to complete his task. Carefully, he wedged the jar next to the others in a shallow recess in the rear wall of the chamber, which looked now like the nest of some giant reptile, filled with earthen eggs. He checked the lid to make sure it was sealed and the contents secure. "They'll be safe in here," he thought, "at least until the trouble passes." He crawled back toward the opening, squeezed out into the blinding sunlight, and rolled the boulder over the mouth of the cave.*

Outside, a sudden squall of hot wind whistled and moaned through the deep fissures in the rugged marl above the wadi, roiling the silvery blue waters of the Dead Sea in the valley below. But the young man thought he heard something more—the sound of frenzied commotion, of anxious voices shouting in the distance. He called out to his elderly companion, but there was no answer. Stumbling up the rocky crevice, he raced toward the top of the cliff. And then he stopped.

There was the old man, his silent gaze fixed on the ridge beyond the panic-filled village of Qumran, on the rising cloud of dust kicked up by countless marching feet, on the brilliant glitter of sunlight glinting off the sharpened blades and polished armor of the approaching Roman legion.

The time of trouble had arrived. The year was 68 CE.

## CHAPTER 13

# SECRETS
# FROM THE
# DESERT

## THE DISCOVERY
## AT QUMRAN

THEY WERE THE ARCHAEOLOGICAL DISCOVERY OF THE CENTURY—A
priceless trove of sacred writings that had lain hidden in the Judean desert for
nearly two thousand years. Since their discovery in 1947 by Bedouin shepherds
in caves near Khirbet Qumran, just ten miles east of Jerusalem, the Dead Sea
Scrolls have been the subject of intense study, speculation, and controversy.
They have excited the imagination of biblical scholars and historians, offered
new insights into the origins and veracity of the Bible, and provided tantalizing
glimpses into the turbulent times that gave birth to Christianity and modern
Judaism.

And although a half-century has passed since their discovery, they continue
to reveal their secrets. The intensely difficult task of translating and analyzing
the ancient Jewish texts still is not complete. Bible scholars and paleographers
who have been working for decades on the most indecipherable of the brittle
parchment fragments still are a year or two away from publishing the last of
their findings. The often passionate and sometimes rancorous debates that have
ensued over the meaning and the biblical significance of the writings from
Qumran are certain to go on for many more years to come.

What continues to make the Dead Sea Scrolls so momentous and so controversial is their absolute uniqueness, not only as an archaeological discovery but as an unmediated literary link to a profoundly important time and place in history. Suddenly (and for the first time), in the middle of the twentieth century, the modern world had at its disposal an entire religious library from first-century Palestine, from the days of Jesus and Paul and the years just preceding the destruction of Jerusalem—an event that forever changed the course of Judaism.

The library's "catalog" is surprisingly extensive. The entire Qumran cache consists of 830 distinct documents salvaged from eleven different caves between 1947 and 1956. Most are written either in Hebrew or Aramaic, although a few Greek fragments also were found. The texts, most scholars believe, were composed or copied between about 250 BCE and 65 CE—probably by members of an ascetic Jewish sect known as Essenes who are thought to have lived in the isolated village adjacent to the caves.

Roughly one-fourth of the documents, 202 in all, are biblical texts, and these include at least a portion (generally in many fragments) of every Old Testament book except Esther—the only book of the Bible that does not mention God. Also found were copies of familiar apocryphal literature—quasi-biblical books such as Enoch, Tobit, Sirach, and Jubilees. But the bulk of the Qumran writings were unknown to the modern world; in fact, many scholars believe that they were unique to the scroll community. These include sectarian commentaries on the Hebrew Scriptures, psalm-like hymns and prayers, vivid apocalyptic prophecies, and intricate rules and instructions for religious and community life. Scholars have found these sectarian writings of special interest because of what they reveal about the pious people who wrote and fervently studied them and, by extension, about the broader religious climate in Palestine at this important moment in history.

That the scrolls survived at all for two millennia is almost a miracle in itself. It was the custom in ancient Judaism to give worn-out biblical manuscripts a reverent burial so that the sacred pieces of parchment would return to the dust of the earth. That is why so few ancient Hebrew biblical texts exist today. But the scrolls at Qumran were not buried like that; they were sealed in clay jars, for the most part. Most scholars believe that they were hidden in the caves, probably during the Jewish Revolt of 66–73 CE, not as a burial but as protection against Roman attack. And that was a wise move. The Roman legions burned and leveled Qumran in 68 CE.

How the long-forgotten scrolls eventually found their way out of their dark desert depository to be studied by a new generation of devoted readers is a fascinating story, and one that still deserves to be told. In its telling in the past, minor variations have arisen and certain details have been disputed. But here, in broad brush strokes, is the intriguing story that has emerged.[1]

## OUT OF THE CAVES

It was early 1947, some say late 1946. Three Bedouin cousins—members of the Ta'amireh tribe—were tending their goats on the plateau below the rocky cliffs of the Wadi Qumran on the northwest shore of the Dead Sea. One of the cousins, Jum'a Muhammad Khalil, was tossing stones at a nimble-footed goat that had wandered too far up into the rocks, when one of the stones skipped into a narrow hole in the side of the cliff and audibly shattered something inside.

Jum'a climbed up to investigate. There in the cliff he found two small openings, but they were too narrow for him to enter through and it was too dark inside to see anything. He tossed in another stone and again heard the sound of cracking pottery. Thinking that perhaps he had found a hidden treasure, he called to his cousins and told them what had happened. They listened attentively, but it was getting late and there wasn't time to explore the cave. So the three cousins left to gather their herd for the night, agreeing that they would come back another day.

In the morning, they took their goats to a fresh-water spring about a mile to the south, and by the time they returned to the previous day's camp, it was again too late to explore the cave. But on the following day, the youngest of the three cousins, Muhammad Ahmed el-Hamed, nicknamed edh-Dhib ("the Wolf"), awoke early and climbed up to the cave alone. He squeezed through the opening and lowered himself feet first into the dark chamber.

Inside, he found the floor littered with broken pottery and other debris. Against the wall were ten unbroken jars, each about two feet high and some with their lids still in place. Anxiously, he tore off the lid of the first jar and reached inside. It was empty. He went to the next. Nothing. To his dismay, jar after jar proved to be empty. He reached into the ninth jar and found it full of sand. Finally, he took the lid off the last jar and felt inside. His fingers closed around a cloth bundle. When he pulled it out, he saw that it was a leather scroll, carefully wrapped in linen. The jar yielded two more scrolls, one without a cloth wrapper. The three scrolls later would be identified as the Great Isaiah Scroll, the Manual of Discipline, and a commentary on the book of Habakkuk. Muhammad edh-Dhib gathered up his treasure and left the cave.

Once edh-Dhib's cousins overcame their initial disappointment that their "hidden treasure" had turned out to be nothing more than three brittle rolls of parchment, they decided they could probably sell them for a modest price to an antiquities dealer. They agreed that they would take the scrolls to the Ta'amireh market in Bethlehem. Before they did that, however, Jum'a returned to the cave—which scholars would come to refer to as Cave 1—with some Bedouin tribesmen. They found and removed four additional scrolls that edh-Dhib apparently had overlooked. Those would turn out to be another partial copy of the book of Isaiah, a collection of hymns known as the Thanksgiving Hymn Scroll, a book of apocalyptic writings known as the War Scroll, and the Genesis Apocryphon, a fanciful amplification of stories found in the biblical book of Genesis. The Bedouin also removed two old jars that had encased the scrolls. These, too, they thought, might fetch a price on the antiquities market.

Sometime in April 1947, Jum'a and his older cousin, Khalil Musa, stuffed the fragile scrolls into a bag and took them to Bethlehem. There they apparently divided the scrolls into two lots and began talking to antiquities dealers. One was Khalil Iskander Shahin, also known as Kando—a cobbler and a Syrian Orthodox Christian. Kando agreed to find a buyer for the four scrolls he was shown, in exchange for one-third of the sale price. He did not know yet what the scrolls contained or what they were worth, but thinking they might be written in the Syriac language, he and another church member, Isaiah George, arranged to show one of the scrolls to the Syrian Orthodox metropolitan of Jerusalem, Athanasius Yeshue Samuel.

A week later at St. Mark's Monastery in the Old City of Jerusalem, Metropolitan Samuel examined the scroll—it was the Manual of Discipline—and recognized immediately that it was written in Hebrew, not Syriac. After Kando and George told him that it had come from the desert near the Dead Sea, he suspected that it must be old: the area had been uninhabited since early Christian times. The metropolitan agreed to buy the scroll and any others the Bedouin wished to sell from the same lot. A meeting was arranged that summer between the metropolitan and two of the Bedouin cousins at the monastery.

This was a turbulent time in Jerusalem. The British Mandate was drawing to a close, and the United Nations was debating the partitioning of Palestine and the creation of a new Jewish state. The gradual withdrawal of the British had spawned deadly violence between Arab, Jew, and Briton. Travel in and out of the city was a dangerous venture. Kando had convinced the two Bedouin to take the scrolls themselves to St. Mark's to negotiate the terms of sale directly with the metropolitan. But when the tattered-looking cousins arrived at the monastery door carrying their dirty bundle, they were turned away by a monk who had not been told of the meeting. The cousins took their scrolls, boarded a bus, and returned to Bethlehem.

When the metropolitan learned of this later in the day, he was horrified. Had the deal been blown? Immediately, he called Kando and apologized for the tragic snub. The cobbler understood what had happened and agreed to bring the scrolls to Jerusalem himself. At that meeting two weeks later, the metropolitan finally had the chance to closely examine what now were five scrolls—the one containing the Manual of Discipline had been broken in two. He listened intently to the story of the discovery in the cave at Qumran. Although he could not read Hebrew and still did not know exactly what he was holding in his hands, the metropolitan was now convinced that these indeed were ancient manuscripts, perhaps early Christian writings. The deal was quickly struck. The metropolitan paid Kando twenty-four pounds, about one hundred dollars at the time, for the five (four) scrolls. Two-thirds would go to the Bedouin cousins, Jum'a and Kahlil. The Dead Sea Scrolls now had a new home in St. Mark's Monastery.

Almost at once, Metropolitan Samuel set out to learn what he could about the age and content of the manuscripts now in his possession. But it would take six months before he learned anything definitive. He consulted with a number of antiquities experts, but because of the perilous conditions in the city and the reluctance of some authorities to be party to what might be a hoax, he had difficulty getting anyone to actually examine the manuscripts. One who was willing—he was eager, in fact—was Professor Eleazer Sukenik of the Hebrew University of Jerusalem.

Sukenik was a highly respected archaeologist who always kept a watchful eye on the antiquities market in Palestine. (His son, Yigael Yadin, then a commander in the underground army, would later become a famous Israeli archaeologist and a distinguished scroll scholar.) Unknown to almost everyone at the time, Sukenik already had in his possession the other three scrolls from Cave 1 at Qumran— the Thanksgiving Hymn Scroll, the War Scroll, and the partial Isaiah scroll. He had bought them from a Bethlehem antiquities dealer on November 29, 1947— the very day that the United Nations approved the partitioning of Palestine. Years later, Yadin would write of the extraordinary symbolism in the confluence of those two dramatic events:

> *It is as if the manuscripts had been waiting in the caves for two thousand years, ever since the destruction of Israel's independence, until the people of Israel had returned to their home and regained their freedom.*[2]

Sukenik had first heard about the scrolls at St. Mark's in December from a Hebrew University librarian who had gone to the monastery some months earlier to look at the manuscripts. The librarian told Sukenik that he had judged the scrolls to be Samaritan and probably not very old. But Sukenik suspected otherwise. He felt sure they were companions of the scrolls that he now had. He tried to reach Metropolitan Samuel, but to no avail.

A month later, in January 1948, Sukenik heard from an acquaintance by the name of Anton Kiraz, who was a parishioner at St. Mark's and who offered to show him some scrolls that were for sale at the monastery. Sukenik was thrilled at his good fortune. Kiraz arranged for Sukenik to view the manuscripts at the local YMCA—a neutral site in the fractured city. As soon as he saw the scrolls, Sukenik knew they indeed were part of the same collection, and expressed an interest in buying them. Kiraz permitted Sukenik to take one of the manuscripts—the Great Isaiah Scroll—back to the university for a few days. When he returned it, Sukenik proposed that Metropolitan Samuel and the president of Hebrew University meet to personally negotiate a selling price. Kiraz took the scrolls back to the monastery. A few days later, he called and told Sukenik that the metropolitan did not wish to sell at the moment; he wanted to wait until hostilities died down so that he could better test the market. Sukenik would never see the scrolls again.

By then, Metropolitan Samuel had learned that one of his scrolls was an ancient copy of the book of Isaiah. But he still was not sure just how old it was. Sukenik, on the other hand, had a strong hunch that the scrolls were from some time around the turn of the era. Perhaps they were to be associated with the Essenes, a first-century Jewish sect known from ancient sources to have lived near En Gedi on the western shore of the Dead Sea. Sukenik knew that there had been reports in the early Christian centuries of scrolls having been found in jars near Jericho, just to the north of the Dead Sea. But he did not share his knowledge of history or his hunch with the Syrian priest.

Still seeking answers, the metropolitan contacted the American School of Oriental Research in Jerusalem. John Trever, a recent Ph.D. recipient and an accomplished photographer who was on duty there at the time, arranged to have the four scrolls brought to the school and photographed. Trever's pictures would turn out to be an invaluable record over the years, as the manuscripts continued to deteriorate. As Trever examined the scrolls, he was amazed at the antiquated style of the Hebrew text. He guessed that they could be as old as the Nash Papyrus—a second-century BCE fragment that contained the oldest biblical Hebrew writing then known. He sent a photographic sample on to the founder of the American School, the famous biblical archaeologist and epigrapher William F. Albright, at Johns Hopkins University in Baltimore. Albright wrote back a few weeks later and confirmed Trever's theory:

*My heartiest congratulations on the greatest manuscript discovery of modern times! There is no doubt in my mind that the script is more archaic than that of the Nash Papyrus. . . . And there can happily not be the slightest doubt in the world about the genuineness of the manuscript.[3]*

It was only then, more than a year after Bedouin herdsmen had lugged the first scrolls down the rocky hillside at Qumran, that news of the discovery of the Dead Sea Scrolls—then known only to a small circle of scholars, clergy, and antiquities dealers in Palestine—was announced to the world. On April 11, 1948, the New Haven, Connecticut, office of the American School of Oriental Research issued a press release that was carried by the *Times* of London the following day, announcing "the discovery in Palestine of the earliest known manuscript of the Book of Isaiah" along with "three other ancient Hebrew scrolls" dating to "about the first century BCE." The newspaper reported incorrectly, however, that the scrolls had been found at St. Mark's, an error that American School officials said was not a part of their original press release.[4] A few days later, Sukenik issued his own announcement, breaking the news of his discovery not only to the public but to the scholars of the American School, who until then had not been aware that there were other scrolls. The *New York Times* carried a story on April 25 reporting that scrolls had been found "some time ago in a hillside cave near En-Geddi, halfway down the shore of the Dead Sea."[5]

The word was finally out. Fearing for the safety of his scrolls and still hoping to score a big sale, Metropolitan Samuel moved his manuscripts from the monastery in Jerusalem to Beirut, and eventually to the United States. There, with help from officials at the American School, he arranged to have them put on display at the Library of Congress and at a number of prestigious museums and galleries. Americans were intensely curious and flocked to see the scrolls from the Dead Sea. But still no big-time buyer emerged. Major institutions appeared reluctant to bid on antiquities whose ownership was in dispute. The Jordanian government by then was claiming title to the scrolls, since they had been found in territory under its control. The legality of removing antiquities from Palestine to Lebanon was in serious doubt.

Finally, in desperation, Metropolitan Samuel, who by then was living in New Jersey, took out a now-famous ad in the *Wall Street Journal* on June 1, 1954:

*"The Four Dead Sea Scrolls"*

*Biblical Manuscripts dating to at least 200 BC, are for sale. This would be an ideal gift to an educational or religious institution by an individual or group.*

*Box F 206, The Wall Street Journal*

The advertisement seemed to do the trick. On July 1, after careful negotiations, the metropolitan brought the scrolls to the Waldorf-Astoria Hotel in New York to a meeting with the purchaser, a man by the name of Sidney Etheridge. The agreed-upon price for the lot was $250,000. The metropolitan had arranged to have the proceeds go into a trust fund that would provide assistance to Syrian Orthodox churches. The deal was consummated, and the scrolls were passed to

Etheridge. It appeared that the Dead Sea Scrolls would end up in a private American collection.

But a few months later, in February 1955, the prime minister of Israel made the surprise announcement that the four scrolls were back in Israel. The mysterious Mr. Etheridge, it turned out, had been a middleman working for Yigael Yadin and the Israeli government. Yadin had seen the newspaper ad and been determined to secure the scrolls that his father, who had passed away the year before, had wanted so much for his country. Now the four wandering scrolls from St. Mark's Monastery would be reunited with Sukenik's three and reside at the Shrine of the Book in Jerusalem.

For Metropolitan Samuel, there would be one more disappointment. Despite his careful preparations, the bill of sale had not been properly drawn up. The Internal Revenue Service declared that the proceeds of the sale counted as personal income, so most of his profit went to the United States government as taxes.

As dramatic as it had been, the biggest archaeological story of the twentieth century was only beginning to unfold. Back in Palestine, archaeologists and Bedouin relic hunters had been combing the cliffs and hillsides near Qumran in search of more scrolls. Their labors had been fruitful beyond expectation. Between 1948 and 1956 they would find ten more caves and hundreds more manuscripts—biblical books and other religious writings all from the same era and, presumably, the same ancient source. The Dead Sea Scrolls, as Albright had proclaimed years earlier, indeed had proven to be the "greatest manuscript discovery of modern times."

Most of the newly discovered material, however, was found to be in much worse condition than the original seven scrolls from Cave 1. Many of the manuscripts were badly decomposed and barely legible fragments. It would take painstaking effort to assemble, identify, and analyze this huge cache of ancient writings. The pieces were gathered up and deposited at the Rockefeller Museum, then known as the Palestine Archaeological Museum in Jordanian-controlled East Jerusalem. It was left to the president of the museum, Father Roland de Vaux of the Ecole Biblique, a French Dominican school in Jerusalem, to assemble a team of scholars to conduct the arduous work. De Vaux picked seven men, all highly credentialed European and American scholars—but no Israelis—and installed himself as head of the team.

As they set about their task in the early 1950s, the team of scholars had no way of knowing just how rigorous, time-consuming, and controversial their historic project would turn out to be. Over the next five decades, the scrolls from Qumran would excite and enlighten the world of biblical scholarship. But they also would provoke rancorous debate and arouse seething academic jealousy. Before it was finished, the momentous and difficult task of deciphering the secrets of the Dead Sea Scrolls—the greatest archaeological discovery of modern times—would be called the "scandal par excellence of the twentieth century."

## CHAPTER 14

# SCROLLS, SCHOLARS, AND SCANDALS

## FIFTY YEARS OF SCROLL RESEARCH

IT DID NOT TAKE LONG, ONCE THE SCROLLS FOUND THEIR WAY INTO THE hands of biblical scholars, before the world began to grasp the historic magnitude of the discovery at Qumran. Suddenly a window had been opened to the distant past—and not to just any past. Here was a library compiled, if not composed, during the seminal period of both Christianity and modern Judaism—a time when the biblical canons of both faiths were taking shape. It was the first surviving Hebrew and Aramaic evidence written by and for a group of Palestinian Jews who were contemporaries of Hillel, Gamaliel, and Jesus of Nazareth. Within a year of the discovery, the famous biblical archaeologist William F. Albright prophetically predicted that the scrolls would "revolutionize intertestamental studies" and "antiquate all present handbooks on the background of the New Testament and on the textual criticism and interpretation of the Old Testament."[1]

The prospects were at once exciting and disquieting. What would these ancient documents reveal about the origins and perhaps evolution of the Bible? Would they confirm or challenge the integrity of the Scriptures that untold millions of Christians and Jews had revered over the centuries as God-inspired and worthy of belief? Would they be found to include some previously unknown manuscript from the hand of a Hebrew prophet, a Christian apostle, or even Jesus himself?

Shortly after the first scrolls were published, speculation arose that they contained explosive information that would devastate traditional views of Christianity. In 1952, Andre Dupont-Sommer, a French biblical scholar who was not a member of the scroll team, suggested that the ancient manuscripts revealed astonishing parallels between Jesus of Nazareth and the mysterious leader of the Qumran sect, who is identified in the scrolls only as the Teacher of Righteousness.[2] The Frenchman's dramatic suppositions, some of which were based on severe misreadings of the Qumran texts, influenced American literary critic Edmund Wilson to write a series of provocative articles in the *New Yorker* claiming that the Qumran sect and Christianity were "successive phases of a [single] movement." There had been nothing miraculous or uniquely revelatory in the birth of the Christian faith, Wilson asserted. It had simply evolved out of this strange, apocalyptic Jewish sect. Referring to the archaeological ruins of Qumran, Wilson wrote, "[Th]is structure of stone that endures between the waters and precipitous cliffs, with its oven and its inkwells, its mill and its cesspool, its constellations of sacred fonts and the unadorned graves of its dead, is perhaps, more than Bethlehem or Nazareth, the cradle of Christianity."[3]

Such fanciful speculation dissipated rather quickly as scroll research advanced and more of the manuscripts were published during the 1950s. But as the years passed, the pace of publication would slow to a near standstill, and frustration and suspicion would reemerge with a vengeance.

In the early stages, work on the scrolls went relatively smoothly as scholars pored over manuscripts from Cave 1—documents that were nearly intact and fairly easy to translate. In 1950, the American School of Oriental Research in Jerusalem produced the first complete edition of any of the scrolls, a volume on the Great Isaiah Scroll and the Habakkuk Commentary that had been acquired from St. Mark's Monastery. A second volume on the Manual of Discipline followed in 1951. Eleazer Sukenik's three scrolls—the partial manuscript of Isaiah, the War Scroll, and the Thanksgiving Hymn Scroll—were published posthumously in 1954, with Yigael Yadin helping to complete the editing of his father's work. The last of the original seven scrolls, the Genesis Apocryphon, was published in 1956, again with Yadin and Israeli scholar Nahman Avigad as editors. All of those volumes included photographs of the manuscripts and Hebrew transcriptions of the texts.

In 1955, the team of scholars assembled by Father de Vaux produced its first publication in the Oxford *Discoveries in the Judean Desert* series—a volume dealing with hundreds of small fragments that had turned up in Cave 1 after the original seven scrolls had been removed.

By the end of 1956, then, all of the manuscripts from Cave 1 had been published and were available for public inspection. But that had been the easy part. All of the remaining documents were in considerably worse shape than the Cave 1 trove, and all were in the hands of de Vaux and his team, which held exclusive publication rights. Biblical scholars outside of that small elite circle now would have to wait for de Vaux and his colleagues to complete their work before they would have a chance to see the remaining manuscripts for themselves. And wait they did.

Six years would pass before de Vaux's team produced its second volume, an analysis of the documents found at the Wadi Murabba'at south of Qumran. The third volume came out a year later with all of the remaining texts from the "minor caves"—caves 2 and 3 and 5 through 10, where relatively few scrolls had been discovered. The fourth volume, containing just one manuscript—a copy of the book of Psalms found in Cave 11—was published three years later, in 1965. Finally, in 1968, the first documents from the huge cache in Cave 4 were published in Oxford's fifth *Discoveries* volume.

At that point, the already slackening pace of publication seemed to bog down completely. Twenty years had passed since the initial scroll discovery, and only five Oxford volumes had been published. It would take de Vaux's team another twenty-four years to pump out the next four volumes, bringing the total in 1992 to just nine out of what ultimately would be a thirty-eight-volume series.

## BITS AND PIECES

At least in part, the slowdown after the Cave 1 documents reflected the intense difficulty of the work that remained.

The material from Cave 4 was by far the most plentiful. It also was in the worst shape. More than 570 documents in all had been found in the now-famous marl cave directly adjacent to the village plateau. While some of the material had been carefully extracted by archaeologists, much of it had been gathered by Bedouin tribesmen and sold to the Palestine Archaeological Museum. And the documents hadn't been in good shape to begin with: the brittle manuscripts had been shattered centuries earlier into tens of thousands of fragments, some no larger than a dime. The pieces were found scattered about the floor of the cave or buried in the sand, where they had been gnawed by worms and stained with corrosive bat droppings. Virtually the entire cache of material was in an advanced state of decay.

One leading scholar who worked on the fragments, Harvard professor Frank Moore Cross, wrote vividly of the difficulties the team faced in those days in reconstructing the Cave 4 manuscripts:

*The fragments when they are purchased from tribesmen generally come in boxes; cigarette boxes, film boxes, or shoe boxes, depending on the size of the fragments. . . . Many fragments are so brittle or friable that they can scarcely be touched with a camel's-hair brush. Most are warped, crinkled, or shrunken, crusted with soil chemical, blackened by moisture and age. The problems of cleaning, flattening, identifying, and piecing them together are formidable.*[4]

The task was understandably time-consuming. Finding and joining the right fragments was like trying to solve a jigsaw puzzle with half the pieces missing. Some fragments contained no more than a letter or two and seemingly could have fit almost anywhere. Many pieces were simply gone, disintegrated, so that often when a document was "completed," it resembled a piece of lace. Translating and making sense of a text in that condition was next to impossible.

What was less understandable, however, given the difficulty of the task, was why the team refused to call in reinforcements. An entire world of talented biblical scholars and expert paleographers stood on the sidelines, anxious to apply their skills to a project of such historical significance. Instead, de Vaux and his team stuck to the original plan—eight scholars, each with an assigned batch of fragments, each having exclusive rights to analyze those documents and to publish his work whenever and however he saw fit. Years later, Harvard professor John Strugnell—one of the original eight, and later the chief editor of the project—conceded to an interviewer that he regretted not having "had the foresight to see already by 1960 that we were absurdly top-heavy; too few scholars were working on the project."[5]

To make matters worse, the scholars had been given no firm deadlines by which to complete their work. Already by the early 1960s it was clear that the team considered its exclusivity arrangement good for a lifetime. And it appeared that some members were perfectly willing to take that long to finish the job. With so few ambitious hands trying to accomplish so much, the publication process ground to a halt.

The Six-Day War of June 1967 would create additional complications. The victorious Israelis had taken control of East Jerusalem, and along with it the Palestine Archaeological Museum and the Dead Sea Scrolls. Who now was the rightful owner of the Cave 4 manuscripts? What would become of the team of scholars assembled under Jordanian authority? Even if they were invited to stay, some members had strong anti-Zionist sentiments and were reluctant to continue the work under Israel's auspices.[6]

But the Israel Department of Antiquities had no desire to disrupt the work. Its top officials sought to reassure the team that they would not interfere with the project and would even honor the team's exclusive publication rights.[7]

As a result, very little changed. And for the many scholars who found themselves shut out of the process, growing frustration was slowly turning to fury. In 1976, Theodor Gaster, a professor at Columbia University, complained that "by the hazards of mortality," the tightly held monopoly over the scrolls would "prevent a whole generation of older scholars from making their contribution."[8] Unless drastic measures were taken at once, warned Oxford University professor Geza Vermes a year later, "the greatest and most valuable of all Hebrew and Aramaic manuscript discoveries is likely to become the academic scandal *par excellence* of the twentieth century."[9]

Indeed, that first generation of scroll scholars had already begun to fade. De Vaux died in 1971 and was succeeded as editor-in-chief by his fellow priest and colleague from the Ecole Biblique, Pierre Benoit. Claus-Hunno Hunzinger, a German Lutheran scholar, had resigned in 1958, leaving his material to the French priest Maurice Baillet. And John Allegro, an Oxford University scholar, ruptured his relationship with his colleagues and ceased to function as a member of the scroll team. His scroll work had been found to be rife with errors and in need of massive corrections.[10] Allegro tarnished his reputation further in 1970 by writing a book depicting the Jesus movement as a drug and fertility cult. Then he accused his teammates of taking orders from the Vatican to suppress controversial material contained in the scroll manuscripts—a sensational charge that was never borne out.[11]

The problem in those years was that as scholars died or resigned, their unpublished work was passed on to a hand-picked replacement. But for years the team itself was not expanded. Only after Pierre Benoit, de Vaux's successor as head of the team, died in 1987, and the leadership mantle fell to Strugnell of Harvard, did the team begin to grow. Strugnell expanded the number of scholars working on the scrolls to about twenty and, for the first time, included some Jewish scholars.

But Strugnell was forced to resign in 1990 after giving a vitriolic interview to an Israeli journalist during which he described himself as an "anti-Judaist" and called Judaism "a horrible religion."[12] The Israeli Antiquities Authority, formerly the Department of Antiquities, installed as his successor Emanuel Tov, a professor at the Hebrew University in Jerusalem and a relative newcomer to the team. For the first time, the leadership of the scroll research project was in Israeli hands.

Under Tov's stewardship as editor-in-chief, the team was widened to about fifty scholars, and the pace of research and publication picked up considerably. Eugene Ulrich, a University of Notre Dame scholar who had been named chief editor over the Cave 4 biblical material, began granting occasional outside requests for access to the scrolls, including requests from teams of scholars working on new Bible translations. "Whatever delays or problems may have occurred in the past," Ulrich said in 1991, "it certainly isn't happening today."[13]

But such claims did not satisfy the many outside scholars who still were being denied access to the unpublished manuscripts. Their discontent over the scroll monopoly and the glacial pace of publication during the previous decades had long since turned to bitter indignation. In 1985, more than half of the Cave 4 documents still had not been seen by any but the small circle of "official" scroll scholars and a few privileged outsiders. That same year, Hershel Shanks, head of the Washington, D.C.–based Biblical Archaeology Society, launched the opening salvos of a crusade in the pages of his popular magazine *Biblical Archaeology Review*, to break the monopoly and liberate the Dead Sea Scrolls. "The insiders," Shanks wrote, "have the goodies—to drip out bit by bit. This gives them status, scholarly power and a wonderful ego trip. Why squander it? Obviously, the existence of this factor is controversial and disputed."[14]

Shanks's efforts would prove instrumental in moving the controversy out of the ivy-covered halls and esoteric journals of biblical academia and into the public limelight. Breaking the decades-long monopoly over the Dead Sea Scrolls soon would become a *cause célèbre* in the national media, as major newspapers and national magazines reported the grievances of the excluded scholars and editorialized for an end to the scholarly blockade. As scroll scholar James VanderKam of Notre Dame recalls of that period, "The language of monopoly gave way to talk of a scrolls 'cartel'—a term normally used for Colombian drug lords or unpopular oil producers."[15] With public pressure mounting, Israeli authorities finally began pressing the scroll team to come up with a specific timetable for completion of their work.

## THE LIBERATION

But a dramatic sequence of events, unforeseen at the time, was about to quickly change the entire terrain. In September of 1991, two scholars at Hebrew Union College in Cincinnati produced a surprisingly accurate but unofficial—some would call it "pirated"—version of the unpublished manuscripts and released it in a book entitled *A Preliminary Edition of the Unpublished Dead Sea Scrolls*. The two scholars—Professor Ben Wacholder and Martin Abegg, who was then a graduate student—reconstructed the text from a concordance that the team had assembled in the 1960s. The concordance listed each occurrence of every major word that appeared in the unpublished fragments, along with its location and its context—the word or two on either side of it. It was intended to be used by team members as they translated and analyzed the manuscript fragments. But Strugnell, prior to his departure, had made copies available to certain academic libraries. One ended up in Wacholder's possession. Using a desktop computer to make the right connections, Wacholder and Abegg were able to accurately link the words of the concordance into complete phrases and sentences, essentially reassembling entire texts in the process. Now anyone who bought the book could see, at least in preliminary form, the long-hidden manuscripts from Qumran.

That moment of liberation was quickly followed by another. Later that same month, the Huntington Library in San Marino, California, startled the academic world by announcing that it had in its possession a complete set of scroll photographs and would make them available to any scholar who wished to see them. Anyone who could read ancient Hebrew or Aramaic script now could have access to essentially the same raw data that until then had been the exclusive property of the scroll team. In many cases, the photographic images were better than the actual scrolls, which had continued to deteriorate over the years. The photos had been taken years earlier for security purposes, in the event anything should ever happen to the original manuscripts. Complete sets had been deposited at Oxford University, Hebrew Union College, and the Ancient Biblical Manuscript Center in Claremont, California, on the condition that no one be allowed to see them without permission of the scroll editors.

Unknown to almost anyone at the time, however, duplicates of the Claremont photos had been placed in the Huntington Library by Elizabeth Hay Bechtel, a wealthy supporter of the Ancient Biblical Manuscript Center. After Bechtel died in 1987, the Huntington photos were all but forgotten until they were noticed by the library's new director, William A. Moffett. Once Moffett learned that the library had never signed a privacy agreement, as the other depositories had, he decided to release the photos in the name of intellectual freedom. "We could not go along with protecting the position of anachronistic privilege," he said.[16]

The nation's media responded with resounding approval. A *New York Times* editorial applauded the two Hebrew Union College scholars who had "amazingly . . . broken the scroll cartel. . . . The two Cincinnatians seem to known what the scroll committee forgot: that the scrolls and what they say about the common roots of Christianity and Rabbinic Judaism belong to civilization, not to a few sequestered professors."[17] Syndicated columnist William Safire, who is not ordinarily a commentator on things biblical, hailed the liberation of the scrolls from the "Judases to academic freedom" who had represented "no interest but their own arrogant selfishness."[18] And Hershel Shanks, who had campaigned so tirelessly for this moment, and whose Biblical Archaeology Society soon would publish the photographs in book form, declared victory: "The struggle to free the scrolls was over."[19]

Israeli authorities, nonetheless, were incensed by it all and initially threat-ened to take legal action. But after gauging the strong worldwide outpouring in support of the disclosures, and recognizing that there was no way to recapture what now was in the public's hands, Emanuel Tov, the scroll teams' recently in-stalled editor-in-chief, did the only reasonable thing left to do. He announced in November 1991 that all scholars would have unconditional access to all of the official scroll photographs. After more than four decades, the Dead Sea Scrolls were free at last.

The resolution of that long and bitter dispute, as welcome as it was, did not bring an end to controversies surrounding the scrolls. In the latter years of the debate, some scroll editors had suggested that providing unfettered access to the raw manuscripts would be inviting mischief. They worried that self-appointed "experts" out to tap the intense public interest in the scrolls would rush to pub-lish material that was beyond their ken and would clutter the field with shoddy scholarship and confusion. Their concerns, as it turned out—initially, at least—were not unfounded.

## COVER-UP CONSPIRACY

Within a year of the scrolls' release, two provocative books appeared that claimed to reveal startling new information about the content of the Qumran manu-scripts and the identity of the people who had written them. Both seemed in-tent on reviving the discredited notion that the scroll editors had deliberately suppressed material that would pose a threat to Christian tradition.

In their 1991 book *The Dead Sea Scrolls Deception,* journalists Michael Baigent and Richard Leigh picked up the tattered threads of John Allegro's "Vati-can conspiracy" theory and wove them into a sensational tale of intrigue and de-ceit. The Catholic-dominated team of scholars, the authors suggested, had almost certainly acted at Rome's behest to conceal explosive evidence contained in the unpublished scrolls—evidence that the two authors now were free to reveal.

What the Roman Catholic Church did not want known, according to Baigent and Leigh, was that the mysterious people of Qumran were not part of an obscure Jewish sect known as Essenes, as was the predominant view among scroll scholars. Rather, they were members of the early Christian church, and their leader—the Teacher of Righteousness, who figures so prominently in the Qumran manuscripts—was none other than the apostle James, who is depicted in the gospels as the brother of Jesus and the leader of the church in Jerusalem.

Baigent and Leigh's book, which leaned heavily on the idiosyncratic views of Robert Eisenman, a California State University professor, initially attracted considerable attention in the media and briefly stirred some public excitement. After all, if the ascetic Jewish sect at Qumran—with its pointed emphasis on strict adherence to the Mosaic law—turned out to be practicing a primitive form of Christianity, it would reveal how radically far the church had wandered from its roots.

But in the fields of biblical and scroll scholarship, Baigent and Leigh's theory barely stirred a ripple; it was almost universally rejected out of hand. As the highly regarded Oxford professor and scroll scholar Geza Vermes pointed out at the time, the Christians-at-Qumran scenario ran up against "three harsh realities." First and foremost, the time factor was all wrong. Some of the key sectarian writings found at Qumran had been composed decades, if not centuries, before Christianity came on the scene. The founder of the sect, the Teacher of Righteousness, according to most scholars, had lived in the first and perhaps the second centuries BCE.[20] Second, the two ideologies differed fundamentally. Their divergence over the primacy of the Mosaic law was perhaps the most striking example. And finally, despite a few unsubstantiated claims to the contrary, no New Testament fragment had been discovered in any Qumran cave. The most that could be said about an intersection of early Christianity and the sect at Qumran, said Vermes, was that the two movements "spring from the same common stock, the Judaism of the period."[21]

As for the inflammatory allegation that the Vatican had been suppressing the scrolls, it was an argument based on insinuation rather than evidence. And even the insinuations did not add up. Hershel Shanks, a persistent critic of the scroll team's monopolistic practices, perhaps best summed up the response of mainstream biblical scholars. The Roman Catholic conspiracy theory, he wrote in 1991, was "hogwash." De Vaux and his colleagues from the Ecole Biblique had proven themselves to be independent-minded scholars highly regarded in the profession, noted Shanks. Like many of their Catholic colleagues in biblical academia, they were "at the forefront of modern critical biblical scholarship"— a position that often placed them at odds with official church doctrine. Moreover, some of the most persistent and vocal critics of the scroll publication team had been Catholic scholars who, if there had been a Vatican conspiracy, said Shanks, apparently "never got the word." In any event, the scrolls had been under the control of the Israeli government since 1967, and Jewish scholars had been part of the team for years. Baigent and Leigh, said Shanks, "do not explain how the Israelis were enticed to join a conspiracy whose purpose is to preserve the purity of church doctrine." The Vatican conspiracy theory, he summarized, was "so badly flawed as to be ludicrous."[22]

The ultimate repudiation of the cover-up allegation came from the scrolls themselves. Once the unpublished documents had been released, it quickly became apparent that there were, in fact, no hidden bombshells—just as the editors had been saying for years. There was nothing in the scrolls that would have warranted a cover-up in the first place.

No sooner had that dustup begun to settle than a second eye-catching book appeared on the scene. This one was even more bizarre. *Jesus and the Riddle of the Dead Sea Scrolls,* a 1992 tome written by University of Sydney (Australia) professor Barbara Thiering, agreed with both Eisenman and Baigent/Leigh that Qumran had been an early Christian community. But Professor Thiering added a mind-boggling new twist. As members of the early Christian church, she argued, the scribes of Qumran wrote not only the sectarian scrolls that were found in the caves, but also the gospels and the book of Acts. Moreover, they composed the New Testament writings in a secretive and highly symbolic code that she alone had managed to crack. Once deciphered, said Thiering, the Bible revealed a detailed and dramatic history of the early church quite unlike the traditional story.

Thiering built her fanciful theory on the notion that the New Testament writers—the Qumran scribes, as she saw it—had employed a technique called *pesher,* which simply means "interpretation." It is a term associated in the Bible with a spiritual ability to interpret dreams, as is demonstrated in the Old Testament stories of Joseph and Daniel. As Thiering accurately noted, the Qumran community was known to have used a pesher method as they studied the Hebrew prophets, which they interpreted as applying to themselves and to their times. They did this, for example, in the Habakkuk Commentary (1QpHab), one of the scrolls from St. Mark's Monastery. As the passage below illustrates, they would quote a line from the biblical book of Habakkuk and follow it with a pesher, and then proceed line by line, extracting what they saw as portents of their own struggle against Roman oppression:

> "Dire and dreadful are they; their law and their fame come from themselves alone" (1:7).
> This refers to the Kittim [Romans], the fear and [dread] of whom are on all nations. By intention their only thought is to do evil, and in deceit and trickery they conduct themselves with all the peoples.
> "Swifter than panthers their horses, faster than desert wolves. Their horses, galloping, spread out, from afar they fly like a vulture intent on food, all of them bent on violence, their faces ever forward" (1:8–9a).
> This refers to the Kittim, who trample the land with [their] horses and with their beasts. From far away they come, from the sea coasts, to eat up all the people like an insatiable vulture. In anger and [hostility] and in wrath and arrogance they speak with all [the peoples, for] that is what it means when it says ["their faces ever forward."]23

Not only were the Qumranites applying the text from Habakkuk to their own situation; apparently, they were interpreting the scriptural passage as if it had been written expressly for and about them. Their use of this pesher technique has been widely recognized by biblical scholars.

But in an amazing leap unsupported by textual evidence from Qumran, the gospels, or anywhere else, Thiering hypothesized that "if a group holding such a view of scripture had set out to write a new scripture, they would have set it up as being capable of a pesher. It would be a 'mystery,' a kind of puzzle, capable of solution by those with special knowledge."[24] Based on that supposition, and apparently applying her own special knowledge, she proceeded to decipher the sensational secrets that she claimed had been encoded into the gospels by the scribes of Qumran.

In the gospel according to Thiering, people, places, and events were not at all what they seemed. John the Baptist, when stripped of his symbolic disguise, was the Teacher of Righteousness, the leader of the Qumran community. Jesus was revealed to be the Wicked Priest who is vilified in the Qumran texts. He was deemed wicked, according to Thiering, because he had donned the robes of the high priest unworthily. The Sea of Galilee stood in the encrypted gospels for the Dead Sea, and Jerusalem represented Qumran, the new holy city.

Jesus was born, it turns out, not in Bethlehem but in a building south of the Qumran plateau. He was married to Mary Magdalene, who bore him three children and then divorced him. He was crucified by Pontius Pilate as an insurgent, but survived the crucifixion. (His accomplices had administered a drug causing him to swoon at the appropriate time, and later revived him with herbs.) His "ascension" meant that he returned to live in celibate seclusion in Qumran after his first marriage. Later he married Lydia, a bishop of Philippi, and accompanied the apostle Paul on missionary trips. He ended up in Rome, where he died as an old man sometime after 64 CE. His family then probably settled in the south of France.

All of these amazing details, according to Professor Thiering, could be found hidden in the text of the New Testament. One needed only to understand the symbolism that had been employed in the writing and that, she asserted, the scrolls from Qumran had revealed to her.

Needless to say, biblical scholars dismissed Thiering's theory as pure rubbish. Its basic premise, like that of Baigent and Leigh's theory, was that the key sectarian scrolls had been written no earlier than the middle of the first century CE—much later than the preponderance of evidence would bear. Setting that fatal flaw aside, biblical scholars noted that Thiering had badly misconstrued the literary function of pesher. As demonstrated in the Qumran texts, it was a method of *interpreting* Scripture—not of writing it. As the noted British biblical scholar N. T. Wright pointed out, "Pesher was a way of saying 'we are the people spoken of by the prophets,' not 'we are the people who can set new crossword puzzles for others to solve.'"[25] Jonathan Campbell, a British lecturer in Jewish studies at the University of Bristol, was even more scathing in his critique:

> *We have absolutely no evidence whatsoever to suggest that the writers [of the Gospels] shaped their accounts so as to conceal under the surface additional data which only Thiering has been able to decipher. In reality, she has cast her own projections into the void created by her fanciful rejection of a more sober account of the sectarian Dead Sea Scrolls. The cumulative evidence shows her conclusions are nonsense.*[26]

Nonsense or not, both Thiering and Baigent/Leigh succeeded in attracting a sizable audience with their sensational claims. Their books hit the shelves at a time when public interest in the Dead Sea Scrolls was near its peak, due to news coverage surrounding the release of unpublished manuscripts. But whatever success they might have achieved in book sales did not carry over into the world of biblical scholarship. They found few buyers in the marketplace of ideas. Indeed, any market for ecclesial conspiracies and fantasy theories all but disappeared with the release of the unpublished scrolls. Now the evidence was available for all to see.

From this point forward, scroll scholarship would proceed in a more orderly, if less titillating, fashion. The significance of the Qumran manuscripts and the contribution they would make to biblical understanding would continue to grow. And so would the debates and controversies surrounding them.

## KEEPERS OF THE SCROLLS

One of the most interesting and intense of the remaining debates concerns the identity of the people who wrote the documents and hid them from Roman invaders in the caves of Qumran. Even though scholars today are nearly unanimous in ruling out the early Christians, they are divided over a range of other possibilities.

Nothing in the scrolls themselves directly identifies the scroll community. But almost from the earliest days after the Qumran discoveries, the evidence seemed to point to an apocalyptic sect of ascetic Jews known as Essenes as the inhabitants of Qumran and the custodians (and probably the writers) of the ancient manuscripts. Hebrew University scholar Eleazer Sukenik, one of the first to lay eyes on the Qumran sectarian scrolls, drew that conclusion based on the match between the writings and what was known of the Essenes from other first-century-CE sources.

The Jewish historian Flavius Josephus, for example, writing for a Roman audience in the late 70s CE, described three "schools of philosophy" flourishing in Palestine in the years preceding the Jewish revolt that began in 66 CE—the Sadducees, the Pharisees, and the Essenes.[27] What Sukenik and others found persuasive were the important similarities in how Josephus depicted the Essenes in his books *Antiquities of the Jews* and *The Jewish War* and the image of the community that emerged from the Qumran sectarian writings, particularly the Manual of Discipline (1QS).

According to Josephus, the Essenes required newcomers to the sect to "transfer their property to the order" to be held in common (*The Jewish War*, 2.122). The Manual of Discipline (6:17–22) spells out that very procedure. The sect emphasized the role of Providence in all of life's details much more than either the Pharisees or Sadducees, according to Josephus, and believed that "nothing befalls men unless it be in accordance" with divine will (*Antiquities of the Jews*, 13.171–173). The Qumran texts are rife with predeterminism, scholars note, as exemplified in the Manual (3:15–16): "From the God of Knowledge comes all that is and shall be. Before ever they existed He established their whole design, and when, as ordained for them, they come into being, it is in accord with his glorious design that they accomplish their task without change."[28]

And even in some minor rules and practices, the two communities seemed to correspond. The Essenes, for example, said Josephus, "are careful not to spit into the midst of the company or to the right" (*The Jewish War*, 2.147). The Manual of Discipline warns that "whoever has spat in an Assembly of the Congregation shall do penance for thirty days" (7:13).[29]

For many scholars, all of this added up to convincing evidence that the Qumran community was, in fact, an outpost of Essenes. What sealed the verdict for many was a passage found in the writings of Pliny the Elder, a first-century Roman geographer who wrote of a "solitary tribe of the Essenes" living "on the west side of the Dead Sea" above En Gedi. That fit precisely Qumran's location—between En Gedi to the south and Jericho to the north, near the Dead Sea's western shore. In his *Natural History*, written in about 77 CE, Pliny went on to describe the sect as "remarkable beyond all the other tribes in the whole world, as it has no women and has renounced all sexual desire, has no money, and has only palm-trees for company."[30] Josephus, meanwhile, told of "another order of Essenes" who did marry, but their motive in marrying "is not self-indulgence but the procreation of children" (*The Jewish War*, 2.160–161).

That seemed to fit better with the situation at Qumran, where archaeologists have discovered graves of women and children outside the village enclosure.

The composite picture of the Qumran community that many scholars have come to embrace is that of a group of Essenes who migrated—or perhaps were expelled—from Jerusalem sometime in the middle of the second century BCE, because of their opposition to the temple priests—the Hasmoneans—and their Sadducean supporters, both of whom dominated the temple. Led into the wilderness by their Righteous Teacher, the Qumranites saw their sojourn as a time of purification and of awaiting the arrival of the Messiah, who they believed would vindicate them and defeat the Wicked Priest in Jerusalem and his followers.

In 1966, scroll scholar Frank Moore Cross of Harvard was so convinced of the Essene hypothesis that he articulated what by then had already become a consensus among the official scroll team and today remains the predominant view of outside scholars as well.

> *The scholar who would "exercise caution" in identifying the sect of Qumran with the Essenes places himself in an astonishing position: He must suggest seriously that two major parties formed communalistic religious communities in the same district of the desert of the Dead Sea and lived together in effect for two centuries, holding similar bizarre views, performing similar or rather identical lustrations, ritual meals and ceremonies. He must suppose that one, carefully described by classical authors, disappeared without leaving building remains or even potsherds behind; the other, systematically ignored by classical sources, left extensive ruins, and indeed a great library. I prefer to be reckless and flatly identify the men of Qumran with their perennial houseguests, the Essenes.*[31]

Nonetheless, some scholars continue to argue that there are other, equally plausible explanations for the scrolls' turning up in the caves of Qumran. One minority position holds that the manuscripts did not belong to the Qumran settlement but were smuggled into the countryside from Jerusalem shortly before the Roman legions attacked the city in 67 CE. Norman Golb, of the University of Chicago's Oriental Institute and a chief proponent of that view, argues that the ideas and writing styles in the Qumran texts "are so diverse and sometimes conflicting that they could not possibly have been the work of one small sect."[32]

For example, Golb says, the Genesis Apocryphon, an embellished version of the book of Genesis, shows nothing of Essene ideas. Likewise, another text—one called Some of the Works of the Torah (4QMMT)—cites twenty reasons why a group of dissenters broke away from the temple in Jerusalem, and yet, Golb says, only two of the twenty points are associated in any way with what is known of Essene beliefs. But the scroll that most damns the Essene theory, in Golb's view, is the Copper Scroll—a virtual treasure map describing riches buried throughout the Judean wilderness. "The types of treasures and documents described on the scroll could only have come from a major center," argues Golb, not from an isolated sect that rejected material wealth.[33]

If Golb is correct and the scrolls were not the property of a small ascetic sect, the Qumran literature would seem to point to a first-century Jewish culture that was in greater intellectual turmoil than scholars had previously thought. Such a diversity of views reflected in a major Jerusalem library, says Shanks of the *Biblical Archaeology Review*, would suggest that "mainstream Judaism" of the era "was much more pluralistic" than anyone could have imagined.[34]

Another noted scholar, Lawrence Schiffman of New York University, has argued that the people of Qumran were a splinter group of Sadducees who considered themselves the sons of Zadok, the chief priest during the days of David and Solomon, and therefore the rightful heirs to the temple priesthood. And still others have posited that the Qumranites might have been members of any of a number of other groups—the radical revolutionary Zealots, perhaps, or the Sicarii, who later would commit mass suicide during the Roman siege at Masada, a few miles down the Dead Sea coast, in 73 CE.

Thus, while the Essene theory continues to dominate the field in explaining the identity of the Qumran community and the origins of the Dead Sea Scrolls, the question is far from settled. It may well take the discovery of additional ancient manuscripts to remove the remaining uncertainties. And scholars say that the prospect of new manuscript discoveries is not as remote as it may seem. Some even speculate that other scrolls may already have been found and now lie squirreled away in private collections or in bank vaults, their owners awaiting an opportune moment to put them on the market, where they would be worth thousands of times their weight in gold. Presumably, the empty and broken jars found in the Qumran caves had not always been empty. Where did their contents go?

The scroll discoveries in the 1940s and 1950s near Qumran certainly were not the first, scholars say, and are unlikely to be the last. The second-century Christian scholar Origen of Alexandria is said to have had a Greek manuscript of the Psalms that had been found in a jar near Jericho.[35] The church historian Eusebius (ca. 260–340 CE) wrote of Greek and Hebrew manuscripts that had been found in jars near Jericho during the reign of Caracalla, Roman emperor in the early third century.[36] And in about the year 800 CE, the Nestorian patriarch Timotheus I wrote a letter to a fellow churchman in which he reported:

> We have learnt from trustworthy Jews who were then being instructed as catechumens in the Christian religion that some books were found ten years ago in a rock-dwelling near Jericho. The story was that the dog of an Arab out hunting, while in pursuit of game, went into a cave and did not come out again; its owner went in after it and found a chamber, in which there were many books, in the rock. The hunter went off to Jerusalem and told his story to the Jews, who came out in great numbers and found books of the Old Testament and others in the Hebrew script.[37]

The caves and cliffs along the Dead Sea shore, it seems, have been yielding their sacred secrets for centuries. Yet it is almost certain, antiquities experts say, that other stashes of ancient writings still lie hidden and undisturbed in chambers not yet discovered. In 1993, Israeli authorities sent teams of archaeologists into the Dead Sea region in a hurried search for new caves and treasures before Israel relinquished control of Jericho to the Palestinians as part of the Mideast peace agreement. While they found a few fragments and artifacts—including a 5,000-year-old skeleton—no new major troves of documents were discovered. Still, archaeologists believe that they have only scratched the surface. It is only a matter of time, they say, before some startling new discovery will open yet another window to the ancient past.

In the meantime, the secrets of the Dead Sea Scrolls have not nearly been exhausted. After a half-century of research and controversy, they continue to shed new light on the Bible and its times. What they have revealed about the origins and veracity of the Scriptures already has revolutionized biblical scholarship and shaken some traditional notions of history. The debate over their meaning and significance will surely go on for years to come.

## CHAPTER 15

# SCRIPTURES
# FIXED AND
# FLUID

## THE SCROLLS AND

## THE OLD TESTAMENT

BEFORE THE DISCOVERY OF THE DEAD SEA SCROLLS, THE OLDEST SURVIVING manuscripts of the Hebrew Bible were traditional Masoretic texts dating from the ninth century CE. Some copies of the Greek Old Testament—the Septuagint—were older, dating to the third and fourth centuries CE. But those were widely considered to be edited versions of Greek translations that had been drawn from the Hebrew text, perhaps in the second or third centuries BCE. The discovery at Qumran would give the world manuscripts of the Hebrew Bible that were a thousand years older than anything previously known.

Now scholars could lay the modern Old Testament alongside these most ancient Hebrew texts and judge just how well it had weathered the centuries. At last they could determine how severely the Scriptures had been altered by inadvertent scribal errors, as well as deliberate redactions during the turbulent years when both nascent Christianity and Rabbinic Judaism were forging their doctrines and traditions.

As they carefully examined the fragile parchment scrolls and assembled hundreds of brittle fragments into page after page of biblical text, the scholars were astonished at what they found. There, in the faded markings of ancient Hebrew and Aramaic script, were the familiar lilting passages of David's Psalms, the unforgettable words of Moses at Sinai, the stern warnings of the prophet

Jeremiah. The Bible had navigated the centuries well. Scholars indeed would find some intriguing variations within the massive trove of biblical documents. But overall, as Notre Dame professor Eugene Ulrich, chief editor of the Qumran biblical texts for the Oxford *Discoveries in the Judean Desert* series, observed, "The scrolls have shown that our traditional Bible has been amazingly accurately preserved for over 2,000 years."[1]

A dramatic example of that textual preservation was found in the Great Isaiah Scroll, the only fully intact biblical document salvaged from the Qumran caves. Now on display at the Shrine of the Book in Jerusalem, it contains all sixty-six chapters of the book of Isaiah that are found in the traditional Bible. Beyond some incidental copying errors, scholars have found only thirteen relatively small variations—a phrase or a verse or two missing or added—when compared to the modern text. The average reader today, says Ulrich, "would look at these differences and say, 'It's no big deal.'"[2] For the most part, they do nothing to alter the meaning of the text, and taken as a whole they attest to the meticulous accuracy of the Masoretic scribes who hand-copied the Hebrew Bible through the first thousand years of the common era.

But editors working on the scrolls also have found fascinating and sometimes puzzling variations in some of the biblical documents. Included among the scrolls were multiple copies of most of the biblical books—thirty-six partial copies of the book of Psalms, for example, twenty-nine of Deuteronomy, twenty-one of Isaiah, seventeen of Exodus, fifteen of Genesis, thirteen of Leviticus, and so on.[3] Despite the close correspondence of many of them to the Masoretic text (and thus to the traditional Bible), the scholars discovered that some of the copies were quite different from other copies.

Some versions of the book of Jeremiah, for example, were found to be significantly shorter than either the traditional Hebrew text or other Qumran copies, and much of the material appeared in a different order. Several renderings of the books of Exodus and Numbers from Qumran, on the other hand, had material that other copies and the traditional Bible did not. In all, roughly half of the biblical texts from Qumran were found either to contain passages that do not appear in modern translations, or to lack passages that appear in the traditional Bible. Some of these differences are especially intriguing, and we turn now to them.

## "NEW" PSALMS

Among the many copies of the book of Psalms found at Qumran are several that contain nine "new" compositions from the hand of King David. Scholars think that these collections may be a variant edition of the biblical Psalter that was in liturgical use at Qumran, and perhaps elsewhere, at the turn of the era. In addition to the extrabiblical writings, the Qumran Psalter appears to include most of the 150 songs and hymns found in the canonical book of Psalms, although they are arranged in a different order.

In their English translation, the "new" psalms attributed to David read pretty much like the traditional Davidic hymns and poems found in the Bible. One, for example, reads in part:

> *Render to us, O Lord, by Your goodness;*
> *according to Your boundless compassion,*
> *Your Myriad righteous acts.*
> *The Lord hears the voice of those who love His name,*
> *of His loving-kindness He deprives them not.*
> *Blessed be the Lord, worker of righteousness,*
> *who crowns the pious with mercy and compassion.*[4]

Most scholars doubt that David actually wrote the new Qumran psalms. "The language of these compositions is a late form of biblical Hebrew—much later than the time of David," explains Michael Wise, a professor at Northwestern College and a co-author of *The Dead Sea Scrolls: A New Translation*. Nevertheless, says Wise, the fact that they were attributed to the great king of Israel "illustrates a trend in Second-Temple Judaism, whereby writings of unknown authors were attributed to great luminaries of the past."[5] So prolific were those pseudonymous writers in the three centuries before and the two centuries after the start of the Christian era that a collection of their works, now known as the Pseudepigrapha, totals sixty-five separate writings—none of which made it into the biblical canon.

Even so, scholars think it is likely that when the people of Qumran read these apocryphal psalms some two thousand years ago, they figured they were reading David's work. For one thing, they kept several copies in their library, notes Ulrich, and there is no indication that the compositions originated there. Three of the nine, in fact, had been seen prior to the discovery of the Dead Sea Scrolls. One appears in the Septuagint as Psalm 151. Two others are preserved in the ancient Scriptures of Syrian Christians, where they are numbered Psalm 154 and Psalm 155. The remaining six are altogether "new."[6]

More intriguing, and perhaps more significant, than the questionable provenance of the Qumran psalms is the bold claim in one scroll fragment as to the ultimate source of David's writings. In a prose prologue that scholars identify as 11Q5, the text declares that God gave to David "a brilliant and discerning spirit" so that he was able to write "four thousand and fifty" songs and psalms. "All of these," the text concludes, "he composed through prophecy given him by the Most High."[7]

Such a direct assertion of the divine inspiration of the Psalms does not appear within the traditional Hebrew Psalter. Yet it is clear that well before the turn of the era the Psalms held a place of high regard in Judaism, alongside the law and the prophets. Could this text explain why?

The Psalms clearly were considered sacred to the writer of the book of 2 Maccabees, a document written before the end of the second century BCE that is included in the Septuagint and in the modern Roman Catholic Bible. In the second chapter, he refers to "the writings of David" along with "the law," and the "kings and the prophets," as texts that were providentially preserved for God's people through the turbulent years of Israel's exile.

The Jewish philosopher Philo of Alexandria (20 BCE–50 CE) affirms that the Psalms were an important part of Jewish devotional life by the turn of the era. In his treatise *On the Contemplative Life,* he describes the daily devotional practices of a Jewish group in Egypt whose members would closet themselves in a consecrated room: "They take nothing into it, either drink or food or any other of the things necessary for the needs of the body, but laws and oracles delivered through the mouths of prophets, *and psalms* and anything else which fosters and perfects knowledge and piety."[8]

And the Jewish historian Josephus, writing in *Against Apion* in about 90 CE, includes in a description of writings "justly accredited" in Judaism "four books [that] contain hymns to God and precepts for the conduct of human life"—a presumed reference to Psalms and Proverbs and possibly Job and Ecclesiastes.[9]

Finally, it is clear from the New Testament that Jesus held the Psalms in high regard and equated David's writings with Scripture. In the gospel of Luke, the resurrected Jesus tells his disciples, "These are my words that I spoke to you while I was still with you—that everything written about me in the law of Moses, the prophets, *and the psalms* must be fulfilled" (Luke 24:44). Throughout the gospels, Jesus quotes the Psalms more than any other part of the Hebrew Bible. And in Mark 12:35, he precedes a quotation of Psalm 110 by declaring that its author, David, said it "by the Holy Spirit."

What was it about the Psalms that set them above other collections of Jewish hymns, devotional poems, and prayers of the time—even those that might have claimed celebrity authorship? Might this long-lost declaration found at Qumran reveal what was by then becoming the prevalent view within Judaism—that the Psalms were written by David through the inspiration of God? "Perhaps in this scroll," says Ulrich, "we have unearthed the claim by which the Psalter moved from being a book of human songs in response to what God has done to humanity to, now, God's word given to David."[10]

## THE "MISSING PROPHECY"

A previously unknown passage in a copy of the book of 1 Samuel found at Qumran may help explain the mysterious "missing prophecy" referred to in the nativity story in the gospel of Matthew. In the first two chapters of that story, Matthew recites five vignettes associated with the birth of Jesus and concludes each by quoting from Hebrew Scripture to show that this was done "to fulfill what had been spoken by the Lord through the prophet." Four of those references are easily found in the traditional Old Testament—that the Messiah would be born of a virgin[11] and would be called Immanuel (Isa. 7:14); that Bethlehem would be his birthplace (Mic. 5:2); that he would come out of Egypt (Hos. 11:1); and that there would be mourning over Herod's slaughter of the children of Bethlehem (Jer. 31:15).

But the fifth prophecy, that "he will be called a Nazarene" (or Nazorean)—explaining why Jesus and his parents settled in Nazareth—is nowhere to be found in the traditional Hebrew Bible. In fact, there is no mention of the Galilean town of Nazareth at all in the Old Testament.

The verse in Matthew has puzzled Bible scholars for centuries. Some modern biblical commentaries suggest that the writer of Matthew may have intended to link Jesus to the messianic "branch" (*netzer,* in Hebrew) that Isaiah 11:1 says shall grow out of the root of Jesse, or to the strict-living Nazirites such as Sampson, ancient Israel's deliverer from the Philistines, who is described in Judges 13:5 as one who was "consecrated" (*nazir,* in Hebrew) to God.[12]

But could Matthew's author simply have been reading from a different version of the Bible—one that includes a prophecy of a messianic connection to Nazareth? The mystery has not been satisfactorily resolved. But scholars who have studied the scrolls say a previously unknown line of text found in a Qumran version of 1 Samuel (4QSam^a) contains language that is startlingly close to Matthew's. It appears at the end of 1 Samuel 1:22, where Hannah, mother of the prophet Samuel, vows to take her newborn son to the temple at Shiloh, "that he may appear in the presence of the Lord, and remain there forever." The Qumran fragment adds a final clause that does not appear in the traditional text: "and I will make him a Nazir forever."

Ulrich says he is "not prepared to claim that this precise passage was the source" of the Matthew citation. Indeed, to do so would seem to require establishing either a misreading of the Hebrew prophets on Matthew's part or a mistranslation of Matthew's gospel in its early form.[13] But the similarity of the language is striking, he says, and so is its context. Just as in Matthew, it appears in a birth narrative. In this case, it is the story of the birth of the prophet who would be chosen by God to anoint King David—the forebear of Israel's Messiah.

Even if this is not the basis of Matthew's "missing prophecy," says Ulrich, "all reasonable indicators point toward the occurrence" in the Scripture in Matthew's hands "of a line, now no longer extant, that could serve as the basis for that quote."[14]

While no other ancient biblical manuscripts contain the passage found at Qumran, the Jewish historian Josephus included it in his close paraphrase in *Antiquities of the Jews*, suggesting that he too knew of this version of 1 Samuel.[15] Convinced of its authenticity, editors of the New Revised Standard Version of the Bible have inserted the line into the modern biblical text, along with a footnote attributing it to the Qumran scrolls.

## FURTHER CORRECTIONS

Other "corrections" based on comparisons with the Qumran texts have been incorporated into some recent editions of the Bible. Most are relatively minor. In the New International Version, for example, a footnote on Exodus 1:5 explains that the number of family members who accompanied the Hebrew patriarch Jacob into Egypt is seventy-five in both the Qumran text and the Septuagint—rather than seventy as the traditional Hebrew text has it. That also agrees with the Christian evangelist Stephen's recitation of the story as told in Acts 7:14. Since most New Testament books are believed to have been composed in Greek, it has been assumed that the writer of Acts was relying on the Septuagint, the Greek translation of the Hebrew Scriptures. Now we have a Hebrew text that, on this point at least, agrees with and may be the source of the Greek.

A few changes to the modern Bible have been more substantive. The New Revised Standard Version, for example, has inserted a relatively lengthy clarifying passage from the Qumran Bible into a narrative involving King Saul. In the traditional Bible, 1 Samuel 11 tells the story of Israel's newly anointed king leading his people in battle against the Ammonites. As the story begins, the Ammonite king Nahash has laid siege against the village of Jabesh-gilead, and men in the village attempt to negotiate peace. But the ruthless Nahash demands a gory price: he wants to gouge out the right eye of every man in the village. It is a strange demand, to say the least, and the traditional text leaves it unexplained.

The Qumran text, however, introduces the story with a paragraph missing from the traditional Bible that puts the entire episode into clearer context. The passage now appears in the New Revised Standard Version as an unnumbered paragraph after 1 Samuel 11:27:

> *Now Nahash, king of the Ammonites, had been grievously oppressing the Gadites and the Reubenites. He would gouge out the right eye of each of them and would not grant Israel a deliverer. No one was left of the Israelites*

*across the Jordan whose right eye Nahash, king of the Ammonites, had not gouged out. But there were seven thousand men who had escaped from the Ammonites and had entered Jabesh-gilead.*[16]

This also appears to match the copy of the Bible Josephus was using as he prepared his history of Israel. He paraphrased the "missing passage" as he wrote about this episode in *Antiquities of the Jews* late in the first century CE:

> *He [Nahash] also reduced their cities into slavery, and that not by subduing them for the present, which he did by force and violence, but by weakening them by subtlety and cunning . . . for he put out the right eyes of those that either delivered themselves to him upon terms, or were taken by him in war; and this he did that when their left eyes were covered by their shields, they might be wholly useless in war.*[17]

Why was it left out of the traditional text? James VanderKam of Notre Dame theorizes that an early Hebrew scribe may have inadvertently skipped over the paragraph while hand-copying the book. He notes that a phrase just preceding the passage ("But he held his peace," 10:27) and one just after it ("About a month later," 11:1) look almost the same in Hebrew. "It appears that a scribe skipped from the end of the first [phrase] to the end of the second," says VanderKam, and unintentionally omitted the intervening paragraph in the process.[18] The Dead Sea Scrolls have proven to be an invaluable resource in finding and correcting copying errors of this type.

## JOSHUA'S ALTAR

One Qumran version of the book of Joshua offers a slightly different take on the sequence of events during the early Israelite battles in the Promised Land. In the traditional Bible, Joshua leads the Israelites across the Jordan River to begin their military conquest. They destroy the fortified cities of Jericho and Ai. Then suddenly, at the end of chapter 8, they are up on Mount Ebal—some twenty-three miles to the north—building an altar to the Lord, offering burnt sacrifices, and renewing their covenant "just as Moses the servant of the Lord had commanded" (v. 31; cf. Deut. 27:4). In the very next scene they are back south at Gilgal, resuming their military exploits.

The Qumran version (4QJosh[a]) casts the sequence differently and, some scholars say, more sensibly. It has the Israelites building the altar and conducting their rituals at their camp at Gilgal immediately after crossing the Jordan River and *before* launching their attacks. The Israelites forego the forty-six-mile side trip to erect the altar on a mountain that has no further role to play in the Hebrew Bible. And once again, when Josephus paraphrases the episode in *Antiquities of the Jews,* he has it the same as in the scrolls.[19]

Some scholars think the Qumran version is closer to how the story originally was told. They theorize that Judean scribes at some point may have switched the episode from Gilgal to Mount Ebal intentionally in the Hebrew text in order to discredit their religious rivals, the Samaritans, who regarded Mount Gerizim—which is directly across the Shechem Pass from Mount Ebal—as a holy place and built their temple there. That seems a plausible enough explanation. But the recent discovery of what some experts believe to be the ruins of an Israelite altar on Mount Ebal would indicate, if correct, that the Hebrew text may be right after all. The question as to which version is the more accurate remains wide open.[20]

## ABRAHAM'S TEST

In addition to the Bible and sectarian writings, the Qumran library includes a number of works categorized as biblical commentaries or paraphrases that were used to explain the meaning of Scriptures to the community. One such book, a "retelling" of the books of Genesis and Exodus (4Q225), puts a provocative new spin on the difficult story in Genesis 22 of Abraham's near sacrifice of his own son. It may offer insight into at least one strain of theological thinking within Judaism prior to the turn of the era.

In the traditional Bible, God tests his servant Abraham by commanding him to offer his only son, Isaac, as a burnt offering. Abraham obeys unquestioningly. He binds his young son, places him on an altar piled high with wood, and puts a knife to his throat. At the last possible moment, an angel stays Abraham's knife and points to a ram trapped in a thicket as a substitute offering.

The biblical story has always posed difficult theological questions. How could God tempt Abraham to slay his own son? If God did not intend Abraham to go through with it in the first place, was God being deceitful? Modern Bible commentaries have tried to explain that God "tested Abraham to see how strong his faith was"[21] or that God did it to "prove Abraham, not to draw him to sin, as Satan tempts."[22] The writer of the Qumran text attempts to answer those questions in another way by bringing a Satan figure, called Mastemah (or "Prince of Malevolence"), into the story. In the Qumran version, it is Mastemah who goads God into the test, much as the Satan figure does in the biblical story of Job. In the Qumran text, therefore, God does not originate the evil of the temptation but merely tolerates it, and by doing so permits Abraham to prove his faithfulness.

What is the significance of all of these variations within the biblical books from Qumran? Why do they occur? Some of the differences, scholars say, may be explained merely as haphazard variations or the result of scribal errors. But not all. To Ulrich and others, it appears as though two or three distinct "variant literary editions" of the biblical books existed side by side in the Qumran library. Some closely resemble the text-rich Masoretic version that is reflected in the modern Hebrew Bible. But others display characteristics that place them closer to the Septuagint or to the Samaritan Pentateuch, a version of the Bible's first five books believed to have originated among Samaritans in Palestine in the second century BCE.[23]

That they were found together and in multiple copies, however, suggests to many scholars that there was no single "authorized version" of the Bible in first-century Judaism—at least not at Qumran. While there had long been core writings in Judaism that were widely considered to be standard, authoritative, and perhaps even divinely inspired, there was not yet a formally recognized Hebrew canon. That would not arise until sometime after the fall of Jerusalem in 70 CE, and perhaps as late as 135 CE. Scholars disagree on precisely when and how that occurred.

Though some books were more highly regarded than others as "Scripture" within first-century Judaism (as we saw in the discussion of the Psalms), scholars say the evidence from Qumran offers no hint that any one of the various editions of those books was preferred, or considered more or less authoritative, in comparison to the others. There is no clear-cut evidence, they say, on which to judge which if any of the versions was in widest use. Nor is there any indication that the perceived merits of one version over another was even a matter of discussion among religious leaders—Christian or Jew—during the first two-thirds of the first century. "Absolutely every source of evidence we have," says Ulrich—the scrolls, the Masoretic text, the Septuagint, the Samaritan Pentateuch—points to "a fully accepted pluriformity of the biblical text" until near the end of the first century. It was only then, when the Jews of Palestine saw themselves facing the double threat of losing their culture—and their lives—to the Romans, and "their ancient identity as 'Israel' to the Christians," says Ulrich, that their religious leaders found it necessary to settle on preferred editions of the Bible and to "freeze" the content of those texts.[24]

Even then, the ultimate embrace of what we now call the Masoretic text as the official Hebrew Bible may have been more the result of accident than of conscious selection, Ulrich says. Rather than weighing the pros and cons of one set of texts over another, the Jewish leaders simply may have adopted the version they happened to have in their possession after the crisis. "When the house catches fire," says Ulrich, "you grab stuff and run."[25]

But what to one may appear accidental may to another be explained as "fate"—or as Providence. How and why particular versions of the Bible arose, gained or lost acceptance, were preserved or revised, and ultimately survived the centuries are questions that scholars might never succeed in answering satisfactorily.

What seems clear, however, is that the Dead Sea Scrolls have revealed a Bible whose text was unsettled at the turn of the era. For some people of faith, that fact itself may be unsettling. But in many respects, what Ulrich describes as the textual "pluriformity" that appears to have characterized the Bible two thousand years ago has never really ceased to exist. Differences in the canons of Christianity's assorted branches today mirror, and perhaps even amplify, the "variant editions" that scholars now find in the scrolls of Qumran. The process of translating, explaining, clarifying, and refining the lines of Scripture—the very process that spawned variations in the biblical text in ancient times—is a process that probably did not begin and certainly did not end in the centuries straddling the turn of the era. It continues today, as the explosion of new Bible editions, translations, paraphrases, and commentaries in recent decades attests. The scholarly task of ensuring that the Bible remains accessible and understandable to its readers is a task for every age. It has never been a once-and-for-all proposition.

## CHAPTER 16

# REDISCOVERING CHRISTIANITY'S ROOTS

## THE SCROLLS AND

## THE NEW TESTAMENT

NO CHRISTIAN WRITINGS WERE FOUND AMONG THE DEAD SEA SCROLLS. No evidence has turned up suggesting that Jesus, or Paul, or any of the apostles ever went to Qumran. No characters from the New Testament are mentioned in the Qumran documents. Despite earlier suspicions and fanciful speculation to the contrary, there is virtual unanimity now among reputable scholars that the Dead Sea Scroll community was neither the birthplace nor an outpost of Christianity.[1]

Nonetheless, scroll scholars during the past decade have discovered some intriguing similarities—along with striking contrasts—between the beliefs and practices of the early Christian church and the conservative brand of Judaism that was practiced at Qumran. Scholars also have found amazingly close parallels between some of the language and imagery of the New Testament and that of the sect at Qumran. The surprising appearance in some scroll fragments of terms such as "Son of God" and the "Son of the Most High," and depictions of spiritual warfare between the powers of darkness and light—long thought to be exclusively Christian concepts—suggest that those ideas and motifs were present in the Jewish milieu years before the New Testament was written.

How directly the Christian Scriptures may have been influenced by the thinking represented in the Qumran scrolls is a matter of ongoing conjecture and debate. But there is now a broad consensus among biblical scholars that the Dead Sea Scrolls reveal a fledgling Christianity that was far more Jewish and a first-century Judaism that was far more diverse than contemporary researchers had imagined.

## QUMRANITES AND CHRISTIANS: HOW THEY WERE ALIKE

Even though the Qumranites and early Christians represented separate and distinct movements, scholars say that they were remarkably close in their theological vocabulary and shared some important doctrinal tenets and practices. For example:

*Both considered themselves recipients of a new covenant with God.* That covenant was seen as superseding or renewing the divine covenants neglected by the Israelites prior to the Babylonian exile. For the Christians, Jesus was "the mediator of a new covenant, so that those who are called may receive the promised eternal inheritance" (Heb. 9:15). Jesus had told his disciples that the eucharistic cup was "the new covenant in my blood" (Luke 22:20). The Qumranites believed that they were the obedient remnant of Israel with whom God had made a "new covenant in the land of Damascus" (Damascus Document 6:19).[2] Each year during the Festival of Weeks, they engaged in a ritual of covenant renewal that is spelled out in the Manual of Discipline (1QS).

*Both were convinced that the end was near and that the Messiah would appear soon*—or reappear, in the case of the Christians (John 14:3). Both expected the Messiah to establish an eschatological kingdom and to reign as both a priest and a king. The people of Qumran may have expected the arrival of two Messiahs to fill the two roles separately (Manual of Discipline 9:9–11). But both groups believed that the prophets were referring to them when they spoke of the final messianic events. As Oxford University scholar Geza Vermes notes:

> The prophecy: "A voice crying in the wilderness: 'Prepare ye the way of the Lord'" (Isa. 40:3), was heard at Qumran as meaning the retirement into the desert of the Teacher of Righteousness and his followers to prepare for the coming of the Messiah. For the New Testament, the voice is that of John the Baptist carrying out a similar mission (Mk. 1:3–8; Mt. 3:1–12; Lk. 3:2–17).[3]

*Both engaged in a sacred ritual meal of bread and wine.* The celebration of the Eucharist, modeled after the Last Supper and instituted by Jesus "on the night when he was betrayed" (1 Cor. 11:23), was a regular feature of Christian worship. It served both as a reminder and reenactment of the messianic sacrifice ("Do this . . . in remembrance of me") and as a precursor of a sacred meal Jesus would celebrate with his followers in the eschatological future ("I will never again drink of this fruit of the vine until that day when I drink it anew with you in my Father's kingdom").[4] At Qumran, detailed rules and instructions for a ritualistic community meal appear in the Manual of Discipline ("[T]he Priest shall be the first to stretch out his hand to bless the first-fruits of the bread and new wine"). Another part of the text describes how the meal was to be celebrated once the Messiah arrived at the community.[5]

*Both conducted a ritual of baptism that was associated with repentance and cleansing.* A prominent part of Christian teaching was that converts must "repent, and be baptized . . . in the name of Jesus Christ for the remission of sins" (Acts 2:38)—a one-time event. The Qumranites were required to perform ritual ablutions, perhaps daily, to preserve purity. "And when his flesh is sprinkled with purifying water and sanctified by cleansing water, it shall be made clean by the humble submission of his soul to all the precepts of God" (Manual of Discipline 3).

*Both practiced a form of communalism—merging their resources for the common good.* The book of Acts (2:44–45) says that the early Christians in Jerusalem "had all things in common; they would sell their possessions and goods and distribute the proceeds to all, as any had need." At Qumran, the Manual of Discipline (6:17–22) spells out how new members were to go about merging their property with the community and when they would be eligible to draw from the shared resources.

## QUMRANITES AND CHRISTIANS: HOW THEY DIFFERED

Despite all of these similarities, there can be no confusing the Dead Sea Scroll community with their first-century contemporaries in the nascent Jesus movement. Profound differences in fundamental beliefs sharply divided the two. Among their basic points of disagreement were these:

*They differed in their understanding of the person of Jesus.* The preacher from Nazareth stands at the center of the New Testament. Through his life, death, and resurrection, he is proclaimed in Christian Scriptures to be Israel's Messiah, the Son of God, and the Savior of the world. Yet he is nowhere to be found in the writings of Qumran. If the Dead Sea Scroll community knew about Jesus at all, scholars say, it is obvious that they did not consider him to be their Messiah.

*They differed in their attitude toward the law of Moses.* The teachings of Paul saw the law as having served a temporary function for the people of Israel— preparing them for and pointing them toward the coming of Jesus Christ. "Therefore the law was our disciplinarian until Christ came," Paul wrote, "so that we might be justified by faith. But now that faith has come, we are no longer subject to a disciplinarian, for in Christ Jesus you are all children of God through faith" (Gal. 3:24–26). For the sect at Qumran, observance of the law of Moses was central and absolutely essential. Proper observance was a defining characteristic of their identity as the obedient ones, in contrast to the lawlessness of their religious rivals.

*They differed in their relationship with the outside world.* The early Christians, after Pentecost, were zealous in carrying out the Great Commission to "go therefore and make disciples of all nations" (Matt. 28:19–20). They became missionaries seeking converts not only among their fellow Jews but among Gentiles and foreigners as well. The Qumran community, on the other hand, kept mostly to themselves, engaging in fervent prayer and study and concentrating on preserving their own purity, which would have been sullied by contact with outsiders.

Even though such clear distinctions between the two groups are widely recognized, most scholars are fascinated by the sometimes striking parallels they find between the New Testament and the Dead Sea Scrolls. More than once in the past fifty years, the rarified world of scroll scholarship has made headlines with sensational theories about connections between the two written records.

## LUKE'S ANNUNCIATION?

One highly publicized Qumran document, which some scholars believe may be a messianic prophecy, bears a striking resemblance to the annunciation scene in Luke 1:32–33. In the Luke account an angel appears to Mary and tells her that she will bear a son who will be called "Son of God" and "Son of the Most High . . . and of his kingdom there will be no end." A Qumran fragment known as 4Q246, written in Aramaic several decades before Luke's gospel, depicts a powerful figure who was to appear during a time of great tribulation: "He will be called the Son of God, they will call him the Son of the Most High. . . . Their kingdom will be an eternal kingdom."[6]

The similarity between the two passages is so striking that when a small portion of the Qumran text was first published in 1974, some scholars speculated that it was an early prototype of Luke's annunciation scene. It was suggested then that the New Testament writers might even have borrowed the idea. Others, however, found the Qumran text to be something far different. They saw the "Son of God" figure depicted in the scrolls not as a Messiah but as a villain who ultimately would be defeated by God's true followers. Now that the full text has become available and the context can be more carefully examined, many reputable scholars lean toward the second interpretation.[7]

Edward Cook, an expert in Aramaic at Hebrew Union College in Cincinnati, for example, suggests that the passage may be an apocalyptic reflection on Antiochus Epiphanes, a ruthless Syrian tyrant and self-styled god whose persecution of Jews and desecration of the temple in Jerusalem in 167 BCE spawned the Maccabean Revolt.[8] Antiochus was named after his father, Antiochus III, another tyrant who had ruled Syria and conquered both Palestine and Phoenicia decades earlier. Antiochus Epiphanes was a warrior as well, having conquered Egypt prior to turning his atrocious attentions to Jerusalem. If we look at this extended portion of the Qumran fragment in the light of that historical background, the merits of Cook's argument become clear:

> [Amid] great [signs], tribulation is coming upon the land. . . . [After much killing] and slaughter, a prince of nations [will arise . . . ] the king of Assyria and Egypt [ . . . ] he will be ruler over the land [ . . . ] will be subject to him and will obey [him]. [Also his son] will be called The Great, and be designated by his name. He will be called the Son of God, they will call him the son of the Most High. But like the meteors that you saw in your vision, so will be their kingdom. They will reign only a few years over the land, while people tramples people and nation tramples nation until the people of God arise; then all will have rest from warfare. Their kingdom will be an eternal kingdom, and all their paths will be righteous.[9]

Whether the Qumran text is, in fact, a precursor of Luke's messianic announcement or an apocalyptic vision based on a tyrant's oppression is still a matter of some debate. In either case, the passage from the scrolls dramatically illustrates that terminology once considered distinctly Christian was part of the earlier Judaic lexicon.

## A "PIERCED" MESSIAH

Another text from Qumran that made headlines a few years back is the "pierced Messiah" fragment. In 1991, within weeks of the release of photographic copies of the scrolls in California, a scholar who had been instrumental in getting the photographs published announced that he had found a fragment containing a startling parallel to the Christian proclamation of a crucified Christ. Robert Eisenman, a religious studies professor at California State University, Long Beach, observed that the Qumran text identified as 4Q285 seemed to dramatically prefigure the Christian claim that the Messiah Jesus was wounded or "pierced" in fulfillment of the prophecy in Isaiah 53:5: "He was wounded for our transgressions, he was bruised for our iniquities." Eisenman translated one line in the Aramaic fragment as reading, ". . . and they killed [*or:* will kill] the prince of the congregation, the branch of David." The next line, Eisenman said, contained a word he translated as "his wounds" or "his piercings."10

The discovery, Eisenman said at the time, amounted to what might be a "missing link" between Christianity and Judaism.11 The implications were stunning. Either the religion of Qumran was a primitive form of Christianity that was radically different from what the faith would eventually become, or the notion of an executed Messiah was not unique to Christianity. That all of this was said to appear in a still-unpublished text was seized upon by some critics as evidence that the scroll editors indeed had conspired to keep under wraps anything that might prove embarrassing to Christianity. It was a bombshell waiting to explode.

But once other scholars took a good look at the controversial document, they discovered that the bombshell was a dud. A team of British Bible scholars led by Professor Geza Vermes of Oxford University carefully examined the scroll fragment that would later become known as the War Rule. They found that Eisenman's translation was far off the mark. The messianic figure in the text was the one doing the killing, they said, and not the other way around. The Messiah, Vermes explained, "appears as triumphant—as is usually the case. That is the normal Jewish tradition."12

Meanwhile, Lawrence Schiffman, a scroll editor and professor of Hebrew studies at New York University, found that the "piercings" and "wounds" that initially had drawn so much attention did not even appear in the text. The Hebrew word that had been translated "pierced" *(mehollal)* was actually "dances" *(mehollot)*. So rather than presaging a pierced and wounded Messiah, said Schiffman, the text was describing a celebration, complete with drums and dances, of the Messiah's defeat of the *Kittim*—the hated Romans—as the now reconstructed fragment makes clear:

> [ . . . *As it is written in the book of*] *Isaiah the prophet:* [*The thickets of the forest*] *shall be hacked away* [*with iron, and the Lebanon trees in their majesty shall*] *fall. But a shoot shall grow out of the stump of Jesse,* [*a twig*

*shall sprout from his stock . . . ] shoot of David, and they will be judged,*
*the . . . and the Prince of the Congregation will kill him, the arm[y] of . . .*
*[with drum]s and with dances. And the [high] priest commanded . . . [the*
*c]orpse[s] of the Kittim . . .*[13]

At the end of the day, as scroll editor James VanderKam later observed, one
"eye-catching parallel to the New Testament" had fallen by the wayside.[14] Even
Eisenman later publicly recanted, saying that he had never really believed in the
parallel in the first place.[15]

## JEWISH ROOTS AND THE GOSPEL OF JOHN

The absence of bombshells, it seems, has been a consistent characteristic of fifty
years of scroll research. Even so, scholars have found plenty of similarities of a
less explosive nature in the ideas and imagery of the New Testament and the
Dead Sea Scrolls. Rather than suggesting a direct relationship between Christianity and the Judaism of Qumran, however, these similarities serve as a vivid
reminder that these two contemporaneous movements sprouted from the same
religious soil.

For some scholars, that realization not only underscores the Jewish roots of
Christianity but adds weight to arguments for the early dating and authenticity
of the gospels—particularly for the frequently assailed gospel of John. Thanks
largely to the Dead Sea Scrolls, many Bible scholars today are taking a fresh and
more respectful look at the origins and historicity of the fourth gospel.

Because it was the last of the gospels to be written—somewhere between 90
and 110 CE, by most estimates—John often has been characterized in modern
biblical academia as the least reliable as a source of history. Before the discovery
of the scrolls, many Bible scholars assumed that much of John's language and
imagery reflected later Greek influences on the early church and its developing
theology rather than material that originated from first-century Palestine.

In the highly theological prologue to his gospel, for example, John's description of Jesus as "the Word" or *Logos* reflects what many scholars have assumed to be the influence of Stoic or pre-Socratic philosophy. They also claim
to see Greek fingerprints on the dualism apparent in passages such as John
12:35–36, where Jesus tells his disciples, "You are going to have the light just a
little while longer. Walk while you have the light, before darkness overtakes
you. The man who walks in the dark does not know where he is going. Put your
trust in the light while you have it, so that you may become sons of light" (NIV).

Such dualistic imagery, especially the use of the term "sons of light," was viewed by many scholars as foreign to Hebrew thinking in Jesus' time and thus a clear indication that John's gospel had to have been written no earlier than the mid to late second century CE. That would make it far too late to have been an eyewitness account, let alone the writing of an apostle of Jesus, which has been the traditional claim.

But now, based in part on their studies of the Dead Sea Scrolls, many scholars have concluded that the gospel of John may contain some of the oldest material in all of the gospels. Rather than a late Hellenistic writing, says James H. Charlesworth, a scroll scholar at Princeton Theological Seminary, "the Gospel of John is now widely and wisely judged to be the most Jewish of the gospels."[16] The same light-versus-darkness dichotomy reflected in Jesus' teaching in John, Charlesworth observes, has been found to be a prominent feature of the earlier teachings at Qumran.

One important text known as the Manual of Discipline (1QS), for example, written perhaps two hundred years before John's gospel, declares that "the master shall instruct and teach the Sons of Light." It goes on to draw a vivid contrast between the cosmic realms of light and darkness, which represented righteousness and evil to the fervently pious Jews at Qumran (just as it did to the Christians):

> *He has created the human for the dominion of the world, designing for him two spirits in which to walk until the appointed time for his visitation, namely, the spirits of truth and deceit. In a spring of light emanate the nature of truth and deceit. In the hand of the Prince of Lights [is] the dominion of all the Sons of Righteousness, in the ways of light they walk. But in the hand of the Angel of Darkness [is] the dominion of the Sons of Deceit, and in the ways of darkness they walk.[17]*

The same scroll, sometimes called the Rule of the Community, warns that those who are not Sons of Light will receive "eternal perdition by the fury of God's vengeful wrath, everlasting terror and endless shame, along with disgrace of annihilation in the fire of murky Hell."[18] That closely tracks the warnings in John 3:16–21, that while those who believe (who "love the light") will "have eternal life," those who do not "will perish" because "God's wrath remains on [them]" (3:36).

The parallels are unmistakable. "Nowhere in the ancient world," says Charlesworth, "do we find the dualism of light and darkness developed so thoroughly as in the Rule of the Community and the Gospel of John."[19] Indeed, the

Dead Sea Scrolls confirm that the imagery in John was not at all foreign to first-century Palestine; it was woven throughout the writings of Qumran's conservative Jewish sect.

Does all of this point to a direct connection between John's gospel and the Dead Sea Scrolls? Might the writer of John have been an Essene, for example, or even a former resident of Qumran? Although that would certainly explain the similarities in language and outlook, few scholars attempt to make that argument. What Charlesworth and others find more reasonable is that John had some amount of familiarity with Qumran ideas. It is even possible, they argue, that John might have borrowed some of the Essene terminology and imagery and reshaped it to communicate the central message of his gospel—namely, that Jesus "was none other than the promised Messiah to the Jews."[20]

Some scholars even suggest that John's community may have included some former Qumranites who escaped the Roman destruction of their village in 68 CE, later joining the Jesus movement. That, they say, could be what is referred to in Acts 6:7, where after Pentecost "the word of God increased; and the number of the disciples in Jerusalem multiplied greatly, and a great crowd of priests followed in the faith." These were unlikely to have been Sadducees, the sect of the temple priests, since the Sadducees rejected the notion of bodily resurrection. And the Pharisees, another major party in first-century Judaism, were not led by priests. But the Essenes, many scholars believe, were Zadokite priests who bitterly opposed the temple establishment and may even have lived in Jerusalem before moving out to the desert to await the Messiah. Archaeologists have uncovered what they think is an Essene quarter in the southwest sector of the Old City.[21] If some of the Essenes later joined the Jesus movement and became part of John's community, John may well have appropriated some of their vivid language and imagery as he crafted his gospel.


## PAUL AND THE ESSENES

John's gospel is not the only New Testament writing in which some scholars find signs of Essene, or at least Qumran, influence. Another striking example is found in an unusual passage in one of the apostle Paul's letters to the church at Corinth (2 Cor. 6:14–7:1):

> *Do not be mismatched with unbelievers. For what partnership is there between righteousness and lawlessness? Or what fellowship is there between light and darkness? What agreement does Christ have with Beliar [Satan]? Or what does a believer share with an unbeliever? What agreement has the*

*temple of God with idols? For we are the temple of the living God. . . . Since we have these promises, beloved, let us cleanse ourselves from every defilement of body and spirit, making holiness perfect in the fear of God.*

These Pauline phrases evoking the dichotomy of light and darkness and the separation of the righteous from the wicked would have been right at home in the writings from Qumran, notes VanderKam of Notre Dame. So would his exhortations to holiness and the avoidance of defilement—both central concerns of the Qumran sect. Paul's admonition that believers should cleanse themselves—an admonition that appears nowhere else in his writings—seems to fit more comfortably with the Qumran practice of ritual cleansing than with the more familiar Pauline teaching of justification by faith. The above passage also is the only time Paul advocates a separatist posture toward nonbelievers—an attitude seemingly more characteristic of the monastic exclusivism of Qumran than of Paul's own calling as a missionary to the Gentiles. Perhaps most curious of all is his use of the word "Beliar," a term for Satan that appears nowhere else in the New Testament but is common in the literature of Qumran.[22]

Could Paul have borrowed all of this from the Essenes? "It is not possible to prove that Paul took these words from an Essene or even Qumran work," says VanderKam, "but in 2 Corinthians he does indeed employ language that is best known from Qumran texts."[23]

But there is another explanation for the striking similarities between the writings of Paul and other New Testament writers, on the one hand, and the Qumran texts on the other. It lies in the diversity of the religious and philosophical boiling pot that characterized Judaism in the first century CE.

If the historian Josephus can be believed, the Essenes were a familiar, if not ubiquitous, part of the Jewish milieu of Paul's time. As we noted earlier, Josephus identifies the Essenes as one of three major sects in first-century Judaism, along with the Sadducees and the Pharisees.[24] Paul, on the other hand, aligns himself in Philippians 3:5 with the Pharisees. Josephus reports that the Essenes in Palestine in the first century numbered more than four thousand—far more than could have lived at the tiny village of Qumran. He even asserts in *The Jewish War* that they "occupy no one city, but settle in large numbers in every town."[25]

The three groups, then, were not hermetically sealed off from one another, physically or intellectually. Thus it is likely that Paul the Pharisee—an educated and traveled man—as well as the other apostles, would have been familiar with the ideas, the terminology, and perhaps the literature of the Essenes.

He might even have shared some of their views. While the three sects had differences, no doubt they also had much in common, not the least of which would have been their devotion to the Torah. Most assuredly, Paul's own ideas and his letters were informed by the Hebrew Scriptures, which he would have heard expounded and debated by teachers of varying viewpoints throughout his life. Some of them almost certainly would have been Essene.

It is hardly surprising, then, to find what appear to be points of intersection in the outlook and language of Paul and the Essenes as reflected in the writings from Qumran. But as with similarities between John and the Essenes, these points of intersection highlight the Jewishness of the apostles and the diversity of the Judaism from which Christianity emerged, rather than suggesting any direct link with the Qumranites—a link for which there is no real evidence.

After a half-century of study, the Dead Sea Scrolls have shown more dramatically than anyone could have anticipated how deeply Christianity was rooted in the Judaism of its time. The Jesus movement was not merely a religious mutation spun out of the fusion of Judaism and Hellenism. It grew out of the soil of ancient Palestine, among a people whose biblical faith had prepared them to look for a Messiah who would be called the Son of God and the Son of the Most High.

Perhaps the major contribution of the scrolls to our understanding of the New Testament, as VanderKam states so eloquently, is to highlight "the simple but profound fact that the uniqueness of the early Christian faith lies less in its communal practices and eschatological expectations than in its central confession that the son of a humble woman and a carpenter from Nazareth in Galilee was indeed the messiah and son of God who taught, healed, suffered, died, rose, ascended, and promised to return in glory to judge the living and the dead."[26]

# PART FOUR

# THE BIBLE
# AND THE
# HISTORICAL
# JESUS

## CHAPTER 17

# IN SEARCH
# OF JESUS

## THE HISTORICAL

## QUEST

FIFTEEN MINUTES BEFORE THE PROGRAM BEGAN, THE ASIA ROOM AT THE Dolphin Hotel at Walt Disney World in Orlando was packed way beyond its capacity. Every chair was filled, and people lined the walls, sprawled cross-legged in the carpeted aisles, and spilled out the doorway into the cooler air of the corridor beyond. This was not your ordinary Disney crowd. They had come not to see the latest attraction at the Magic Kingdom, but to hear a panel of Bible experts discuss historical research into the life of Jesus, and why it matters.

It was one of hundreds of sessions during a four-day gathering of the American Academy of Religion and the Society of Biblical Literature, an annual event that draws some eight thousand Bible scholars and religion professors from throughout the United States and Canada and from some other countries as well. The popularity of this particular session at the November 1998 meeting was just the latest illustration of the intense fascination among biblical scholars with the ambitious enterprise that has become known as "the quest for the historical Jesus."

For more than two centuries, Bible scholars and historians have tried to peer behind the familiar images of Jesus drawn from the Bible and Christian tradition to uncover what they think may be a more historically accurate portrait of the man and his teachings. Using the tools of modern textual study, archaeology, and social research, they have attempted to explore the distinctions between the

"Jesus of history"—the man who lived and died in Roman-occupied Palestine at the turn of the era—and the "Christ of faith" as experienced by Christian believers and enshrined in the creeds of the church. No issue within the biblical academy has stirred more activity, excitement, or controversy.

Fascination with the Jesus quest has not stopped there. In the past decade alone, the search for "the real Jesus" has made the front pages of major daily newspapers and the covers of national newsmagazines, and has become the standard fare of cable television docudramas. Dozens of books have been written, some by respected scholars and others by armchair theorists and theologians, purporting to offer new and improved versions of Jesus. The more recent revisionist portraits have run the gamut from "Jesus the Cynic Sage" and "Jesus the Palestinian Revolutionary" to "Jesus the Spirit Person and Social Prophet" and even "Jesus the Stand-up Comic." In this burgeoning scholarly genre, traditional notions of divinity, miracle, and resurrection have often seemed decidedly passé.

Understandably, the historical quest has been denounced by some as a frontal assault on the Christian faith and an attempt to undermine the Bible's authority. And in some instances, that is precisely what it has been. Yet such sinister motivations are often too quickly and too broadly ascribed. In its ebb and flow over the years, the Jesus quest has been far from monolithic. Its proponents have included many who sincerely hoped to find in the endeavor a more rational basis for Christian belief and a clearer essence of Jesus and his teachings than they have gleaned from traditional interpretations.

Some others, on the other hand, as we shall see, indeed have disclosed a more blatantly ideological agenda, declaring with unrestrained hubris their intent to debunk and demythologize the gospels, to break the back of biblical literalism come what may, and to "reinvent Christianity" in the process. But their work has not gone unanswered, and their influence to date has not extended much beyond their own circle of ideological allies.

Ever since the quest for the historical Jesus began in earnest during the heightened skepticism of the Enlightenment, it has focused as much on the veracity of the gospels as on the figure of Jesus himself. A starting point for many questers over the years has been the premise that the gospels are unreliable records because they were written as religious proclamation, not objective history, decades after Jesus' death. While the gospels may contain a kernel of history, according to these scholars, it lies buried beneath layers of mythology and ideology that became attached to the Jesus story after the events happened but before they were recorded.

Finding the true words and deeds of Jesus then, these scholars say, requires clearing away the accretion of church tradition within the gospels as well as looking to other presumably more objective sources of information outside of the biblical canon. As one might imagine, excavating the biblical text for these hidden nuggets has tended to be a rather freewheeling venture—one that has often seemed guided more by subjective judgment and philosophical assumption than by hard rules of evidence. The entire process, as we shall see, has been sharply contested.

Even though it is not a monolithic movement, the quest over the years has proven to be more than a little lopsided, generally attracting scholars of a theologically liberal and philosophically skeptical bent. For obvious reasons, conservatives and traditionalists have shown little abiding interest in the enterprise: they find no deficiency in the Jesus of the gospels and generally are quite satisfied with the Bible as a source of history. Consequently, the few conservatives who have ventured into the fray have done so more to refute the revisionists' arguments than to engage in primary historical research of their own.

There have been a few noteworthy exceptions, however. Some evangelical stalwarts, including British biblical scholars N. T. Wright, dean of the Lichfield Cathedral in Staffordshire, and James D. G. Dunn, of the University of Durham, not only have waged powerful defenses of biblical orthodoxy in response to the skeptics, but have found in their own historical surveys some enriching details that provide a sometimes surprising context of the life and times of Jesus.

Still, it comes as no surprise that the Jesus scholarship that consistently attracts the most attention and stirs the most controversy is that which offers the most shocking and iconoclastic challenges to traditional views. There is no better contemporary example of that than the work of the Jesus Seminar. Since the mid-1980s, this loosely knit collection of New Testament scholars has made a cottage industry of deconstructing the gospels and broadly disseminating their own learned pronouncements on what the historical Jesus *really* said and did. They have concluded that Jesus spoke only a small fraction of the sayings and performed even fewer of the deeds that are ascribed to him in the gospels. Now they have set their sights on the written works of the apostle Paul, the historic Christian creeds, and the outlines of the biblical canon. There are even plans for a movie on the life of Jesus. The seminar and its work will be examined more closely in Chapter 19.

What has all of this Jesus scholarship revealed about the veracity of the Bible? After more than two centuries of critical scrutiny, can the gospels still be considered a reasonable and reliable source of history? Or is the voice of Jesus forever lost to us, buried beneath the literary inventions and theological fantasies of the early Christian writers? We begin our search for answers by exploring briefly the origins and evolution of the quest itself.

## CHAPTER 18

# THE QUEST
# AND ITS
# ORIGINS

## FROM THE OLD QUEST
## TO THE THIRD QUEST

THE BEGINNING OF THE JESUS QUEST IS OFTEN TRACED TO THE POLEMICAL writings of eighteenth- and nineteenth-century German scholars who set out to undercut the veracity of the gospels and expose traditional depictions of Jesus as a pious fraud. But in a sense, as one leading Jesus scholar has noted, the real genesis of the Jesus quest can be located even earlier, in the rise of modern biblical criticism—a development that itself was "the child of two parents": the Protestant Reformation and the Enlightenment.[1]

In their sixteenth-century rebellion against the magisterium of the Roman Catholic Church, the Protestant Reformers had declared that the Bible—as opposed to church tradition—was the only legitimate authority in matters of faith and practice. Out of the Reformation dictum *sola Scriptura* sprang a new emphasis on the study of the Bible as God's Holy Word and on the importance of making the Scriptures widely accessible.

Meanwhile, as the Enlightenment gathered steam in Europe about a century later, it ignited a revolution in epistemology that would challenge many of the existing presuppositions of science, philosophy, and religion. Under the newly ascendant rationalism, true knowledge was to be found in investigation and reason, not in supernatural revelation. The deists of the era believed in the divine but disdained notions of received truth and ecclesiastical authority. The Bible, in their estimation, was first and foremost a human artifact; its truth-claims were undeserving of either sacred status or deferential trust.[2] What the Reformers had exalted as Christianity's central authority became a target of Enlightenment iconoclasts.

## THE OLD QUEST

It was in that skeptical spirit of Enlightenment rationalism that Hermann Samuel Reimarus (1694–1768), a professor of Semitic languages at Hamburg University, fired the opening salvos against the Jesus of the gospels. In a lengthy critique of Christianity published posthumously in the late 1770s, Reimarus depicted Jesus as a Jewish revolutionary who failed in his vision to become Israel's political liberator. To keep the movement alive after the crucifixion, according to Reimarus, Jesus' disciples stole his body and publicly proclaimed him the resurrected Lord, whose imminent return would bring about God's kingdom and Israel's vindication.

This "new system of a suffering spiritual savior," Reimarus wrote, "was invented only because the first hopes had failed." When Jesus did not return, the second hopes failed as well, proving, in Reimarus's estimation, that Christianity—with its outrageous claims of miracle and resurrection—was "an intentional, deliberate fabrication" that rational moderns could summarily dismiss.[3]

In reaction to Reimarus, some Enlightenment scholars who were not prepared to jettison Christianity entirely stepped forward with pale new versions of the Jesus story. They offered a variety of natural explanations for the miracles—he used pharmacology to heal people, the "dead" he raised were only in a coma, he walked in shallow water on the Sea of Galilee. There may have been nothing miraculous in Jesus, according to these scholars, but the power of his words nonetheless commended him as a teacher worth following.[4]

Such arguments, of course, were denounced and refuted by defenders of biblical orthodoxy in the churches and seminaries of Europe who found nothing deficient in the Jesus of the gospels. But the critical approach to biblical studies, with its skeptical and anti-supernaturalist presuppositions, was increasingly de rigueur at the more secular-minded institutions of the continent.

The assault on the gospels was intensified in the nineteenth century when a young German scholar, David Friedrich Strauss, wrote *The Life of Jesus Critically Examined.*[5] Strauss argued that the gospel accounts of Jesus were pure mythology and, as such, were devoid of any real history. It was pointless to try to give natural explanations for the miracles, Strauss asserted, since the miracle stories were mere inventions intended to communicate what the gospel writers believed about Jesus. Strauss's book stirred such a scandal that he was banned from teaching. But his notion of the gospels as myth and his *a priori* rejection of the supernatural would influence the Jesus quest for generations to come.

By the turn of the century, other "lives of Jesus" would emerge, depicting him variously as a benign moralist, a teacher of timeless ethics, and an apocalyptic prophet. But after more than one hundred years, the Jesus quest had failed to produce a consensus. A young Albert Schweitzer, in a brilliant summation of the quest to that point, concluded in 1906 that the historical Jesus was as elusive and mysterious as ever. The mild-mannered, ethics-preaching Jesus of the nineteenth-century historians, Schweitzer wrote in his now famous *Quest of the Historical Jesus,* "never had any existence. He is a figure designed by rationalism, endowed with life by liberalism, and clothed by modern theology in an historical garb."[6] The truly historical Jesus—who in Schweitzer's estimation had been an eschatological prophet—remained beyond reach, "a stranger to our times." But that really did not matter, wrote Schweitzer, because it was after all the spiritual Christ—not the historical Jesus—who still made himself known to believers and who called his followers "to the tasks which He has to fulfill for our time."[7]

## THE "NO QUEST"

Schweitzer's thesis marked the end of the Old Quest and the beginning of a period of No Quest. Through the first half of the twentieth century, the pursuit of the historical Jesus seemed to many scholars futile and irrelevant. The failure of the Old Quest, as N. T. Wright has noted, had left a "deep ditch" separating the Jesus of history from the Christ of faith.[8] Prominent theologians and biblical scholars of the era, from Karl Barth (1886–1968) to Rudolf Bultmann (1884–1976), insisted that it was the Jesus of Christian proclamation, the kerygmatic Christ, and not a sketchy historical reconstruction who mattered most to Christian faith and practice. In any event, they argued, a historical "life of Jesus" as envisioned by the nineteenth-century questers simply could not be written.[9] Post-Enlightenment skepticism, it seemed, had cast a daunting shadow on the gospels as a credible source of history.

Consequently, the focus of biblical studies during those years shifted away from Jesus and history to the gospels and tradition. Critical scholars had become more interested in exploring the New Testament for what it revealed about the early church and its evolving message.

They also modified their methodologies. During the previous century, biblical scholarship had been dominated by *source criticism*—an approach aimed at discerning the earliest sources behind the gospels, the assumption being that earlier sources were better than later ones in providing reliable information about Jesus. Out of that approach came the two-source hypothesis discussed in Chapter 3, which posited that Mark's gospel and a sayings source known as *Q* were behind the gospels of Matthew and Luke. But once it became fashionable to view Mark as no more credible than the other gospels, source criticism had nowhere further to go in the quest for Jesus.

Arising to take its place in some parts of the biblical academy was *form criticism*. Not an altogether new discipline, it sought to draw distinctions between various literary forms within the gospels—parables, pronouncements, proverbs, and so on—and to identify the stages of development of the texts and the traditions behind them as they passed from oral to written form. Through this process, scholars presumed they could trace the pre-history of a text back to its *sitz im leben*—its original "life setting"—and thereby come to a better understanding of its meaning and context. But many of those who engaged in form criticism applied it with a set of skeptical philosophical presuppositions—miracles do not happen, the early church fabricated much of the Jesus tradition, and so on—all but assuring that their ultimate conclusions would reflect a generally low view of biblical historiography.[10]

No one applied form criticism in that skeptical manner more deftly than Bultmann. Unquestionably the most influential New Testament scholar of the No Quest period, the University of Marburg professor argued that most of the gospel material had originated in the life of the church, not in the life of Jesus, and was so permeated with first-century mythology that it made finding the historical Jesus hopeless. In any event, all one really needed to know about Jesus was that he once lived and that he died on the cross. Only by carefully translating out the mythological language of the gospels, Bultmann argued, could one recapture the essential message of the early church, which in his view was an existentialist call to a "decision for God."[11] That "demythologization" of the gospels became Bultmann's agenda—one that has continued to hold sway in the more liberal precincts of New Testament scholarship to this day.


## THE NEW QUEST

But by the early 1950s, some of Bultmann's disciples had grown increasingly uncomfortable with their teacher's pessimistic notion that the Christ of the church must remain forever detached from Jesus the man. In 1953, Bultmann protégé Ernst Käsemann delivered a stinging lecture in which he argued that, even though Bultmann was correct in concluding that a "life of Jesus" could not be written, the doctrines of the church could not be left totally divorced from their historical roots. By emphasizing a spiritual Christ disconnected from the earthly Jesus, Käsemann warned, Christianity risked falling into a form of Docetism in which Jesus would become little more than a vaporous wisp and an existentialist illusion. It was important, therefore, Käsemann argued, that critical Bible scholars attempt to salvage whatever they could of the Jesus of history.[12]

Käsemann's arguments were persuasive. The quest for the historical Jesus sprang back to life. The "New Quest," as it was called, would be carried forward by scholars who, for the most part, shared Bultmann's naturalistic philosophy and meticulously employed his critical methods. Though it lacked the fanfare and optimism of the Old Quest, and ultimately would produce few solid results, it would nonetheless influence New Testament scholarship for the remainder of the twentieth century.[13]

Among the early New Questers were German scholars Günther Bornkamm and Joachim Jeremias, whose works in the 1950s and 1960s focused heavily on recovering the message of Jesus rather than on reconstructing a full-blooded biography. That emphasis on Jesus' sayings would dominate much of the post-Bultmannian quest, including and especially its most notorious modern incarnation in the work of the Jesus Seminar. In the United States, the groundwork for the New Quest was laid by the eminent New Testament scholar James Robinson of the Claremont School of Theology, whose 1959 book *A New Quest of the Historical Jesus* defined many of the issues that would come to dominate the scholarly debate for decades.[14]

Typical of more recent New Quest scholarship, American scholars such as John Dominic Crossan and Burton Mack in the 1980s and 1990s began looking outside the biblical canon to early Gnostic writings and to the modern social sciences for material with which to sketch their more expansive and decidedly unorthodox portraits of Jesus—a Jesus who would turn out, however, to be only marginally different from the tepid teacher of the Old Quest. We will briefly survey some of those contemporary portraits in the next chapter.

The New Quest also would become a testing ground for what seemed to some a promising new tool of modern biblical scholarship: *redaction criticism*. Like form criticism, it assumes that the biblical texts evolved as they passed from oral to written form. It also assumes that the texts were redacted (that is, edited) in the process to reflect the various theological agendas of the many editors. The dual task of the redaction critic, then, is to find the precise points in a text where redactions have occurred and to analyze the redactor's purpose in making those changes. By working through an entire gospel in this way, one could begin to identify the primary themes and theological concerns of the gospel writer and, presumably, the extent to which those concerns shaped the gospel's depiction of Jesus.

In theory, an adept scholar could then begin to peel away the theological husks and draw closer to the historical kernels, or at least to the more primitive traditions underlying the gospels. But in practice, rather than moving scholars closer to the Jesus of history, as Gregory Boyd, theology professor at Bethel College in St. Paul, Minnesota, has noted, redaction criticism has tended to "raise a new barrier between the reader of the Gospels and the historical Jesus: namely, the 'creativity' of the biblical authors themselves."[15] After peeling away the layers of "creative theology," the more skeptical redaction critics often found themselves left with little more than a table full of husks. The New Quest, in that respect, has gone back nearly full circle to the No Quest pessimism of Bultmann.

But it was the scholars' willingness to plumb new pools of information—the Dead Sea Scrolls, the Gnostic texts from Nag Hammadi, archaeological data, and modern anthropological theories regarding ancient Near Eastern culture—that kept the New Quest from fully collapsing into Bultmannian despair. Unlike the nineteenth-century questers, modern searchers for the historical Jesus felt they no longer had to rely solely on the gospels of the biblical canon. Crossan and others, for example, would come to view the second-century Gospel of Thomas, a brief collection of purported sayings of Jesus found at Nag Hammadi, as having as much claim to historical authenticity as the canonical gospels.[16]

## THE THIRD QUEST

Even as the New Quest continues, another current in Jesus scholarship has emerged during the past twenty years, largely in reaction to (and distinct from) the post-Bultmannian stream. Christened the Third Quest by some, it includes a much wider diversity of scholars, many of whom owe little allegiance to the Bultmann legacy of skepticism, philosophical naturalism, and biblical minimalism.

Works to date by such scholars as Geza Vermes, E. P. Sanders, and N. T. Wright have focused on the Jewish context of Jesus and the diversity of the early church, the aims of Jesus as seen against the backdrop of the political and religious aspirations of his Jewish contemporaries, and the nature of the gospels as literature capable of disclosing new historical insights into Jesus' life and times.

Some, such as Marcus Borg, have gone beyond mere questions of history to explore in addition the spiritual significance that images of Jesus can have for Christian faith.

In some corners of the Third Quest, there is a greater openness to the possibility of the supernatural at work in the life of Jesus and the world. There is also a greater willingness to weigh the evidence, whether from the gospels or non-biblical sources, unfiltered by the ideological orthodoxies of either the left or the right. That cannot but bode well for the future of the scholarly inquiry. The quest goes on—with less uniformity, to be certain, but also with undiminished vigor.

If the Jesus scholarship of two centuries has revealed anything clearly, it is that regardless of how reliable they may ultimately prove to be, the gospels of the New Testament remain the single most salient record of the life and times of Jesus. While other external sources may help color the background and fill in the gaps, the gospel images of Jesus still are the most vivid and complete we have. As a consequence, questions concerning the historical veracity of the gospels assume even greater significance for those who would see Jesus. And those questions, for some scholars, remain very much at issue.

The continuing historical enterprise has underscored, as well, the strong interrelationship between the quester and the quest—the extent to which the worldview of the inquirer influences the outcome of the inquiry. Schweitzer recognized this correlation nearly a century ago when he chided the liberal skeptics of the Old Quest for vainly casting about for a Jesus in their own image.[17] In seeking to understand and evaluate the modern portraits of Jesus, then, it is helpful to consider not only the work but the backgrounds and agendas of the portrait-makers themselves. It is to this task that we turn next.

## CHAPTER 19

# JESUS AND
# HIS SEEKERS

## SCHOLARS OF
## THE QUEST

WHO ARE THE LEARNED SCHOLARS WHOSE SOMETIMES STARTLING
pronouncements about the life and times of Jesus have stirred so much controversy in the press and the pews of America during the past decade? What level
of professional expertise and personal insight qualify them to assess (and often
challenge) the accuracy of the Bible and Christian tradition in relating the
words and deeds of Jesus? How might the scholars' own histories—their personal religious and educational backgrounds and their ideological and philosophical biases—influence the course of their investigations and the conclusions
they draw?

In the following pages are brief profiles of five leading scholars of the Jesus
quest. While their names may not be household words, their work is widely
known in the vast field of modern biblical scholarship. Each is currently engaged in historical-Jesus research as part of either the "New" or "Third" quests,
discussed in the previous chapter. Each has written extensively and thoughtfully
on the life of Jesus and on the gospels and other literary sources that reveal him.
And even though they sometimes arrive at radically different conclusions, each
in his own way has left an indelible mark on the search for new insights into the
Jesus of history.

## ROBERT FUNK:
## JESUS THE SAGE AND SOCIAL CRITIC

Even now, when Robert Funk addresses an audience, there are hints of the pre-cocious young preacher who once led revival meetings in rural Texas. In a field characterized more often by esoteric discourse than revivalist fervor, the renowned biblical scholar and founder of the controversial Jesus Seminar still has an evangelist's dramatic flair, frequently cajoling listeners to repent of their erroneous ways and behold the true Jesus.

But the Jesus whom Funk commends to his audiences these days bears little resemblance to the Savior of his gospel-preaching youth. Stripped of what he considers to be the mythological accretions of centuries of church tradition, the historical Jesus (in Funk's view) was probably more akin to a Jewish Socrates—or perhaps a Lenny Bruce—than the divine Son of God. It is the goal of the Jesus Seminar, says Funk, to "set Jesus free" from the "scriptural and creedal and experiential prisons in which we have incarcerated him. We aspire to no less than to roll away the stone from the door of the rock-cut tomb." And if a "radical reformation" of Christianity should happen to be ignited in the process, he adds, so much the better.

It is Funk's evangelistic zeal as much as his unorthodox views that has placed him and his California-based seminar at the forefront of the modern historical-Jesus quest and at the center of the scholarly storm. He and his organization have drawn criticism both from mainstream academia, where Funk is viewed as something of a publicity hound, and from conservative scholars, who consider him an enemy of traditional Christianity and of the Bible.

Schooled in biblical studies at Vanderbilt University, he taught briefly at Texas Christian, Harvard, and Emory Universities, among other places, and became a leader in the Society of Biblical Literature, an organization of several thousand biblical scholars. But he split from the group in 1980, frustrated in his attempts to prod his colleagues into bridging the gap between the insular world of biblical academia and real-world religious practice. "I tried to get them to go public with what we were doing to raise the literacy level of the public," he explains. "Without that, our religious traditions become crass, unhealthy, and even demonic."

Funk organized the seminar in 1985 and set it to work, first examining the historicity of the words and deeds of Jesus as recorded in the gospels and then reporting the results in press releases and popular books. From the outset, the group has been chided by other academicians for its "gimmickry." At their semiannual meetings in Santa Rosa, California, the seminar's fifty or so members present papers and carry on spirited discussion of the relative merits and demerits of particular Scripture passages. Then they vote by casting colored beads: red indicates an authentic saying or deed, pink indicates something that Jesus *may* have said or done, gray denotes material that is probably inauthentic, and black indicates material that is definitely not from Jesus. The whole notion of voting on the authenticity of scriptural passages has struck many scholars as a rather brazen and ill-conceived attempt to find a shortcut to scholarly consensus—something that traditionally arises, if and when it does, only after years of painstaking argumentation and peer review.

Following the vote-casting procedure and applying some conventional methods of textual analysis and other more disputed rules of evidence, the seminar has concluded that no more than 20 percent of the sayings and even fewer of the deeds attributed to Jesus are authentic. Among the seminar's castoffs are the Lord's Prayer, the sayings from the cross, the claims of Jesus to divinity, the virgin birth, most of Jesus' miracles, and his bodily resurrection.

The Jesus that remains, which Funk described in his 1996 book *Honest to Jesus,* is a secular sage and a social critic who satirized the pious and championed society's poor and marginalized. He spoke in parables and aphorisms, often using humor or irony to make a point. "Jesus was perhaps the first stand-up Jewish comic," says Funk. He was "not political, not programmatic," and offered no detailed prescriptions for dealing with the issues of the world. Starting a new religion, says Funk, "would have been the farthest thing from his mind."

Funk now sees the seminar's role as laying the foundations for a new Reformation. "Christianity as we have known it is anemic and wasting away," Funk told a California audience at one seminar meeting. It is time, he said, to "reinvent Christianity," complete with new symbols, new stories, and a new understanding of Jesus. The new Christianity that Funk envisions would, among other things, emphasize Jesus as a teacher rather than as a divine being. It would also replace the Eucharist with a common meal, stress forgiveness and freedom over punishment and piety, and endorse "protected recreational sex among consenting adults."[1]

More recently, the seminar has turned its attention to revising the Christian creeds and canon and evaluating the authenticity of the writings of St. Paul. Meanwhile, filmmaker Paul Verhoeven, director of *Basic Instinct* and *Showgirls* and a voting member of the seminar, is planning a movie on the life of Jesus based in part on the group's work.

The seminar also has taken its controversial message on the road, dispatching teams of scholars to conduct public forums throughout the country. Their aim is to further the seminar's goal of raising the public literacy level, disseminating knowledge that Funk says has been hoarded by scholars for years. So far, the audience for these sessions has been small but receptive—and generally outside the theological mainstream.

At one meeting at the Universal Truth Center in Miami, for example, Funk told an enthusiastic group of about seventy-five people that modern Christians "can no longer swallow the kind of mythology that has dominated the faith for the past two thousand years." Funk and seminar member Robert J. Miller, a religion professor at Midway College in Kentucky, described the historical Jesus as a remarkable but thoroughly human teacher, one more interested in the plight of the poor than in speculation about an afterlife. Jesus attracted followers, the scholars said, by subverting conventional wisdom and advocating an "unbrokered relationship with God." According to the Reverend Mary Tumpkin of the Universal Truth Center, the seminar's message was exactly the kind of thing her congregants needed to hear. "It helped our people to see that traditional Christianity doesn't have all the answers."

A few ministers who are sympathetic with the seminar's views have begun incorporating the group's teachings into their ministries. During Sunday services at her United Methodist congregation in Davis, California, the Reverend Eileen Lindsay says she no longer introduces the Lord's Prayer as "the prayer that Jesus taught his disciples." Instead, she calls it "the prayer that Christians have prayed through the ages." The prayer is meaningful, says Lindsay, "even if it didn't come from Jesus." The Reverend Jon Brown, a United Methodist pastor in Nampa, Idaho, says he uses the seminar's heavily edited version of the gospels when he teaches a class on the parables of Jesus. "It has helped my people deal with questions and doubts they didn't feel free to talk about before," he says.

Yet not all the seminar's controversial opinions play well in public. At one "seminar-on-the-road" meeting in Boise, the audience seemed supportive when scholars Roy Hoover, a retired professor from Whitman College in Walla Walla, Washington, and Lane McGaughy of Willamette University in Salem, Oregon, explained why the seminar thinks there is little solid history in the biblical stories of Jesus' birth and death. But some of the fifty or so participants grew fidgety when Hoover explained the implications of the seminar's disbelief in the bodily resurrection of Jesus. "The whole idea of resurrection," Hoover said, "is embedded in an ancient worldview" that is outdated in a scientific age. The Christian belief in a "general resurrection of the dead . . . simply cannot stand as an article of faith." The entire notion of life after death, Hoover said, has become difficult to affirm.

No afterlife? Christianity without a hope of heaven? "As a minister," said the Reverend Judy Johnson, a United Methodist pastor in Aston, Idaho, who attended the event, "I don't think that helps me when I'm counseling a grieving family."

The seminar's critics are confident that the long-term impact of Funk and his disciples on Christianity will not be anything close to what Funk intends. "You don't just go out and start a Reformation," says Gregory Boyd of Bethel College in St. Paul, Minnesota. Most of what the seminar is saying about Jesus, Boyd says, "is old standard liberal theology. It didn't take off before, and I don't think it's going to take off now."

Even the seminar fellows are divided on the more theological elements of Funk's agenda. Some are uncertain that reforming Christianity or revising the scriptural canon is an appropriate role for academic Bible scholars and historians. "It's not our place to act as a canonical council," says Perry Kea, a seminar member and an associate professor of biblical studies at the University of Indianapolis. To add or subtract from the Scriptures, adds Stephen Patterson of the Eden Theological Seminary in St. Louis, "is a function of a community of faith. We are not a community of faith."

If the seminar expects to have any impact at all on Christian doctrine and praxis, say Kea and others, it will have to broaden its membership to engage theologians and perhaps even church officials in the process. But even with the discussion thus expanded, seminar members say, change will come congregation by congregation and will take generations to accomplish. Few of the current fellows are likely to be around to see the results. It will be up to future historians to decide whether Funk and the Jesus Seminar will be hailed as reformers, repudiated as heretics, or simply forgotten.[2]


## MARCUS J. BORG:
## JESUS THE SPIRIT PERSON

While the fellows of the Jesus Seminar may be a decidedly liberal bunch, they are not entirely monolithic in their outlook. Marcus Borg, one of the leading fellows, shares many of the post-Bultmannian presuppositions of his colleagues. But in his own spiritual journey Borg has found a much more mystical Jesus than most of his fellow seminarians can abide. As an author and lecturer, his impact on Jesus research has extended far beyond his role as a member of the seminar.

A long and winding road has led Borg to the conclusion that the historical Jesus was a "spirit person, subversive sage, social prophet, and movement founder." Born and raised of Scandinavian stock in North Dakota, Borg began his journey with childhood Lutheran hymns and continued with his study in college in Minnesota. His spiritual evolution, which he sometimes calls "Tao," after the ancient Chinese philosophy, included bouts of serious skepticism; at times he was a "closet agnostic" and even a "closet atheist." He says of that period: "The bottom line was that I finally did not know what to do with the notion of God. On the whole, I thought there probably was no such reality."

At Union Theological Seminary in New York and then at Oxford University, where he received his doctorate, Borg found himself on a less traveled path. "The news that the 'Jesus of history' was very different from the Jesus I had heard about growing up in church seemed important to me," he wrote in his 1994 book *Meeting Jesus Again for the First Time*. He was on the road to discovering a Jesus who was more concerned about this life than the afterlife, who taught subversive wisdom, and who was intent on revitalizing Israel. He was also a "healer or holy person"—something of a Jewish mystic. "It seemed vaguely scandalous, and something I shouldn't tell my mother about," Borg wrote. "But I was hooked."

After studying sources as varied as the mystic novelist Carlos Castenada, the psychologist and philosopher William James, and the Buddha, Borg concluded that there were two Jesuses. One was the "pre-Easter Jesus, a powerful witness to the reality and character of God" and a radical cultural critic who preached the politics of compassion. The other was the "post-Easter Jesus, a living spiritual reality, God with a human face." Taken together, says Borg, these two Jesuses "made it possible for me to be a Christian again." To follow Jesus, he says, "means in some sense to be 'like him,' to take seriously what he took seriously," which can then provide "an alternative vision of life."

Partly because of new archaeological evidence contained in finds such as the Dead Sea Scrolls, but mainly because of new methods for interpreting centuries of previous studies, Borg believes that contemporary scholars understand "the world of Jesus better than any generation since perhaps A.D. 200."[3]

## JOHN DOMINIC CROSSAN:
## JESUS THE REVOLUTIONARY PEASANT

Like Borg, John Dominic Crossan has left an indelible mark on Jesus scholarship quite apart from his participation in the Jesus Seminar, which he co-founded with Funk and over which he continues to hold considerable sway. One of the most prolific of the modern questers, he broke controversial new ground in the field of Jesus research with his 1991 book, *The Historical Jesus: The Life of a Mediterranean Jewish Peasant*. In the intervening years, the former Roman Catholic priest and professor emeritus at DePaul University in Chicago has written several more works both for scholars and for popular audiences.

The gospel according to Crossan goes something like this: Jesus was a revolutionary peasant who resisted economic and social tyranny in Roman-occupied Palestine. He was a Jewish Cynic (in the original sense of that word: an adherent of the philosophy that virtue and self-control were the only good) who wandered from town to town, teaching unconventional wisdom and subverting oppressive social customs. He was a preacher who proclaimed "God's radical justice" and lived the idea so powerfully that it inspired a movement that changed the course of history. And if the clarity of his life and message, now long obscured, could be fully grasped today, the same could happen again.

Born and raised in Ireland, Crossan considers himself "Catholic through and through," despite the fact that he quit the Servite order to marry in 1969 and has not attended mass regularly since then. "There has never been a more empowering figure than Jesus," he explains. "If you are empowered by Jesus' life, in my judgment that makes you a Christian."

Like many of his colleagues in the post-Bultmannian quest, Crossan rejects most of the gospel record as inaccurate. Using modern sociological and anthropological studies of ancient Palestine as a backdrop, he attempts to reconstruct the historical Jesus from early "Jesus traditions" that he says are embedded within the gospels and other noncanonical texts from the early church. He relies heavily, for example, on the Gnostic *Gospel of Thomas*—a sayings source most scholars consider apocryphal and of second-century origin—and on the theoretical Q sayings source, a text many scholars still are not sure ever existed.

While he has come up with a vivid description of the man and a short list of sayings he believes can be traced to Jesus, Crossan thinks that the evidence he has gathered would rule out most of Christianity's traditional teachings. He sees biblical accounts of the Last Supper and appearances of the risen Jesus, for example, as attempts by Jesus' devout followers to express their "continued experience" of his presence after the crucifixion.

While Crossan's Jesus seems much more of a political animal than the traditional version, he warns that it would be "the ultimate betrayal of Jesus" to make him either "totally political—he tried to start a political movement" or "totally religious—he was talking about the afterlife." The historical Jesus, says Crossan, "proclaimed God's radical justice, which is extremely critical of the structures of almost any society—including ours."[4]

## JOHN MEIER:
## JESUS "THE MARGINAL JEW"

The small book on the historical Jesus that John Meier set out to write in 1989 was supposed to have been a brief warm-up for a much weightier project he had long anticipated—a definitive, multivolume explication of the gospel of Matthew. The brief diversion turned into *A Marginal Jew: Rethinking the Historical Jesus,* a two-volume work of sixteen hundred pages. Now Meier is working on a third volume, and he is not certain it will be the last. Meanwhile, Matthew is still waiting. That, says Meier, a professor at the University at Notre Dame, is the compelling nature of the historical-Jesus quest. "It seems to have a life of its own."

Like many of his academic colleagues in the Jesus quest, Meier believes that the New Testament gospels have limited value as historical records. Still, he considers them to be the best information source available on Jesus' life, offering far richer historical detail than the biographies of many other ancient figures. Among the conclusions Meier draws regarding the life of Jesus:

> ➤ He was born probably around 7 BCE in Nazareth, not in Bethlehem as the gospels of Luke and Matthew say.
> ➤ Despite official Catholic teaching that Mary, the mother of Jesus, remained a virgin all of her life, Meier says that Jesus had four brothers and at least two sisters, details that emerge from the gospels of Mark and John and from the writings of Paul. The virgin birth of Jesus, says Meier, "cannot be proven or disproven" by historical investigation.
> ➤ He had a brief ministry in Galilee as a teacher, prophet, and worker of deeds that were perceived by some as miracles.
> ➤ He was arrested in Jerusalem and crucified under Pontius Pilate somewhere around 30 CE. His followers claimed that he rose from the dead.

Yet as interesting and as accurate as those facts may be, says Meier, they do not constitute "the real Jesus." The best that historians can hope for, says Meier, is "sufficient data to draw a rough sketch" of Jesus' life.

Meier is widely regarded by his peers as meticulous and tidy as a historian, although some criticize his work as unimaginative and too beholden to official Catholic doctrine. A priest in the Roman Catholic Archdiocese of New York,

Meier was raised in a Catholic neighborhood in the South Bronx and educated and ordained in Rome. He taught in a New York seminary before moving to Washington. He remains close friends with New York's Cardinal John O'Connor.

The suggestion that his objectivity as a scholar is somehow compromised by his sound Catholic credentials is a criticism Meier finds particularly stinging. He works hard to keep his academic work and his faith separate. He notes, for example, that while he firmly believes in the virgin birth, the miracles, and the resurrection of Jesus, "as a historian, I cannot claim the ability to either confirm or deny those." Too often, he says, "historical scholars make theological claims about Jesus" that "go beyond the realm of historical research. You can't mix theology and historical research without causing tremendous confusion."

Even so, says Meier, good historical data on Jesus "can help inform theology." And while such data will never "create faith where there is none, it does say to the ordinary believer: You are not putting your faith in a fairy tale or some ahistorical symbol, but in a real person who was crucified in the first century."[5]

## N. T. WRIGHT:
## "JESUS AND THE VICTORY OF GOD"

In the rarefied ranks of Jesus questers, N. T. Wright stands as an imposing if somewhat lonely figure in a field dominated by skeptics. An Anglican cleric, New Testament scholar, and prolific writer, he is a staunch defender of Christian orthodoxy who finds plenty of reliable history in the gospels. And he loves nothing better than to engage in spirited debate with members of the Jesus Seminar and others who "write silly things about the Bible."[6]

Yet Wright is no mere apologist. He takes historical-Jesus research seriously and thinks traditional Christianity can stand to learn plenty about Jesus and his world, even from sources outside the Bible. In his 1996 book, *Jesus and the Victory of God,* he depicts a thoroughly orthodox Jesus who is firmly rooted in history but does not always fit neatly into the niches of tradition.

As Wright sees him, the historical Jesus is very much the Jesus of the gospels: a first-century Palestinian Jew who announced and inaugurated the kingdom of God, performed "mighty works," and believed himself to be Israel's Messiah who would save his people through his death and resurrection. "He believed himself called," in other words, says Wright, "to do and be what, in the scriptures, only Israel's God did and was."[7]

Dean of the Lichfield Cathedral in Staffordshire, Wright studied the New Testament at Oxford under the same professor as Borg, whom he counts as a personal friend and sometime debating partner. He makes no apologies for his orthodox views of the Bible, which he calls "the book of my life. It's the book I live with, the book I live by, the book I want to die by."[8]

Yet despite his high view of Scripture and its historical reliability, Wright warns those who share his conservative theological perspective that there is a "danger of idolatry" in becoming "overly protective about particular readings of the Bible." The Bible, he says, "is God's book for God's people." But the "security of God's people is ultimately in God."[9] It is not only possible, he says, but "actually highly likely that the church has distorted the real Jesus, and needs to repent of this and rediscover who its Lord actually is." That does not mean, he says, that traditional Christianity "has been wrong in everything it has said about Jesus. Only real no-holds-barred history can tell us whether that is so."[10]

That, says Wright, is why he is engaged in the historical-Jesus quest. It is not acceptable, he says, to merely hang around the periphery waiting to refute those who make scurrilous attacks on the Bible's integrity. "What we need are people out there making contributions and feeding the stuff into the stream higher up. I guess that is the reason I am doing my work."[11]

When all is said and done, says Wright, "Christianity ought to emerge from historical enquiry more solid and robust, not watered down or thinned out. Instead of bad portraits" of the historical Jesus, says Wright, "we need good ones."[12]

There are, of course, many others who are engaged in the Jesus quest. Whether they set out to compose comprehensive portraits or merely to fill in small pieces of the puzzle, they are part of an endeavor that over the years has produced a seemingly endless stream of conflicting theories, provocative proposals, and controversies. And the Jesus quest is a process that will no doubt continue for years to come.

What has the more recent of this research revealed about the life and times of Jesus? How reliable are the accounts of his birth, death, and resurrection as reported in the gospels? What can be known about his authentic words and deeds as he ministered for those few short years in Galilee? And what does all of this reveal about the origins of the movement that began in his name? It is to those important questions that we now turn.

## CHAPTER 20

# NATIVITY AND NUANCE

## THE BIRTH OF JESUS

> For unto us a child is born, unto us a son is given:
> and the government shall be upon his shoulder: and his
> name shall be called Wonderful, Counsellor, The mighty
> God, The everlasting Father, The Prince of Peace.
>
> *Isaiah 9:6 (KJV)*

TO CHRISTIANS THROUGH THE AGES, THE CHRISTMAS STORY PROCLAIMS the advent of a Savior, the imponderable miracle of God's invasion of human history through a stable in Bethlehem over two thousand years ago. Yet like the rest of the Bible, the accounts of Jesus' birth have come under intense scrutiny. New Testament scholars continue to debate whether the nativity stories should be understood as history, religious legend, theological proclamation, or perhaps some combination of the three. While many scholars question the historical veracity of at least some of the details, many others have found little reason to alter traditional understandings of a story that, at its heart, is a call to faith in a self-revealing God.

While recent archaeological discoveries and ancient nonbiblical writings have shed some new light on the historical context of the events of Jesus' life, the New Testament remains virtually the only source of details concerning his birth. Even there, nativity stories appear in only two places—the gospels of Matthew and Luke.

The fact that neither Mark, widely considered to be the first gospel, nor John provides an account of Jesus' birth has led many scholars to conclude that the nativity stories were not part of the Jesus movement's earliest oral traditions. The first Christian preaching, as recorded in the book of Acts and in the epistles of Paul, focused on the resurrection as evidence that Jesus was the Christ. It made no mention of a miraculous birth accompanied by the acclaim of angels and visiting Magi. Some scholars have tried to put a negative spin on the omission by suggesting that if the apostles had been aware of the dramatic events associated with Jesus' birth, surely they would have trumpeted the details as evidence that Jesus was indeed God's anointed one.

Yet there are other, more reasonable explanations for the somewhat later development of the nativity traditions. Most scholars agree that the birth narratives took shape as a result of the growing curiosity of the early Christians, who—believing Jesus to be both human and divine—sought to understand his origins. Skeptics argue that the gospel writers filled the information void by inventing their delightful-but-ahistorical tales of angels, wise men, shepherds, and a miraculous virgin birth. Others, however, find every reason to believe the gospel writers drew upon credible sources still very much at their disposal in the early Christian decades as they reconstructed the events surrounding the birth of Jesus. The writer of Luke explains in his opening lines that he "investigated everything carefully" in order to write "the exact truth" about events he had not personally witnessed.

While the gospels do not identify their sources, some traditions suggest that Matthew's version is based on the recollections of Joseph and that Mary may have been the source of Luke's narrative. There is, of course, no way to substantiate such claims. Many have argued that apparent disagreements on some of the birth details make it unlikely that family members could have been the source of the infancy material. Matthew, for example, has Mary and Joseph taking their infant son to Egypt to escape a plot on his life. Luke, on the other hand, has them staying in Bethlehem and Jerusalem for at least a month and then going home to Nazareth. He seems to know nothing of a flight to Egypt.

The accounts are surely different. But are they contradictory? Some scholars have tried to harmonize the differences by explaining that the writers merely selected different anecdotes in order to address the questions of their different communities. Others see the apparent discrepancies as far more problematic. "The two narratives are not only different," writes the eminent New Testament scholar Raymond E. Brown, "they are contrary to each other in a number of details"—some of which we will soon explore. In his widely cited book *The Birth of the Messiah,* Brown concludes that it is "unlikely that either account is completely historical."[1] That, of course, remains a matter of vigorous debate.

While scholars disagree on the significance of apparent divergences, most acknowledge that writing an objective history or a complete biography was not at all what the gospel writers had in mind. Indeed, perhaps neither of the gospel writers who addressed the nativity knew all that went on in connection with Jesus' birth. "The main question for the people at the time was 'What does this birth mean for our faith?'" says Brennan Hill, a theology professor at Xavier University in Cincinnati. "They did not spend much time with the question that we might ask today: 'What really happened?'"[2] The nativity story, adds Donald Hagner, professor of New Testament at Fuller Theological Seminary in Pasadena, California, "was not told for the sake of facts alone, but in order to illustrate a deeper meaning—the theological significance of Jesus as the fulfillment of Old Testament prophecy."[3] On that score, says Professor Brown, regardless of questions concerning certain of the details, the gospel narratives remain "dramatically persuasive" in their proclamation of the birth of the Messiah.[4]

## THE BIRTH

> And Joseph also went up from Galilee . . . unto the city of David which is called Bethlehem . . . to be taxed with Mary, his espoused wife. . . . And so it was that while they were there . . . she brought forth her firstborn son, and wrapped him in swaddling clothes and laid him in a manger.
>
> *Luke 2:4–7 KJV*

Whatever their apparent differences, the two gospels agree on the main points of the nativity story: Jesus was born in Bethlehem near the end of the reign of Herod the Great—perhaps between 6 and 4 BCE—to a virgin named Mary whose husband, Joseph, was a descendant of King David. All of this, according to the gospel writers, was to fulfill the Hebrew prophecies that "a virgin shall conceive and bear a son, and shall call his name Immanuel" (Isa. 7:14) and that out of Bethlehem "one will go forth . . . to be ruler in Israel" (Mic. 5:2).

While the virginal conception of Jesus seems not to have been a part of the earliest Christian preaching, the fact that both Matthew and Luke make note of it suggests to many scholars that it is firmly rooted in early Christian tradition. Yet whether it is strictly historical or is merely a vehicle for theological teaching is, as it has been for centuries, a subject of considerable dispute.

In 178 CE, the pagan writer Celsus wrote a lengthy polemic against Christianity in which he portrayed Jesus as the illegitimate son of a Roman soldier.[5] In a more modern attack on the doctrine, Episcopal Bishop John Spong, in a

1992 book *Born of a Woman,* describes the virginal conception as a myth and asserts that Jesus may have been born to a sexually violated girl.[6] The quality of the argument against the virgin birth, it appears, has not improved with age.

Of course, there is no way modern historians can approach the question decisively. There are no witnesses to cross-examine, no polygraphs to administer, no DNA samples to test. As John Meier notes, judging the historicity of the virgin birth must ultimately depend on "one's own philosophical and theological presuppositions, as well as the weight one gives Church teaching."[7]

N. T. Wright, however, argues that it is unlikely that Matthew and Luke would have invented such a story, since in telling it they "were taking an enormous risk" with little potential payoff. Claiming a miraculous conception could —and did—expose the Christian writers to the charge of covering up "sexual misbehavior." The inhabitants of ancient Palestine may not have been as scientifically sophisticated as we moderns are, but they certainly knew how babies were made. The more prudent course would have been to simply keep silent. The fact that they spoke out, Wright surmises, "makes it clear that the early church . . . was aware of something strange surrounding Jesus' birth, and that they were writing to clarify the matter."[8]

Moreover, stories of miraculous births associated with divine figures were relatively common in the pagan world. To have borrowed from a pagan motif— which is precisely what some critical scholars claim the gospel writers did— Wright says would not have made the Christian gospel more attractive either to Jews, "to whom such ideas would have been anathema," or to pagans, who likely would have considered the move shameless me-tooism. Nor was a virgin birth necessary, especially in light of the early Christians' belief in the resurrection, for the gospel writers to make the case for Jesus' divinity.[9]

Why, then, did Matthew and Luke include the virgin birth in their gospels? The best explanation, says Wright, "is that they firmly believed it to be true."[10] The fact that their independent accounts agree on the core of the story—that Jesus was born in Bethlehem to a virgin named Mary—suggests that at least those basic facts were widely known within the early Christian movement. The two writers then set about to provide details that would help the members of their separate communities understand the significance of the Bethlehem birth.

The setting of Jesus' birth in the Christmas story is nearly as important as its nature. The fact that Jesus was known during his ministry to have come from Nazareth rather than from Bethlehem "constituted a problem" for the writers of Matthew and Luke, says Hagner. Listeners familiar with Old Testament prophecies no doubt would have questioned how a native son of Nazareth could be the Messiah. That complication, says Hagner, may explain why both Matthew and Luke emphasize Bethlehem as Jesus' birthplace and why they tell intricate and seemingly differing stories to get him back to Nazareth.[11]

In Luke's gospel, Joseph and Mary go to Bethlehem from their home in Nazareth to be counted in a census "of the entire Roman world" (2:1, NIV), ordered by Caesar Augustus. It was, Luke says, "the first census that took place while Quirinius was governor of Syria" (2:2), and it required that all people go to their native cities to be counted. Some scholars who see this part of the story more as myth than history ask why a very pregnant Mary would make such an arduous eighty- to ninety-mile trip when Joseph could easily have responded to the census alone. But Paul Maier, professor of ancient history at Western Michigan University, in his 1991 book, *In the Fullness of Time,* suggests that Mary "had every reason to make the trip." She probably knew of the Old Testament prophecies that the Messiah was to be born in Bethlehem, says Maier, and no doubt was puzzled about why God had chosen a girl from Nazareth. The Roman emperor's census decree, says Maier, "placed the last piece of the divine-human puzzle into place."[12]

Many scholars also have found Luke's reference to an empire-wide census puzzling. Outside of the Bible, there is no historical record either of a universal census ordered by Caesar Augustus or, as Brown has noted, of a "census requirement that people be registered in their ancestral cities."[13] While records do exist of censuses ordered by Augustus in 28 BCE, 8 BCE, and 14 CE, they all apparently involved only Roman citizens.[14]

There also are records of many smaller counts of non-Romans in the provinces, mainly for taxing purposes. Some scholars suggest that it may have been one of those that Luke recalled. However, the only known census involving Quirinius as governor of Syria occurred in 6–7 CE.[15] That was nearly a decade after the death of Herod the Great, a key figure in Matthew's nativity story.

So has Luke confused the facts? Not necessarily. Some scholars argue that the apparent discrepancy is the result of a modern translating error. The problem is resolved, claims Nigel Turner, a Greek scholar from the University of Edinburgh, if the passage is translated correctly: "This census was *before* the census taken when Quirinius was governor."[16] The Greek word *protos,* Turner explains, which is translated "first" in Luke's passage, can also mean "before" when it is followed by the genitive case, as it is in this verse. This alternative translation also corrects what Wright calls another "otherwise odd problem" in the text. "Why should Luke say that Quirinius' census was the first? Which later ones was he thinking of?"[17]

Another possible mistranslation from the Greek in Luke also may require a revision of the popular depiction of the Christmas crèche. In the traditional telling of the Christmas story, Joseph and Mary arrive late in Bethlehem and, finding no room at the inn, spend the night in a stable or cave, where the baby is born. But Kenneth E. Bailey, professor of New Testament at the Tantur

Ecumenical Institute in Jerusalem, describes that as a creative expansion of Luke's gospel, which mentions neither stable nor cave. It simply says that after Mary gave birth to Jesus, she "laid him in a manger because there was no room in the inn."

Bailey thinks that Jesus was born not in a stable at all, but on the ground floor of a typical two-level Bethlehem house, in the upper portion of a split-level room where animals were kept at night. He argues that the Greek word most commonly translated as "inn" is *pandocheion*—the same word Luke uses in the parable of the Good Samaritan (10:34). But in the nativity story, Luke says there was no room in the *kataluma,* which Bailey says normally is translated "guest chamber" or "guest room." Mary and Joseph, says Bailey, probably were invited into the ground-floor room because the guest room was already taken. Instead of being turned away by a callous innkeeper and sent to a cave or a drafty stable, says Bailey, "Joseph finds shelter for his family in a simple peasant home."[18]

Matthew's gospel seems to offer a much different picture of events surrounding the birth. There are no depictions of the nativity scene itself, nor of Joseph and Mary traveling from Nazareth. The narrative skips the preliminaries and begins by noting that "when Jesus was born in Bethlehem" he was visited by Magi from the East. When they arrived, the Magi entered "into the house." While many scholars believe that Matthew simply chose to omit the details of Mary and Joseph's travels, others conclude from the gospel that the couple lived in Bethlehem all along. It is a plausible enough argument, but one that is drawn largely from silence.

For Matthew, the more fascinating chapter of the Christmas story entails the holy family's move from Bethlehem to Nazareth following the birth. It is a dramatic story of a wicked king and a terrifying plot against Jesus' life that is absent from Luke's account.

## THE VISITORS

> There came wise men . . . to Jerusalem saying, Where is he that is born King of the Jews? For we have seen his star in the East and are come to worship him.
>
> *Matthew 2:1–2 KJV*

The holy family did not celebrate the nativity alone. In Luke's gospel, an angel announced the royal birth to local shepherds, who found their way to the baby's side. In Matthew's account, Magi—or "wise men," in some translations—arrived sometime later, bearing precious gifts to pay homage to the newborn king.

But the Magi's courtesy call, as Matthew tells it, was just the beginning of a harrowing chapter in the Christmas story. When the Magi stopped in Jerusalem to ask directions, their inquiries about a newborn king stirred up trouble. A jealous King Herod, hearing of the Magi's quest, secretly plotted to find and kill the child—a plot that sent Joseph, Mary, and their newborn son into Egypt and resulted in the slaughter of the children of Bethlehem.

While these are easily the most dramatic of the nativity events, Matthew's visit of the Magi and "slaughter of the innocents" also have drawn fire from skeptics through the years. Many scholars have simply dismissed the stories as ahistorical, citing a lack of corroboration from other sources both for the atrocity in Bethlehem and for an astral phenomenon over the Middle Eastern skies that might have been the Magi's guiding star. Some of these skeptics, including Bishop Spong, view the stories as *midrash*—theological elaborations of other biblical motifs—or as allegories intended to evoke the story of Moses, who also escaped an infant slaughter and "came out of Egypt." Some view the Magi mainly as an allegorical symbol representing those Gentiles of Matthew's time who responded as believers to the Christian message when many Jews did not.[19]

Many scholars, however, are now convinced that the stories have been dismissed too easily. They contend that there is reason to believe that the Magi, the star, and the atrocity at Bethlehem are indeed rooted in history—although getting to those historical roots requires peeling away some nonbiblical embellishments that popular tradition has attached to the story.

The Magi, for example, often are depicted as "three kings from the Orient," even though Matthew does not describe them as royalty or say how many there were. This tradition, scholars note, grew up in the church between the second and fifth centuries. The number three was probably affixed based on the three gifts of gold, frankincense, and myrrh that Matthew describes. By the sixth century, the tradition had been elaborated to the point of assigning the Magi names—Gaspar, Melchior, and Balthasar—as well as ages and skin color.[20] Little weight is given to these embellishments today. In any event, they do not taint the veracity of the gospel texts themselves.

What seems more likely to some biblical scholars is that the Magi of Matthew were astrologers from Persia or Mesopotamia who were drawn to Bethlehem by a significant alignment of stars and planets indicating to them that a ruler had been born. As Maier and others note, just such a configuration occurred in 6 BCE, when Jupiter, Saturn, and Mars drew close together in the constellation of Pisces—an event that occurs every 805 years. In ancient astrology, says Maier, Jupiter was considered the "king's planet" and Saturn the shield of Palestine, while Pisces represented epochal events. So to astrologers of the time, he says, the conjunction "would have meant that a cosmic ruler or king was to appear in Palestine at the culmination of history."[21]

To many scholars, this is more plausible than the sudden appearance of a spectacular star in the night sky, as depicted by tradition. It also would explain why Herod and his court seemed unaware of the star and why no other historical sources mention it. But it does not explain what Matthew seems to describe as a star moving and standing over the house "where the young child was" (2:9). While a few have suggested that the Bethlehem star might have been a comet or a nova, those scenarios have drawn fewer supporters. Some biblical commentators argue simply that the Bethlehem star must be understood as a unique astral event that cannot be explained.

Well-worn arguments against the historicity of the Bethlehem slaughter also are getting new scrutiny today. The presumption in most academic circles long has been that an atrocity of the magnitude that Matthew describes—the killing of all boys up to two years old in the town and vicinity—certainly would have been noted by the first-century historian Josephus, who documented the final years of Herod's reign. The Bible does not say how many were slain, but some church traditions have estimated the death toll as high as sixty-four thousand.[22]

Some scholars now argue that the incident probably was much smaller in scope. Hagner, for example, estimates that the population of Bethlehem in those days was probably no more than one thousand, meaning that there could have been as few as twenty infants under the age of two—roughly half of whom would have been male. Though despicable, says Hagner, the massacre of ten or twelve babies in a small town might well have escaped Josephus's attention, especially when compared with other grisly deeds committed by Herod that *were* known to the historian.[23]

For example, Herod had a number of Torah scholars burned alive for removing Rome's golden eagle from the Temple Gate in Jerusalem. He also had his wife and some of his sons murdered because he considered them a threat to his throne. To assure that there would be universal mourning associated with his death, he ordered thousands of men locked inside the hippodrome in Jericho to be massacred when he died—an order that was never carried out.[24] If Josephus *had* heard of the Bethlehem murders, would they have been eclipsed by other atrocities? Maier asks, "Which [events] do you include in your history as you are trying to wind up Herod's rotting life?"[25]

While scholars who make such arguments concede that there is no direct evidence outside of the Bible to corroborate Matthew's account of the Bethlehem slaughter, they say that the story is far from implausible. The manic Herod who appears in Matthew's gospel, says Hagner, is "entirely consistent" with Josephus's portrait and "reflects the way Herod would have responded to the Magi."[26] Even Caesar Augustus is quoted as saying of his Judean pawn, "I'd rather be Herod's pig than his son."[27]

Ultimately more important in Matthew's story is the fact that Joseph, alerted to the peril by an angelic messenger, escaped with his wife and child to Egypt unharmed. Exactly where they lived and how long they stayed in Egypt, Matthew does not say, although a number of legends have survived. In Old Cairo's Coptic quarter, a crypt under the church of St. Sergius is venerated as the place where the holy family stayed for three months. At another site outside Cairo, near the Heliopolis, Christians since the fifth century have honored the "Tree of Mary," a sycamore under which Mary is said to have sought shade.[28]

Apocryphal writings from the second century purport to provide some additional details about the family's life in exile. The Arabic *Gospel of the Infancy*, for example, describes the holy family's being waylaid by robbers on a road in Sinai. When the highwaymen found nothing worth stealing, they took pity on the family and sent them on their way with fresh provisions. According to the tale, one of the robbers turned up thirty years later as one of the two thieves crucified with Jesus—the repentant one to whom Jesus said, "Today you will be with me in paradise" (Luke 23:43).[29]

The sojourn in Egypt ended, according to Matthew's gospel, when Herod died and an angel gave Joseph the all-clear to return with his family to Israel. But when Joseph and Mary learned that the new ruler, Herod's son Archelaus, had begun his reign by slaughtering three thousand Jews in Jerusalem, they decided to look north toward the more pastoral region of Galilee. They settled in the dusty little town of Nazareth.

## THE HIDDEN YEARS

> And Jesus increased in wisdom and stature,
> and in favor with God and man.
>
> *Luke 2:52 (KJV)*

Virtually nothing is known of the details of Jesus' life during the nearly three decades between his infancy and the start of his ministry—a period Bible scholars have come to call "the hidden years." Except for a brief episode where Jesus visits the temple in Jerusalem at age twelve, the New Testament is silent on his coming of age. While those details may never be recovered, new archaeological and historical research is providing some revealing glimpses into the personal, religious, and social influences that may have shaped the humanity of the Holy Child of Bethlehem.

The age-old desire to fill the gaps in Jesus' biography is evident in non-canonical writings dating to the second century CE, some of which purport to tell miracle stories from Jesus' childhood. The apocryphal *Infancy Gospel of*

*Thomas,* for example, depicts a five-year-old Jesus bringing dried fish and clay sparrows to life.[30] It also portrays him displaying an ornery streak: a playmate drops dead after Jesus curses him for accidentally hitting his shoulder, and when Joseph reprimands him for it, Jesus warns, "I am not thine. Vex me not!"[31] Though such accounts make fascinating reading, scholars say they have no historical basis.

Perhaps more importantly, they illustrate that while there was, indeed, a penchant in the early Christian centuries for inventing dramatic legends that would fill in the gaps in Jesus' biography, those legends stand in stark contrast to the accounts in the canonical gospels. As N. T. Wright notes, "When we read all the legends that did grow up later about the birth and childhood of Jesus, one thing is very striking. The gospels themselves, our earliest documents about Jesus, are sober, restrained and understated by comparison."[32]

While few details are known, there is a broad scholarly consensus on some facts of Jesus' boyhood. Most agree that he grew up in Nazareth, where he likely learned the carpenter's trade from Joseph. According to Justin Martyr (ca. 100–165 CE), an early church father, Jesus and Joseph specialized in making wooden yokes and plows. They were of such excellent quality, Justin wrote, that some were still in use in the mid–second century.[33]

As a child, Jesus no doubt was schooled in the synagogue, where he would have studied the Torah and Hebrew. He probably also learned to speak Greek and perhaps Latin. The New Testament says that Jesus had four brothers—James, Joses, Jude, and Simon—and at least two unnamed sisters, although these may have been cousins.[34] As the firstborn, he probably received special attention, which no doubt produced some sibling rivalry. John's gospel notes that during Jesus' ministry, his brothers did not believe in him. His father probably had little chance to witness that ministry; unlike Mary, Joseph does not reappear in the gospels, suggesting that he may have died before Jesus turned thirty.[35]

Even though Jesus' hometown was a peaceful rural village of about sixteen hundred people, the lower Galilee region surrounding Nazareth was no rural backwater. Recently uncovered archaeological ruins of numerous cities and towns in the area suggest to some that the region was one of the most densely populated of the Roman Empire. Life in lower Galilee, says J. Andrew Overman, a religion professor at the University of Rochester, New York, who has directed excavations in Galilee, was "as urbanized and urbane as anywhere else in the empire."[36] It was also considered a hotbed of anti-Roman feeling and messianic hope—an area, says Brennan Hill, where "bands of brigands and robbers roamed looking for victims."[37] That may help explain why during his ministry Jesus was sometimes branded a rebel and a troublemaker.

Though he was raised in a religious home and may not have traveled far, Jesus was probably exposed to considerable intellectual diversity. Just four miles from Nazareth, about a one-hour walk, was the provincial capital of Sepphoris, a cosmopolitan center of culture and commerce. Some scholars speculate that as a young man, Jesus may well have found carpentry work there; if so, he would have come into contact with the urban culture of a major Hellenistic city.

Just how much Jesus was influenced by his world is ultimately a question for theologians. Was he always aware of his special calling? Did he know what lay ahead? As the child "increased in wisdom and in years" (Luke 2:52), there must have been discoveries that fascinated him. Perhaps he, too, marveled at stories of angels, shepherds, and Magi at a Bethlehem manger.

There is every reason to see real history in the outlines of the birth narratives. The two versions clearly are told from different perspectives and offer different emphases. While it is true that they also differ in some of their details, the fact that the authors apparently summarized, skipped over, and telescoped some events, and were simply unaware of others, does not mean that the birth narratives should be jettisoned as contradictory.

One certainly need not attempt a complete harmonization of the texts in order to recognize that at least some of the apparent difficulties can, in fact, be plausibly explained. How long, for example, after the Bethlehem birth did the Magi arrive, prompting Joseph and his family to flee to Egypt, as recounted in Matthew? The story does not say. It is certainly conceivable that there was a sufficient lapse of time for the infant to have been circumcised (eight days after birth) and presented at the temple, thus making it more compatible with Luke's mentioning of those events. That Matthew has Herod seeking to kill Bethlehem children up to two years old would suggest that there may, in fact, have been quite a substantial time-lapse.

Even so, it is somewhat incomprehensible that Luke would have known nothing at all of the Egypt sojourn or of the "slaughter of the innocents." Could he simply have chosen to omit those substantial details from his narrative because they were not pertinent to his theological purpose? Clearly, there are major difficulties and incongruities to be explained by anyone who would attempt to establish complete agreement between the two accounts.

Still, the far more compelling fact is the remarkable extent to which these two ancient narratives, independently written and obviously drawn from different sources, agree on the important fundamentals of the story: the infant Jesus, Israel's prophesied Messiah, was born in Bethlehem to a virgin named Mary, whose husband Joseph was of the lineage of David—all in fulfillment of the Hebrew Scriptures. That alone seems strong and striking testimony to the core historicity of the nativity tradition.

## CHAPTER 21

# MESSAGE AND MIRACLE

## JESUS THE MAN

[O]n the way he asked his disciples, "Who do people say
that I am?" And they answered him, "John the Baptist; and
others, Elijah; and still others, one of the prophets." He
asked them, "But who do you say that I am?"

*Mark 8:27–29*

HE WALKED OUT OF THE JUDEAN WILDERNESS NEARLY TWO THOUSAND
years ago, an unknown itinerant preacher, proclaiming to all who would listen
that the kingdom of God was at hand. It was said that he was a healer and a
gifted teacher who challenged conventional wisdom and spoke with authority
and wit.

In the villages and on the hillsides of Galilee, curious crowds would gather
to witness his wondrous deeds and hear his teachings. He spoke of freedom for
the prisoner, power for the meek, comfort for the afflicted. Some followed him,
believing that he was God's Anointed One, while others dismissed him as a pre-
tender and a troublemaker. After all, there had been other self-proclaimed
prophets and would-be messiahs in Roman-occupied Palestine. And when they
all had come and gone, the Jewish people still felt the weight of Caesar's yoke
upon their necks.

Today, as in his own time, Jesus of Nazareth remains one of history's most
intriguing and enigmatic figures. Many still ask the question of the centuries:

Who is Jesus? Scholars have sought the answer by sifting the Scriptures and other sources in an attempt to assess the accuracy of the gospel accounts of his brief years of ministry. What did he really say and do? What was his message? Did he claim to be the Messiah, the divine Son of God? Did his audiences think of him in those ways?

In the gospels, Jesus frequently refers to himself enigmatically as the Son of Man and to God as Father. Yet he shies away from publicly proclaiming himself Israel's Messiah. Only in the gospel of Mark, when asked after his arrest if he is Israel's Promised One, does Jesus respond unambiguously, "I am." Today, some scholars doubt that Jesus ever spoke these words. They argue that the declaration more likely reflects the views of his followers as they came to understand years later the meaning of his life, death, and resurrection.

Many, of course, still take the words to be authentic. But even those who do so say that it is impossible to be certain what Jesus meant by them, or when he came to recognize himself as God's promised Messiah. "The texts don't tell us," says Don Carson, professor of New Testament at Trinity Evangelical Divinity School in Deerfield, Illinois. Yet what seems clear, says Carson, is that by the time Jesus began his public ministry, he knew his special status: "he knows he is going to be a different Messiah from what is expected."[1]

Indeed, scholars have come to learn from the Dead Sea Scrolls and other texts that the messianic title had many and varied meanings in Jesus' time: some people expected a military conqueror, others a prophetic teacher, and still others an apocalyptic figure who would bring down God's wrath and Israel's vindication. It is not surprising, then, that many of Jesus' contemporaries responded either negatively or with confusion when he did not act as they supposed he should. For similar reasons, Jesus elicits much the same response from many people today.

In large measure, those seeking the historical Jesus today must base their judgments on his words and deeds, much as his Galilean audiences had to do in his time. But the assumptions that many modern scholars carry into the task often lead to rather skewed results. Since the middle of the twentieth century, biblical scholars engaged in the so-called New Quest (see Chapter 18) have applied a standard set of criteria for weighing the authenticity of Jesus' sayings—criteria that assume there is relatively little real history in the gospels. It is widely accepted today, for example, that a saying can be considered uniquely from Jesus only if:

> It is *dissimilar* to anything one might expect to find in the
> Judaism of Jesus' day or in the life of the early church. In other
> words, if a saying goes against the grain of conventional Jewish

teaching—"Leave the dead to bury the dead" (Matt. 8:22), for example—or if it does not reflect what are known to be later doctrinal developments within Christianity, then it is more than likely authentic. The shortcoming in this test, as many scholars have pointed out over the years, is that it removes Jesus from his Jewish context and, as Carson notes, "it assumes that the church didn't learn anything from Jesus."[2] One can hardly classify Jesus as a great teacher while maintaining that his students retained so little of his teaching.

➤ It has *multiple attestation;* that is, it appears in more than one tradition or source. That should work well in theory, since two or three witnesses generally are better than one. In practice, however, this criterion has not always proven decisive. Some scholars have rejected sayings of Jesus that are repeated in multiple sources by claiming that one source had merely borrowed from another, or that the sayings reflected the theology of the gospel writers and should be dismissed on that ground alone.[3]

➤ It is *coherent;* that is, it is consistent with other sayings or material previously judged to be authentic. This too seems reasonable at first glance. But as N. T. Wright points out, it "leads one into a circle. Where should we break in, and why?"[4]

➤ It reflects what is known of the *language and culture* of first-century Palestine (as opposed, say, to later Hellenistic thought or rhetorical style). While looking in the right cultural and historical context for the authentic Jesus would seem to make perfect sense, it seems to be at direct odds with the earlier "dissimilarity" argument.

It is easy to see how scholars who apply these criteria have ended up with a bleak assessment of the gospels. At times it has seemed as if the ground rules were applied, if not designed, to predetermine the outcome. In the late 1980s, the Jesus Seminar, for example, laid out sixty-four premises and thirty-seven rules of evidence as it set about judging the authenticity of Jesus' sayings in the gospel of Mark. Many of these read more like summary conclusions than guidelines for an objective investigation. Among the premises and rules with which the Jesus Seminar began its quest are these examples:

➤ "The historical Jesus is to be distinguished from the Gospel portraits of him."

> ➤ "Only a small portion of the sayings attributed to Jesus in the gospels was actually spoken by him."
> ➤ "Quoted speech that is entirely context-bound is probably the product of the storyteller" [i.e., it is not authentic].
> ➤ "Statements attributed to the risen Jesus are not admissible as evidence for the historical Jesus."[5]

Guided by those lights, it is little wonder that the seminar fellows judged only one saying in the entire gospel of Mark to be authentic: "Pay to the emperor whatever belongs to the emperor and to God whatever belongs to God" (Mark 12:17).

Some scholars assert that whatever dependable historical material concerning Jesus may have existed initially, it underwent so much revision during the century following his death that no one can be absolutely certain of the accuracy or authenticity of the gospels, especially of the words the authors attributed to Jesus himself. "In over 40 years of oral transmission, the sayings of Jesus often were paraphrased," asserts Lane McGaughy, professor of religion at Willamette University in Salem, Oregon. That may be true. But does it necessarily follow that errors crept into the gospel record and obliterated the authentic sayings of Jesus? Many scholars think not, and for good reason.

Although some scholars make it out to be, the tradition of oral transmission in the first century was not at all analogous to the modern children's game of "telephone," where the message sent by the players is unavoidably corrupted in each phase of its passing. In the ancient Jewish world, as well as in the wider Greco-Roman culture, memorization skills were highly prized. Rabbis were encouraged to memorize the entire Torah, along with the body of oral law that grew up around it.[6] Oral recitation of such material was not the least haphazard or freewheeling. In any event, there is no reason to think that a full thirty or forty years passed without any of Jesus' sayings being written down in some "pre-gospel" form. As was noted earlier, the hypothetical sayings source often designated as Q would have been just such a record.

Moreover, scholars say it was not uncommon in those days before the invention of digital recorders for a speaker or writer to summarize a speech or an event in a way that accurately conveyed the gist of the material.[7] Providing a verbatim transcript was not expected, nor was it considered the only accurate form of reporting—any more than it is today. "To have accurate summaries of Jesus' teachings is just as historical as to have his actual words," says Darrell Bock of Dallas Theological Seminary.[8] It is a distinction that biblical scholars often make between *ipsissima verba* ("the exact words") and *ipsissima vox* ("the exact voice") of Jesus. "The gospels may not have Jesus' exact words," says Alan Johnson, New Testament professor at Wheaton College in Illinois, "but they accurately report his voice."[9]

One point on which scholars tend to agree almost unanimously is that the central focus of Jesus' teaching was the kingdom of God—its present arrival, its future fulfillment, and its implications for human conduct.[10] In his sermons and discourses recorded in the gospels, he declared love the greatest of the biblical commandments and spoke reassuringly to the poor, the powerless, and the peacemakers. Yet he also warned of divine judgment and declared paradoxically that he had come "not to bring peace, but a sword" (Matt. 10:34) that would divide nations and families.

To his curious listeners in Galilee, chafing under Roman rule and longing for a restoration of Israel's kingdom after long years of exile, the arrival of God's kingdom would have been a tantalizing but puzzling message, note biblical scholars. In the gospels, Jesus seldom spoke explicitly concerning the nature of God's kingdom, but instead described it in parables with sometimes hidden meanings.

In fact, to many of his listeners, scholars say, it is likely that Jesus' message would have sounded subversive. He seemed to challenge the bounds of the Jewish law by declaring that "the Sabbath was made for man, not man for the Sabbath" (Mark 2:27), and "not what enters into the mouth defiles the man, but what proceeds out of the mouth" (Matt. 15:11). He often accused the Pharisees—the leaders of the synagogues—of hypocrisy for following the letter of the law but not its spirit.

The kingdom of God that Jesus described would include the Gentiles—an egalitarian vision that seriously challenged many of Israel's cherished traditions. "It would be like announcing in a Muslim country that one was fulfilling the will of Allah while apparently vilifying Muhammad and burning a copy of the Koran," says Wright. "It's no wonder Jesus needed to use parables to say all this."[11] While some of Jesus' listeners were prepared to follow him, forsaking all, says Edwin Yamauchi of Miami University of Ohio, "many more were either skeptical or aghast at his apparent disregard of Moses' teachings and his claim of a special relation with God the Father."[12]

For modern inquirers, more astounding and problematic than Jesus' words are the reports of his miraculous deeds. What can historians possibly make of stories that depict Jesus walking on water, restoring sight to the blind, and raising the dead? As Craig Blomberg of Denver Seminary notes, "even the most devout believer must share the tension that the skeptic feels when it comes to the credibility of miracle stories."[13]

Most scholars, conservatives and skeptics alike, would agree that there is no way traditional historical methodology can directly prove or disprove the miracles as reported in the gospels. "It is simply beyond our reach," says Paul Maier.[14] Yet by examining some important indirect evidence—the corroborative testimony of nonbiblical sources, the historical "fallout" of certain miracle episodes, and so on—it is possible to draw some reasonable conclusions about the veracity of the gospel accounts.

In all, the gospels directly record thirty-five miracles performed by Jesus during his brief years of ministry, and they allude to at least twelve others.[15] These events generally fall into three categories: healings, exorcisms, and "nature miracles" (such as calming a storm or turning water into wine). Perhaps surprisingly, recent critical scholarship has been generally supportive of the notion of miracles in Jesus' life, at least to those in the first two categories. "Despite the difficulty which miracles pose for the modern mind," says Marcus Borg, "on historical grounds it is virtually indisputable that Jesus was a healer and exorcist."[16] John Dominic Crossan agrees that "throughout his life, Jesus performed healings and exorcisms for ordinary people."[17]

Moreover, there is broad consensus among even the most skeptical of scholars that extrabiblical evidence supports the fact that Jesus' reputation as a miracle worker extended beyond his own circle of followers. Josephus, for example, notes that Jesus was widely known as "a doer of amazing deeds" and a teacher who "won over many Jews and many of the Greeks."[18] And the Babylonian Talmud—a compendium of Jewish law and commentary—relates that "on the eve of Passover, Yeshu was hanged . . . because he has practiced sorcery and led Israel astray."[19]

Yet the precise nature and the significance of those "amazing deeds" are matters of vigorous debate in current scholarship. Were they unique and supernatural acts given as signs of the arrival of God's kingdom? Or were they otherwise naturally explicable occurrences that would not have been considered altogether surprising in a time when traveling healers and exorcists were relatively common?

More often than not, the conclusions scholars draw in response to those questions hinge heavily on their own philosophical predispositions. As the leaders of the Jesus Seminar have observed, "The contemporary religious controversy . . . turns on whether the worldview reflected in the Bible can be carried forward into this scientific age."[20] For those who assume *a priori* that the inviolable laws of a fixed universe do not allow for such occurrences as the gospels describe, the conclusion is foregone. But for others who hold, as A. M. Hunter suggests, that "Jesus was, and is, what Christians have always believed him to be, the Son of God," there is "nothing inherently incredible in the belief that such a person as Jesus may have had control over the great frame of nature itself."[21]

It has been observed that critical scholars who grant that Jesus probably did perform healings and exorcisms are careful to qualify their conclusion in two ways: (1) some if not all of Jesus' cures were "cognitive and psychosomatic" rather than biological, and (2) others in Jesus' time were known to both heal and perform exorcisms (Matt. 12:27–28; Mark 9:38–40), making Jesus' actions not particularly unique.[22]

Without question, Jesus was not the first, last, or only "doer of wondrous deeds" known in the ancient Near East. Historians note that every culture—before, during, and after Jesus' time—has had stories of healings. Therefore, to declare that Jesus was a healer and to tell stories of healings by Jesus, says Stevan Davies, a New Testament scholar at College Misericordia in Pennsylvania, is "no more exciting than to say he was a carpenter."[23]

Moreover, says Davies, even without invoking the supernatural, one could conclude that Jesus successfully healed certain psychosomatic illnesses (skin disorders, lameness, and some types of blindness, for example)—illnesses that were the result of "internalized guilt" that the sufferer associated with sin. By pronouncing forgiveness of sins, Davies theorizes, Jesus was able to heal such people of their ailments.[24] Such attempts to explain away the Bible's miracles naturalistically go back at least to the Old Quest liberalism of the nineteenth century, as we saw in Chapter 18. Today as then, however, few find such explanations entirely satisfying.

Jesus also was widely known as an exorcist—one who was able to cure persons who believed that they were possessed by demons. The gospels record four instances in which he came upon individuals said to be demon-possessed. In one story, he sent a "legion" of demons into a herd of pigs, which then threw themselves off a cliff. "Jesus certainly performed exorcisms as they were practiced in the first century," says John J. Rousseau, an archaeologist and member of the Jesus Seminar. "It would have been natural for an itinerant charismatic healer and teacher to do so."[25]

Exorcisms, Rousseau explains, clearly were a part of the Jewish milieu in first-century Palestine. The Judaism of Jesus' time had been influenced by Babylonian, Persian, Egyptian, and Greek cultures. The Persian belief that demons could possess individuals and cause diseases, says Rousseau, "had gained wide acceptance. Therefore, the techniques of exorcism were used for the treatment of illnesses."[26] Often those techniques involved the use of magical devices such as amulets, rings, stones, and other artifacts, many of which have recently been discovered at archaeological sites. One tradition, mentioned by Josephus even held that the ancient Israelite King Solomon was an exorcist.[27] And in addition to the several accounts of Jesus casting out demons, the book of Acts notes that his disciples also performed exorcisms. Many scholars conclude that such a preponderance of evidence suggests that Jesus probably did set the example for his followers.

Regarding the so-called nature miracles, however, critical scholars are far less credulous. They find little that is authentic in stories depicting Jesus calming a stormy sea, walking on water, changing water into wine, and feeding five thousand people with five loaves and two fish. Most difficult of all for skeptics to abide are the accounts of Jesus raising the dead. There are three such stories: Luke tells of Jesus reviving a widow's son in Nain, John records Jesus raising his friend Lazarus in Bethany, and Matthew, Mark, and Luke all relate the story of the raising of the daughter of Jairus.

Many scholars write these off as literary inventions intended to illustrate the authors' belief about the divinity of Jesus and the ongoing activity of the risen Christ within the church. But such feats pose little trouble for those who believe that a divine Jesus was capable of suspending the laws of nature. "It is prudent," says Wright, "to hold back from too hasty a judgment on what is actually possible and what is not in the space-time universe. There are more things in heaven and earth than are dreamed of in post-Enlightenment philosophy."[28]

Beyond merely restating their theological and philosophical presuppositions, however, can Bible scholars and historians offer anything concrete concerning the veracity of these stories?

Some conservatives find that certain ancillary details woven into the gospel texts give the miracle stories what they consider to be a "ring of truth." In the story of Jesus turning water into wine, for example, one scholar argues that it is unlikely that an early church writer would have invented an episode that might have "encouraged those who criticized Jesus for being a glutton and a drunkard."[29] Nor is the story particularly flattering in its depiction of Jesus, who addresses his mother rather harshly. And in the raising of Jairus's daughter, another scholar sees the vivid extraneous details, such as Jairus "prostrating himself before Jesus, the pressing throng, Jesus overhearing the message of Jairus' servants," and so on, and the absence of "wild features often found in miracle accounts in the apocryphal gospels," as lending credibility to the story.[30] The same may be said for the story of Lazarus.

Maier also sees circumstantial corroboration for the Lazarus story in the subsequent history of Bethany. The town was destroyed when the Romans attacked Jerusalem in 70 CE, but it was rebuilt later and renamed by the Arabs who settled there. "The Israelis today call it Bethanya but the Arabs call it el-Azariyeh, 'the place of Lazarus,'" says Maier. "I find that fascinating. Why would they change the name of the town unless something spectacular happened there?"[31]

Clearly, there is a vast and largely ideological divide over the question of Jesus' deeds. Critical scholars generally accept the notion of Jesus as a healer and an exorcist but not as one who performed miracles of nature. And whatever curative abilities he may have had they find reducible to natural explanations; those abilities do not make him divine, nor even particularly unique.

Scholars with a higher view of Scripture maintain a greater openness to the notion of divine sovereignty over nature's laws and consider the essential accuracy of the miracle accounts to be supported by secondary textual and historical evidence. And yet they agree that the miracles of Jesus cannot be proven.

Where does all of this leave the Jesus of the gospels? If the skeptics are correct and he was not unique in working "wondrous acts," are his claims diminished? Can the Bible still be true?

This, as some perceptive scholars note, is where the debate over the words and deeds of Jesus has so often gone astray. What was Jesus' real purpose in healing the sick and performing other amazing deeds? Was it to gain a following and prove his divinity? Wright and others make a convincing argument that it was not. Rather, they contend, Jesus' miracles were a direct extension of his teaching of the kingdom of God—a teaching that some considered to be a threat to the social and religious order but that brought liberation and restoration to those who received it.

Without giving an inch on the authenticity of Jesus' miracles, Wright notes that in describing Jesus' deeds, the writers of the gospels used Greek words such as *paradoxa* ("the unexpected"), *dunameis* ("displays of power"), and words connoting "signs and portents," rather than terms that today would be equated with a supernatural display or an "invasion from another world."[32]

Though there were other healers, Jesus' unexpected displays of power, says Wright, would have been understood by first-century Jews as unique in that they were "signs of the long-awaited fulfillment of prophecy." The healings were "in exact parallel with the welcome of sinners" and could be seen as the "restoration to membership in Israel of those who, through sickness or whatever, had been excluded as ritually unclean."[33] Wright concludes:

> *Within the public career of Jesus, therefore, the mighty works were not simply showy magic, nor the attempt to win support from crowds, and certainly not in themselves indications or hints that Jesus was "divine." ... They were signs which were intended as, and would have been perceived as, the physical inauguration of the kingdom of Israel's god, the putting into action of the welcome and the warning which were the central*

*message of the kingdom and its redefinition. They were an integral part of the entire ministry, part of the same seamless robe as the parables, and on a level with Jesus' other characteristic actions.*[34]

Seen in that light, the gospel portrait of Jesus of Nazareth appears far clearer, more consistent, and more credible than contentious scholarly discourse often makes it out to be. The Jesus of the gospels emerges as a bearer of hope, a doer and sayer of the unexpected. His message and miracle correspond. And the unknown man from Galilee becomes less of a stranger to our times.

## CHAPTER 22

# DEATH AND
# RESURRECTION

## THE LAST DAYS

## OF JESUS

THE PASSION OF CHRIST—HIS SUFFERING, DEATH, AND RESURRECTION, so vividly described in the gospels—forms the foundation of the Christian faith. For the apostle Paul, it was "the good news," the very heart of the gospel, and "the power of God unto salvation."[1] Yet, for events so momentous, the crucifixion and its aftermath have been subjects of endless controversy.

Prior to the eighteenth century, few biblical scholars or theologians challenged the basic historical accuracy of the Passion story as it is related in various levels of detail in all four gospels. But as post-Enlightenment scholars began critically examining the Scriptures and other records in their quest for the historical Jesus, attention became focused on how the gospels differed as to some important details of the story and on certain dramatic elements that some skeptical scholars simply found too incredible to believe. Over the centuries, it is safe to say, no other execution has been examined more carefully or debated with more intensity.

What has all of this study produced? While some scholars have come to reject the Passion narratives as pure fiction, others have found evidence to buttress their belief in the solid historical core of the gospel accounts. That might seem to suggest that the truth lies somewhere in between. But does it? How accurate are the gospels as they tell the familiar story of the arrest, trial, and crucifixion of Jesus? How credible is their testimony concerning the imponderable events of that miraculous "third day" in Jerusalem? As the ongoing debate suggests, the evidence is not clear-cut in every respect. But modern scholarship has shed important new light on the Bible's account of Jesus' last days.

## THE TRIUMPHAL ENTRY

Then they brought the colt to Jesus and threw their cloaks on it; and he sat on it. Many people spread their cloaks on the road, and others spread leafy branches that they had cut in the fields. Then those who went ahead and those who followed were shouting, "Hosanna! Blessed is the one who comes in the name of the Lord!"

*Mark 11:7–9*

It was a hero's welcome, the early Palestinian equivalent of a ticker-tape parade, that greeted the Galilean preacher and his band of followers as they rode into Jerusalem for the Passover observance. In Palm Sunday sermons, the story of Jesus' triumphal entry into the City of David often is cited to demonstrate the fickleness of the Jerusalem crowd, whose excited messianic shouts of "Hosanna!" would soon give way to vengeful cries of "Crucify him!"

But after examining the Scriptures and other more recently discovered ancient texts, some scholars now take a more sympathetic view of the actions of the Jerusalem crowd. That there was widespread confusion about the political and theological significance of Jesus is not the least surprising, given what historians now know about the religious turmoil of the times. While people no doubt found Jesus to be powerfully captivating and charismatic, he constantly surprised them by saying and doing the unexpected. He defied easy labels. Then as now, the Man from Nazareth was for many a great enigma.

In any event, few scholars now believe that the Palm Sunday procession was the spontaneous outpouring of acclaim that tradition has depicted. They note, for instance, that Luke's gospel says that Jesus "sent messengers ahead of him" (9:52)—advance men, as it were, who presumably spread word of his amazing deeds and his authoritative teachings. Stories of his run-ins with local religious leaders in nearby towns likely would have played well with the people of Jerusalem, who not only despised the Romans but were disenchanted with their collaborators in the temple hierarchy. Even those who did not believe Jesus to be Israel's Messiah, says Donald Senior, a New Testament scholar and president of the Catholic Theological Union of Chicago, "would have been willing to band around someone who was seen as an anti-establishment figure."[2]

Although many of the Palm Sunday revelers no doubt thought they were cheering the Messiah, their understanding of that term was almost certainly different from that embraced by Christian orthodoxy today. Judaism in Jesus' time was wracked by sectarian rivalry. The Pharisees, a lay reform movement strong in the village synagogues, were at odds with the Sadducees, the party of the priests who dominated the temple. In the Judean wilderness were the Essenes, a radical apocalyptic sect that rejected the temple establishment, and the insurrectionist Zealots, whose main objective was throwing off Roman rule. Each would have had different expectations for the Messiah: a military deliverer, a priestly king who would restore Israel's religious fervor, a mystical figure who would usher in a new age.

Whomever they thought Jesus to be, it is likely that many in the Jerusalem crowd that day expected him to march into the city and lead an attack on the Roman garrison. Instead, he attacked the abuses of the temple court, challenging the very power structure of Jerusalem.

In the traditional story, Jesus often is described as suddenly enraged when he enters the temple and sees the rampant buying and selling. But some modern commentators contend that his actions were carefully premeditated. They note that Mark's gospel indicates that when Jesus arrived in Jerusalem, he "went into the temple; and when he had looked around at everything, as it was already late, he went out to Bethany with the twelve" (11:11), and there considered what action he would take. When he returned the following day to drive out the money-changers, it amounted to open and premeditated defiance of the temple authorities.

Some scholars doubt whether the incident happened exactly the way the gospels describe. The story, says Paula Fredriksen, professor of ancient Christianity at Boston University, "is excellent theology. It's just terrible history."[3] The selling of sacrificial animals in the temple court, she notes, was a long-standing practice that enabled pilgrims to meet their religious obligations. And portraying Jesus as chasing the money-changers from the temple, says Robert Funk of the Jesus Seminar, "is not a realistic picture. There must have been hundreds of them, especially on a festival day."[4] Some scholars also argue that an apparent chronological discrepancy casts further doubt on the story's historicity. While Matthew, Mark, and Luke report the temple incident as occurring after Jesus' final entry into Jerusalem just days before his arrest, John's gospel seems to have him performing the deed at the very beginning of his ministry.

Not all scholars find such arguments persuasive—certainly not to the point of dismissing the entire account as fiction. In fact, there is broad consensus that an incident at the temple at least somewhat akin to the gospel accounts of Jesus' provocative act lies behind the biblical narratives. The fact alone that all four gospels attest to it—the "multiple attestation" argument—makes it reasonable to conclude that the story has a historical basis.

The exact nature of the incident, however, and the historicity of each of the details are matters of ongoing debate. Some have suggested that Jesus may have protested the temple tax or the use of coins with pagan images. Others theorize that he was angered that the selling of animals had taken over the only area in the temple where Gentiles were permitted to pray.[5] Many are convinced that Jesus was purging the temple of commercial corruption—purifying what the gospels said had become "a den of thieves"—and that in doing so he was showing himself to be the Messiah who would restore Israel.[6] Still others believe that he was challenging the temple establishment itself as a first step toward establishing a new religious order.

Whatever the exact nature of Jesus' deed, says Bruce Chilton, professor of religion at Bard College in Annandale-on-Hudson, New York, "an act against the Temple would have been perceived by the Romans as an attack on the status quo." And that would have made Jesus a prime candidate for arrest. The temple, after all, was not only the religious and social center of the city; it was of prime commercial importance as well. As Raymond Brown notes, the temple was being rebuilt at the time, "and a great number of people were employed in the rebuilding."[7] Whenever pilgrims came to Jerusalem for Jewish festivals, the temple brought in money for food, lodging, and sacrifices. Historians note that years earlier, the Jewish high priest had led an army north to destroy the Samaritan temple because it had been perceived as a dangerous rival.[8] "What Jesus did," says New Testament professor Jerome Neyrey of the University of Notre Dame, "was like attacking the Bank of America, and they simply squished him."[9]

## THE ARREST AND TRIAL

> Then they seized him and led him away, bringing him into the
> high priest's house. . . . When day came, the assembly of the elders
> of the people, both chief priests and scribes, gathered together, and
> they brought him to their council. They said, "If you are the
> Messiah, tell us." He replied, "If I tell you, you will not believe." . . .
> Then the assembly rose as a body and brought Jesus before Pilate.
> They began to accuse him. Then Pilate asked him, "Are you the
> king of the Jews?" He answered, "You say so." Then Pilate said
> to the chief priests and the crowds, "I find no basis for an
> accusation against this man."
>
> *Luke 22:54, 66–68; 23:1–4*

The arrest and trial of Jesus have long attracted the interest of historians and Bible scholars seeking to answer the compelling central question of the Passion: Why did Jesus die? It is a question that traditionally has yielded a theological response: Jesus died to atone for sin and to provide salvation for the world. But for generations, scholars have looked for a more historical understanding by seeking to unravel the legal and political intricacies of what is without question the world's most celebrated case of capital punishment.

Stripped to the essentials, scholars say, the charges against Jesus were blasphemy and sedition. He was accused by religious leaders of claiming to be the Messiah and of threatening the temple. And he was accused before Pontius Pilate, the Roman procurator, of claiming to be "King of the Jews"—a title that the ancient chronicler Josephus notes was commonly assumed by revolutionaries of that era. It is that charge, scholars believe, that accounts for Jesus' execution at the hands of the Romans. "The Romans," says Senior, "would hardly become excited about any Jew's claims to be a Son of God or a Messiah, unless those claims implied political power, as Jesus' enemies suggested they did."[10]

The extent to which Jewish authorities contributed to the death of Jesus is a complicated and sensitive issue, given the anti-Semitic theologies that have used the New Testament accounts to promote their legitimacy. In fact, the gospels suggest that opposition to Jesus among Jewish leaders was by no means unanimous. At least two members of the Jewish high council—Joseph of Arimathea and Nicodemus—are portrayed as sympathizers. Today, theologies that seek to use the Passion narratives to excuse anti-Semitism are universally repudiated.

Even so, Jesus did have plenty of enemies among Jewish leaders in Jerusalem. He had accused the Pharisees of hypocrisy, challenged the Sadducees' theology, and espoused unconventional interpretations of Mosaic law. Most important, he was perceived as having threatened to "destroy the temple"—an affront that the priests could not tolerate. They saw little choice but to move against Jesus.

But what had Jesus *really* said about the temple's destruction? The gospel authors attribute to him a *prediction* that the temple would be destroyed—"Do you see these great buildings? Not one stone will be left here upon another; all will be thrown down" (Mark 13:2 and parallels)—and attribute to his accusers at his trial the false testimony that he *threatened* to destroy the temple (Mark 14:58; Matt. 26:61).

Some modern scholars argue that Jesus probably never said anything like the words reported in the gospel narratives. His "prediction" so closely presages what the Romans actually did in 70 CE, they argue, that it almost certainly reflects an attempt by the authors, writing *after* the destruction of Jerusalem, to enhance Jesus' reputation as a prophet. But as E. P. Sanders points out, Jesus' prediction was not precisely fulfilled. When the Romans destroyed the city some forty years later, they left much of the temple's support-work intact. Indeed, the massive stones are still standing today along the western wall of the Temple Mount. Sanders observes that "when a later writer composes a bogus prophecy—the prophecy and the event are usually in perfect agreement. Had the prediction of Mark . . . been written after 70, we would expect it to say that the Temple would be destroyed by fire, not that the stone walls would be completely torn down." This prophecy, Sanders concludes, "is probably pre-70, and it may be Jesus' own."[11]

It certainly is understandable, given that Jesus' words (assuming they were authentic) were coupled with his symbolic action of overturning temple tables, that some people may have perceived Jesus as threatening the temple. "This created deep offense," notes Sanders, which surfaced not only during the trial, and again when Jesus hung on the cross (Mark 15:29; Matt. 27:40), but also later in accusations against the martyr Stephen (Acts 6:14). "We cannot attribute this persistent tradition of a threat against the Temple to the authors of the gospels," says Sanders. "They wished it would go away."[12]

Both Jesus' seeming indifference to the charges against him and the manner in which he testified in his own defense puzzle modern historians seeking to reconstruct the events. Each of the synoptic gospels depicts a taciturn Jesus responding somewhat differently when asked by the priests if he is the Messiah: "I am," in Mark; "That is what you say," in Matthew; "If I tell you, you will not believe," in Luke. To Pilate's question, "Are you the king of the Jews?" he responds in each account, "You say so." In John's Gospel, a more talkative Jesus engages the high priest in a verbal sparring match and tells Pilate that his kingdom "is not of this world."[13]

Even though the gospels indicate that Peter and perhaps another disciple witnessed the proceedings, some modern scholars doubt that any of Jesus' followers were present. On that basis, they conclude that the trial narratives are literary inventions—a rather radical way of accounting for relatively minor variations in the dialogue. As Dallas Theological Seminary professor Darrell Bock and others have noted, while the dialogue may not reflect the consistency of a tape-recorded transcript, the accounts accurately summarize the gist of the event. Bock explains: "Whether Jesus said 'I am' or used the idiom 'You are right in saying I am' [Luke 22:70, NIV]—an ancient expression that means, 'It is as you say but not with the sense you mean'—he affirmed his identification as Messiah, Son of God."[14]

In any event, the question of titles was not the real issue in the trial. As Sanders notes, Caiaphas, the high priest, had had Jesus arrested because of his actions against the temple, but the testimony of witnesses as Caiaphas pursued the matter had been inconsistent. Unwilling to drop the case, says Sanders, Caiaphas "fell back on titles, and declared that Jesus' answer was blasphemy—no matter what he said. We do not have to decide whether Jesus answered 'yes' or 'maybe.' The high priest had already made up his mind."[15] The rest of the court went along.

While Caiaphas traditionally is depicted as the villain of the story, history may have treated him too harshly. The high priest in those days was responsible for keeping order in and around the temple. If he failed to do so, the Roman prefect would intervene militarily. The safety of the populace and the preservation of the temple itself depended on his doing his job. Any perceived threat against the temple—especially one accompanied by a violent table-turning demonstration—could not be tolerated. "It is highly probable," says Sanders, "that Caiaphas was . . . concerned with the possibility that Jesus would incite a riot. He sent armed guards to arrest Jesus, he gave him a hearing, and he recommended execution to Pilate, who promptly complied."[16] The life of one man would have seemed to Caiaphas a small price to pay to preserve order in Jerusalem.

Pilate's actions as well may have been misunderstood. In each of the gospel accounts, the apparently indecisive and weak-willed Roman procurator declares Jesus innocent, yet ultimately yields to the demands of the priests and the angry crowd to condemn him. But like Caiaphas, say some historians, Pilate may have been concerned primarily to prevent anti-Roman sentiments from exploding in a city crowded with Passover pilgrims—though he could not have failed to consider the deleterious effect such an explosion would have had on his own career.

He was justifiably concerned, as well, about offending the chief priest and Herod Antipas, the governor of Galilee. First-century historians note that Pilate had been reprimanded by the emperor Tiberius for offending the Jewish leaders on at least two previous occasions. On one of those occasions, Pilate infuriated the temple priests by allowing his troops to carry insignias bearing the image of Tiberius into Jerusalem, in violation of the Jewish law against graven images. Later, Pilate set up golden shields in his Jerusalem headquarters that bore inscriptions honoring Tiberius. Herod Antipas angrily protested that action directly to the emperor, who responded with a scathing letter warning Pilate to uphold the religious and political customs of his Jewish subjects.[17] Pilate was put on a short leash. He could not afford another incident.

That, say scholars, is why in Luke's account a frustrated Pilate sends Jesus to Herod. Rather than an act of indecision or of principled reluctance to condemn an innocent man, suggests Harold Hoehner, professor of New Testament at Dallas Theological Seminary, it was a "diplomatic courtesy" to improve relations with Herod by acknowledging his jurisdiction in affairs involving Galileans.

The strategy worked. Pilate and Herod later became friends.[18] An incident had been averted. Now if the temple priests wanted Jesus condemned, Pilate would oblige.

## THE CRUCIFIXION

So they took Jesus; and carrying the cross by himself, he went out to
what is called The Place of the Skull . . . There they crucified him, and
with him two others.

*John 19:17–18*

Just twenty years after the trial and crucifixion of Jesus in Jerusalem, the
apostle Paul, a former Pharisee, would write to Christians in Corinth: "Jews demand signs and Greeks desire wisdom, but we proclaim Christ crucified . . . the
power of God and the wisdom of God" (1 Cor. 1:22–24). In that relatively
short time, the followers of Jesus had come to see his brutal execution on a hill
outside of Jerusalem as a source of triumph, and the instrument of his death—
the cross—as a symbol of hope.

But on the day of the crucifixion, the cross was an object of suffering and
horror. According to the gospels, Jesus was flogged and beaten and forced to
carry a heavy wooden beam through the city to the place of his execution.
There he was attached to the cross with iron nails driven through his feet and
hands. He died within six hours, probably of asphyxiation. A spear was thrust
into his side to assure his death.

While some of the details may be disputed, the central fact that Jesus, a
man in his late twenties or early thirties, was executed in Roman-occupied
Palestine is well corroborated by extrabiblical sources. The Roman historian
Tacitus, writing in 110 CE of the persecution of Christians under the emperor
Nero, refers to followers of "Christ whom the procurator Pontius Pilate had executed in the reign of Tiberius."[19] And the Babylonian Talmud, as noted in the
previous chapter, mentions the execution of Jesus "on the eve of Passover . . .
because he has practiced sorcery and led Israel astray."[20]

Yet the mode of Jesus' execution, as graphically described in the gospels, has
long been a subject of historical inquiry (and, until recently, some skepticism).
During the nineteenth and early twentieth centuries, some scholars questioned
the crucifixion story on a number of counts. Some argued, for instance, that it
was more common in first-century Palestine for criminals to be executed by
some other means—stoning, burning, beheading, or strangling—and then (already dead) "hanged on a tree" as a warning to others. Others added that because crucifixion was a Roman mode of execution—one not permitted in
Jewish law—it is unlikely that the temple priests would have called for Jesus to
be crucified, as the gospels report.[21] Still other scholars questioned the historicity of such details as the shape of the cross depicted in Christian tradition and
the use of nails rather than bindings to attach the victim to the cross.

But archaeological discoveries and textual research in recent years have added considerable weight to the gospel accounts. Two manuscripts found among the Dead Sea Scrolls—the Temple Scroll and the so-called Pesher of Nahum—suggest that Mosaic law may have been understood in Jesus' time to prescribe crucifixion in certain cases.[22] The German scholar Ernst Bammel has noted that execution by crucifixion had been used in Palestine since the second century BCE—even by Jewish courts. Because it was a particularly gruesome form of punishment, notes Bammel, "it was used especially in political cases," such as those involving perceived rebellion against the Romans.[23] Striking corroboration of the type of crucifixion described in the gospels was provided by the discovery of the remains of the crucified man Yehohanan in Jerusalem in 1968, as was discussed in Chapter 11.

Another aspect of the crucifixion account that has been challenged is the description of midday darkness over the city as Jesus hung on the cross. Using computer models, astronomers have ruled out a solar eclipse in Palestine at that time. And while they say a lunar eclipse did occur on April 3 in 33 CE, it would not have been seen in Jerusalem during the daylight hours (and in any event would not have accounted for daytime darkness).

However, some scholars speculate that a spring sirocco—a high-altitude, dust-laden wind common to that part of the Middle East—could easily have darkened the midday sky just as the gospel writers described.[24]

## THE BURIAL

> Now when evening had come, there came a rich man from Arimathea, named Joseph, who himself had also become a disciple of Jesus. This man went to Pilate and asked for the body of Jesus. . . . And when Joseph had taken the body, he wrapped it in a clean linen cloth and laid it in his new tomb which he had hewn out of the rock; and he rolled a large stone against the door of the tomb and departed.
>
> *Matthew 27:57–60*

After the dramatic events at Golgotha, site of the crucifixion, the burial scene depicted in the gospels seems subdued and anticlimactic. Yet it serves an important function in the Passion story by confirming the somber reality of the crucifixion: Jesus was indeed dead.

With the confused and frightened disciples in hiding, according to all four gospels, a member of the Sanhedrin stepped forward to claim the body and give it an honorable burial in a rock-cut tomb. In the days that followed, the tomb would take on great significance as friends and foes of the crucified carpenter were confronted with one of the greatest paradoxes of history.

Although many questions concerning Jesus' fate have echoed through the centuries, his actual death on the cross has never been convincingly contested. The "swoon theory"—that Jesus was put into a drug-induced coma and was later revived—first was suggested by the second-century pagan philosopher Celsus, and it still gets an occasional airing in polemical works.[25] But according to the gospels, there were many witnesses at Golgotha, including the Roman soldiers specifically charged with overseeing the execution. Additionally, Mark's narrative notes that Pilate personally confirmed Jesus' death. There was no reason to suspect that Jesus had survived the cross. Even when anti-Christian propaganda later attempted to challenge the resurrection claim, it tended to allege that the body had been taken, not that Jesus had not died.

Despite general agreement on the death of Jesus, however, some modern critics question what they consider to be incongruent details in the accounts of the burial. Why, for example, would Pontius Pilate have given the body to a known disciple of Jesus, as two of the gospels describe Joseph of Arimathea— or, for that matter, to a member of the Sanhedrin who, according to Luke, had sided with Jesus during the trial? Doing either would have seemed to invite mischief. The narratives make clear that Pilate and the Jerusalem authorities were concerned that Jesus' followers might attempt to steal the body in order to claim a miracle that would keep the movement alive. Matthew even relates that Pilate posted a guard at the tomb, although some skeptics believe that that convenient detail may have been deliberately incorporated into the story to refute the theft theory.

One current explanation is that Joseph was not a disciple at the time, but became one later. In that case, some scholars argue, Matthew may be understood as having incorporated Joseph's post-resurrection career into the burial account by describing him as a disciple. Other text critics consider it implausible that an observant Jew like Joseph would have handled a corpse—let alone that of a crucified criminal—on the eve of Passover. Such an act would have rendered him unclean under Mosaic law.

However, Raymond Brown has noted that a "pious, law-observant member of the Sanhedrin" also would have been aware of the law's requirement in Deuteronomy 21:22–23 regarding the disposal of the remains of those who have been hanged: "His body shall not remain all night on the tree; but you shall bury him the same day, for a hanged man is accursed by God." In the Temple Scroll from Qumran and in the writings of Philo, Brown notes, the Deuteronomy text is cited as pertaining to crucifixion as well. Joseph, says Brown, would have understood that a body must not be left on the cross after sunset, a situation perhaps made even more urgent by the approach of the Sabbath. Burial, then, would have been seen "as a necessary good that overshadowed the accompanying impurity."[26]

Other evidence favoring Joseph's role in the burial is that he is one of just a handful of lesser characters in the Passion story whose names were remembered through the period of oral tradition. Another is Simon of Cyrene, whom the gospels describe as having helped Jesus carry the cross and who, tradition says, became a disciple sometime after the events of Easter.

Others question whether the borrowed tomb of Jesus actually belonged to Joseph, as only Matthew states. Some Bible scholars deem it unlikely that a wealthy member of the Sanhedrin would have owned a tomb so close to a crucifixion site, an area where criminals were buried. Others speculate that Joseph did not own the tomb at the time but bought it later, after the Easter event had transformed it into a site of reverence and awe.

Some scholars, John Dominic Crossan perhaps the most prominent, have argued that Jesus' corpse probably was not buried at all, but was left hanging on the cross to be devoured by birds and wild dogs, since that was the common treatment of rebels and traitors executed by the Romans.[27] However, there is nothing in early anti-Christian propaganda to suggest that that is what happened, nor can it be deduced from anything hidden between the lines of Scripture. It is the kind of speculative conclusion that is born of necessity if one rejects the story's ending as it is recorded in the gospels.

## THE RESURRECTION

> Very early in the morning, on the first day of the week, they came to the
> tomb when the sun had risen. . . . But when they looked up, they saw
> that the stone had been rolled away. . . . And entering the tomb, they
> saw a young man clothed in a long white robe sitting on the right side;
> and they were alarmed. But he said to them, "Do not be alarmed. You
> seek Jesus of Nazareth, who was crucified. He is risen! He is not here."

*Mark 16:2–6a*

It is Christianity's most irreducible tenet: on the third day, Jesus arose from the grave. From the very beginning, Christians have proclaimed the resurrection a validation of all that Jesus taught and all that they believe him to be. It is the foundation upon which all else rests. The apostle Paul recognized this when he wrote to the church in Corinth in 56 CE, saying that "if Christ has not been raised, then our proclamation has been in vain and your faith has been in vain" (1 Cor. 15:14).

Yet despite its centrality, or perhaps because of it, the resurrection has been subjected to more historical second-guessing and theological dispute than perhaps any other tenet of Christianity. What occurred on that Easter morning that would turn a defeated and disoriented movement into a vibrant new faith? If the cameras had been rolling in that tomb outside the walls of Jerusalem, what would they have recorded? Are the gospel narratives an accurate reflection of a real, historical event? As Sanders observes, "Nothing is more mysterious than the stories of [the] resurrection, which attempt to portray an experience that the authors could not themselves comprehend."[28]

There are no resurrection stories per se in the Bible, no eyewitness accounts of Jesus rising from the dead. For modern readers of the gospels, as for the first hearers of the Christian proclamation, the resurrection is largely a deduction drawn from two pieces of data: the discovery of an empty tomb and the testimony of Jesus' disciples that he appeared to them in Jerusalem and Galilee. How do those data stand up under scholarly examination today?

Although there may be conflicting testimony on some of the details, the weight of textual evidence presents a strong case that the empty tomb was indeed a part of the earliest gospel tradition. All four accounts relate the surprising early-morning discovery by Mary Magdalene and others. Yet they seem to disagree on the particulars. Were there three women visitors (Mark), two (Matthew), or one (John)? Did the women arrive before dawn (Matthew, John) or after (Mark)? Was the stone rolled away after (Matthew) or before they arrived (Mark, Luke, John)? Were angels present (Matthew, Mark, and Luke, yes; John, no)? Such textual disagreements often are portrayed as evidence that the stories were invented, or at least embellished, by later Christian tradition. Scholars with a higher view of biblical historicity have attempted over the years to harmonize the differences—with varying degrees of success.[29] In any event, few New Testament experts think those differences obscure the basic fact that on that first Easter morning the tomb was empty.

Archaeological evidence is sometimes cited as indirectly supporting the finding of an empty tomb. It was customary in Judaism at the time for relatives of the deceased to return to a grave a year afterward to gather up the skeletal remains and place them in a box called an *ossuary*. For many Jews, the practice was associated with the belief in a general resurrection that would occur at the end of the age. Storing the remains in an ossuary was a way of ensuring that God would have all the parts, as it were, with which to "reconstruct" the body on that Day of the Lord. There was, in other words, a distinct physicality to the

Jewish concept of resurrection. It was not seen as some vaguely spiritual event. It involved real bodies reanimated and restored in an inexplicable and surely miraculous act of God.

The physicality of the concept is significant as we attempt to weigh the claims of Jesus' disciples. Their testimony, after all, was that Jesus had been resurrected—not translated and directly ascended in the manner of the prophet Elijah. Unless there had been a tomb into which Jesus was known to have been laid and which subsequently was found empty, says James Dunn, of the University of Durham, the claims of the disciples that Jesus had been resurrected "would not have cut much ice."[30] Nor would their testimony have been given much credence had it been widely known at the time that some other fate had befallen Jesus' body—that it had been thrown into a mass grave with other criminals, for example, or left for wild dogs and birds to devour. "The absence of such a counter claim in any available literature of the period (Christian or Jewish) is therefore important," says Dunn.[31] Significant, too, is the fact that when the resurrection claim *was* disputed, the argument was based on the suspicion that Jesus' disciples came by night and stole the body away. In other words, it was a counterexplanation as to why the tomb had been found empty, not a dispute of the fact of an empty tomb.[32]

Interestingly, as Dunn notes, the earliest gospel—Mark, written between 50 and 70 CE—ends with an empty tomb but includes no resurrection appearances. Meanwhile, the earliest nongospel account of resurrection appearances—Paul's first letter to the Corinthians, written in about 55 CE—makes no reference to an empty tomb. "This degree of independence and lack of correlation between the two earliest records," says Dunn, "speaks favorably for the value of each. There is nothing to indicate that one was contrived to bolster the other."[33]

Indeed, if the gospel stories of an empty tomb were merely pious inventions to support the Christian proclamation of the resurrection, they were poorly conceived. As Stephen Davis, a professor of philosophy and religious studies at Claremont McKenna College, observes:

> If the story is an apologetic legend invented by later Christians, why does it (in Mark's original version) lead only to fear, flight, and silence on the part of the women? If the story is an apologetic legend . . . why is it so openly admitted that some of Jesus' followers were suspiciously in the vicinity of the tomb early on the morning of the discovery of the empty tomb? And why is there no mention made of any thorough investigation of the tomb or its environs, or of some verifying word from Joseph of Arimathea? As an apologetic argument, this one seems weak.[34]

Moreover, if the gospel writers were hoping to concoct the strongest possible story, they undermined their own cause—as they would have known—by depicting women as the discoverers of the empty tomb. In the heavily patriarchal Jewish culture of the first century, notes Boyd, "the testimony of women generally counted for nothing. Indeed, in most cases they were not even allowed to testify in court."[35] The only logical reason for including them, then, is to relate what really happened: the women discovered the empty tomb.

Rather than pious propaganda or religious myth, the far more reasonable conclusion to be drawn from the evidence is that the discovery of the empty tomb is an early and independent tradition—one that is firmly rooted in history.

What of the reports of post-resurrection appearances of the risen Christ? The earliest attestation comes from the apostle Paul in his first letter to the Corinthians (15:3–8). Writing two to four decades before the gospels were composed, Paul recited what seems to have been a formula—one that he no doubt repeated often as he proclaimed the gospel on his missionary journeys:

> *For I handed on to you as of first importance what I in turn had received: that Christ died for our sins in accordance with the scriptures, and that he was buried, and that he was raised on the third day in accordance with the scriptures, and that he appeared to Cephas, then to the twelve. Then he appeared to more than five hundred brothers and sisters at one time, most of whom are still alive, though some have died. Then he appeared to James, then to all the apostles. Last of all, as to one untimely born, he appeared also to me.*

In all four gospels, these basic facts of Christ's appearances are woven into richly detailed narratives. The details are so rich, in fact, that at times they seem to disagree. Here too, however, the "problem" of diversity of details must be properly weighed.

In all, the gospels seem to report ten separate occasions on which the risen Christ appears to his followers. Matthew and John have him appearing first at the tomb; Mark puts him elsewhere. And while Matthew, Mark, and John describe appearances in Galilee, Luke seems to limit Jesus to Jerusalem. The writers also differ in how they describe the risen Jesus. Luke and John depict him in concrete, physical terms: he eats; he invites a doubting disciple to touch his wounds. Paul's risen Christ, who appears later on the road to Damascus, is more spiritual than physical.

Some scholars—members of the Jesus Seminar, for instance—consider these to be "egregious contradictions" that undercut any possible claim to credibility.[36]

Seminar member Thomas Sheehan, a philosophy professor at Loyola University in Chicago, captures the gist of the skeptics' argument against the post-resurrection appearances:

> The reasons both for the patent inconsistencies and the physical unrecordability of these miraculous "events" come down to one thing: The gospel stories about Easter are not historical accounts but religious myths. . . . They are myths and legends; and it is absurd to take them literally and to create a chronology of preternatural events that supposedly occurred in Jerusalem and Galilee during the weeks after Jesus died.[37]

There is little question that the four gospels offer differing details as they attempt to describe appearances of the risen Christ. Those differences cannot be ignored, nor can they easily be harmonized into a single intelligible chronology—although many have tried. But rather than undercutting the historicity of the gospel accounts, or exposing them as a pious fabrication, the variations on certain details make the testimony of the gospels all the more credible, according to many scholars.

As was noted in Chapter 3, most scholars acknowledge a degree of interdependence among the gospels. It seems clear by the sometimes word-for-word duplication in their accounts of Jesus' ministry that some sharing of sources or borrowing of material went on, particularly among the three synoptic gospels: Matthew, Mark, and Luke. Yet significantly, this does not seem true of their accounts of the resurrection. While the gospels agree on the core facts—women finding the tomb empty and Jesus appearing to various disciples—they diverge on many of the details surrounding those facts. The details are so different, in fact, that as Boyd observes, "it is impossible to explain them as mere editorial alterations of a single source."[38]

Instead, the gospel writers seem to have drawn on independent sources for their resurrection material. To many scholars, the fact that those independent and sometimes diverging sources agree on the central fact that the risen Christ appeared to his disciples is a powerful indicator that they are reporting authentic history. As the German historian Hans Stier has written:

> [T]he sources for the resurrection of Jesus, with their relatively big contradictions over details, present for the historian for this very reason a criterion of extraordinary credibility. For if that were the fabrication of a congregation or of a similar group of people, then the tale would be consistently and obviously complete. For that reason every historian is especially skeptical at

*that moment when an extraordinary happening is only reported in accounts which are completely free of contradictions.*[39]

In that respect, the testimony of the gospels, as Brown notes, is not unlike that of the courtroom:

*The same event looks different to different people, especially when they look at it with hindsight. . . . The evidence is that of human witnesses, and courtroom experiences show that such evidence needs to be probed to determine exactly what happened. The fact of the Resurrection, not the how, is what comes across persuasively.*[40]

In some circles, the term *resurrection* itself has become a matter of debate. What does the Bible mean when it says God raised Jesus from the dead? Christian tradition says Jesus was physically resurrected, that his dead flesh and bones were miraculously reanimated. But some theologians have sought to reconcile the resurrection with a more rationalistic worldview by describing it as a metaphor appropriated by early Christians who "thought mythically" and for whom a resurrection of their fallen leader had occurred "in their hearts and minds." Sheehan, for example, supposes "it is difficult to let go of someone who has liberated you from the yoke of traditional religion." The disciples, therefore, must have been "so entranced" by the words and deeds of Jesus that, for them, "Jesus had to be alive." Thus their affirmations of the resurrection and of Jesus' appearances, says Sheehan, "are not statements about the post mortem history of Jesus but religious interpretations" of their own subjective experience.[41]

But if that were the case, why would the disciples have bothered to describe what happened to Jesus as a resurrection? As Craig Blomberg points out, "They could simply have referred to Jesus being exalted or glorified, as the rest of the New Testament does, without using language which more naturally implies an empty tomb and a living body."[42] By using resurrection language, the disciples were only making their story more difficult for their contemporaries to comprehend. In first-century Judaism, as we previously noted, resurrection was associated with the end of the age, when it was believed that all the righteous would be raised. It was not regarded as something that would happen to a single individual—not even to the Messiah.

It seems unlikely, then, that the disciples would have described what had happened to Jesus as a resurrection—unless, of course, they believed that is exactly what it was. As Reginald Fuller, New Testament professor emeritus at Virginia Theological Seminary, observes, "Resurrection faith rests upon eyewitnesses who testify not merely to their own belief, but to something which 'happened' additionally to and outside of their belief: God revealed his Son to them as risen from the dead."[43]

What, then, is it reasonable to conclude concerning the gospel accounts of the resurrection?

The New Testament, as we have seen, bears strong and credible witness to two important pieces of historical data: an empty tomb and reports of post-resurrection appearances of the risen Christ. That, of course, falls far short of proving as incontestable objective fact the gospel claim that Jesus of Nazareth was raised from the dead. But it is no small thing. It establishes a credible historical foundation—a basis beyond mere fantasy or wishful thinking—upon which a resurrection faith can stand.

Even the most skeptical of scholars concede that something extraordinary happened in Jerusalem after Good Friday to account for the radical change in the behavior of the disciples who fled in fear at Jesus' arrest. Could Jesus' resurrection account for the fact that within a few weeks they were boldly preaching their message to the very people who had sought to crush them? The historicity of the resurrection is a question that academic inquiry alone is incapable of answering to everyone's satisfaction. Ultimately, the events of the "third day" in Jerusalem must remain, as they have for two thousand years, in the realm of things unprovable—matters to be grasped by faith informed by the credible historical witness of the gospels.

While historical issues continue to dominate modern debates over the Bible, a surprising new controversy has arisen in recent years that raises profound questions concerning the very nature and purpose of the Scriptures. It is a controversy sparked by the startling claims of a small cadre of experts that the true message of the Bible has little to do with the familiar teachings of the ancient text. The Bible's real message, these experts claim, is urgent and for our times—and it lies hidden in a sophisticated secret code that only now can be deciphered. We turn our attention next to the amazing mystery of the "Bible code."

# PART FIVE

# THE BIBLE
# CODE AND
# PROPHECY

# THE AMAZING
# BIBLE CODE

## SECRET MESSAGES FROM GOD?

> The rule is that all that was, is, and will be unto the end of
> time is included in the Torah, from the first word to the
> last word. And not merely in a general sense, but as to the
> details of every species and each one individually, and
> details of details of everything that happened to him from
> the day of his birth until his end.
>
> *Eliyahu ben Shlomo, the Gaon of Vilna, eighteenth century* [1]

> The Bible is not only a book—it is also a computer
> program. It was first chiseled in stone and handwritten on
> a parchment scroll, finally printed as a book, waiting for us
> to catch up with it by inventing a computer. Now it can be
> read as it was always intended to be read.
>
> *Michael Drosnin,* The Bible Code, *1997* [2]

IT IS DIFFICULT TO IMAGINE A MORE COMPELLING MYSTERY: A SECRET
code of acrostic word patterns hidden in the text of the Bible thousands of years
ago that is said to reveal with amazing accuracy the details of events in our time—
and in our future.

Reading the code with a specially designed computer program in 1994,
American journalist Michael Drosnin came across the name of Israeli Prime

Minister Yitzhak Rabin encoded in a skip sequence of Hebrew letters in the Torah—the first five books of the Old Testament. Intersecting Rabin's name in an acrostic pattern was the ominous phrase "assassin that will assassinate." Without delay, Drosnin went to Israel to warn the prime minister that his life was in danger. The encrypted prediction, the journalist told Rabin in a hand-delivered letter, "should not be ignored, because the assassinations of Anwar Sadat and both John and Robert Kennedy are also encoded in the Bible—in the case of Sadat with the first and last names of his killer, and the date of the murder, and the place, and how it was done."[3]

But the warning went unheeded. Fourteen months later, on November 4, 1995, Rabin was shot and killed in Tel Aviv by a man who believed he was on a mission from God. "The assassination of Rabin," Drosnin wrote in his 1997 book *The Bible Code,* "is dramatic confirmation of the reality of the Bible code, the hidden text in the Old Testament that reveals the future."[4]

That was just the beginning. The code is said to have accurately predicted the start of the Gulf War in 1991 and the election of President Clinton in 1992. It knew about President Nixon and Watergate, Adolf Hitler, and Auschwitz, the stock market crash of 1929, and much more. And chillingly, it seems to point to cataclysmic events yet to come: devastating earthquakes in California and China, a comet's catastrophic collision with the earth, and a nuclear holocaust in the Middle East that ignites an apocalyptic World War III—all early in the next century.

What human possibly could have foreseen these events when the Torah was written three thousand years ago, let alone known how to encode messages that would remain indecipherable until the age of computers? Is the code, as some have suggested, proof of the Bible's divine authorship? Is it God's way of revealing himself to a cynical and scientifically sophisticated world? Or is it, as some skeptics have contended from the beginning, merely the product of chance and mathematical manipulation—perhaps even a deliberate hoax?

Whatever it is, the Bible code has found an enthusiastic and credulous audience at the end of the twentieth century. Drosnin's book quickly became an international bestseller, and a major Hollywood studio has reportedly bought the movie rights. Since its publication, at least a half-dozen other books promoting or attacking the code have appeared, including psychiatrist Jeffrey Satinover's *Cracking the Bible Code,* a more technical and less sensational but equally credulous treatment of the subject. Online entrepreneurs, meanwhile, are busy hawking commercial software and elaborate multimedia guides designed to help amateur code-breakers find their own secret messages in the Bible. Some Christian evangelists and Jewish outreach groups have happily embraced the code phenomenon, proclaiming it to be scientific evidence for the existence of God and the truth of the Scriptures.

By all outward appearances, the Bible code has been embraced as a made-for-the-millennium miracle. As *Time* magazine observed, "the mix of Scripture, Jewish mysticism, cyberwizardry and existential dread is year 2000 catnip."[5]

## A CHALLENGING PUZZLE

Almost as amazing as the phenomenon itself is the degree of credibility that the Bible code has managed to maintain within the scientific community. The code as we know it was discovered more than a decade ago by three respected Israeli scientists—physicist Doron Witzum, mathematics professor Eliyahu Rips of Hebrew University, and computer scientist Yoav Rosenberg of the Jerusalem College of Technology. Using a powerful computer program to search the text of the Hebrew Bible, the three claimed to have found unusual pairings of some three hundred conceptually related words embedded in cryptographic sequences in the book of Genesis. For example, "anvil" might be found encoded in close proximity to "hammer," or "table" might be located surprisingly close to "chair" in hidden acrostic patterns. The consistency of the patterns and the proximity of the related words, they said, far exceeded what normal mathematical odds would allow.

The scientists conducted their search by feeding the Hebrew text into a computer and eliminating all spaces between words, so that the entire book of Genesis was one continuous strand of Hebrew letters. In that process, Drosnin contends, the scientists were "restoring the Torah to what great sages say was its original form. According to legend, it was the way Moses received the Bible from God—'contiguous, without break of words.' "[6] Then the scientists used a computer program to search through the strand at progressively larger skip sequences—every third letter, every fourth, every fifth, and so on—until the word they were seeking appeared. Once they found the word, they then would repeat the process in search of related words nearby.

In one amazing and highly publicized experiment, the Israeli scholars found the names of thirty-four famous rabbis from the ninth to the eighteenth centuries, along with their dates of birth or death, hidden in equidistant-letter sequences (ELS) in the Hebrew text of Genesis. The odds of finding such detailed and accurate information in close proximity in so short a text, they said, were less than 1 in 62,500. In most scientific journals, a chance level less than 1 in 20 is said to be considered significant.[7] As a control test, the scholars ran the same search on a similarly sized segment of the Hebrew translation of Tolstoy's *War and Peace* and found virtually no meaningful correlation. The code seemed to apply only to the Bible. Whatever the explanation, the scholars concluded, the phenomenon clearly was "not due to chance."[8]

In drawing such a startling conclusion, the Israeli scientists did not expect to be taken at their word. They submitted their findings to rigorous examination by a peer-reviewed scientific journal, *Statistical Science*, which published their report in 1994. The journal's editor at the time was Robert E. Kass, chairman of the Department of Statistics at Carnegie Mellon University, who explained in an introductory note:

> *Our referees were baffled: their prior beliefs made them think the Book of Genesis could not possibly contain meaningful references to modern-day individuals, yet when the authors carried out additional analyses and checks the effect persisted. The paper is thus offered to* Statistical Science *readers as a challenging puzzle.*[9]

The ELS study also was reviewed by mathematicians at Harvard, Yale, and Hebrew Universities who called the Israeli scholars' work "serious research carried out by serious investigators." While the phenomenon in question, the reviewers said, was "enigmatic and controversial . . . the results obtained are sufficiently striking to deserve a wider audience and to encourage further study."[10] Though not a ringing endorsement, this affirmation clearly added to the code's cachet in the scientific community.

A more dramatic gesture of approbation came later when a skeptical senior code-breaker at the U.S. National Security Agency set out to debunk the Bible code and ended up seemingly doing the opposite. When he first read about the code, Harold Gans, a mathematician and statistics expert fluent in Hebrew, was convinced that it was "off the wall, ridiculous."[11] Using a computer program he had written himself, he went in search of the names and dates that Witzum, Rips, and Rosenberg had sought in their "famous rabbis" experiment. To his great astonishment, the names and dates were there—exactly as the three Israelis had discovered them.

Still not convinced, Gans went looking for more information. "If this was real," he said, "then I figured that the cities where these men were born and died ought to be encoded as well." He also added the names of dozens more famous Jewish sages and their cities to the search list, making a total of sixty-six names in all. Again, the results were positive, this time reflecting a "significance level" of 1 in 200,000.[12] "It sent a chill up my spine," Gans recalls. It also made him a convert. Gans now conducts Bible-code classes in synagogues, claiming that the code is proof of God's authorship of the Bible.[13]

Not everyone in the scientific community is convinced of the code's authenticity, of course. Many scholars understandably remain skeptical, reserving judgment pending further investigation. Others, meanwhile, have offered withering critiques that challenge both the premise and the procedures of the Bible code. We will examine their arguments in some detail in the next chapter. Nonetheless, it has become clear that the Bible-code phenomenon—the occurrence of significant ELS word patterns in the Hebrew Scriptures—cannot be easily brushed aside as a crudely crafted hoax. It has shown itself to be a "challenging puzzle" indeed.

## MYSTICAL ROOTS

Although it took the invention of modern computers to fully explore ELS patterns in the Scriptures, the notion of a Bible code has centuries-old roots in Jewish mysticism. Many scholars trace the notion to the Kabbalah, a tradition of esoteric wisdom dating to the Middle Ages that holds, among other things, that every word, letter, and number that appears in the Torah has mystical significance beyond the plain meaning of the text. "When the Holy One, blessed be He, created the world," declares the Zohar, a sacred Kabbalistic text, "He created it by means of the letters of the Torah . . . by means of the secret power of letters."[14]

Echoes of the Bible-code technique can be seen in the three principal methods used by Kabbalism for searching the hidden meanings of Scripture: *timurah,* a system of uniformly substituting one Hebrew letter for another so that, for example, *aleph,* the first letter, becomes *lamed* by interchange with the twelfth, the second, *beth,* becomes *mem,* the thirteenth, and so on; *gematria,* which interprets words based on their Hebrew numerical value; and *notarikon,* an acrostic system of taking the first letter (or the second or third, etc.) of words in a sentence to make new words.[15]

The great thirteenth-century mystic and sage Rabbi Moses ben Nachman, also known as Nachmanides, referred in several of his writings to hidden words and messages in the Torah. A student of Nachmanides, Rabbenu Bachya ben Asher, found an assortment of significant words spelled out in discernible skip patterns in the Torah. He discovered, for example, that the word "Torah" appears in a skip sequence of fifty letters in four of the first five books of the Bible.[16] And the sixteenth-century Spanish sage Rabbi Moshe Cordevaro, in his often-quoted commentary on the Zohar, observed:

> *The secrets of our holy Torah are revealed through knowledge of combinations, numerology* (gematria), *switching letters, first-and-last letters, shapes of letters, first- and last-verses,* skipping of letters (dilug otiot) *and letter combinations. These matters are powerful, hidden and enormous secrets.*

Because of their great hiddenness, we don't have the ability to fully comprehend them. *Further, to see different angles through these methods is infinite and without limit. On this the Torah says, "its measure is longer than the world."*[17]

By the eighteenth century, the Gaon (genius) of Vilna, the great Lithuanian rabbi and Kabbalist whose words began this chapter, was such a believer in the hidden content of the Torah that he could proclaim that it included "all that was, is, and will be unto the end of time." And finally, in the twentieth century, the brilliant Czechoslovakian rabbi Michael Dov Weissmandl—who is most noted for his heroic efforts during World War II to rescue European Jews from the Holocaust—built on Rabbenu Bachya's work and manually found scores of other related words and names hidden in skip sequences within the Torah. As a precocious youth, Weissmandl had written out the entire 304,805-letter Hebrew text of the Torah in ten-by-ten grids so that he could better visualize the acrostic patterns that would emerge at ten-letter intervals.[18] It was largely Weissmandl's work that inspired scholars in Israel to begin their own word searches of the Torah—searches that eventually would come to include the groundbreaking computer-enhanced research of Witzum, Rips, and Rosenberg.[19]

## PROPHETIC MESSAGES?

Beyond the intriguing scientific questions raised by the ELS phenomenon—whether it can be validated or disproved mathematically—what has made the Bible code so fascinating and so controversial for most people today is its alleged predictive capability and the astounding theological and paranormal explanations some proponents offer to account for its origins. On those most compelling of questions, the code's leading modern proponents are not of one mind.

Can the Bible code predict the future? Drosnin is absolutely convinced it can. The former *Wall Street Journal* reporter made the code's capacity to prognosticate the central thesis of his book. "The Bible code for the first time gives us a direct line to the future," he says. "Instead of relying on prophets who see visions and interpret dreams, we can now access by computer an ancient code hidden in the Bible."[20] Drosnin stops short, however, of saying that the future foretold in the Bible code is foreordained and inalterable. Instead, he sees the code's sometimes foreboding message as a benevolent warning of avoidable calamity. "It is not a promise of divine salvation. It is not a threat of inevitable doom. It is just information. The message of the Bible code is that we can save ourselves."[21]

But Drosnin is virtually alone among the Bible code's key proponents in holding that view. Witzum, Gans, and Rips all emphatically reject any suggestion that ELS patterns in the Bible can be used to foretell future events. "Mr. Drosnin's book," says Witzum, "is based on a false claim. It is impossible to use Torah codes to predict the future." Gans adds that "there is no scientific or mathematical basis for such a statement." And Rips, with whom Drosnin claims to have worked closely in researching his book, flatly declares that "all attempts to extract messages from Torah codes, or to make predictions based on them, are futile and are of no value. This is not only my own opinion, but the opinion of every scientist who has been involved in serious Codes research."[22] In the next chapter, we will visit more closely some of the reasons why scientists, even those who promote the code, reject the validity of alleged Bible-code predictions.

Yet even if the code cannot augur the future, say the scholars, the fact that the Torah seems to contain such accurate historical information encrypted in ELS patterns is itself so extraordinary that it defies conventional explanation. "Every scientist, every mathematician and physicist who understands the code," says Drosnin, "agrees that not even the fastest super-computers we have today—not all the Crays in the war room of the Pentagon, or all of the mainframes at IBM, not all of the computers in the world working together—could have encoded the Bible in the way it was done 3000 years ago."[23]

Who or what, then, is behind the Bible code? As a mathematician and theorist, Rips remains the most cautious in his assessment. "The only conclusion that can be drawn from the scientific research regarding the Torah codes," he says, "is that they exist and that they are not a mere coincidence." The physicist Witzum ventures a bit farther, allowing that the "repercussions of our discovery touch on the very nature of human existence. It can be looked at as the same feeling Robinson Crusoe had when he first discovered the tracks in the sand, that he wasn't alone on the island." Gans, the former American cryptographer, is much more exuberant in declaring that the code "points to a divine author of the Bible. . . . [It is] yet another piece of 'evidence' that this anchor of faith, on which entire belief systems and ways of life have been built, merits careful and serious study." And Satinover, the psychiatrist and author, also sees the code as "the Author's signature"—a latter-day revelation to a cynical and scientifically sophisticated world that "God is precisely who he had said he is" and that the Bible is his handiwork.[24]

Interestingly, it is once again Drosnin—who claims that he does not believe in God—who finds himself alone in his assessment of the source of the Bible code. "I am persuaded only that no human could have encoded the Bible in this way. We do have the first scientific proof that some intelligence outside our own does exist, or at least did exist at the time the Bible was written."[25] Later in his book, Drosnin comes more fully clean on his personal hypothesis: "If the Bible code came from an all-powerful God, he would not need to tell us the future. He could change it himself." Instead, Drosnin theorizes, the Bible code is "the long-awaited contact from another intelligence"—an "alien artifact" from beyond our planet, dictated to Moses by "someone good, but not all-powerful, who wanted to warn us of terrible danger so we could prevent it ourselves."[26]

So whether the Torah was given to Moses by God or by space aliens, believers in the code are convinced that it proves there is much more to the ancient sacred text than meets the eye. The Bible code, virtually all such believers would aver, presents itself as a distinctly and dramatically new way of understanding the Bible. Some even contend, as did some of the Kabbalistic sages of the past, that the encoded messages represent the true significance of the Scriptures.[27] Drosnin, for example, in describing the Bible code as "the Bible beneath the Bible," suggests that the scriptural text is of secondary importance (if not altogether meaningless except as a repository of encrypted messages).[28] If the Bible code could be proven valid beyond a doubt, the repercussions for biblical faith would indeed be immense. It is little wonder that the phenomenon has drawn such intense interest among ordinary readers of the Bible.

Nor is it surprising, given such weighty implications, that the code's validity continues to be challenged by experts in the field of mathematics and probability. While no one yet has claimed to have fully debunked the Bible code, there have been plenty of potent attacks—some of which have cast significant doubt over some of the claims of the code's promoters. We turn now to an examination of the case against the Bible code and of the dark side of the code phenomenon.

## CHAPTER 24

# CRACKING
# THE CODE

## HOW IT WORKS—

## AND DOESN'T

I am the Lord, and there is no other. I did
not speak in secret, in a land of darkness; I did not
say to the offspring of Jacob, "Seek me in chaos."
I the Lord speak the truth, I declare what is right.

*Isaiah 45:18–19*

CONSIDERING THE AMAZING ALLURE OF THE BIBLE-CODE PHENOMENON
and the stunning degree of credulity with which it has been received, it is hardly
surprising that some of its leading proponents have seemed at times to indulge
in a bit of hubris. As his book was rapidly climbing the bestseller lists in 1997,
an obviously annoyed Drosnin responded to the tedious carping of Bible-code
critics and would-be debunkers with a derisive challenge: "When my critics
find a message about the assassination of a prime minister encrypted in *Moby
Dick,*" Drosnin told *Newsweek* magazine, "I'll believe them."[1]

It was a challenge Brendan McKay simply could not resist. A mathematician in the Department of Computer Science at the Australian National University in Canberra, McKay was skeptical from the moment he first heard of a
mysterious Bible code that was said to have predicted Rabin's murder. Since
the 1970s, McKay had written blistering critiques of other notorious "mathematical miracles" purported to exist in Christian, Islamic, and Mormon Scriptures.[2] "I have nothing against religion per se," McKay says of his avocation as a

debunker. "I just have a strong distaste for nonsense that masquerades as science, especially when innocent people are being duped by it."[3]

Taking up the gauntlet Drosnin had cast down, McKay fired up his computer and went searching the Melville classic for ELS-encoded references to assassinated prime ministers. Immediately he found two. The name of Rabin appeared acrostically in the English text near that of his assassin, Igal Amir, and the words "shot dead." Another skip sequence revealed the name of Indian Prime Minister Indira Gandhi, who was shot to death in 1984, intersected by the phrase "the bloody deed."[4]

But that was not all McKay found hidden in the "Moby Dick code." In addition to the prime ministers, he discovered other victims of political assassination. There were the names of Lebanese President Rene Moawad, killed in 1989 when a bomb exploded beside his car ("Moawad" intersected by "car" and "an exploding bomb"); Bolshevik leader Leon Trotsky, who was stabbed to death with an ice pick in 1940 ("Trotsky" near "executed" and "steel head of the lance"); and Austrian Chancellor Englebert Dollfuss, killed by Nazis in Vienna in 1934 ("Dollfuss" and "Wien" intersected by "assassins of a good fellow"). McKay also found references to the deaths of Presidents Kennedy and Lincoln, Martin Luther King, and Princess Diana.[5]

Amazing? McKay doesn't think so. "Once you learn Drosnin's rules (none) and the method (a bit of messy programming) you can find things like this anywhere," says McKay. "The reason it looks amazing is that the number of possible things to look for, and the number of places to look, is much greater than you imagine."[6]

Of course, Drosnin is not the only Bible-code theorist, and meeting his *Moby Dick* challenge does not in itself disprove the existence of significant ELS patterns in the Hebrew text of the Torah. But increasingly intense scrutiny focused on the Bible code by mathematicians such as McKay and scholars in other fields has begun to reveal what some persuasively argue are serious flaws in Bible-code data and methodology and in the premise of the code itself—that divinely encrypted messages lie hidden in the biblical text. All of which suggests that there may be far less to the Bible code than its proponents claim.

## DISSECTING THE CODE

Until recently, most of the debate over the veracity of the Bible code has taken the form of polemical articles posted on Internet Websites and in a few nontechnical publications, such as *Bible Review* and the statistical magazine *Chance*.[7]

That is why the publication of the Witzum, Rips, and Rosenberg "famous rabbis" study in the refereed mathematics journal *Statistical Science* in 1994 seemed to carry such weight. As Drosnin correctly noted in 1997, "in the nearly three years since the Rips-Witzum paper was published, no one has submitted a rebuttal to the math journal."[8]

However, that is no longer the case. In the May 1999 issue of *Statistical Science,* McKay and three other respected scholars—Dror Bar-Natan and Gil Kalai, both of the Department of Mathematics at the Hebrew University of Jerusalem, and Maya Bar-Hillel, of the Department of Psychology and the Center for the Study of Rationality, also at the Hebrew University—offered a carefully crafted and withering refutation of the Witzum-Rips-Rosenberg (WRR) experiment. The four scholars, in a paper subjected to the same rigorous peer-review process as the original study, claim to expose "serious flaws" in WRR's selection and use of data, including "significant circumstantial evidence" that the data was "selectively biased towards a positive result."[9]

McKay and his colleagues found, for example, that there was "enormous 'wiggle-room' available" in the choice of names for the famous rabbis that were run through the computer search. "The literature contains a considerable number of variations in names and their spellings, as well as other appellations such as nicknames and acronyms, but WRR used only a fraction of them," the scholars noted.[10] Coincidentally perhaps, when the four scholars re-ran the famous rabbis experiment using any form of the names other than those used by WRR, the results were "weaker in the great majority of cases. This appears very unlikely to have occurred by chance, suggesting that WRR's data suffers from systematic bias."[11]

The question, say the scholars, is not whether interesting ELS sequences exist in the Bible. Of course they do, just as they do in *Moby Dick* or any other sufficiently long text. McKay and his colleagues even found skip-sequence messages in Ted Kaczynski's "Unabomber" manifesto ("mail," "bomb," and "Free Ted").[12] "The question," say McKay and company, "is whether, as WRR claim, the Bible contains them in compact formations more often than expected by chance."[13] The answer to that, say the four scholars, is an emphatic no:

> *Our most telling evidence against the "codes" is that we cannot find them. All of our many earnest experiments produced results in line with random chance. These included a reenactment of the famous rabbis experiment with the help of an independent expert. In light of these findings, we believe that [Statistical Science former editor] Kass's "challenging puzzle" has been solved.[14]*

Kass thinks so, too. In an introduction to the McKay-and-colleagues paper in *Statistical Science,* the Carnegie Mellon statistics scholar describes the refutation of WRR as "very convincing":

> *Because minor variations in data definitions and the procedure used by Witzum, et al., produce much less striking results, there is good reason to think that the particular forms of words those authors chose effectively "tuned" their method to their data, thus invalidating their statistical test. Considering the work of McKay, Bar-Natan, Bar-Hillel, and Kalai as a whole it indeed appears, as they conclude, that the puzzle has been solved.[15]*

## LETTER FOR LETTER?

Beyond the criticisms leveled against the math and methodology of the WRR study, an array of compelling arguments against the veracity of the Bible code have been raised not only by McKay and his colleagues, but by a host of other scholarly skeptics.

One of the most stinging of these indictments pertains to the dramatic but misleading claim of some Bible-code proponents concerning the unique character of the code's database—the Hebrew text of the Torah itself. Drosnin misstates the point most grievously. "The Bible code," he says, "was discovered in the original Hebrew version of the Old Testament, the Bible as it was first written."[16] He depicts the text as having been dictated to Moses in a continuous strand of Hebrew letters without spaces or punctuation. It is that very text, says Drosnin, that we have today. "Every Hebrew Bible that now exists," he says, "is the same letter for letter. A Torah—the first five books—cannot be used if even one letter is missing or out of place. And the Bible code uses that now universally accepted Hebrew text."[17]

This is simply dead wrong. As dependable and accurately preserved as the Bible may be, there is virtual unanimity among biblical scholars today that no surviving text of either testament can be rightly considered an exact, letter-for-letter replica of the original autograph—the manuscript as it was first written.

The version of the Hebrew Bible used by WRR, and which Drosnin describes as the original, is indeed the standard text in modern Judaism. It is known as the Koren edition, and it was published in Jerusalem just a few decades ago. The committee of scholars who produced the Koren Bible in the early 1960s drew upon some of the oldest and most authoritative Masoretic manuscripts available, some dating to the ninth and tenth centuries CE. But their editorial work required reconciling differences between those texts—relatively minor differences that had little bearing on the meaning of the text but that certainly affected its overall length and letter count. And in a code that is based on a uniform sequence of skips between letters, scholars say, any variation in the number of letters in the text can have a devastating effect.

As we saw in Chapter 15, the Dead Sea Scrolls have demonstrated the remarkable degree to which the Masoretic text of the Hebrew Bible has survived largely unchanged since the Second Temple period—roughly from the third century BCE through the first century CE. That certainly is an amazing testimony to the overall textual integrity of the Hebrew Scriptures. Yet as Jeffrey H. Tigay, a professor of Hebrew and Semitic languages at the University of Pennsylvania, observes, "the phrase 'largely unchanged' masks a large number of minor variant readings."[18] Some of those variant readings, says Tigay, are "probably more original" than those of the Masoretic text. He explains:

> In Gen. 4:8, the Masoretic text reads: "And Cain said to his brother Abel, and when they were in the field, Cain set upon his brother Abel and killed him." The verb "said" begs to be completed with Cain's actual words, but they are absent from the Masoretic text and appear to have fallen out. Ancient versions of the text, such as the Samaritan Pentateuch, the Greek Septuagint, and some of the Aramaic translations, give Cain's words as: "come let us go out into the field," which is probably more or less what the text originally said.[19]

Along with numerous minor variations in spelling and grammar, the length and structure of the Koren edition of the Hebrew Bible, scholars say, are clearly different from those of the Bible in its original form (or even the Scriptures of one or two thousand years ago). For example, in the oldest complete manuscript of the entire Hebrew Bible—the Leningrad Codex, which was completed around 1009 CE—the Torah contains approximately forty-five letters more than the 304,805 letters of the Koren edition. The vast majority of those differences, Tigay observes, reflect spelling variations and "do not affect the sense of the text but do affect the number of letters in each verse."[20]

Frequent variations in spelling in the Torah, moreover, are documented by the great rabbinic sages. Rabbi Abraham ibn Ezra (ca. 1089–1164) wrote that the use of vowels was a matter of ongoing scribal discretion, clearly implying that they were not part of divine revelation.[21] Some of the oldest known Hebrew texts, in fact, omitted vowels altogether, scholars say, while later writings used them sporadically. Virtually all versions of the Hebrew Bible known to us today employ a complex mixture of full and defective spelling that is not even consistent for the same words.[22] It was only with the rise of printing that greater textual uniformity was achieved. "There is hardly any chance that the Koren edition is close in letter-by-letter detail to the original text," says McKay. "If the text of Genesis were to be consistently spelled in the style of the inscriptions closest to the time it was traditionally written, the differences would number in the thousands (even without any change of meaning)."[23]

A revealing passage in the Babylonian Talmud dramatically illustrates the extent to which these minor variations have altered the Bible's letter count. According to one Talmudic writer, early biblical scholars identified the middle letter in the Torah as a particular letter in Leviticus 11:42, and the middle pair of words as occurring in Leviticus 10:16. However, in the Koren and all the other texts used today, the middle letter appears 4,830 letters earlier in Leviticus 8:28, and the middle words appear 933 words earlier in Leviticus 8:15.[24] "Unless the Talmudic passage is based on erroneous calculations," says Tigay, "it seems to have been based on a text of the Torah that was either shorter than today's text or had the pertinent passages in Leviticus in a different order than they are today."[25]

Even though the Koren edition used by the Bible-code promoters is widely considered the standard Hebrew text, scholars note that there is no universally agreed-upon version of the Masoretic text. Yemenite Torah scrolls, for example, differ from the Koren edition in the spelling of nine words. Their readings, which are used by some Orthodox Jews today, reduce the total number of letters in the Torah by four. They also agree with the Aleppo Codex, which the great twelfth-century sage Maimonides is said to have considered the most reliable text in his time.[26] "This," says Tigay, "is a point for the decoders to ponder: they are relying on a text that not only disagrees with the Talmud, but also disagrees with the text used by Maimonides, arguably the greatest authority on Jewish law in history."[27]

In other words, archaeological and manuscript evidence about the history of the Hebrew text has independent corroboration. As Tigay notes, "Explicit statements in Talmudic and later Jewish sources make it crystal clear that we do not possess the original text" of the Hebrew Bible. Even the editors of the Koren edition have stated as much. Tigay explains:

> When this edition was first published in 1962, at a public program celebrating its publication one of the editors who prepared the text stated, "We do not claim that we have established our edition on the basis of the tablets that Moses brought down from Mount Sinai." He was absolutely correct.[28]

What impact does all of this have on the veracity of the Bible code? McKay calls the consequences "catastrophic." Clearly, he says, "an ELS is destroyed if any letter is inserted or deleted within its overall span. Our experiments show that deletion of 10 letters in random places is enough to degrade the result by an average factor of 4000, and deleting 50 letters [is] enough to eliminate it completely." Of course, he adds, the effect has a "very large variance, as it depends on which of a comparatively small number of important ELSs are 'hit' by a deletion." But 10 letters deleted in random places are "on average enough to eliminate its significance altogether."[29]

Another serious flaw in the Bible code, critics argue, is the unfettered license that "decoders" often take in interpreting messages by creatively redividing the continuous strand of Hebrew letters to form words. In English, for example, one might take the phrase "he took ill suddenly" and redivide in part to say "he too kills." In Hebrew, many words are formed by three letters, making opportunities for such mischief almost limitless.

In Drosnin's "discovery" of a reference in the Torah to a 1996 terrorist attack on a bus in Jerusalem, for example, he found "autobus" in a vertical skip-sequence grid that was intersected horizontally by the words "fire, great noise" in the regular Hebrew text of Genesis.[30] But to arrive at those words, Drosnin redivided the Hebrew letters in Genesis 35:4, which spell out the phrase "which is near." And in a sequence that spans Exodus 19:12 through Deuteronomy 4:48, letters were lifted from the phrase "You will be my people. I am the Lord your God" (Lev. 26:12–13) and taken to mean "July to Amman"—a prediction of a planned trip by Israeli Prime Minister Binyamin Netanyahu to Amman in July 1996.

Just how much mischief can be done by this method, says Tigay, was shown to him when he was in Hebrew high school by a teacher who pointed out that the words "In the beginning God created" (Gen. 1:1) could be redivided into "At first the god of the sea created himself." By such methods, says Tigay, "one can produce messages not only undreamed of by the Torah, but contrary to its most fundamental, monotheistic teaching."[31]

Similarly, Tigay and others note that parts of dramatic messages often are produced not by finding ELS patterns but by reading horizontal lines of actual biblical text and "arbitrarily selecting certain letters as part of the message and ignoring the rest."[32] For example, a horizontal phrase in Deuteronomy 4:42 marked by Drosnin as predicting the assassination of Rabin means "a slayer who happens to have killed" and deals with cities of refuge where accidental killers can find asylum. Harvard University mathematician Rabbi Shlomo Sternberg, writing in *Bible Review,* notes that Drosnin mistranslates these words as "assassin that will assassinate." With this method, says Sternberg, "it is pretty clear that you can predict anything."[33]

Moreover, adds Tigay, Drosnin ignores the word "unwittingly" that immediately follows the phrase. "In this case, then, the message would refer to an accidental killing of (or by) Rabin and it would therefore be wrong." And in the alleged description of the Jerusalem bus bombing in Genesis 35:4, the phrase Drosnin translates as "fire, great noise" is followed in the actual text by the name of the biblical town of Shechem. "If the phrase does tell of a bus bombing," asks Tigay, "why not take it to indicate that it would be in Nablus, the site of ancient Shechem?"[34]

## SEEING THE FUTURE?

Without a doubt, the most sensational claim of Bible-code promoters is its alleged ability to foretell the future. But as we noted in the previous chapter, even the Israeli mathematicians who first uncovered the ELS phenomenon have rejected such claims as "absolutely unfounded."[35] And Harold Gans, the former American government cryptographer, declares that while some historical events "have been shown to be encoded in the Book of Genesis in certain configurations, it is absolutely not true that every similar configuration of 'encoded' words necessarily represents a potential historical event. In fact, quite the opposite is true: most such configurations will be quite random and are expected to occur in any text of sufficient length."[36] Regarding the seemingly dramatic prediction of Rabin's assassination, Gans says, "A single success, regardless of how spectacular, or even several such 'successful' predictions proves absolutely nothing unless the predictions are made and evaluated under carefully controlled conditions. Any respectable scientist knows that 'anecdotal' evidence never proves anything."[37] Witzum, who calls himself "the original researcher of the phenomenon of Torah codes," goes even farther. Having "investigated thoroughly" the question of predicting the future, he reports:

> I reached the conclusion that [predicting the future via the Bible code] is impossible. I saw this through experimentation and also as a simple point of logic. There are several reasons why it's impossible. I will give the most basic reason. In general, we always have difficulty understanding a text where we don't have any syntax or punctuation. In the plain Hebrew text of the Torah, without punctuation, I could easily read the ten commandments as telling me to steal and murder. There's a verse that describes Moses being commanded to bring incense. I could easily read it as a commandment to use drugs. All we have is a few isolated encoded words of a hidden text. Maybe we're missing some very critical words. It's literally impossible to learn a coherent story out of the juxtaposition of a few words that may be somehow related. Additionally, just like there is a code that Rabin will be assassinated, I also found a code saying that Churchill will be assassinated!

*Even regarding past events, there are ELSs of words that appear near*
*each other that have no relation to each other. It is therefore unwise, and*
*one could say irresponsible, to make "predictions" based on ELSs of words*
*appearing near each other.*[38]

But if the very meaning of the alleged messages in the Bible code is apparent only after the fact, of what use are they? What did their author hope to
achieve by encoding them? As Tigay notes, "They become no better than the
Delphic oracles who told Croesus that if he attacked the Persians he would destroy a mighty empire. When he was defeated and complained to the oracles, he
was told that if he had been wise he would have inquired whether the Persian
empire or his own was meant; he therefore had only himself to blame for the result (Herodotus 1:53, 91)."[39]

Beyond the devastating questions raised against the math, logic, and methods of interpretation of the Bible code, the most compelling argument against
its authenticity, for many biblical scholars, is the internal theological inconsistency that a fortune-telling code in the Scriptures would represent. Use of a code
to predict the future, notes Rabbi Sternberg of Harvard, "violates the explicit
biblical prohibition against augury, necromancy and the like."[40] Deuteronomy
18:10–12, for example, seems to make the point clearly:

*No one shall be found among you who makes a son or daughter pass*
*through fire, or who practices divination, or is a soothsayer, or an augur, or*
*a sorcerer, or one who casts spells, or who consults ghosts or spirits, or who*
*seeks oracles from the dead. For whoever does these things is abhorrent to*
*the Lord.*

If the God of the Bible prohibits divination, scholars note, why would he
allow—or, indeed, design—the Bible itself to be used as such a tool?[41] As New
Age experts John Ankerberg and John Weldon observe:

*By seeking to know future events, divination promises to allow the individ-*
*ual to control his future. In this sense, it represents a fundamental rejection*
*of God's infinite, wise, and perfect will, replacing it with the limited and*
*self-serving perspective of the human will. Because it represents a conscious*
*abdication of divine sovereignty for human 'control,' it is ultimately a con-*
*frontation with God. This is why the Bible strictly opposes divination.*
*While it acknowledges that people use divination (e.g., Genesis 4:4–5), it*
*condemns and never endorses such practices.*[42]

Even Drosnin—quoting Rips—concedes the danger inherent in buying fully into the sensational claims of the Bible code: "The worst thing that could happen," says Rips, "is that some people might interpret what they find in the Bible code as commandments, as telling them what to do—and it's not that, it is only information, and it may only be probabilities."[43]

There are other dangers. As Weldon notes, many people—including Bible-believing Christians—are using the Bible code and their own computers to try to discover their futures or to convince their unbelieving friends of the Bible's divine origins. "If the Bible code is disproved some years from now," he says, "what are millions of people going to conclude about the credibility of Christians . . . or the Bible?"[44]

Perhaps the most serious repercussions of the Bible-code phenomenon are the implications of what it suggests about the nature of the Bible itself. If Drosnin is correct and the Bible code is "the Bible beneath the Bible"—the text "as it always was intended to be read"—then the Scriptures are little more than an object of curiosity to be manipulated like a genie's lamp or a diviner's rod. The text itself is quite meaningless, other than as a repository for encoded messages.

But that is hardly what the evidence of centuries of biblical and historical scholarship has shown the Bible to be. Nor is it what the faith experience of millions of Bible readers and believers has proven: that the real prophetic power of the Scriptures is in the inspired message of the text itself. The phenomenon of the Bible code will no doubt continue to strike many as a fascinating puzzle, but it has demonstrated little credibility as a revealer of the true character of the book that so many find to be a sacred revelation. One hardly needs the gimmickry of laptops and logarithms to prove the veracity of the Scriptures.

# PART SIX

# THE BIBLE
# AND BELIEF

## CHAPTER 25

# IS THE
# BIBLE TRUE?

## CONCLUSION

AT THE BEGINNING OF THIS BOOK, I LAID OUT SOME GUIDING questions that I have tried to follow carefully and objectively throughout this investigation: In light of the conflicting claims and the often equivocal evidence of modern scholarship, what can be known about the Bible? What can be proved? What is reasonable for modern readers to believe about its authority, its authenticity, and its reliability as a historical witness?

In subsequent pages I inquired into the Bible's genre and the credibility of its sources, examined archaeological evidence and exegetical arguments for and against its historical claims, and explored the testimony of other ancient texts that illuminate the content and the context of the Scriptures. And I have tried where appropriate to assess the extent to which the philosophical predilections of scholars sometimes influence both their conclusions and our perceptions regarding the essential historicity of the Bible.

The answers we have discovered along the way have seldom been simple or singular; indeed, sometimes they have remained elusive, a necessary reflection of the complexity of both the methods of modern historiography and the Bible itself. As we noted at the outset, many of the Bible's most pivotal claims—the existence of a personal and communicative God, the divine incarnation in the person of Jesus Christ, the reality of miracles and of the resurrection—are theological in nature and thus ultimately must remain beyond the reach of historical inquiry and verification.

And yet, as we have seen, the Bible and the faith it commends are by no means entirely detached from historical examination. To the contrary, we have discovered an abundance of evidence—both direct and indirect—that sheds light on the historical claims and the context of the Scriptures. As we have examined that evidence and considered the scholarly arguments drawn from it, and as we have compared the Scriptures to other written histories from the ancient Near East, we have found the Bible consistently and substantially affirmed as a credible and reliable source of history.

The Bible is affirmed by the weight of evidence and the strength of early traditions relating to the formation of the scriptural canon. The authority and authentic origins of the Bible, though often perceived today through the haze of intervening centuries as largely obscure and unknowable, were seen much more clearly in the first generations of the Christian era. As we saw in Part One, among those early church fathers—men such as Papias and Polycarp, who were personally acquainted with apostles—there was little serious question as to the identity and authenticity of the New Testament authors. Nor was there any hint of doubt among the leaders of the churches and synagogues of the first and second centuries that the Hebrew Scriptures, long recognized as sacred and inspired, had been written by "men moved by the Holy Spirit [who] spoke from God" (2 Pet. 1:21). What now are widely viewed as ancient and questionable traditions of source and provenance were considered common knowledge and uncontested fact in those early centuries.

More important than authorship was the virtually spontaneous acceptance and discernment within the early church's far-flung precincts of the innate authority of the writings that later would be recognized as the Christian canon—in contrast to a plethora of apocryphal and pseudonymous writings that were circulating at the same time. That early functional recognition, which preceded by more than a century any formal canonical decree, is a powerful testimony to the authenticity and authority of the Scriptures.

The Bible is affirmed by the weight of evidence from archaeology. As we noted in Part Two, archaeology cannot prove the Scriptures. And there are numerous instances where particular biblical narratives and current archaeological data simply do not match or where archaeology thus far is silent. Yet the wealth of ancient artifacts, inscriptions, and architectural ruins discovered and analyzed during the past century has provided important corroboration for some key episodes of biblical history and has helped to establish a plausible historical and cultural context for many others. Sometimes the corroboration has been dramatic and direct, as in the match between the Bible and ancient Assyrian records of the invasion of Judah by King Sennacherib. In other instances, the evidence is indirect but no less dramatic, as in the discovery of the "house of David" inscription in upper Galilee. The impact overall has been to affirm the historical essence of the Scriptures, to disclose its solid roots in the knowable material past, and often, in the process, to confute the bedrock skeptics who dismiss the Bible as nothing more than a collection of myths and legends.

The Bible is affirmed by the testimony of the Dead Sea Scrolls. While the ancient manuscripts from Qumran have revealed some intriguing variations in the text of the Bible as it existed at the turn of the era, scholars have found the overall picture emerging from the scrolls to be that of a Bible that has been amazingly accurately preserved for over two millennia. As we saw in Part Three, the language and imagery contained in the sectarian writings from Qumran refute the argument of some modern scholars that certain New Testament concepts were late inventions, reflecting second-century Greek influences on the evolving church rather than authentic first-century content from the days of Jesus. The dualistic imagery of the gospels depicting spiritual warfare between the powers of darkness and light, for example, and messianic references using the terminology "Son of God" and "Son of the Most High" were there in the scrolls—a dramatic demonstration that those ideas were clearly part of the Jewish lexicon by the middle of the first century. The scrolls have shown how deeply Christianity was rooted in the Judaism of the time.

The Bible is affirmed by the intense scholarly scrutiny that has been directed at the gospels in the quest for the historical Jesus. Much has been made of apparent disagreements between the gospels over some of the details in their portraits of Jesus. Those differences, as we noted in Chapter One, did not escape the attention or concern of leaders of the early church. And yet, as perceptive scholars have recognized from that day to this, it is the substantial agreement of the four gospels on the important central facts of Jesus' birth, his ministry, and his death and resurrection (while allowing for different recollections of peripheral details) that makes their combined testimony so credible. While the synoptic gospels indeed show signs of having shared some proto-gospel sources of information, each also demonstrates an independent perspective and the use of independent source material as well. And still they agree on the basics. The testimony of the gospels would be much more suspect had they been in lock-step on every detail. As we saw in Parts One and Four, the gospels are far more, but certainly no less, than history. They impart historical information, but it is information interpreted and packaged as "good news" proclamation. And while other external sources may help color the background and fill in some gaps, the gospel images of Jesus remain the most vivid, credible, and complete.

Finally, the Bible is affirmed amid fleeting controversies over the so-called Bible code. As the sensational theories falter and the hyperbole fades, we are reminded that the value and veracity of the Scriptures do not depend on the cleverness of computer scientists and cryptologists in finding secret messages hidden in sacred texts, that the real prophetic power of the Bible is to be found in the wisdom of its words and the truth of its teachings—not in the mathematical manipulation of its component parts.

Without question, historical accuracy is an essential feature of the Bible's integrity and authority. As the biblical archaeologist G. Ernest Wright once observed, "In biblical faith, everything depends upon whether the central events actually occurred."[1] Indeed, the Bible cannot be rendered comprehensible apart from its historical claims.

Yet as we have been reminded at various points in our investigation, it is not merely to ancient history that the Bible directs our attention. It is to the God who is active in history, redeeming it and infusing it with meaning, that the Scriptures ultimately point. The inspired authors and editors of the Bible perceived giving an account of Israel's past as telling "his story." They saw God's hand at work in the calling forth of a consecrated people in patriarchal times, in the deliverance of Hebrew slaves from Egyptian captivity, and in the rise of a mighty Israelite nation in a land God provided. They heard God's voice in the ancient precepts from Sinai, in the lilting songs of David, in the sage wisdom of the prophets and apostles, and in the profound aphorisms of the Sermon on the Mount. They perceived God's faithfulness in the resilience and restoration of an often wayward people through times of oppression and exile. And they sensed God's love in the utter selflessness of a carpenter from Nazareth who "while we still were sinners . . . died for us" (Romans 5:8).

It is as a witness to that sacred history, to the mighty acts of Israel's God in the affairs of nations and in the lives of people of faith, that the Bible most resoundingly sets itself apart from other ancient texts. More than the precision of its historiography, it is the power of its inspired testimony and the resonance of its timeless message that has earned the Bible the fidelity and trust of countless millions through the centuries who, having read and believed, have encountered in their own experience the self-revealing God of the universe.

INTRODUCTION

1. N. T. Wright, *Jesus and the Victory of God* (Minneapolis: Fortress Press, 1996), 662.

CHAPTER 1

1. Origen, *Against Celsus,* 4:43, as it appears at the "Early Church Fathers" Internet site: http://ccel.wheaton.edu/fathers2/
Origen's essay contains major excerpts of Celsus's anti-Christian polemic *True Doctrine,* which is no longer extant.
2. Origen, *Against Celsus,* 1:33.
3. See, for example, Joseph W. Trigg, "Origen," *Anchor Bible Dictionary,* ed. David Noel Freedman (New York: Doubleday, 1992), 5:44.
4. A March 1994 poll commissioned by *U.S. News & World Report* found that 34 percent of Americans believe the Bible is "the actual word of God to be taken literally word for word," 46 percent view the Bible as "the inspired word of God, but not everything in it can be taken literally," and 16 percent see it as "an ancient book of legends, history and moral precepts, recorded by man." The poll of one thousand registered voters was conducted by Celinda Lake of Mellman-Lazarus-Lake and Ed Goeas of the Tarrance Group, and appeared in the magazine's April 4, 1994, issue.
5. See Craig Blomberg, *The Historical Reliability of the Gospels* (Downers Grove, Ill.: InterVarsity Press, 1987), 2–5.
6. For a brief but cogent summary of the conservative reaction to biblical criticism, see Martin Marty, "North America: Conservative Reaction in Protestantism," *The Oxford Illustrated History of Christianity,* ed. John McManners (Oxford: Oxford University Press, 1992), 412–413. Also see Marty's more complete work on fundamentalism, with R. Scott Appleby, *The Fundamentalism Project,* vols. 1–5 (Chicago: University of Chicago Press, 1991–1995).
7. James K. Hoffmeier, *Israel in Egypt: The Evidence for the Authenticity of the Exodus Tradition* (New York/Oxford: Oxford University Press, 1996), 10.
8. See, for example, Yale University Assyriologist and Hebrew Bible expert William W. Hallo's article "The Limits of Skepticism," *Journal of the American Oriental Society* 110, no. 2 (1990): 187–199; and Harvard University professor Jon D. Levenson's critique of "the hermeneutics of suspicion" in *The Hebrew Bible, the Old Testament, and Historical Criticism* (Louisville: Westminster/John Knox Press, 1993), 116. Both are cited by Hoffmeier, a professor of biblical studies and archaeology at Wheaton College, in *Israel in Egypt,* 14.
9. Hallo, "The Limits of Skepticism," 189. Hallo is speaking here about texts from the ancient Near East in general, but he makes it clear later in the paper that the treatment he prescribes applies to the Bible as well.
10. Hallo, "The Limits of Skepticism," 194.
11. Hallo, "The Limits of Skepticism," 187–188.

CHAPTER 2

1. Nahum M. Sarna, "Canon: Order of the Books in the Hebrew Bible," *The Oxford Companion to the Bible,* ed. Bruce M. Metzger and Michael D. Coogan (New York/Oxford: Oxford University Press, 1993), 99.

2. See the discussion in Chapter 15.
3. Flavius Josephus, *Against Apion,* as it appears in *The Complete Works of Josephus,* trans. William Whiston (Grand Rapids: Kregel Publications, 1981), 1:38–41.
4. See F. F. Bruce, *The Canon of Scripture* (Downers Grove, Ill.: InterVarsity Press, 1988), 22–23.
5. Josephus, *Against Apion,* 1:42.
6. See Bruce, *The Canon of Scripture,* 29–30.
7. L. William Countryman, "Canon," *HarperCollins Bible Dictionary,* rev. ed., ed. Paul J. Achtemeier (San Francisco: HarperSanFrancisco, 1996), 167–68.
8. The Old Testament of Protestant and most of Eastern Orthodox Christianity contains the same books as the Hebrew Bible, although some are subdivided so that the number totals thirty-nine rather than twenty-four. The books also appear in a somewhat different order. The Bible of the Roman Catholic and some Orthodox churches includes additional books from the Septuagint: Tobit, Judith, Wisdom of Solomon, Sirach, Baruch, 1 and 2 Maccabees, and additions to the books of Esther and Daniel. They were added to the Roman Catholic canon in 1546 at the Council of Trent.
9. In 1 Clement, the Didache, and the writings of Ignatius and Papias, for example, the "living voice" of the oral teachings was preferred over the written testimony of the gospels well toward the middle of the first century. See Andrie B. Du Toit, "Canon: New Testament," *The Oxford Companion to the Bible,* ed. Bruce M. Metzger and Michael D. Coogan (New York/Oxford: Oxford University Press, 1993), 103.
10. D. A. Carson, Douglas J. Moo, and Leon Morris, *An Introduction to the New Testament* (Grand Rapids: Zondervan, 1992), 494.
11. See Du Toit, "Canon," 103; also see Helmut Koester, *Ancient Christian Gospels: Their History and Development* (Philadelphia: Trinity International Press, 1990), 35–36.
12. Glenn W. Barker, William L. Lane, and J. Ramsey Michaels, *The New Testament Speaks* (San Francisco: Harper & Row, 1969), 29, as cited in Carson, Moo, and Morris, *An Introduction to the New Testament,* 494.
13. Barker, Lane, and Michaels, *The New Testament Speaks.*
14. Brevard S. Childs, *The New Testament As Canon: An Introduction* (Philadelphia: Fortress Press, 1984), 28–29.

## CHAPTER 3

1. See William H. Barnes, "Inspiration and Inerrancy," *The Oxford Companion to the Bible,* ed. Bruce M. Metzger and Michael D. Coogan (New York/Oxford: Oxford University Press, 1993), 303.
2. 2 Pet. 1:21.
3. See James Barr, "History of Interpretation," *The Oxford Companion to the Bible,* 321–322.
4. Wellhausen expounded this theory in two monumental works, *Die Composition Des Hexateuch,* published in 1877, and *Prolegomena zur Geschichte Israels,* published in German in 1883 and in English in 1885. Good summaries of his theory can be found in Edward L. Greenstein, "Sources of the Pentateuch," *HarperCollins Bible Dictionary,* rev. ed., Paul J. Achtemeier (San Francisco: HarperSanFrancisco, 1996), 1055–1054; David J. A. Clines, "Pentateuch," *The Oxford Companion to the Bible,* 580; and Raymond B. Dillard and Tremper Longman III, *An Introduction to the Old Testament* (Grand Rapids: Zondervan, 1994), 39–42.
5. Richard Elliott Friedman, *Who Wrote the Bible?* rev. ed. (San Francisco: HarperSanFrancisco, 1997), 86.
6. Friedman, *Who Wrote the Bible?* 87.
7. Friedman, *Who Wrote the Bible?* 210.
8. Friedman, *Who Wrote the Bible?* 147.
9. Friedman, *Who Wrote the Bible?* 218, 224.
10. Clines, "Pentateuch," 580.
11. For summaries, see James K. Hoffmeier, *Israel in Egypt* (New York/Oxford: Oxford University Press, 1996), 7–10; Dillard and Longman, *An Introduction to the Old Testament,* 42–48; and Edwin Yamauchi, "The Current State of Old Testament Historiography," *Faith, Tradition, and History,* ed. A. R. Millard, J. K. Hoffmeier, and D. W. Baker (Winona Lake, Ind.: Eisenbrauns, 1994), 7–8.
12. Friedman, *Who Wrote the Bible?* 28.

13. From an interview with the author, February 22, 1999.

14. For the minimalist position see, for example, John Van Seters, *In Search of History: Historiography in the Ancient World and the Origins of Biblical History* (New Haven: Yale University Press, 1983), and Thomas L. Thompson, *The Mythic Past: Biblical Archaeology and the Myth of Israel* (New York: Basic Books, 1999).

15. See Dillard and Longman, *An Introduction to the Old Testament*, 40.

16. Greenstein, "Sources of the Pentateuch," 1056.

17. Clines, "Pentateuch," 580.

18. Clines, "Pentateuch," 580.

19. From an interview with the author, February 22, 1999.

20. Babylonian Talmud, *Baba' Bathra* 15a.

21. Noth's hypothesis appeared first as *Schriften der Konigersberger Gelehrten Gesellschaft* in 1943, and in a better-known second edition, *Uberlieferungsgeschichtliche Studien* (Tübingen: Max Niemeyer Verlag, 1957; 3rd unaltered edition, 1967). For a summary of Noth, see Russell Fuller, "Deuteronomic History," *The Oxford Companion to the Bible*, 163–164.

22. Dennis R. Bratcher, "Deuteronomy," *Harper's Bible Dictionary*, 220.

23. Josh. 10:12–13; 2 Sam. 1:18–27.

24. See, for example, Leslie J. Hoppe, "Esther," *The Catholic Study Bible* (New York: Oxford University Press, 1990), RG217; also see Dillard and Longman, *An Introduction to the Old Testament*, 207.

25. One case in point, noted by Dillard and Longman, is Psalm 30. The superscription is "A Psalm. A Song at the dedication of the temple. Of David." Yet the psalm itself has no apparent connection to the temple but is the prayer of a man who has recovered from a near-fatal illness. See Dillard and Longman, *An Introduction to the Old Testament*, 215.

26. Dillard and Longman, *An Introduction to the Old Testament*, 236.

27. Dillard and Longman, *An Introduction to the Old Testament*, 264.

28. See, for example, individual discussions on each of the gospels in D. A. Carson, Douglas J. Moo, and Leon Morris, *An Introduction to the New Testament* (Grand Rapids: Zondervan, 1992).

29. From an interview with the author, November 14, 1990.

30. *Apology*, 1:66.3, 1:67.3, as cited by F. F. Bruce, *The Canon of Scripture* (Downers Grove, Ill.: Inter-Varsity Press, 1988), 127.

31. Helmut Koester, *Ancient Christian Gospels: Their History and Development* (Philadelphia: Trinity Press International, 1990), 38.

32. Papias's writing is preserved in Eusebius, *Ecclesiastical History*, 3:39.15.

33. See, for example, Acts 9:26, 11:30, and 15:2 against Gal. 1:18 and 2:1.

34. Irenaeus, *Adversus Haereses*, 2:1.2.

35. See Carson, Moo, and Morris, *An Introduction to the New Testament*, 139.

36. That Papias was a disciple of John is confirmed by Irenaeus, as recorded in Eusebius, *Ecclesiastical History*, 3:39.1. Irenaeus also discusses Polycarp's association with John in "Letter to Florinius," Eusebius, *Ecclesiastical History*, 5:20.4–8.

37. Irenaeus, "Letter to Florinius," in Eusebius, *Ecclesiastical History*, 5:20.4–8.

38. Martin Hengel, *Studies in the Gospel of Mark* (Philadelphia: Fortress, 1985), 64–84.

39. Tertullian, *Against Marcion*, 4:2.

40. For more on this and a fair evaluation of the counterarguments, see Carson, Moo, and Morris, *An Introduction to the New Testament*, 66–67.

41. As with most other questions regarding the composition of the gospels, *where* they were written is uncertain. Rome for Mark, Syria (perhaps Antioch) for Matthew, and Achaia for Luke are commonly posited, however. See, for example, the individual entries for the gospels in *The Oxford Companion to the Bible*.

42. From an interview with the author, November 13, 1990.

43. Carson, Moo, and Morris, *An Introduction to the New Testament*, 38.

44. Cited in Bruce, *The Canon of Scripture*, 303–304.

45. Koester, *Ancient Christian Gospels*, 294.

46. Frederick C. Grant, "Growth of the New Testament Literature," *Encyclopedia Americana* (Danbury, Conn: Grolier, Inc., 1996), 3:700.

47. This is the Chester Beatty manuscript identified as $P^{46}$. It is a codex containing 86 out of an original

104 folios. It apparently did not include 1 and 2 Timothy and Titus but did include Hebrews. For more on this, see Bruce, *The Canon of Scripture,* 130.

48. Carson, Moo, and Morris, *An Introduction to the New Testament,* 233–234.
49. Werner Kümmel delineates these in his *Introduction to the New Testament,* trans. Howard Clark Kee (Nashville/New York: Abingdon Press, 1975), 411. The scriptural citations: son of Zebedee (Mark 1:19; 3:17 par.; Acts 12:2), son of Alphaeus (Mark 3:18), brother of Jesus (Mark 6:3; 1 Cor. 15:7; Gal. 1:19; 2:9, 12; Acts 12:17; 15:13; 21:18; Jude 1), the younger (Mark 15:40; son of a Mary, cf. Mark 16:1), father of Jude (Luke 6:16; Acts 1:13).
50. Kümmel, *An Introduction to the New Testament,* 411–412.
51. Kümmel, *An Introduction to the New Testament,* 406.
52. Kümmel, *An Introduction to the New Testament,* 424.
53. Stevan L. Davies, *The New Testament: A Contemporary Introduction* (San Francisco: Harper & Row, 1988), 204.
54. Kümmel, *An Introduction to the New Testament,* 430.
55. See, for example, Carson, Moo, and Morris, *An Introduction to the New Testament,* 433–437.
56. Papias is cited by Eusebius, *Ecclesiastical History,* 3:39.17; Irenaeus, *Adversus Haereses,* 3:16.18; Clement, *Stromata,* 2:15.66.
57. Carson, Moo, and Morris, *An Introduction to the New Testament,* 459–460.
58. Kümmel, *An Introduction to the New Testament,* 469–470.
59. Kümmel, *An Introduction to the New Testament,* 470–472.
60. James A. Sanders, "Canon," *Anchor Bible Dictionary,* ed. David Noel Freedman (New York: Doubleday, 1992), 1:851.

## CHAPTER 4

1. Raymond B. Dillard and Tremper Longman III, *An Introduction to the Old Testament* (Grand Rapids: Zondervan, 1994), 21.
2. Dillard and Longman, *An Introduction to the Old Testament,* 21.
3. G. W. Coats, *Genesis with an Introduction to Narrative Literature,* Forms of Old Testament Literature Series 1 (Grand Rapids: Eerdmans, 1983), 319.
4. R. W. L. Moberly, "At the Mountain of God: Story and Theology in Exodus," *Journal for the Study of the Old Testament* 22 (1983): 36.
5. Coats, *Genesis with an Introduction to Narrative Literature,* 5–10.
6. Dillard and Longman, *An Introduction to the Old Testament,* 49.
7. N. T. Wright, *Who Was Jesus?* (Grand Rapids: Eerdmans, 1992), 74.
8. G. W. Ahlström, *Who Were the Israelites?* (Winona Lake, Ind.: Eisenbrauns, 1986), 46. Similar arguments against the historical intent or accomplishment of Genesis and Exodus can be found in Thomas L. Thompson, *The Origin Tradition of Ancient Israel,* JSOT Supp. Series, vol. 55 (Sheffield, U.K.: JSOT Press, 1987), and J. Van Seters, *Prologue to History: The Yahwist as Historian in Genesis* (Louisville: Westminster/John Knox, 1992).
9. Edwin Yamauchi, "The Current State of Old Testament Historiography," *Faith, Tradition, and History,* ed. A. R. Millard, J. K. Hoffmeier, and D. W. Baker (Winona Lake, Ind.: Eisenbrauns, 1994), 27–28. He cites A. Momigliano, "Biblical Studies and Classical Studies: Simple Reflections upon Historical Method," *Annali della Scuola Normale Superiore* 11 (1981): 25.
10. Johan Huizinga, "A Definition of the Concept of History," *Philosophy and History: Essays Presented to Ernst Cassirer,* ed. R. Kiblansky and H. J. Paton (New York: Harper Torch Books, 1963), 1–10. Originally published Oxford: Clarendon Press, 1936.
11. Dillard and Longman, *An Introduction to the Old Testament,* 23.
12. *Merriam-Webster's Collegiate Dictionary,* 10th ed.
13. Nahum Sarna, "Israel in Egypt: The Egyptian Sojourn and the Exodus," *Ancient Israel: A Short History from Abraham to the Roman Destruction of the Temple,* ed. Hershel Shanks (Washington, D.C.: Biblical Archaeology Society, 1988), 37.
14. William G. Dever, *Recent Archaeological Discoveries and Biblical Research* (Seattle: University of Washington Press, 1990), 6.
15. Dillard and Longman, *An Introduction to the Old Testament,* 22.

16. Dillard and Longman, *An Introduction to the Old Testament,* 22.
17. See, for example, A. R. Millard, "Story, History, and Theology," *Faith, Tradition, and History,* ed. Millard, J. K. Hoffmeier, and D. W. Baker (Winona Lake, Ind.: Eisenbrauns, 1994), 7, 8.
18. John 1:11 (KJV).
19. Carson, Moo, and Morris, *An Introduction to the New Testament,* 45.
20. See, for example, James Barr, "Story and History in Biblical Theology," *Journal of Religion* 56 (1976): 1–17; reprinted in Barr, *The Scope and Authority of the Bible* (Philadelphia: Westminster Press, 1980), 1–17.
21. Herodotus 4:105 (9 vols.; Loeb Classic Library 117–120; Cambridge: Harvard University Press, 1922–1928).
22. Millard, "Story, History, and Theology," 40. His citations of Herodotus are in the Loeb Classic Library edition, 3:101 and 7:138.
23. Millard, "Story, History, and Theology," 40.
24. The Gallup Organization's poll was conducted November 6–9, 1997. The question that was asked was, "Which of the statements on this card comes closest to describing your views about the origin and development of man? (a) God created man pretty much in his present form at one time within the last 10,000 years. (b) Man has developed over millions of years from less advanced forms of life. God had no part in this process. (c) Man has developed over millions of years from less advanced forms of life, but God guided this process, including man's creation. (d) I don't know." The responses were (a) 44 percent, (b) 10 percent, (c) 39 percent, and (d) 7 percent. The poll appeared in George Bishop, "The Religious Worldview and American Beliefs About Human Origins," *The Public Perspective,* August/September 1998, 39–48.
25. See, for example, Stephen Jay Gould, *Rocks of Ages: Science and Religion in the Fullness of Life* (New York: Ballantine, 1999). Gould argues that both science and religion are legitimate enterprises, each valid within its own framework, but that they are incapable of reaching agreement because they address entirely different questions. They are "nonoverlapping magesteria" that should "coexist peacefully in a position of respectful noninterference" (cover).
26. This figure was cited by financier-philanthropist John M. Templeton, a major benefactor of science-religion dialogue, in remarks at a meeting of scientists and theologians in Chicago in November 1991.
27. Papal message in *Physics, Philosophy, and Theology: A Common Quest for Understanding,* ed. Robert John Russell, William R. Stoeger, and George V. Coyne (Vatican City State: Vatican Observatory, 1988), M13–14.
28. From an interview with the author, December 3, 1991.
29. From an interview with the author, December 4, 1991.
30. From an interview with the author, December 3, 1991.
31. St. Augustine, *The Literal Meaning of Genesis,* trans. and annot. John Hammond Taylor, S.J., 2 vols. (New York: Newman Press, 1982). All page references that follow are to pages in vol. 1.
32. St. Basil, "Nine Homilies of the Hexaemeron," *A Select Library of Nicene and Post-Nicene Fathers of the Christian Church,* ed. Philip Schaff and Henry Wace (New York: The Christian Literature Company, 1890–1900), vol. 8.
33. Davis A. Young, "The Contemporary Relevance of Augustine's View of Creation," *Perspectives on Science and Christian Faith* 40, no. 1 (March 1998): 45.
34. All of the above theories are delineated in Pattle P. T. Pun, *Evolution: Nature and Scripture in Conflict?* (Grand Rapids: Zondervan, 1982).
35. From an interview with the author, December 3, 1991.
36. From an interview with *U.S. News & World Report* staffer Joannie Schrof, 12/3/91.
37. That late date is discussed and disputed by K. A. Kitchen and T. C. Mitchell in "Creation," *Illustrated Bible Dictionary,* ed. James D. Douglas and N. Hillyer (Leicester, England: InterVarsity Press; Wheaton, Ill.: Tyndale House, 1980), 1:269.
38. See, for example, "The Geophysics of God: A Scientist Embraces Plate Tectonics—and Noah's Flood," *U.S. News & World Report,* June 16, 1997, 55–58. This article may be viewed online at: http://www.usnews.com/usnews/issue/970616/16terr.htm.
39. Michael D. Coogan, "In the Beginning: The Earliest History," *The Oxford History of the Biblical World,* ed. Michael D. Coogan (New York/Oxford: Oxford University Press, 1998), 29.
40. Coogan, "In the Beginning."

41. Coogan, "In the Beginning."

42. See, for example, Clifford Wilson, "The A.B.C. of Biblical Archaeology," in *The Online Bible*, a CD-ROM published by Online Publishing, Bronson, Mich. Wilson cites A. T. Clay, "A Hebrew Deluge Story in Cuneiform" (New Haven, 1922): "Assyriologists, as far as I know, have generally dismissed as an impossibility the idea that there was a common Semitic tradition, which developed in Israel in one way, and in Babylonia in another. They have unreservedly declared that the Biblical stories have been borrowed from Babylonia, in which land they were indigenous. To me it has always seemed perfectly reasonable that both stories had a common origin among the Semites, some of whom entered Babylonia, while others carried their traditions into Palestine."

    Also, see Tikva-Frymer-Kensky, "The Atrahasis Epic and Its Significance for Our Understanding of Genesis 1–9," *Biblical Archaeologist*, December 1977, 40.4:147–155. In part he writes: "Three different Babylonian stories of the flood have survived: the Sumerian Flood Story, the ninth tablet of the Gilgamesh Epic, and the Atrahasis Epic. Details in these stories, such as the placing of animals in the ark, the landing of the ark on a mountain, and the sending forth of birds to see whether the waters had receded, indicate clearly that these stories are intimately related to the biblical flood story and, indeed, that the Babylonian and biblical accounts of the flood represent different retellings of an essentially identical flood tradition."

43. George W. Ramsey, *The Quest for the Historical Israel* (Atlanta: John Knox, 1981), as cited in V. P. Long, *The Art of Biblical History* (Grand Rapids: Zondervan, 1994), 83ff.

44. William G. Dever, "Archaeology: Syro-Palestinian and Biblical," *Anchor Bible Dictionary*, ed. David Noel Freedman (New York: Doubleday, 1992).

45. Siegfried H. Horn, "The Divided Monarchy: The Kingdoms of Judah and Israel," *Ancient Israel: A Short History from Abraham to the Roman Destruction of the Temple*, ed. Hershel Shanks (Washington, D.C.: Biblical Archaeology Society, 1988), 110.

## Chapter 5

1. Avraham Biran, *Biblical Dan* (Jerusalem: The Israel Exploration Society, 1994), 275–278; Biran, "An Aramaic Stele Fragment from Tel Dan," *The Israel Exploration Journal* 43 (1993): 81–98. Also see "David Found at Dan," *Biblical Archaeology Review*, March/April 1994, 33.

2. Biran, "An Aramaic Stele Fragment from Tel Dan," 90.

3. Philip R. Davies, "House of David Built on Sand: The Sins of the Biblical Maximizers," *Biblical Archaeology Review*, July/August 1994, 54–55.

4. Philip R. Davies, *In Search of "Ancient Israel"* (Sheffield, U.K.: Sheffield Academic Press, 1992), 12.

5. Quoted from Jeffery L. Sheler, "Mysteries of the Bible," *U.S. News & World Report*, May 17, 1995, 61.

6. See, for example, Randall Price, *The Stones Cry Out* (Eugene, Ore.: Harvest House, 1997), 173.

7. Davies, "House of David Built on Sand," 54–55.

8. See "Face to Face: Biblical Minimalists Meet Their Challengers," *Biblical Archaeology Review*, July/August 1997, 36–37.

9. See, for example, *Biblical Archaeology Review*, July/August 1997, 34; and James K. Hoffmeier, *Israel in Egypt* (New York/Oxford: Oxford University Press, 1997), 13.

10. From a telephone interview with the author, October 24, 1993.

## Chapter 6

1. As cited in Edward M. Blaiklock, *Out of the Earth: The Witness of Archaeology to the New Testament* (London: Paternoster Press, 1957), 10.

2. For a good survey of the historical development of biblical archaeology and its techniques, see William G. Dever, "Methods of Archaeology," *HarperCollins Bible Dictionary* (San Francisco: HarperSanFrancisco, 1996), 59–66.

3. Dever, "Methods of Archaeology."

4. Gonzalo Baez-Camargo, *Archaeological Commentary on the Bible* (Garden City, N.Y.: Doubleday, 1984), xv.

5. Randall Price, *The Stones Cry Out* (Eugene, Ore.: Harvest House, 1997), 10.

6. As quoted in Baez-Camargo, *Archaeological Commentary on the Bible*, xvi.

7. Baez-Camargo, *Archaeological Commentary on the Bible*, xxii.

8. See Dever, "Methods of Archaeology," 59ff.
9. Dever, "Methods of Archaeology."
10. Dever, "Methods of Archaeology."
11. Dever, "Methods of Archaeology."
12. Dever, "Methods of Archaeology."

CHAPTER 7

1. Gen. 17:5–8.
2. As cited by Kevin D. Miller in "Did the Exodus Never Happen?" *Christianity Today,* September 7, 1998, 44.
3. Miller, "Did the Exodus Never Happen?"
4. Niels Peter Lemche, "History of Israel (Premonarchic Period)," *Anchor Bible Dictionary,* ed. David Noel Freedman (New York: Doubleday, 1992), 3:534.
5. Miller, "Did the Exodus Never Happen?" 44. (The article goes on to enumerate circumstantial evidence for the patriarchal accounts.)
6. Lemche, "History of Israel (Premonarchic Period)," 534.
7. From an interview with the author, March 16, 1995.
8. Kenneth A. Kitchen, "The Patriarchal Age: Myth or History?" *Biblical Archaeology Review,* March/April 1995, 52.
9. Kitchen, "The Patriarchal Age."
10. Kitchen, "The Patriarchal Age."
11. Kitchen, "The Patriarchal Age."
12. Kitchen, "The Patriarchal Age."
13. From an interview with the author, March 16, 1995.
14. P. Kyle McCarter, Jr., "The Patriarchal Age," *Ancient Israel* (Washington, D.C.: Biblical Archaeology Society, 1988), 26–27.
15. See Jack Finegan, *Handbook of Biblical Chronology,* 2nd ed. (Peabody, Mass.: Hendrickson, 1998), 224–225.
16. Flavius Josephus, *Against Apion,* as it appears in *The Complete Works of Josephus,* trans. William Whiston (Grand Rapids: Kregel Publications, 1981), 1:14.
17. See McCarter, "The Patriarchal Age," 27.
18. McCarter, "The Patriarchal Age."
19. Finegan, *Handbook of Biblical Chronology,* 224–225; also see McCarter, "The Patriarchal Age," 226.

CHAPTER 8

1. William G. Dever, *Recent Archaeological Discoveries and Biblical Research* (Seattle: University of Washington Press, 1990), 39.
2. Baruch Halpern, "The Exodus from Egypt: Myth or Reality?" *The Rise of Ancient Israel,* a symposium (Washington, D.C.: Biblical Archaeology Society, 1992), 91. Also see N. P. Lemche, *Early Israel* (Leiden, Neth.: Brill, 1985), 409; and G. W. Ahlström, *Who Were the Israelites?* (Winona Lake, Ind.: Eisenbrauns, 1986), 46.
3. Kenneth A. Kitchen, "The Patriarchal Age: Myth or History?" *Biblical Archaeology Review,* March/April 1995, 50.
4. Nahum Sarna, "Israel in Egypt: The Egyptian Sojourn and the Exodus," *Ancient Israel: A Short History from Abraham to the Roman Destruction of the Temple,* ed. Hershel Shanks (Englewood Cliffs, N.J.: Prentice Hall; Washington, D.C.: Biblical Archaeology Society, 1988), 37.
5. As quoted by David Finnigan, "Ancient Galilee—More Than Jesus," Religion News Service, December 4, 1998.
6. Dever, *Recent Archaeological Discoveries and Biblical Research,* 24.
7. Peter Feinman, "Drama of the Exodus," *Bible Review,* February 1991, 29.
8. Sarna, "Israel in Egypt," 36.
9. Sarna, "Israel in Egypt."
10. Sarna, "Israel in Egypt."
11. James K. Hoffmeier, *Israel in Egypt* (New York/Oxford: Oxford University Press, 1997), 114.

12. Hoffmeier, as cited in Kevin D. Miller, "Did the Exodus Never Happen?" *Christianity Today,* September 7, 1998, 48.
13. Hoffmeier, *Israel in Egypt,* 112–114.
14. Halpern, in *The Rise of Ancient Israel,* 99.
15. J. B. Pritchard, ed., *Ancient Near Eastern Texts Relating to the Old Testament* (Princeton: Princeton University Press, 1955), 376–378.
16. Sarna, "Israel in Egypt," 38.
17. From an interview with the author, January 23, 1994.
18. See "Moses," *Britannica Online:*
    http://www.eb.com:180/cgi-bin/g?DocF=macro/5004/37.html
    Also see Halpern, in *The Rise of Ancient Israel,* 104 n.
19. Halpern, in *The Rise of Ancient Israel,* 104.
20. See *Cambridge Annotated Study Bible NRSV,* ed. Howard Clark Kee (Cambridge University Press, 1993), commentary on Exod. 12:31–42.
21. Halpern, in *The Rise of Ancient Israel,* 105.
22. Halpern, in *The Rise of Ancient Israel.*
23. Miller, "Did the Exodus Never Happen?"
24. Halpern, in *The Rise of Ancient Israel,* 106.
25. Abraham Malamat, "Let My People Go and Go and Go and Go," *Biblical Archaeology Review,* January/February 1998, 62ff.
26. Hoffmeier, *Israel in Egypt,* 225–226.

CHAPTER 9

1. From an interview with the author, January 28, 1994.
2. Josh. 6:21.
3. John Garstang, "Jericho and the Biblical Story," *Wonders of the Past,* ed. J. A. Hammerton (New York: Wise, 1937), 1222.
4. As noted in Hoffmeier, "Did the Exodus Never Happen?" *Christianity Today,* September 7, 1998, 50.
5. Josh. 8:28.
6. Joseph A. Callaway, "Settlement and Judges," *Ancient Israel: A Short History from Abraham to the Roman Destruction of the Temple,* ed. Hershel Shanks (Englewood Cliffs, N.J.: Prentice Hall; Washington, D.C.: Biblical Archaeology Society, 1988), 63.
7. Callaway, "Settlement and Judges," 55.
8. As noted in William G. Dever, *Recent Archaeological Discoveries and Biblical Research* (Seattle: University of Washington Press, 1990), 47.
9. Dever, *Recent Archaeological Discoveries and Biblical Research,* 61.
10. James K. Hoffmeier, *Israel in Egypt* (New York/Oxford: Oxford University Press, 1997), 36.
11. G. Ernest Wright, *Biblical Archaeology* (Philadelphia: Westminster Press, 1957), 69.
12. As noted in Hoffmeier, *Israel in Egypt,* 33.
13. Hoffmeier, *Israel in Egypt,* 34–35.
14. Abraham Malamat, "The Israelite Conduct of War in the Conquest of Canaan," *Symposia Celebrating the Seventy-Fifth Anniversary of the Founding of the American Schools of Oriental Research (1900–1975),* ed. F. M. Cross (Cambridge, Mass.: American Schools of Oriental Research, 1979), 44–54.
15. K. Lawson Younger, *Ancient Conquest Accounts: A Study in Ancient Near Eastern and Biblical History Writing* (Sheffield, U.K.: JSOT Press, 1990), chapters 2–4, as noted in Hoffmeier, *Israel in Egypt,* 39–41.
16. Hoffmeier's translation, as it appears in *Israel in Egypt,* 41, of Egyptian hieroglyphics published in Kurt Sethe, *Urkunden der 18. Dynastie,* 4 vols. (Berlin: Akademie-Verlag, 1961), 614.1–2.
17. Hoffmeier, *Israel in Egypt,* 41.
18. Hoffmeier, *Israel in Egypt,* 41.
19. Dever, *Recent Archaeological Discoveries and Biblical Research,* 48.
20. As noted in Hoffmeier, *Israel in Egypt,* 35.

21. Hershel Shanks, *The Rise of Ancient Israel* (Washington, D.C.: Biblical Archaeology Society, 1992), 15–16.

22. Bryant Wood, "Did the Israelites Conquer Jericho? A New Look at the Archaeological Evidence," *Biblical Archaeology Review,* March/April 1990, 53.

23. Wood, "Did the Israelites Conquer Jericho?"

24. Cited in Callaway, "Settlement and Judges," 73.

25. Lawrence E. Stager, "Forging an Identity," *The Oxford History of the Biblical World,* ed. Michael D. Coogan (New York/Oxford: Oxford University Press, 1998), 134.

26. William G. Dever, "Philology, Theology, and Archaeology: What Kinds of History of Israel Do We Want, and What Is Possible?" in *The Archaeology of Israel: Constructing the Past, Interpreting the Present,* ed. Neil Asher Silberman and David Small (Sheffield, U.K.: Sheffield Academic Press, 1997), 301.

27. Callaway, "Settlement and Judges," 73.

28. Callaway, "Settlement and Judges," 71.

29. Callaway, "Settlement and Judges," 71.

30. Stager, "Forging an Identity," 139.

31. As summarized in Stager, "Forging an Identity," 139–140; in Dever, *Recent Archaeological Discoveries and Biblical Research,* 54–56; and in Edwin Yamauchi, "The Current State of Old Testament Historiography," *Faith, Tradition, and History,* ed. A. R. Millard, J. K. Hoffmeier, and D. W. Baker (Winona Lake, Ind.: Eisenbrauns, 1994), 17–21.

32. See, for example, Yamauchi, "The Current State of Old Testament Historiography," 18–20.

33. See Callaway, "Settlement and Judges," 72–73.

34. Callaway, "Settlement and Judges," 72–73.

35. As noted in Yamauchi, "The Current State of Old Testament Historiography," 20.

36. Yigael Yadin, "Is the Biblical Account of the Israelite Conquest of Canaan Historically Reliable?" *Biblical Archaeology Review,* March/April 1982, 17.

37. Dever, *Recent Archaeological Discoveries and Biblical Research,* 171.

CHAPTER 10

1. From an interview with the author, January 28, 1994.

2. Andre LeMaire, "House of David Restored in Moabite Inscription," *Biblical Archaeology Review,* May/June 1994, 30–37.

3. LeMaire, "House of David Restored in Moabite Inscription."

4. Carol Meyers, "Kinship and Kingship," *The Oxford History of the Biblical World,* ed. Michael D. Coogan (New York/Oxford: Oxford University Press, 1998), 233–234.

5. Meyers, "Kinship and Kingship," *The Oxford History of the Biblical World.*

6. Meyers, "Kinship and Kingship," *The Oxford History of the Biblical World.*

7. Meyers, "Kinship and Kingship," *The Oxford History of the Biblical World.*

8. Gonzalo Baez-Camargo, *Archaeological Commentary on the Bible* (Garden City, N.Y.: Doubleday, 1984), 82.

9. Gerland L. Mattingly, "Philistines," *HarperCollins Bible Dictionary,* rev. ed., ed. Paul J. Achtemeier (San Francisco: HarperSanFrancisco, 1996), 847.

10. Trude Dothan, "Philistines," *Anchor Bible Dictionary,* ed. David Noel Freedman (New York: Doubleday, 1992), 5:329.

11. Dothan, "Philistines," *Anchor Bible Dictionary.*

12. From an interview with the author, January 23, 1994.

13. William G. Dever, "Philology, Theology, and Archaeology: What Kinds of History of Israel Do We Want, and What Is Possible?" *Archaeology of Israel: Constructing the Past, Interpreting the Present,* ed. Neil Asher Silberman and David Small (Sheffield, U.K.: Sheffield Academic Press, 1997), 20.

14. William G. Dever, *Recent Archaeological Discoveries and Biblical Research* (Seattle: University of Washington Press, 1990), 117.

15. "King Solomon's Wall Still Supports the Temple Mount," *Biblical Archaeology Review,* May/June 1987, 34–44.

16. Dever, *Recent Archaeological Discoveries and Biblical Research,* 107–108.

17. Dever, *Recent Archaeological Discoveries and Biblical Research,* 114.

18. Dever, *Recent Archaeological Discoveries and Biblical Research,* 108.

19. Dever, "Philology, Theology, and Archaeology," 21.

20. See Andre LeMaire, "The United Monarchy," *Ancient Israel: A Short History from Abraham to the Roman Destruction of the Temple,* ed. Hershel Shanks (Washington, D.C.: Biblical Archaeology Society, 1988), 107; "Monarchy at Work? The Evidence of Three Gates," *Biblical Archaeology Review,* July/August 1997, 38; and Dever, *Recent Archaeological Discoveries and Biblical Research,* 102–106.

21. Cited in Dever, *Recent Archaeological Discoveries and Biblical Research,* 106.

22. "Monarchy at Work?" 38; Dever, *Recent Archaeological Discoveries and Biblical Research,* 106.

23. H. T. Frank, *An Archaeological Companion to the Bible* (London: SCM Press, 1969), 158–159.

24. Michael D. Coogan, in a presentation to the Biblical Archaeology Society in Orlando, Fla., November 1998.

25. Coogan, November 1998.

26. Coogan, November 1998.

27. Duane L. Christensen, "Omri," *HarperCollins Bible Dictionary,* 784.

28. Mordechai Cogan, "Into Exile: From the Assyrian Conquest of Israel to the Exile," *The Oxford History of the Biblical World,* ed. Michael D. Coogan (New York/Oxford: Oxford University Press, 1998), 331.

29. P. Kyle McCarter, "Siloam Inscription," *HarperCollins Bible Dictionary,* 1024.

30. Mordechai Cogan, "Hezekiah," *HarperCollins Bible Dictionary,* 421.

31. Aikirk Grayson, "Sennacherib," *Anchor Bible Dictionary,* 5:1089.

32. As noted in Siegfried H. Horn, "The Divided Monarchy: The Kingdoms of Judah and Israel," *Ancient Israel: A Short History from Abraham to the Roman Destruction of the Temple,* ed. Hershel Shanks (Washington, D.C.: Biblical Archaeology Society, 1988), 135.

33. Jonathan Rosenbaum, "Hezekiah, King of Judah," *Anchor Bible Dictionary,* 3:192. See also Herodotus 2:14–141 (9 vols.; Loeb Classic Library 117–120; Cambridge: Harvard University Press, 1922–1928); and Flavius Josephus, *Antiquities of the Jews,* as it appears in *The Complete Works of Josephus,* trans. William Whiston (Grand Rapids: Kregel Publications, 1981), 10:1.5.

34. As cited in Cogan, "Into Exile," 334.

35. D. D. Luckenbill, *Ancient Records of Assyria and Babylonia* (Chicago: University of Chicago Press, 1924), 2:116.

36. Baez-Camargo, *Archaeological Commentary on the Bible,* 120.

37. As cited in Cogan, "Into Exile," 350.

38. See Robert Koldewey, *The Excavations at Babylon* (London: Macmillan, 1914); see also "Babylon," *Britannica Online:* http://www.eb.com:180/cgi-bin/g?DocF=micro/44/71.html

39. William G. Dever, quoted in "Is the Bible Right After All?" *Biblical Archaeology Review,* September/October 1996, 36.

40. Leslie J. Hoppe, *What Are They Saying About Biblical Archaeology?* (New York: Paulist Press, 1984), 11; see also Siegfried H. Horn, "The Divided Monarchy," 118.

CHAPTER 11

1. Bargil Pixner, *With Jesus Through Galilee According to the Fifth Gospel* (Collegeville, Minn.: Liturgical Press, 1996), back cover.

2. Gonzalo Baez-Camargo, *Archaeological Commentary on the Bible* (Garden City, N.Y.: Doubleday, 1984), 211. Also see John J. Rousseau and Rami Arav, *Jesus and His World* (Minneapolis: Fortress Press, 1995), 75–76; and "Biblical Archaeology: Good Grounds for Faith," an interview with James Charlesworth, *U.S. Catholic,* July 1994, 18.

   It should be noted that the original anthropological analysis, published in 1970, has been disputed by Israeli anthropologist Joseph Zias, who reappraised the evidence in 1985. He contends that the arms may have been tied rather than nailed to the cross, that the feet were nailed separately to the sides of the upright, and that the shin bones were not broken during the crucifixion. See J. Zias and E. Sekeles, "The Crucified Man from Giv'at ha-Mivtar: A Reappraisal," *Israeli Exploration Journal* 35 (1985): 22–27.

3. See Ronny Reich, "Caiaphas Name Inscribed on Bone Boxes," *Biblical Archaeology Review* 18, no. 5 (September/October 1992): 38–44.

4. Flavius Josephus, *Antiquities of the Jews,* as it appears in *The Complete Works of Josephus,* trans. William Whiston (Grand Rapids: Kregel Publications, 1981), 18:4.3.

5. See Baez-Camargo, *Archaeological Commentary on the Bible,* 208. Also see Robert J. Bull, "Caesarea Maritima: The Search for Herod's City," *Biblical Archaeology Review,* May/June 1982.

6. Josephus, *Antiquities of the Jews,* 18:3.1; also see Rousseau and Arav, *Jesus and His World,* 225.

7. Rousseau and Arav, *Jesus and His World,* 227.

8. See James H. Charlesworth, "Reinterpreting John: How the Dead Sea Scrolls Have Revolutionized Our Understanding of the Gospel of John," *Bible Review,* February 1993, 20.

9. Jack Finegan, *The Archaeology of the New Testament: The Life of Jesus and the Beginning of the Early Church* (Princeton, N.J.: Princeton University Press, 1969), 164.

10. Dan Bahat, "Does the Holy Sepulchre Church Mark the Burial of Jesus?" *Archaeology in the World of Herod, Jesus and Paul,* ed. Hershel Shanks (Washington, D.C.: Biblical Archaeology Society, 1990), 254–256. This is a reprint of an article appearing in *Biblical Archaeological Review,* May/June 1986, 26–45.

11. Dio Cassius, *Roman History,* LXIX 12, as cited in Finegan, *The Archaeology of the New Testament,* 120–121.

12. Eusebius, *The Life of Constantine,* 3:26–29, as translated by John Wilkinson, *Egeria's Travels to the Holy Land,* rev. ed. (Jerusalem: Ariel Pub. House; Warminster, England: Aris & Phillips, 1981).

13. Eusebius, *The Life of Constantine,* 3:33–34.

14. As noted in Bahat, "Does the Holy Sepulchre Church Mark the Burial of Jesus?" 257–258. Eusebius describes this in *Life of Constantine,* 3:33–40. The church and its location also are described by the Bordeaux Pilgrim, an anonymous French writer who visited Jerusalem in 333 CE, and whose account is preserved in *Itinerarium Burdigalense,* trans. Aubrey Stewart (London: Palestine Pilgrim's Text Society, 1887).

15. As quoted in Thomas K. Grose, "Unearthing the Secrets of a Sacred Place," *U.S. News & World Report,* November 9, 1998, 46.

16. See Bahat, "Does the Holy Sepulchre Church Mark the Burial of Jesus?" 248–259.

17. See Kathleen Kenyon, *Jerusalem: Excavating 3000 Years of History* (London: Thames & Hudson, 1967), 153–154. Also see Bruce Schein, "The Second Wall of Jerusalem," *Biblical Archaeologist* 44, no. 1 (Winter 1981): 21–26.

18. John 19:20; Heb. 13:12.

19. Bahat, "Does the Holy Sepulchre Church Mark the Burial of Jesus?" 260.

20. Justin Martyr, *Dialogue with Trypho,* 78, as it appears in *The Ante-Nicene Fathers,* ed. Alexander Roberts and James Donaldson (Buffalo: The Christian Literature Publishing Company, 1885–96).

21. Origen, *Against Celsus,* 1:51, as it appears at the "Early Church Fathers" Internet site: http://ccel.wheaton.edu/fathers.2

22. Finegan, *The Archaeology of the New Testament,* 23.

23. Rousseau and Arav, *Jesus and His World,* 17.

24. Matt. 11:20–22; Luke 10:13–14.

25. Rousseau and Arav, *Jesus and His World,* 52–54.

26. Rousseau and Arav, *Jesus and His World,* 38.

27. James F. Strange and Hershel Shanks, "Synagogue Where Jesus Preached Found at Capernaum," *Archaeology in the World of Herod, Jesus and Paul,* ed. Hershel Shanks (Washington, D.C.: Biblical Archaeology Society, 1990), 201–207. This is a reprint of an article appearing in the *Biblical Archaeology Review,* November/December 1983.

28. James F. Strange and Hershel Shanks, "Has the House Where Jesus Stayed in Capernaum Been Found?" *Archaeology in the World of Herod, Jesus and Paul,* 188–199. This is a reprint of an article appearing in the *Biblical Archaeology Review,* November/December 1982.

29. From the diary of a Spanish nun named Egeria, as noted in Strange and Shanks, "Has the House Where Jesus Stayed in Capernaum Been Found?" 199.

30. Baez-Camargo, *Archaeological Commentary on the Bible,* 216.

CHAPTER 12

1. Nelson Glueck, *Rivers in the Desert: A History of the Negev* (New York: Farrar, Straus and Cudahy, 1959), ix.

2. William F. Albright, *The Archaeology of Palestine and the Bible* (Cambridge, Mass.: American Schools of Oriental Research, 1974), 127.
3. As quoted in G. Ernest Wright and David N. Freedman, eds., *The Biblical Archaeological Reader* (Garden City, N.Y.: Doubleday, 1961–64), 2:199.
4. In an interview with the author in Jerusalem on January 23, 1994.
5. William G. Dever, quoted in "Is the Bible Right After All?" *Biblical Archaeology Review,* September/October 1996, 75.
6. Kenneth A. Kitchen, "The Patriarchal Age: Myth or History? *Biblical Archaeology Review,* March/April 1995, 94.
7. Leslie J. Hoppe, *What Are They Saying About Biblical Archaeology?* (New York: Paulist Press, 1984), 9.
8. In an interview with the author, appearing in "Mysteries of the Bible," *U.S. News & World Report,* April 17, 1995, p. 67.
9. See, for example, Thomas E. Levy, "From Camels to Computers," *Biblical Archaeology Review,* July/August 1995, 44f.

### CHAPTER 13

1. This account is a synthesis of four versions of the story contained in the following works: John C. Trever, *The Dead Sea Scrolls: A Personal Account* (Grand Rapids: Eerdmans, 1965); James C. VanderKam, *The Dead Sea Scrolls Today* (Grand Rapids: Eerdmans, 1994); Harry Thomas Frank, "Discovering the Scrolls," *Understanding the Dead Sea Scrolls,* ed. Hershel Shanks (New York: Random House, 1992); and Hershel Shanks, *The Mystery and Meaning of the Dead Sea Scrolls* (New York: Random House, 1994).
2. Yigael Yadin, *The Message of the Scrolls* (New York: Simon & Schuster, 1957), 13–14.
3. As quoted in Frank, "Discovering the Scrolls," 17.
4. As cited in VanderKam, *The Dead Sea Scrolls Today,* 6.
5. VanderKam, *The Dead Sea Scrolls Today,* 7.

### CHAPTER 14

1. William F. Albright, *Bulletin of the American Schools of Oriental Research* 110 (April 1948): 3.
2. Andre Dupont-Sommer, *The Dead Sea Scrolls: A Preliminary Survey* (Oxford: Basil Blackwell, 1952), 99.
3. A collection of Wilson's essays was reprinted in a book, *The Scrolls from the Dead Sea* (New York: Oxford University Press, 1955), 104.
4. Frank Moore Cross, *The Ancient Library of Qumran and Modern Biblical Studies,* rev. ed. (Grand Rapids: Baker Book House, 1980), 35.
5. From a 1994 interview with Hershel Shanks, as cited in Shanks, *The Mystery and Meaning of the Dead Sea Scrolls* (New York: Random House, 1994), 47.
6. As noted in Shanks, *The Mystery and Meaning of the Dead Sea Scrolls,* 48–49; also see Michael Wise, Martin Abegg, Jr., and Edward Cook, *The Dead Sea Scrolls: A New Translation* (San Francisco: HarperSanFrancisco, 1996), 6–7.
7. Shanks, *The Mystery and Meaning of the Dead Sea Scrolls.*
8. Theodor H. Gaster, *The Dead Sea Scriptures* (New York: Doubleday Anchor Press, 1976), xv.
9. Geza Vermes, *The Dead Sea Scrolls: Qumran in Perspective* (London: Collins, 1977), 23–24.
10. For an account of this, see James C. VanderKam, *The Dead Sea Scrolls Today* (Grand Rapids: Eerdmans, 1994), 191.
11. See John M. Allegro, *The Sacred Mushroom and the Cross* (Garden City, N.Y.: Doubleday, 1970); also see Allegro's *The Dead Sea Scrolls and the Christian Myth* (Buffalo: Prometheus Books, 1992). The first edition was published in England in 1979 and released in the United States in 1984.
12. The interview, conducted by Avi Katzman, first appeared in the Tel Aviv newspaper *Ha'aretz* in the fall of 1990. It was later published in English in the United States: "Chief Dead Sea Scroll Editor Denounces Judaism; Claims to Have Seen Four More Scrolls Found by Bedouin," *Biblical Archaeology Review,* January/February 1991, 64–72.

13. Jeffery L. Sheler and Joannie Shrof, "The Bible's Last Secrets," *U.S. News & World Report,* October 7, 1991, 67.

14. Hershel Shanks, "Failure to Publish Dead Sea Scrolls Is Leit Motif of New York University Scroll Conference," *Biblical Archaeology Review,* September/October 1985, 66.

15. VanderKam, *The Dead Sea Scrolls Today,* 193.

16. As quoted by William Safire, *New York Times* News Service, September 27, 1991.

17. "Breaking the Scroll Cartel," *New York Times,* September 7, 1991.

18. Safire, *New York Times* News Service, September 27, 1991.

19. Shanks, *The Mystery and Meaning of the Dead Sea Scrolls,* 58.

20. One of the most important sectarian writings, the Habakkuk Commentary (1QpHab), contains repeated references to the Teacher of Righteousness and his nemesis, the Wicked Priest. As a result of accelerator mass spectrometry testing and paleographic analysis in 1995, the origin of that manuscript has been firmly dated to the first century BCE. For more on this, see A.J.T. Jull and others, "Radiocarbon Dating of Scrolls and Linen Fragments from the Judean Desert," *Radiocarbon* 37 (1995), 14; also see Jonathan G. Campbell, *Dead Sea Scrolls: The Complete Story* (Berkeley, Calif.: Ulysses Press, 1998), 57–58.

21. Vermes, *The Dead Sea Scrolls: Qumran in Perspective,* 211.

22. Hershel Shanks, "Is the Vatican Suppressing the Dead Sea Scrolls?" *Biblical Archaeology Review,* November/December 1991, 66–71.

23. Translated by Edward Cook as the passage appears in Michael Wise, Martin Abegg, Jr., and Edward Cook, *The Dead Sea Scrolls: A New Translation* (San Francisco: HarperSanFrancisco, 1996), 117.

24. Barbara Thiering, *Jesus and the Riddle of the Dead Sea Scrolls: Unlocking the Secrets of His Life Story* (San Francisco: HarperSanFrancisco, 1992), 22.

25. N. T. Wright, *Who Was Jesus?* (Grand Rapids: Eerdmans, 1992), 27.

26. Campbell, *Dead Sea Scrolls: The Complete Story,* 179–180.

27. Flavius Josephus, *Antiquities of the Jews,* 13:5.9, as it appears in *The Complete Works of Josephus,* trans. William Whiston (Grand Rapids: Kregel Publications, 1981), 274. Subsequent references to Josephus's *Antiquities of the Jews* and *The Jewish War,* cited parenthetically in text, are from the Loeb Classical Library editions.

28. As cited in VanderKam, *The Dead Sea Scrolls Today,* 76.

29. VanderKam, *The Dead Sea Scrolls Today,* 87.

30. VanderKam, *The Dead Sea Scrolls Today,* 72.

31. Frank Moore Cross, "The Early History of the Qumran Community," *New Directions in Biblical Archaeology,* ed. David Noel Freedman and Jonas C. Greenfield (Garden City, N.Y.: Doubleday, 1971), 77.

32. As quoted in Sheler and Shrof, "The Bible's Last Secrets," 64–70.

33. Sheler and Shrof, "The Bible's Last Secrets."

34. From an interview with the author, June 30, 1997.

35. As cited in VanderKam, *The Dead Sea Scrolls Today,* 1.

36. VanderKam, *The Dead Sea Scrolls Today.*

37. VanderKam, *The Dead Sea Scrolls Today.*

## CHAPTER 15

1. From an interview with the author, June 17, 1997.

2. From an interview with the author, January 21, 1999.

3. See James C. VanderKam, *The Dead Sea Scrolls Today* (Grand Rapids: Eerdmans, 1994), 30.

4. Translated by Michael Wise as the passage appears in Michael Wise, Martin Abegg, Jr., and Edward Cook, *The Dead Sea Scrolls: A New Translation* (San Francisco: HarperSanFrancisco, 1996), 450.

5. Wise, *The Dead Sea Scrolls: A New Translation,* 447.

6. Wise, *The Dead Sea Scrolls: A New Translation.*

7. This appears in the scroll designated 11Q5. See Wise, *The Dead Sea Scrolls: A New Translation,* 452.

8. Philo, *On the Contemplative Life,* 25, as cited in VanderKam, *The Dead Sea Scrolls Today,* 145.

9. Flavius Josephus, *Against Apion,* 1:38–41, as cited in VanderKam, *The Dead Sea Scrolls Today,* 148.

10. From an interview with the author, June 17, 1997.

11. The Greek (Septuagint) has it "virgin." It is "young girl" in the Masoretic text.

12. See, for example, Howard Clark Kee, ed., *The Cambridge Annotated Study Bible NRSV* (Cambridge, U.K.: Cambridge University Press, 1993).

13. More than the mistranslation of a single key word, *nazir*-Nazorean, would be at issue here. If *nazir* is authentic, and the Matthew passage refers to the fulfillment of a prophecy involving consecration, it does not fit with the portion of the birth narrative with which it has been paired.

14. Eugene C. Ulrich, "The Qumran Biblical Scrolls: The Scriptures of Late Second Temple Judaism," unpublished paper, University of Notre Dame, 10.

15. Flavius Josephus, *Antiquities of the Jews*, as it appears in *The Complete Works of Josephus*, trans. William Whiston (Grand Rapids: Kregel Publications, 1981), 5:10.2–3.

16. This passage, found in 4QSamᵃ, now appears in the NRSV after 1 Sam. 10:27.

17. Josephus, *Antiquities of the Jews*, 6:5.1.

18. James C. VanderKam, *The Dead Sea Scrolls Today* (Grand Rapids, Mich.: Eerdmans, 1994), 132.

19. Josephus, *Antiquities of the Jews*, 5:1.

20. See Adam Zertal, "Has Joshua's Altar Been Found on Mount Ebal?" *Biblical Archaeology Review*, January/February, 1985, 26–44. A more technical report of Zertal's discovery can be found in "An Early Iron Age Cultic Site on Mount Ebal: Excavation Seasons 1982–1987—A Preliminary Report," *Tel Aviv*, 13–14 (1986–1987), 9–30.

21. Commentary on Gen. 22:1–14, *Cambridge Annotated Study Bible* (Cambridge, U.K.: Cambridge University Press, 1993).

22. Commentary on Gen. 22:1–2, *Matthew Henry's Concise Commentary on the Whole Bible* (Cedar Rapids: Parson's Technology, 1998).

23. Ulrich, "The Qumran Biblical Scrolls: The Scriptures of Late Second Temple Judaism," 9.

24. Ulrich, "The Qumran Biblical Scrolls: The Scriptures of Late Second Temple Judaism."

25. From an interview with the author, January 21, 1999.

CHAPTER 16

1. Prior to the release of the unpublished scrolls in 1991, sensational theories abounded that sought to identify the Righteous Teacher and Wicked Priest of Qumran as any of various combinations of Jesus, John the Baptist, and the apostles James and Paul. The wider circulation of the scrolls since 1991 has deflated those theories. See a discussion of this in James C. VanderKam, *The Dead Sea Scrolls Today* (Grand Rapids: Eerdmans, 1994), 159–162; also see James H. Charlesworth, ed., *Jesus and the Dead Sea Scrolls* (New York: Doubleday, 1992), xxxv.

2. As it appears in Michael Wise, Martin Abegg, Jr., and Edward Cook, *The Dead Sea Scrolls: A New Translation* (San Francisco: HarperSanFrancisco, 1996), 57.

3. Geza Vermes, *The Dead Sea Scrolls: Qumran in Perspective* (London: Collins, 1977), 213.

4. Matt. 26:29; Mark 14:25.

5. Manual of Discipline 6:4–6, as cited in VanderKam, *The Dead Sea Scrolls Today*, 173–175.

6. VanderKam, *The Dead Sea Scrolls Today*, 269–270.

7. See, for example, VanderKam, *The Dead Sea Scrolls Today*, 178–179; and Cook in *The Dead Sea Scrolls: A New Translation*, 269.

8. Cook in *The Dead Sea Scrolls: A New Translation*, 269.

9. This translation of 4Q246 appears in Wise, Abegg, and Cook, *The Dead Sea Scrolls: A New Translation*, 269–270.

10. As noted in VanderKam, *The Dead Sea Scrolls Today*, 179.

11. As reported by Ron Grossman, "Scrolls Suggest Early Jewish-Christian Link," *Chicago Tribune*, November 11, 1991, 1.

12. Quoted by Richard N. Ostling, "Is Jesus in the Dead Sea Scrolls?" *Time*, September 21, 1992, 56.

13. As translated by Lawrence H. Schiffman in *Reclaiming the Dead Sea Scrolls* (Philadelphia/Jerusalem: Jewish Publication Society, 1994), 346.

14. VanderKam, *The Dead Sea Scrolls Today*, 180.

15. As noted by Martin Abegg in Wise, Abegg, and Cook, *The Dead Sea Scrolls: A New Translation*, 292.

16. James H. Charlesworth, "Reinterpreting John," *Bible Review*, February 1993, 19.

17. Charlesworth, "Reinterpreting John," 21.

18. Charlesworth, "Reinterpreting John," 23.

19. Charlesworth, "Reinterpreting John," 24.
20. Charlesworth, "Reinterpreting John," 24.
21. See Rainer Reisner, "Jesus, the Primitive Community, and the Essene Quarter of Jerusalem," in Charlesworth, ed., *Jesus and the Dead Sea Scrolls*, 198–221.
22. It occurs, for example, in the Hymns Scroll and in the halakic letter known as 4QMMT. See James C. VanderKam, "The Dead Sea Scrolls and Christianity," *Understanding the Dead Sea Scrolls*, ed. Hershel Shanks (New York: Random House, 1992), 188.
23. VanderKam, *The Dead Sea Scrolls Today*, 167.
24. For example, Josephus, *Antiquities of the Jews*, as it appears in *The Complete Works of Josephus*, trans. William Whiston (Grand Rapids: Kregel Publications, 1981), 13:5.9.
25. Josephus, *The Jewish War*, 2:124, as cited by Charlesworth in *Jesus and the Dead Sea Scrolls*, 6.
26. VanderKam, *The Dead Sea Scrolls Today*, 184.

CHAPTER 18

1. See Marcus Borg, *Jesus in Contemporary Scholarship* (Valley Forge, Pa.: Trinity Press International, 1994), 184.
2. Borg, *Jesus in Contemporary Scholarship*. Also see Gregory A. Boyd, *Cynic Sage or Son of God?* (Wheaton, Ill.: BridgePoint, 1995), 19–32.
3. *Reimarus: Fragments*, ed. C. H. Talbert, trans. R. S. Frazer (Philadelphia: Fortress, 1970), 151, 243.
4. See Boyd, *Cynic Sage or Son of God?* 24–26.
5. David Friedrich Strauss, *The Life of Jesus Critically Examined*, trans. George Eloit (Ramsey, N.J.: Sigler Press, 1994).
6. Albert Schweitzer, *The Quest of the Historical Jesus: A Critical Study of Its Progress from Reimarus to Wrede*, trans. W. Montgomery (New York: Collier/Macmillan, 1968), 398.
7. Schweitzer, *The Quest of the Historical Jesus*, 403.
8. N. T. Wright, *Who Was Jesus?* (Grand Rapids: Eerdmans, 1992), 7.
9. N. T. Wright, *Who Was Jesus?* 7
10. For more on this, see N. T. Wright, "Quest for the Historical Jesus," *Anchor Bible Dictionary* (New York: Doubleday, 1992), 3:798; also see Boyd, *Cynic Sage or Son of God?* 39.
11. Rudolf Bultmann, *Theology of the New Testament*, 2 vols., trans. K. Grobel (New York: Scribner, 1951), 1:21; also see Wright, "Quest for the Historical Jesus," 3:798.
12. Ernst Käsemann, *Essays on New Testament Themes* (Philadelphia: Fortress, 1982); also see Wright, "Quest for the Historical Jesus," 3:798–799.
13. Some scholars see the New Quest as having been relatively short-lived, coming to a distinct end by the close of the 1970s. Its philosophy and approach were then carried forth in what some refer to as the "Post-Bultmannian Quest," which has continued to the present alongside the more diverse and less ideological "Third Quest." Other scholars, however, hesitate to make such precise labeling distinctions and consider the Post-Bultmannian Quest merely to be a continuation of the New Quest. See, for example, Boyd, *Cynic Sage or Son of God?* 43–67, versus Wright's conclusion in "Quest for the Historical Jesus," 3:800.
14. James M. Robinson, *A New Quest of the Historical Jesus* (London: SCM, 1959; reprint, Philadelphia: Fortress, 1983).
15. Boyd, *Cynic Sage or Son of God?* 44.
16. The Jesus Seminar, for example, of which Crossan is a key member, included the Gospel of Thomas in its 1993 revisionist work, co-authored by Robert W. Funk and Roy W. Hoover, *The Five Gospels: The Search for the Authentic Words of Jesus*, a Polebridge Press Book (New York: Macmillan, 1993; San Francisco: HarperSanFrancisco, 1996).
17. Schweitzer, *The Quest of the Historical Jesus*, 309.

CHAPTER 19

1. These are outlined in some detail in Robert W. Funk, *Honest to Jesus*, a Polebridge Press Book (San Francisco: HarperSanFrancisco, 1996), epilogue.
2. The material in this profile was obtained by the author during in-person and telephone interviews

with Funk during March of 1996, and interviews with others while attending various meetings of the Jesus Seminar between 1994 and 1998.

3. Most of the material in this profile was compiled by my esteemed colleague Mike Tharp, a collaborator in my cover story "In Search of Jesus," in the April 8, 1996, issue of *U.S. News & World Report*. The material appears here in revised form with his permission.

4. The material in this profile was obtained by the author during an interview with Crossan in March 1996.

5. The material in this profile was gathered by the author during the spring of 1996 and from an interview with Meier at the Catholic University of America on March 19 of that year.

6. As quoted in Tim Stafford, "The New Theologians," *Christianity Today*, February 8, 1999, 43.

7. N. T. Wright, with Marcus J. Borg, *The Meaning of Jesus: Two Visions* (San Francisco: HarperSanFrancisco, 1998), 166.

8. Stafford, "The New Theologians," 46.

9. Stafford, "The New Theologians," 46.

10. N. T. Wright, *Who Was Jesus?* (Grand Rapids: Eerdmans, 1992), 18.

11. Stafford, "The New Theologians," 43.

12. Stafford, "The New Theologians," 43.


CHAPTER 20

1. Raymond E. Brown, *The Birth of the Messiah* (New York: Doubleday, 1979), 36.

2. Brennan Hill, *Jesus the Christ: Contemporary Perspectives* (Mystic, Conn.: Twenty-Third Publications, 1991), 149.

3. Donald A. Hagner, *Word Biblical Commentary: Matthew 1–13*, vol. 33a (Nashville: Thomas Nelson, 1993), 16.

4. Brown, *The Birth of the Messiah* (New York: Doubleday, 1979), 38.

5. See John P. Meier, *A Marginal Jew: Rethinking the Historical Jesus* (New York: Doubleday, 1991), 221. As Meier notes, Celsus's writing has been lost, but it was cited and refuted by Origen in *Against Celsus* in about 248 CE.

6. John S. Spong, *Born of a Woman: A Bishop Rethinks the Birth of Jesus* (San Francisco: HarperSanFrancisco, 1992), 126–127.

7. Meier, *A Marginal Jew*, 220.

8. N. T. Wright, *Who Was Jesus?* (Grand Rapids: Eerdmans, 1992), 83.

9. Wright, *Who Was Jesus?* 83.

10. Wright, *Who Was Jesus?* 83.

11. Hagner, *Word Biblical Commentary*, 29.

12. Paul L. Maier, *In the Fullness of Time: A Historian Looks at Christmas, Easter, and the Early Church* (San Francisco: HarperSanFrancisco, 1991), 22.

13. Brown, *The Birth of the Messiah*, 415.

14. Brown, *The Birth of the Messiah*, 549.

15. Brown, *The Birth of the Messiah*, 554.

16. Nigel Turner, *Grammatical Insights into the New Testament* (Edinburgh, U.K.: T & T Clark, 1965), 23–24.

17. Wright, *Who Was Jesus?* 89.

18. Kenneth E. Bailey, "The Manger and the Inn: What the Bible Really Says About Jesus' Birth," *Catholic Digest*, January 1989, 87.

19. See, for example, Brown, *The Birth of the Messiah*, 196.

20. Brown, *The Birth of the Messiah*, 198–199.

21. Maier, *In the Fullness of Time*, 54.

22. Hagner, *Word Biblical Commentary*, 37.

23. Hagner, *Word Biblical Commentary*, 37.

24. Hill, *Jesus the Christ*, 156–157.

25. Paul L. Maier, "The Infant Massacre: History or Myth?" *Christianity Today*, December 19, 1975, 9.

26. Hagner, *Word Biblical Commentary*, 37.

27. Macrobius, *Saturnalia* ii, 4, as cited in Maier, *In the Fullness of Time*, 67.

28. Maier, *In the Fullness of Time,* 73–75.
29. *Arabic Gospel of the Infancy,* xxiii, as cited in Montague R. James, *The Apocryphal New Testament* (Oxford: Clarendon, 1924).
30. *Infancy Gospel of Thomas,* ii.
31. *Infancy Gospel of Thomas,* iv–v.
32. Wright, *Who Was Jesus?* 86.
33. Justin Martyr, *Dialogue with Trypho,* 88, as translated by Maier, *In the Fullness of Time,* 90.
34. See Meier, *A Marginal Jew,* 348.
35. Meier, *A Marginal Jew,* 315.
36. Andrew J. Overman, "Who Were the First Urban Christians? Urbanization in Galilee in the First Century," *Society of Biblical Literature Seminar Papers 1988* (Atlanta: Scholars Press), 165, 168.
37. Hill, *Jesus the Christ,* 9.

## CHAPTER 21

1. From an interview with *U.S. News & World Report,* Montreal, Canada, February 3, 1993.
2. From an interview with the author, June 4, 1991.
3. See Darrell L. Bock's discussion in "The Words of Jesus in the Gospels: Live, Jive, or Memorex?" *Jesus Under Fire: Modern Scholarship Reinvents the Historical Jesus,* ed. Michael J. Wilkins and J. P. Moreland (Grand Rapids: Zondervan, 1995), 92.
4. N. T. Wright, *Who Was Jesus?* (Grand Rapids: Eerdmans, 1992), 9.
5. See "Rules of Evidence," *The Gospel of Mark: Red Letter Edition,* ed. Robert W. Funk and Mahlon H. Smith (Sonoma, Calif.: Polebridge Press, 1991), 29–52.
6. For more on this, see Craig L. Blomberg, "Where Do We Start Studying Jesus?" *Jesus Under Fire: Modern Scholarship Reinvents the Historical Jesus,* ed. Michael J. Wilkins and J. P. Moreland (Grand Rapids: Zondervan, 1995), 32.
7. The fifth-century-BCE Greek historian Thucydides confessed to following such a procedure: "It was difficult for me to remember the exact substance of the speeches I myself heard and for others to remember those they heard elsewhere and told me of." Yet clearly he did not regard that as license to invent or fictionalize his historical account. He went on to explain: "I have given the speeches in the manner in which seemed to me that each of the speakers would best express what needed to be said about the ever-prevailing situation, but I have kept as close as possible to the total opinion expressed by the actual words" (*History of the Peloponnesian War,* New York: Oxford University Press, 1960), 1:22.1.
8. Bock, "The Words of Jesus in the Gospels," 88.
9. From an interview with the author, November 20, 1993.
10. See, for example, G. R. Beasley-Murray, *Jesus and the Kingdom of God* (Exeter, U.K.: Paternoster; Grand Rapids: Eerdmans, 1986); also see Bruce Chilton, *God in Strength: Jesus' Announcement of the Kingdom* (Freistadt, Germany: F. Plochl, 1979).
11. Wright, *Who Was Jesus?* 98–99.
12. From an interview with the author, November 23, 1993.
13. Craig Blomberg, *The Historical Reliability of the Gospels* (Downers Grove, Ill.: 1987), 73.
14. From an interview with the author, November 20, 1993.
15. Many New Testament introductions and indexes delineate these. One such source is the *Ryrie Study Bible* (Chicago: Moody Press, 1976), 1973.
16. Marcus Borg, *Jesus: A New Vision: Spirit, Culture, and the Life of Discipleship* (San Francisco: HarperSanFrancisco, 1987), 61.
17. John Dominic Crossan, *Jesus: A Revolutionary Biography* (San Francisco: HarperSanFrancisco, 1994), 177.
18. Josephus, *Antiquities of the Jews,* as it appears in *The Complete Works of Josephus,* trans. William Whiston (Grand Rapids: Kregel Publications, 1981), 18:3.3.
19. Babylonian Talmud, *b. Sanh.* 43a, as cited in Graham N. Stanton, "Jesus of Nazareth: A Magician and a False Prophet Who Deceived God's People?" *Jesus of Nazareth Lord and Christ: Essays on the Historical Jesus and New Testament Christology,* ed. Joel B. Green and Max Turner (Grand Rapids: Eerdmans, 1994),169.

20. Robert W. Funk, Roy W. Hoover, and the Jesus Seminar, *The Five Gospels: What Did Jesus Really Say?* (New York: Macmillan, 1993), 2.

21. A. M. Hunter, *Bible and Gospel* (Philadelphia: Westminster, 1969), 93, as cited in Gary Habermas, "Did Jesus Perform Miracles?" *Jesus Under Fire: Modern Scholarship Reinvents the Historical Jesus,* ed. Michael J. Wilkins and J. P. Moreland (Grand Rapids: Zondervan, 1995), 126.

22. Habermas, "Did Jesus Perform Miracles?" 125.

23. From an interview with the author, March 5, 1993.

24. Davies presented this argument in an unpublished paper, "Whom Jesus Healed and How," presented at a meeting of the Jesus Seminar in Sonoma, Calif., March 4, 1993.

25. John J. Rousseau and Rami Arav, *Jesus and His World: An Archaeological and Cultural Dictionary* (Minneapolis: Fortress, 1995), 91.

26. Rousseau and Arav, *Jesus and His World,* 89.

27. Rousseau and Arav, *Jesus and His World,* 90. Rousseau and Arav cite Josephus, *Antiquities of the Jews,* 8:2.5, as it appears in *The Complete Works of Josephus,* trans. William Whiston (Grand Rapids: Kregel, 1981).

28. N. T. Wright, *Jesus and the Victory of God* (Minneapolis: Fortress Press, 1996), 187.

29. Habermas, "Did Jesus Perform Miracles?" 131.

30. As paraphrased in Habermas, "Did Jesus Perform Miracles?"

31. From an interview with the author, November 20, 1993.

32. Wright, *Jesus and the Victory of God,* 188.

33. Wright, *Jesus and the Victory of God,* 191.

34. Wright, *Jesus and the Victory of God,* 205.

Chapter 22

1. Rom. 1:16.

2. From an interview with the author, March 7, 1990.

3. From an interview with *U.S. News & World Report,* February 3, 1993.

4. From an interview with *U.S. News & World Report,* February 3, 1993.

5. Both of those arguments surfaced during discussions of the Jesus Seminar in March 1993, regarding the temple incident. The seminar fellows concluded that "Jesus performed some anti-temple act and spoke some anti-temple word . . . the precise nature of which is unknown." See Robert W. Funk and the Jesus Seminar, *The Acts of Jesus: The Search for the Authentic Deeds of Jesus* (San Francisco: HarperSanFrancisco, 1998), 231–232.

6. See, for example, Scot McKnight, "Who Is Jesus? An Introduction to Jesus Studies," *Jesus Under Fire: Modern Scholarship Reinvents the Historical Jesus,* ed. Michael J. Wilkins and J. P. Moreland (Grand Rapids: Zondervan, 1995), 66.

7. Raymond Brown, "A Between-the-Lines Look at Jesus," *U.S. Catholic,* March 1998, 12.

8. Brown, "A Between-the-Lines Look at Jesus."

9. From an interview with the author, March 8, 1990.

10. From an interview with the author, March 8, 1990.

11. E. P. Sanders, *The Historical Figure of Jesus* (London: Penguin Books, 1993), 255–257.

12. Sanders, *The Historical Figure of Jesus,* 259.

13. Matt. 26:64; Mark 14:62; Luke 22:67; John 18:19–23, 36.

14. Darrell L. Bock, "The Words of Jesus in the Gospels: Live, Jive, or Memorex?" *Jesus Under Fire: Modern Scholarship Reinvents the Historical Jesus,* ed. Michael J. Wilkins and J. P. Moreland (Grand Rapids: Zondervan, 1995), 88.

15. Sanders, *The Historical Figure of Jesus,* 271.

16. Sanders, *The Historical Figure of Jesus,* 269.

17. There are actually five incidents involving Pilate that are reported by first-century historians Josephus and Philo. These two, and perhaps others, preceded the arrest and crucifixion of Jesus. See Josephus, *Antiquities of the Jews,* 18:3–4, and Philo, *De Legatione ad Gaium* xxxviii, 299–305, as cited in Paul L. Maier, *In the Fullness of Time: A Historian Looks at Christmas, Easter, and the Early Church* (San Francisco: HarperSanFrancisco, 1991), 148–149.

18. Luke 23:12.

19. Tacitus, *Annals*, 15:44, as cited in "Jesus Christ, Non-Christian Sources," *Encyclopedia Britannica Online:* http://members.eb.com/bol/topic?artcl=106456&seq_nbr=1&page=n&.isctn.2.

20. Babylonian Talmud, *b. Sanh.* 43a, as cited in Stanton, "Jesus of Nazareth: A Magician and a False Prophet Who Deceived God's People?" *Jesus of Nazareth Lord and Christ: Essays on the Historical Jesus and the New Testament Christology,* ed. Joel B. Green and Max Turner (Grand Rapids: Eerdmans, 1994), 169.

21. These arguments are discussed in Joseph A. Fitzmyer, "Crucifixion in Ancient Palestine, Qumran Literature, and the New Testament," *Catholic Biblical Quarterly* 40 (1978): 493–513.

22. Fitzmyer, "Crucifixion in Ancient Palestine, Qumran Literature, and the New Testament," 498–507.

23. Ernst Bammel, ed., *The Trial of Jesus* (Naperville, Ill.: Allenson, 1970), 164–165.

24. Eric F. Bishop, "With Jesus on the Road from Galilee to Calvary: Palestinian Glimpses into the Days Around the Passion," *Catholic Biblical Quarterly* 11 (1949): 442.

25. Origen, *Against Celsus*, trans. Rev. Frederick Crombie, D.D., 2:56. Also see Barbara Thiering, *Jesus and the Riddle of the Dead Sea Scrolls: Unlocking the Secrets of His Life Story* (San Francisco: HarperSanFrancisco, 1992).

26. Raymond Brown, "The Burial of Jesus," *Catholic Biblical Quarterly* 50 (1988): 233–245.

27. John Dominic Crossan, *Jesus: A Revolutionary Biography* (San Francisco: HarperSanFrancisco, 1994), ch. 6.

28. Sanders, *The Historical Figure of Jesus*, 280.

29. See, for example, John Wenham, *Easter Enigma: Do the Resurrection Stories Contradict One Another?* (Exeter, U.K.: Paternoster; Grand Rapids: Zondervan, 1984).

30. James D. G. Dunn, *The Evidence for Jesus* (Louisville: Westminster Press, 1985), 67.

31. Dunn, *The Evidence for Jesus*.

32. Dunn, *The Evidence for Jesus*.

33. Dunn, *The Evidence for Jesus,* 66.

34. Stephen T. Davis, *Risen Indeed: Making Sense of the Resurrection* (Grand Rapids: Eerdmans, 1993), 73.

35. Gregory A. Boyd, *Cynic Sage or Son of God?* (Wheaton, Ill.: BridgePoint, 1995), 278.

36. W. Barnes Tatum, "Bookshelf," *The Fourth R,* January/February 1995, 5.

37. Thomas Sheehan, *The First Coming: How the Kingdom of God Became Christianity* (New York: Random House, 1988), 97–98.

38. Boyd, *Cynic Sage or Son of God?* 277.

39. Hans E. Stier, in *Moderne Exegese und Historische Wissenschaft,* 152, cited in Hugo Staudinger, *The Trustworthiness of the Gospels* (Edinburgh: Handsel, 1981), 77.

40. Brown, "A Between-the-Lines Look at Jesus," 14.

41. Sheehan, *The First Coming,* 170, 107.

42. Craig Blomberg, *The Historical Reliability of the Gospels* (Downers Grove, Ill.: InterVarsity Press, 1987), 104.

43. Reginald H. Fuller, *The Formation of the Resurrection Narratives,* 2nd ed. (Philadelphia: Fortress Press, 1980), 181.

CHAPTER 23

1. From the Gaon's *Book of Hidden Things,* "Sifra Ditzniuta," chap. 5, as quoted in Abraham Rabinowitz, *The Jewish Mind in Its Halachic Talmudic Expression* (Jerusalem: Hillel Press, 1978), 33–34.

2. Michael Drosnin, *The Bible Code* (New York: Simon & Schuster, 1997), 25.

3. Drosnin, *The Bible Code,* 13.

4. Drosnin, *The Bible Code,* 13.

5. David Van Biema, with reporting by Lisa McLoughlin, "Deciphering God's Plan," *Time,* June 9, 1997, 56.

6. Van Biema, with reporting by Lisa McLoughlin, "Deciphering God's Plan," 25. Drosnin is quoting from Nachmanides, *Commentary on the Torah,* ed. Charles Chavel (New York: Shilo, 1971), 1:14.

7. See Jeffrey B. Satinover, "Divine Authorship? Computer Reveals Startling Word Patterns," *Bible Review,* October 1995, 31.

8. Doron Witzum, Eliyahu Rips, and Yoav Rosenberg, "Equidistant Letter Sequences in the Book of Genesis," *Statistical Science: A Review Journal of the Institute of Mathematical Statistics* 9, no. 3 (August 1994): 434.

9. Robert E. Kass, from the introduction to Witzum, Rips, and Rosenberg, "Equidistant Letter Sequences in the Book of Genesis," 306. The article itself appears on 429–438.

10. Remarks of professors H. Furstenberg, Hebrew University; I. Piateski-Shapiro, Yale University; and D. Kazhdan and J. Bernstein, Harvard University, as quoted in Satinover, "Divine Authorship?" 31.

11. All quotations from Gans in this section are from Drosnin, *The Bible Code,* 23.

12. As noted in Jeffrey B. Satinover, *Cracking the Bible Code* (New York: Morrow, 1997), 224.

13. As noted in John Weldon, *Decoding the Bible Code* (Eugene, Ore.: Harvest House, 1998), 26.

14. Zohar II, 204a, and IV, 151b, as cited in Satinover, *Cracking the Bible Code,* 43.

15. For a brief explanation, see Weldon, *Decoding the Bible Code,* 40; also see "Kabbala" in *The Catholic Encyclopedia* online:
    http://www.knight.org/advent/cathen/08590a.htm

16. See Satinover, *Cracking the Bible Code,* 69–70; also see Grant R. Jeffrey, *The Mysterious Bible Codes* (Nashville: Word, 1998), 33–34.

17. *Pardes Rimonim* (68a), emphasis added, as cited on the Aish HaTorah Web site:
    http://www.discoveryseminar.org/Codes/classical.htm

18. See Satinover, *Cracking the Bible Code,* 69.

19. Satinover, *Cracking the Bible Code,* 66–70; also see Jeffrey, *The Mysterious Bible Codes,* 43–44.

20. Drosnin, *The Bible Code,* 100.

21. Drosnin, *The Bible Code,* 179.

22. The statements from Rips, Gans, and Witzum appear on the Aish HaTorah Internet Website.

23. Drosnin, *The Bible Code,* 46.

24. Satinover, "Divine Authorship?" 45.

25. Drosnin, *The Bible Code,* 50–51.

26. Drosnin, *The Bible Code,* 97, 103.

27. "The author of the Zohar, whose belief in the primacy of Kabbalistic interpretation was extreme, actually expressed the opinion [3, 152a] that had the Torah simply been intended as a series of literal narratives he and his contemporaries would have been able to compose a better book!" From *Encyclopedia Judaica* (Jerusalem: Keten, 1972), 10:624.

28. Drosnin, *The Bible Code,* 25.

CHAPTER 24

1. Sharon Begley, "Seek and Ye Shall Find," *Newsweek,* June 9, 1997, 66.

2. McKay's critical analysis of these other alleged anomalies can be found at his Web site:
   http://cs.anu.edu.au/~bdm/dilugim/index.html

3. McKay, in e-mail correspondence with the author, April 30, 1999.

4. See "Assassinations Foretold in *Moby Dick*!" on McKay's Web site.

5. "Assassinations Foretold in *Moby Dick*!"

6. "Assassinations Foretold in *Moby Dick*!"

7. See, for example, Ronald S. Hendel, "The Bible Code: Cracked and Crumbling," *Bible Review,* August 1997, 22–25; Shlomo Sternberg, "Snake Oil for Sale," *Bible Review,* August 1997, 25; Maya Bar-Hillel, Dror Bar-Natan, and Brendan McKay, "The Bible Codes: Puzzle and Solution," *Chance* 2, no. 2 (1998): 13–19.

8. Michael Drosnin, *The Bible Code* (New York: Simon & Schuster, 1997), 31.

9. Brendan McKay, Dror Bar-Natan, Maya Bar-Hillel, and Gil Kalai, "The Bible Code: The Genesis of Equidistant Letter Sequences," *Statistical Science* 14, no. 2 (May 1999): 15. (*Note:* The May issue had not yet gone to press at the time of this writing. The citation is based on a prepublication copy of the approved article obtained from the authors. Actual publication page numbers had not been assigned. The page numbers cited here, therefore, refer to the internal page sequence within the article.)

10. McKay, Bar-Natan, Bar-Hillel, and Kalai, "The Bible Code," 3.
11. McKay, Bar-Natan, Bar-Hillel, and Kalai, "The Bible Code," 4.
12. McKay, Bar-Natan, Bar-Hillel, and Kalai, "The Bible Code," 3.
13. McKay, Bar-Natan, Bar-Hillel, and Kalai, "The Bible Code," 3.
14. McKay, Bar-Natan, Bar-Hillel, and Kalai, "The Bible Code," 30–31.
15. Robert Kass, in an introduction prepared for the May 1999 issue of *Statistical Science.* Kass made a copy available to the author prior to its publication, for which the author is grateful. In the same introduction, Kass suggested that promoters of the Bible code had misinterpreted and exploited his preface to WRR's 1994 paper as a "stamp of approval" of the Bible code. However, none of the journal's referees of the WRR paper, Kass said, "was convinced that the authors had found something genuinely amazing. Instead, what remained intriguing was the difficulty of pinpointing the cause, presumed to be some flaw in their procedure, that produced such apparently remarkable findings. Thus, in introducing that paper, I wrote that it was offered to readers 'as a challenging puzzle.' "
16. Drosnin, *The Bible Code,* 20.
17. Drosnin, *The Bible Code,* 38.
18. Jeffrey H. Tigay, "The Bible 'Codes': A Textual Perspective," a paper appearing on Tigay's Web site: http://www.sas.upenn.edu/~jtigay/codetext.html
19. Tigay, "The Bible 'Codes.' "
20. Tigay, "The Bible 'Codes.' " In his endnotes, Tigay observes, "There are 304,850 letters in the Michigan-Claremont-Westminster (MCW) computerized text of Biblica Hebraica Stuttgartensia (BHS) which is the critical edition of the Leningrad codex currently in use by most scholars (information courtesy of Alan Groves, the final editor of the MCW text). C. D. Ginsburg's edition of the Torah contains 304,807 letters according to the colophon at its end (C. D. Ginsburg, *The Pentateuch* [London: British and Foreign Bible Society, 1926; repr. Jerusalem: Makor, 1970])."
21. Tigay, "The Bible 'Codes.' " Tigay cites *Safah Berurah,* ed. G. Lippmann (Fürth, Germany: Fuerth, 1839), 7a-b (cited and translated in Ginsburg, *The Pentateuch,* 137–138).
22. McKay, Bar-Natan, Bar-Hillel, and Kalai, "The Bible Code," 27–28.
23. McKay, Bar-Natan, Bar-Hillel, and Kalai, "The Bible Code," 28.
24. Tigay, "The Bible 'Codes.' " He cites S. Rosenfeld, *Sefer Mishpahat Sofrim* (Vilna, Lithuania: Romm, 1883), 34–36, 100, who identifies the middle letter as the ALEPH in the word HU', in Lev. 8:28 (the same is true for the Koren edition), and the middle pair of words as 'EL YESOD in Lev. 8:15. According to the Talmud, the middle letter is the VAV in the word GAXON in Lev. 11:42, and the middle words are DAROSH DARASH in Lev. 10:16. The inconsistency between the Talmudic passage and the Masoretic text of today, Tigay says, is also noted by M. M. Kasher, *Torah Shelemah* 28 (Jerusalem: American Biblical Encyclopedia Society/Makhon Torah Shelemah, 1978), 286–289. In the Yemenite, the middle letter is the L of LYHVH in Lev. 8:28; according to Alan Groves, in Biblica Hebraica Stuttgartensia (which has an even number of letters) the middle two letters are HX in HXZH, also in Lev. 8:28.
25. Tigay, "The Bible 'Codes.' "
26. Tigay, "The Bible 'Codes.' "
27. Tigay, "The Bible 'Codes.' "
28. Tigay, "The Bible 'Codes.' " Tigay cites Koren editor M. Medan in "Al haNusah beMahadurat Koren," *Beth Mikra* 3, no. 15 (January 1963): 142.
29. McKay, Bar-Natan, Bar-Hillel, and Kalai, "The Bible Code," 29.
30. Drosnin, *The Bible Code,* 70–71.
31. Tigay, "The Bible 'Codes.' "
32. Tigay, "The Bible 'Codes.' "
33. Sternberg, "Snake Oil for Sale," 25.
34. Tigay, "The Bible 'Codes.' "
35. Harold Gans, in a statement appearing on the Aish HaTorah Web site: http://www.aish.edu/issues/biblecodes/main.htm
36. Gans, in a statement appearing on the Aish HaTorah Web site.
37. Gans, in a statement appearing on the Aish HaTorah Web site.
38. Witzum's statement of June 4, 1997, as it appears on the Aish HaTorah Web site.

39.  Tigay, "The Bible 'Codes.'"
40.  Sternberg, "Snake Oil for Sale," 25.
41.  For more on this point, see John Weldon, *Decoding the Bible Code* (Eugene, Ore.: Harvest House, 1998), 137–139.
42.  John Ankerberg and John Weldon, *Encyclopedia of New Age Beliefs* (Eugene, Ore.: Harvest House, 1996), 124–125.
43.  Quoted by Drosnin in *The Bible Code,* 44.
44.  Weldon, *Decoding the Bible Code,* 101–102.

CHAPTER 25

1.  G. Ernest Wright, *God Who Acts* (London: SCM, 1952), 126–127.